Two years! Thank you, everyone!

NEW!! 04-25 20:05:50
Theme: (None)

I just got back...
...from the ZINGS 2nd Anniversary Concert in Myojo Hall!
Whether you made it to the concert or were sending love from elsewhere,
thank you so much!!! (*^_^*)

Over the last two years, things have sometimes been...complicated...
but this was a fantastic opportunity to look back and realize how grateful
I am for the chance to meet all of our very special fans, and above all,
for getting to be an idol with Yu-kun! (^^)

Myojo Hall is huge!! I got a bit carried away with the camera...
I'll try not to upload them all at once!

In the green room with Yu-kun and our manager Ms. Shinano,
who always has our backs!
There are hardly any photos of just the three of us, so this is a rare shot!

Kazuki Yoshino

Profi

Ther

April
March
Febru
Janua
Decen
Nover
Octob
Septe
Augus
July
June
May
April

Follc

flow

PHANTOM OF THE IDOL ☆ CONTENTS BOT
<<<-----SET 7---P.003-----\>>>

Noriko is not buying merch this month
Apparently Setouchi-kun was spotted near a ZINGS show!
Should I go check out the VIP seats??

PHANTOM OF THE IDOL ☆ CONTENTS BOT
<<<-----SET 8---P.024-----\>>>

Smiling escargot@Summer Campaigning
I cannottttt My bias asked me to smileeee
I will smile UNTIL I DIEEEEEE
I could raise antlions in my dimples

☆ 1

PHANTOM OF THE IDOL ☆ CONTENTS BOT
<<<-----SET 9---P.049-----\>>>

Mehmai@Campaigned
"Go home smiling"! I was like. Wooow. but when I saw the photo on the blog,
okay, 5000000000 points. Niyodo wins

Q 2   ☆ 4

PHANTOM OF THE IDOL ☆ CONTENTS BOT
<<<-----SET 10---P.072-----\>>>

Complaining Alt Account
Just me or do Niyodo's eyes look dead lately? Does he want to be an idol or not?

PHANTOM OF THE IDOL ☆ CONTENTS BOT
<<<-----SET 11---P.097-----\>>>

Ray
When Niyodo started running with Yoshino-kun and crying happy tears, you bet
I started crying too... ZINGS best boys...no competition...THE BEST!!!!

Q 4   ☆ 7

PHANTOM OF THE IDOL ☆ CONTENTS BOT
<<<-----SET 12---P.123-----\>>>

Kazuki Yoshino
Looks like Yu-kun is finally going to start using social media! 😊 I'll check out his
posts when they go up and let you all know about them. Look forward to it! 😊

Q 42   ☆ 86

PHANTOM OF THE IDOL ☆ CONTENTS BOT
<<<-----SET 13---P.149-----\>>>

Yumiko
Lately all we talk about at shows is Mr. Scarf. Who is he???

☆ 1

PHANTOM OF THE IDOL ☆ CONTENTS BOT
<<<-----SET 14---P.179-----\>>>

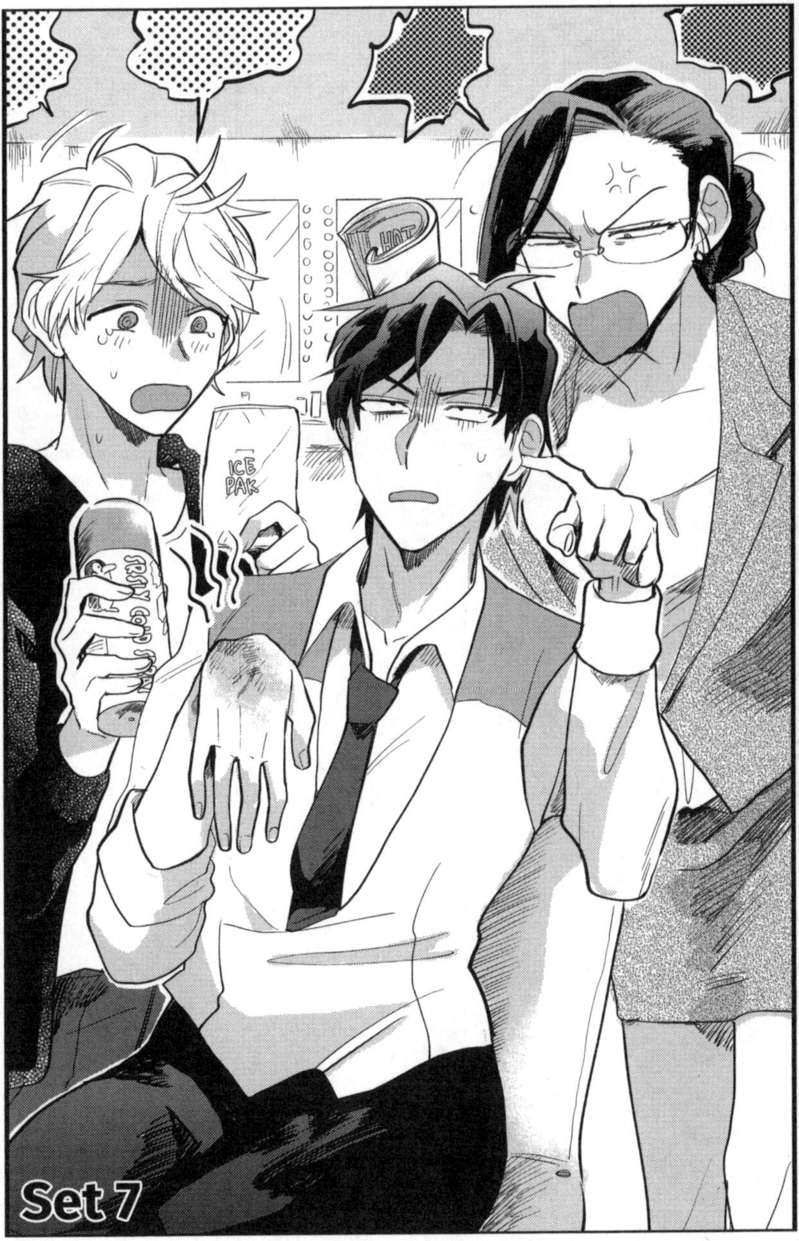
HOT
ICE PAK
Set 7

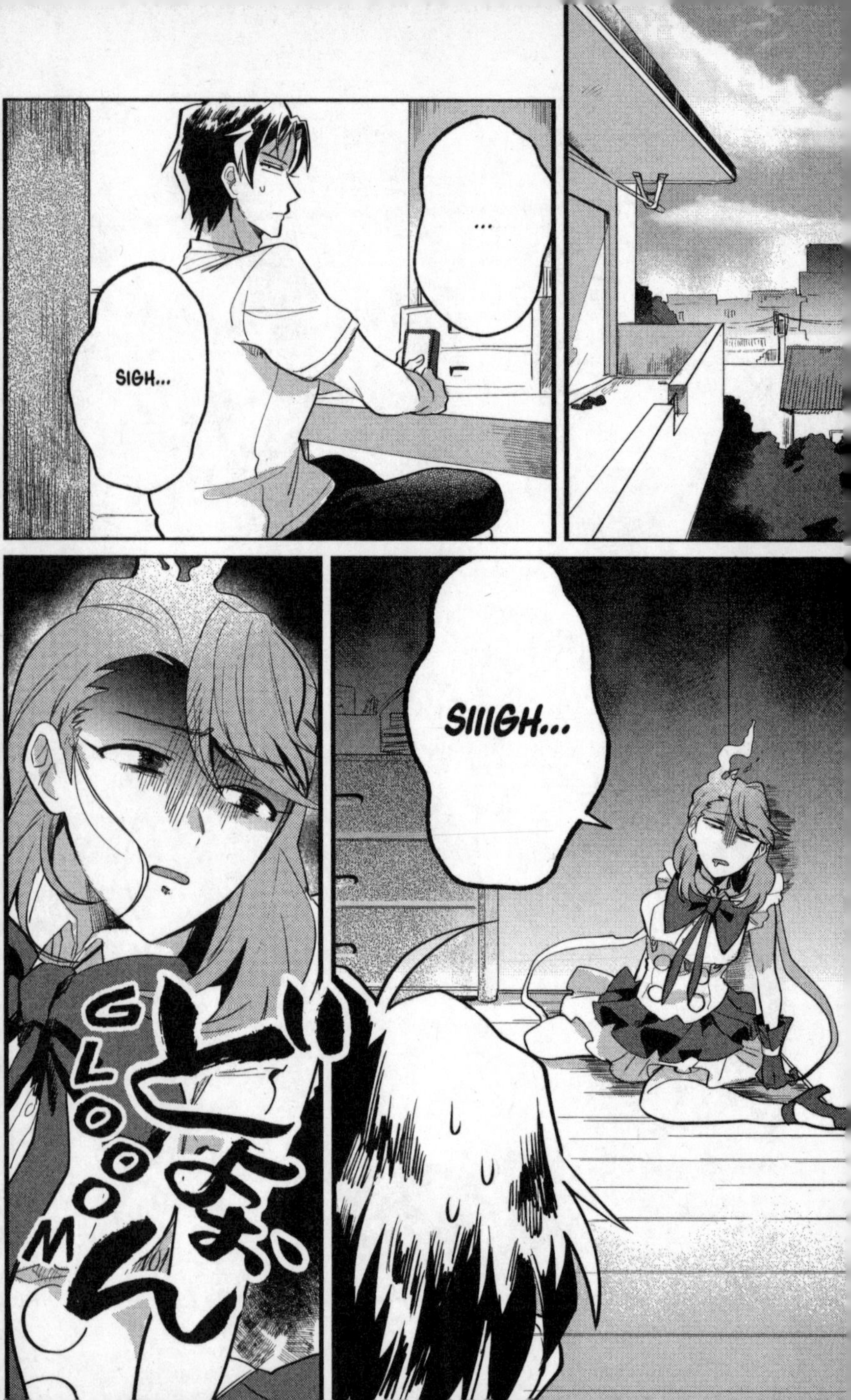
...
SIGH...
SIIIGH...
GLOOOM

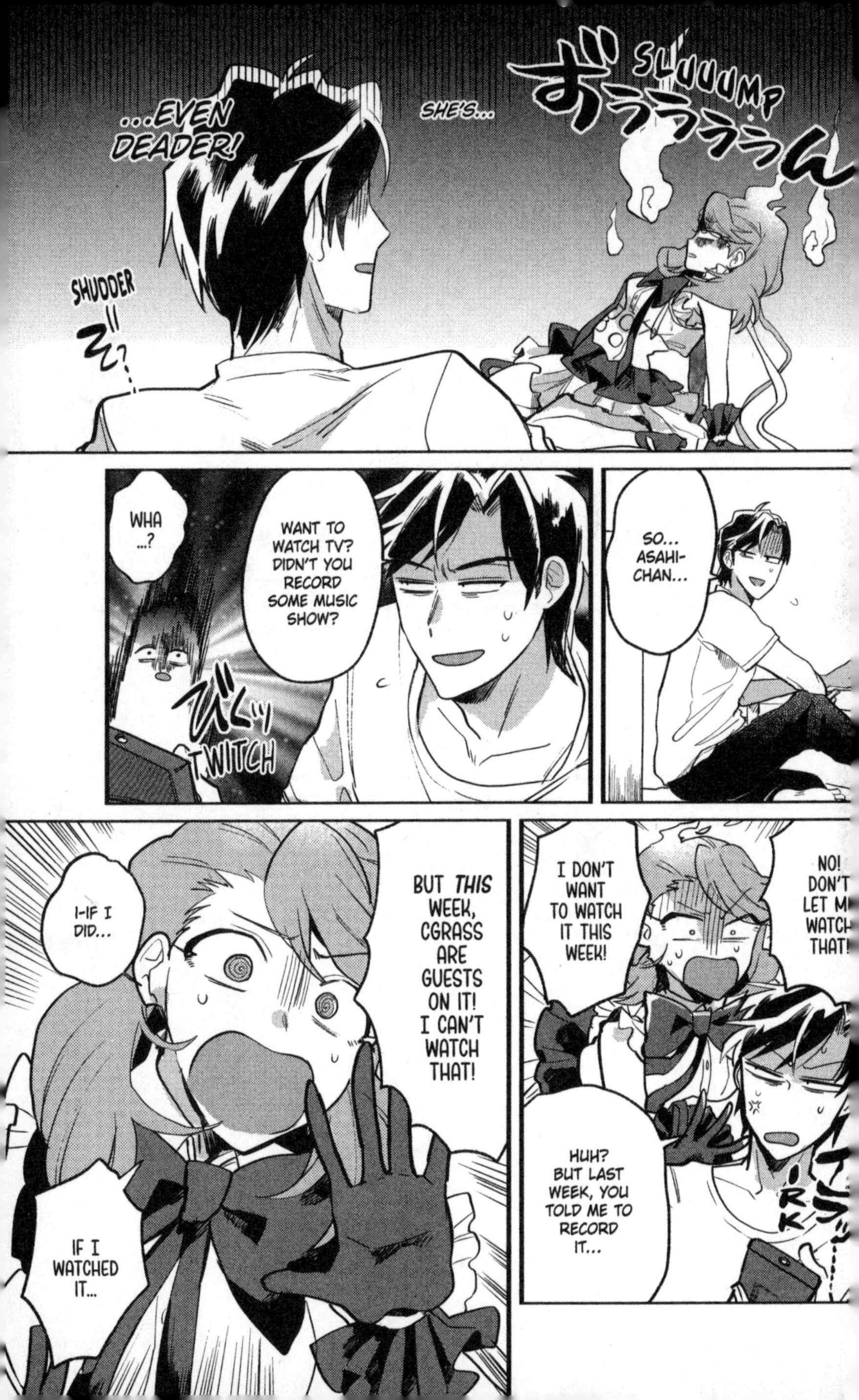
SLUUUUMP
SHE'S...
...EVEN DEADER!
SHUDDER
SO... ASAHI-CHAN...
WANT TO WATCH TV? DIDN'T YOU RECORD SOME MUSIC SHOW?
WHA ...?
TWITCH
NO! DON'T LET M WATCH THAT!
I DON'T WANT TO WATCH IT THIS WEEK!
HUH? BUT LAST WEEK, YOU TOLD ME TO RECORD IT...
BUT *THIS* WEEK, CGRASS ARE GUESTS ON IT! I CAN'T WATCH THAT!
I-IF I DID...
IF I WATCHED IT...

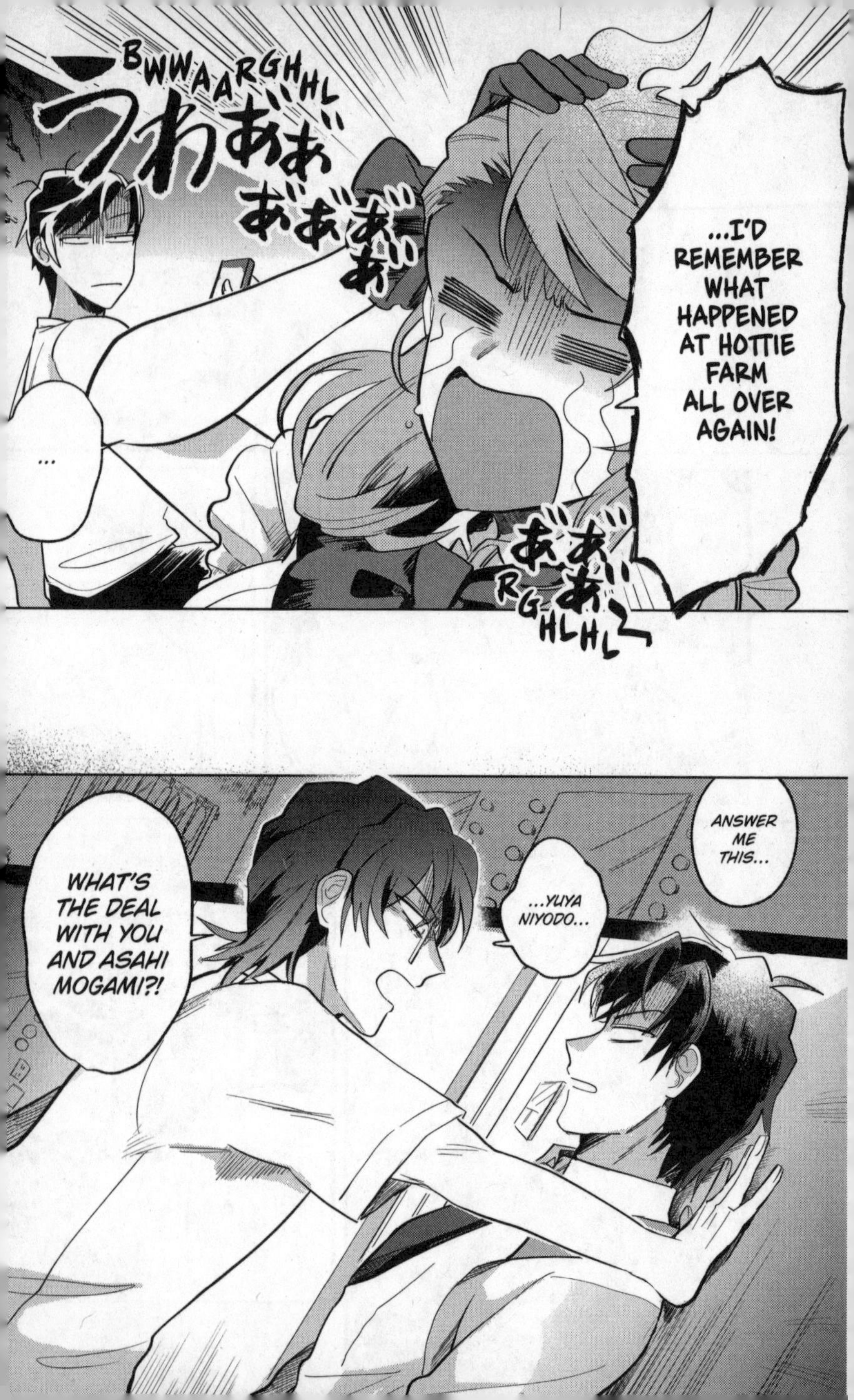
...I'D REMEMBER WHAT HAPPENED AT HOTTIE FARM ALL OVER AGAIN!
BWWAARGHHL
RGHLHL
...
ANSWER ME THIS...
...YUYA NIYODO...
WHAT'S THE DEAL WITH YOU AND ASAHI MOGAMI?!

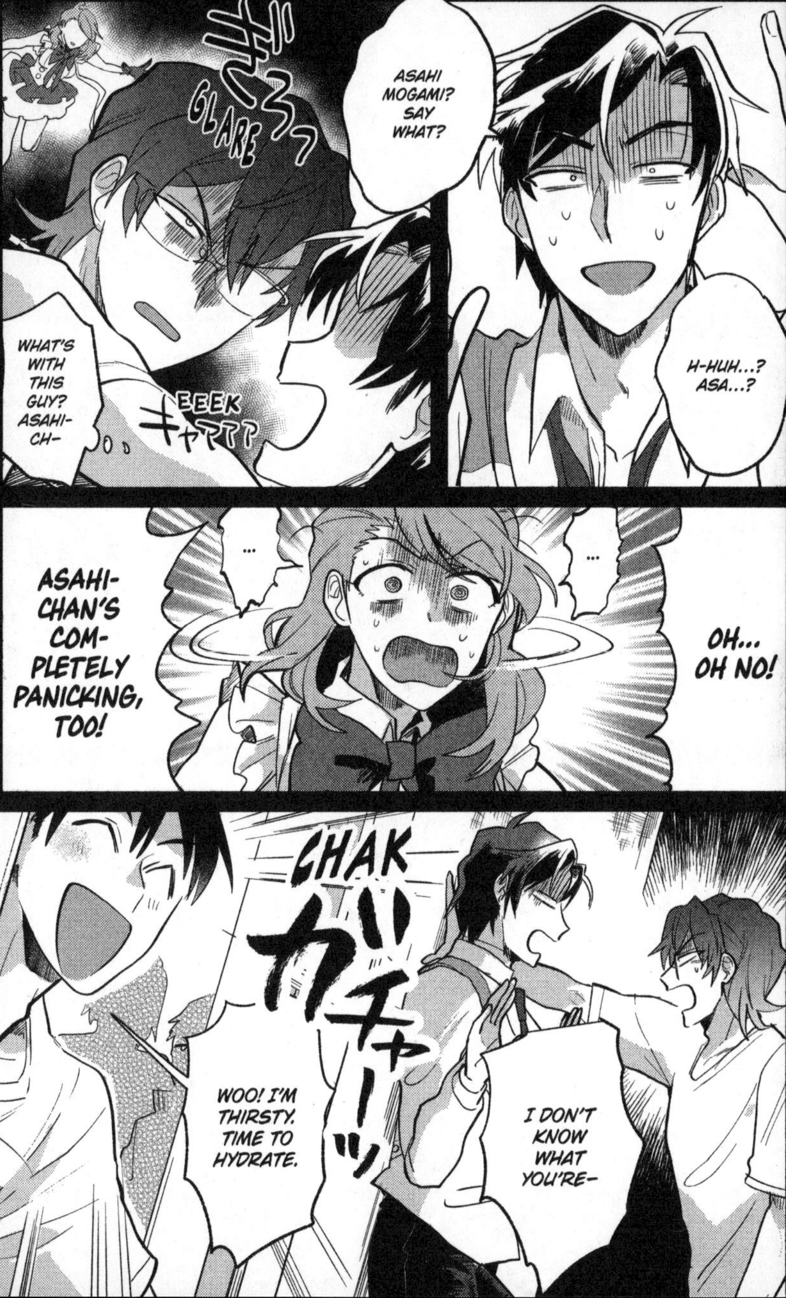
H-HUH...? ASA...?
ASAHI MOGAMI? SAY WHAT?
ぎろっ
GLARE
キャアアア
EEEK
WHAT'S WITH THIS GUY? ASAHI-CH-
...
...
OH... OH NO!
ASAHI-CHAN'S COMPLETELY PANICKING, TOO!
I DON'T KNOW WHAT YOU'RE-
ガチャーッ
CHAK
WOO! I'M THIRSTY. TIME TO HYDRATE.

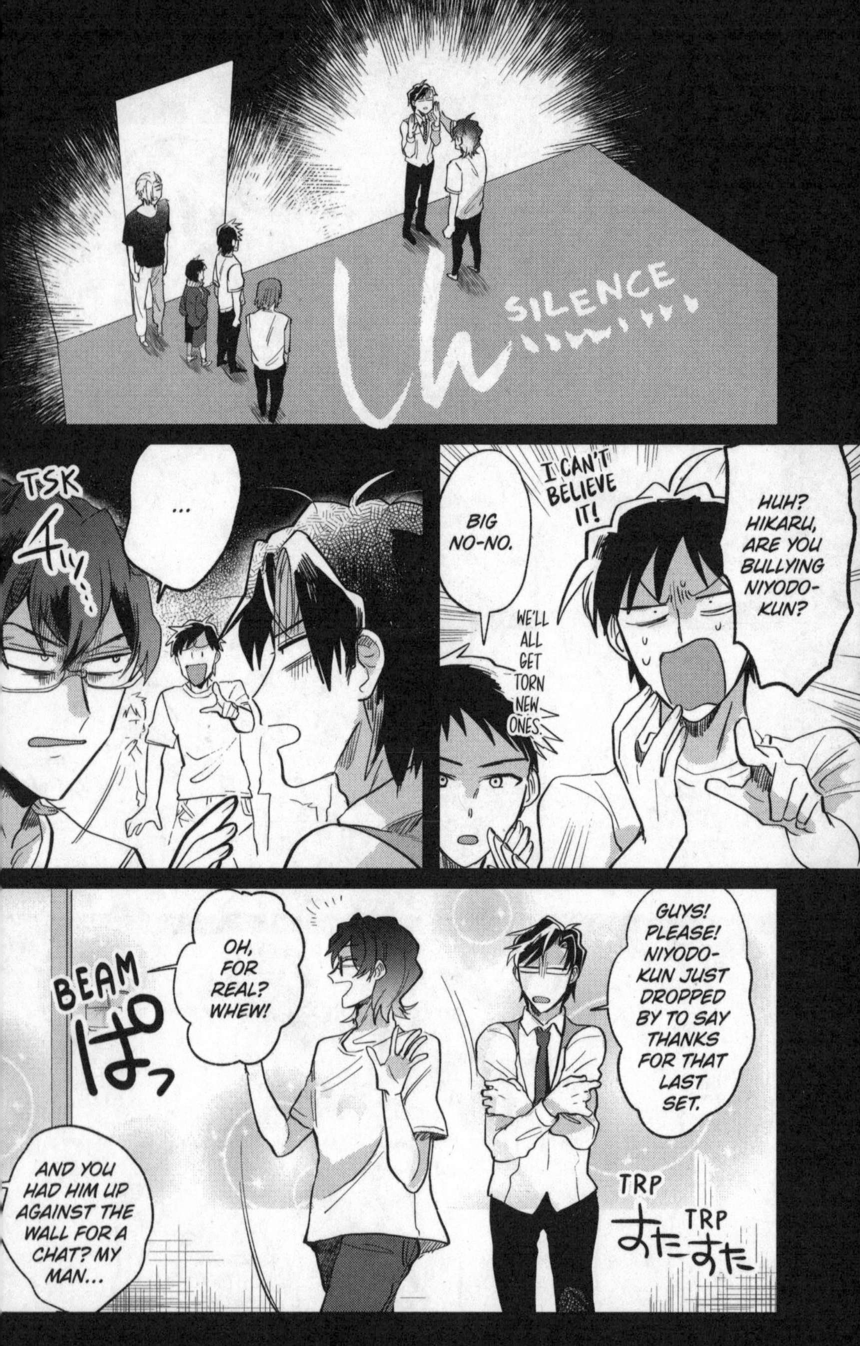

SILENCE
しん
HUH? HIKARU, ARE YOU BULLYING NIYODO-KUN?
I CAN'T BELIEVE IT!
BIG NO-NO.
WE'LL ALL GET TORN NEW ONES.
TSK
...
GUYS! PLEASE! NIYODO-KUN JUST DROPPED BY TO SAY THANKS FOR THAT LAST SET.
TRP TRP
すたすた
OH, FOR REAL? WHEW!
BEAM
ぱっ
AND YOU HAD HIM UP AGAINST THE WALL FOR A CHAT? MY MAN...

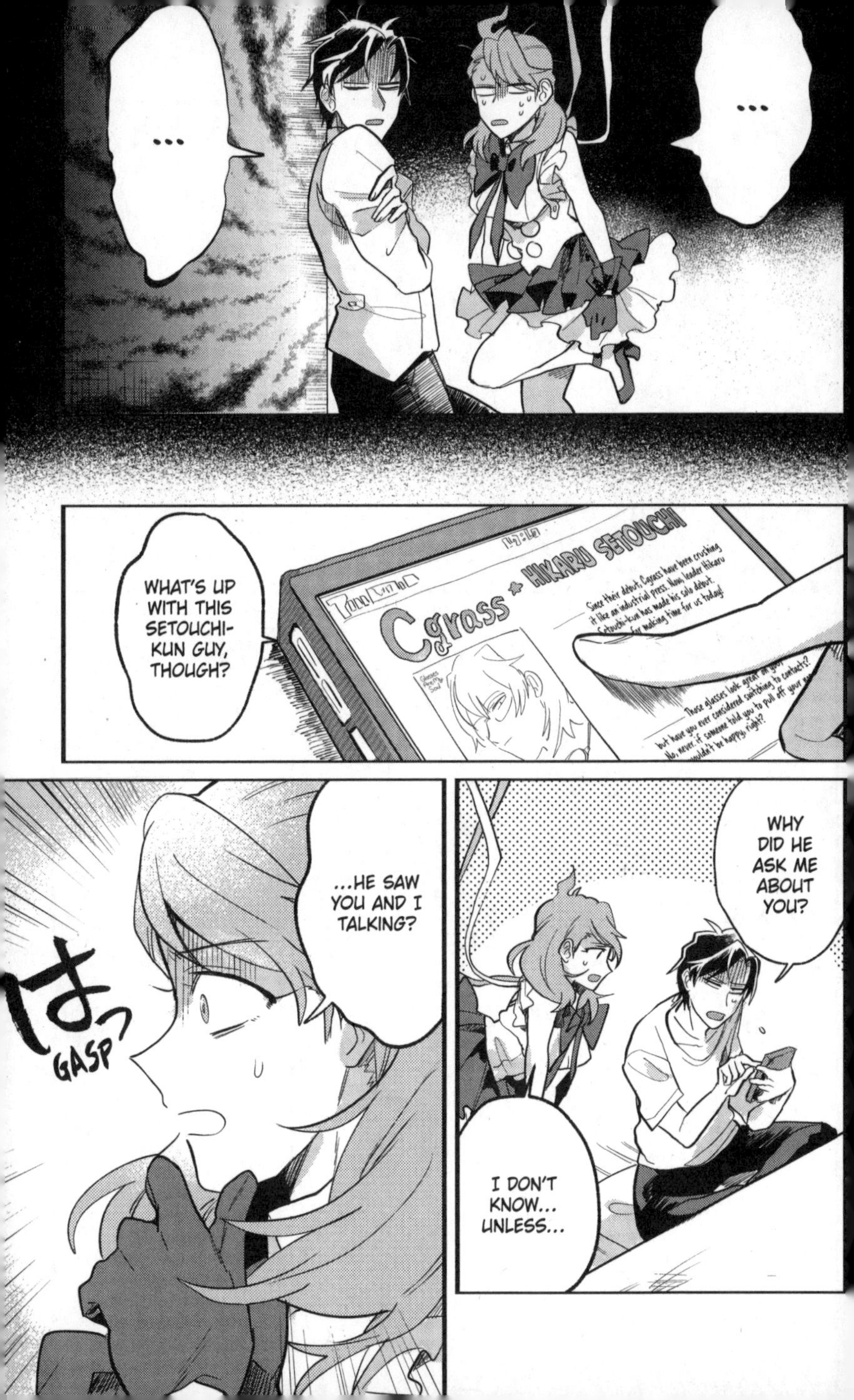
...
...
WHAT'S UP WITH THIS SETOUCHI-KUN GUY, THOUGH?
Cgrass ✿ HIKARU SETOUCHI
Since their debut, Cgrass have been crushing it like an industrial press. Now, leader Hikaru
has made his solo debut.
for making time for us today!
Glasses Are My Soul
Those glasses look great
but have you ever considered switching to contacts?
No, never. If someone told you to pull off your
be happy, right?
WHY DID HE ASK ME ABOUT YOU?
I DON'T KNOW... UNLESS...
...HE SAW YOU AND I TALKING?
はっ
GASP

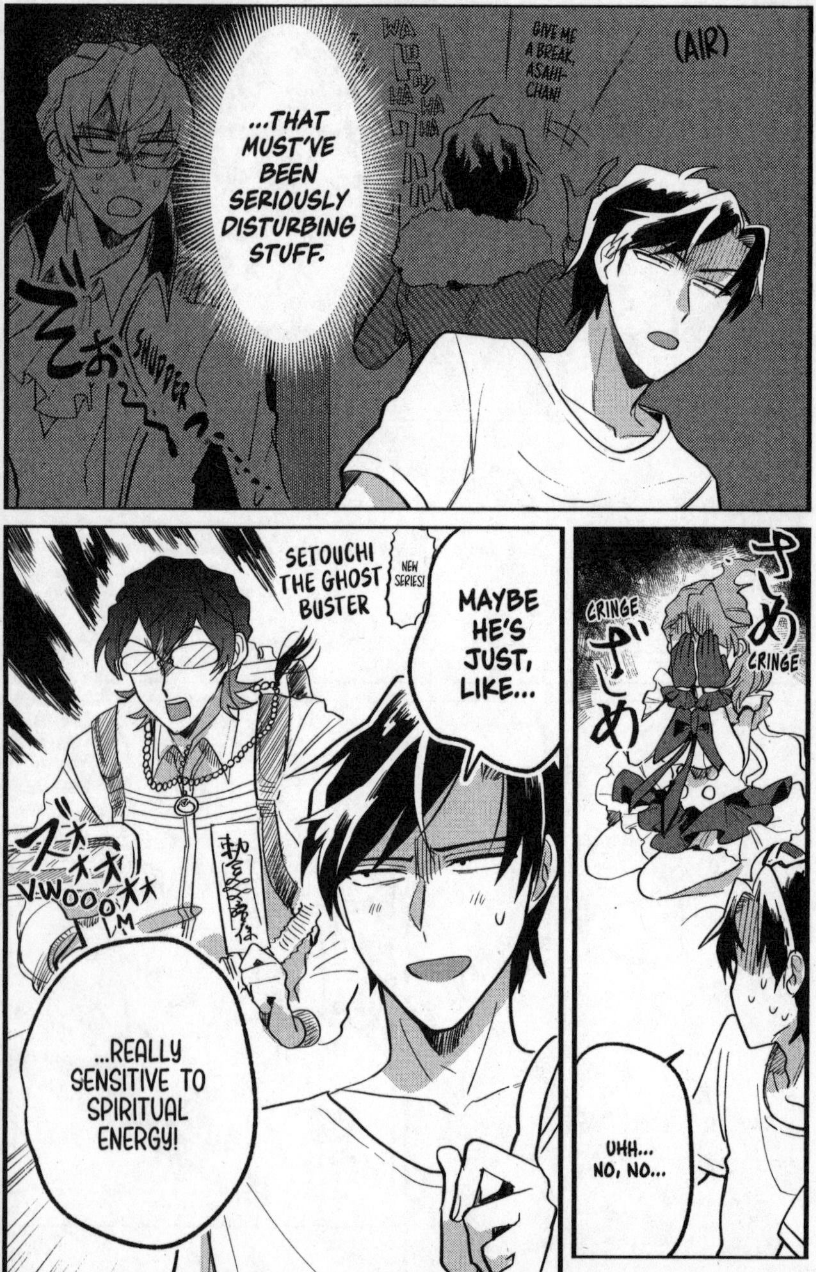
(AIR)
GIVE ME A BREAK, ASAHI-CHAN!
WA HA HA
...THAT MUST'VE BEEN SERIOUSLY DISTURBING STUFF.
SHUDDER
CRINGE
CRINGE
UHH... NO, NO...
MAYBE HE'S JUST, LIKE...
NEW SERIES!
SETOUCHI THE GHOST BUSTER
VWOOOOM
...REALLY SENSITIVE TO SPIRITUAL ENERGY!

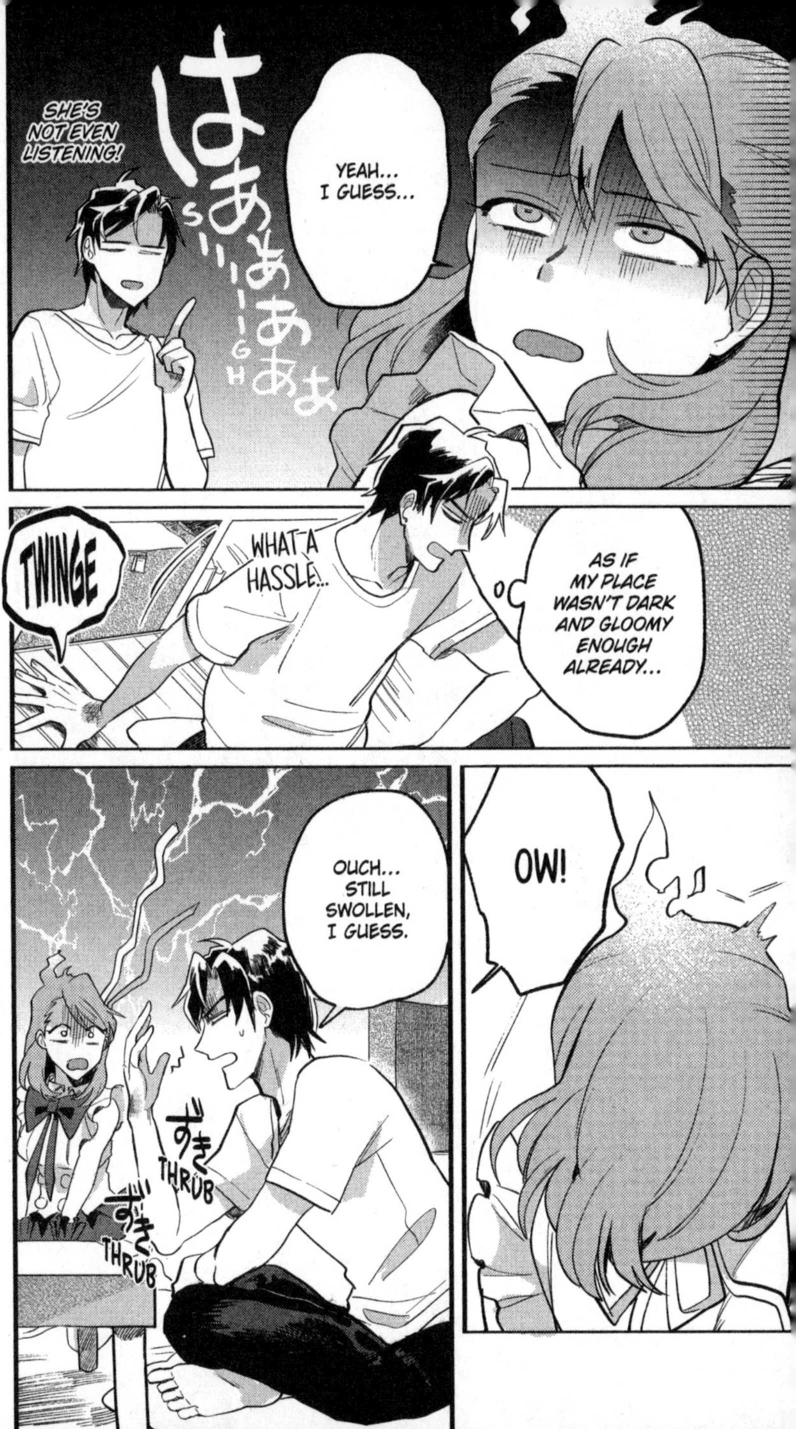
YEAH... I GUESS...
はあぁあああ
SIIIIGH
SHE'S NOT EVEN LISTENING!
AS IF MY PLACE WASN'T DARK AND GLOOMY ENOUGH ALREADY...
WHAT A HASSLE...
TWINGE
OW!
OUCH... STILL SWOLLEN, I GUESS.
ずき
THRUB
ずき
THRUB

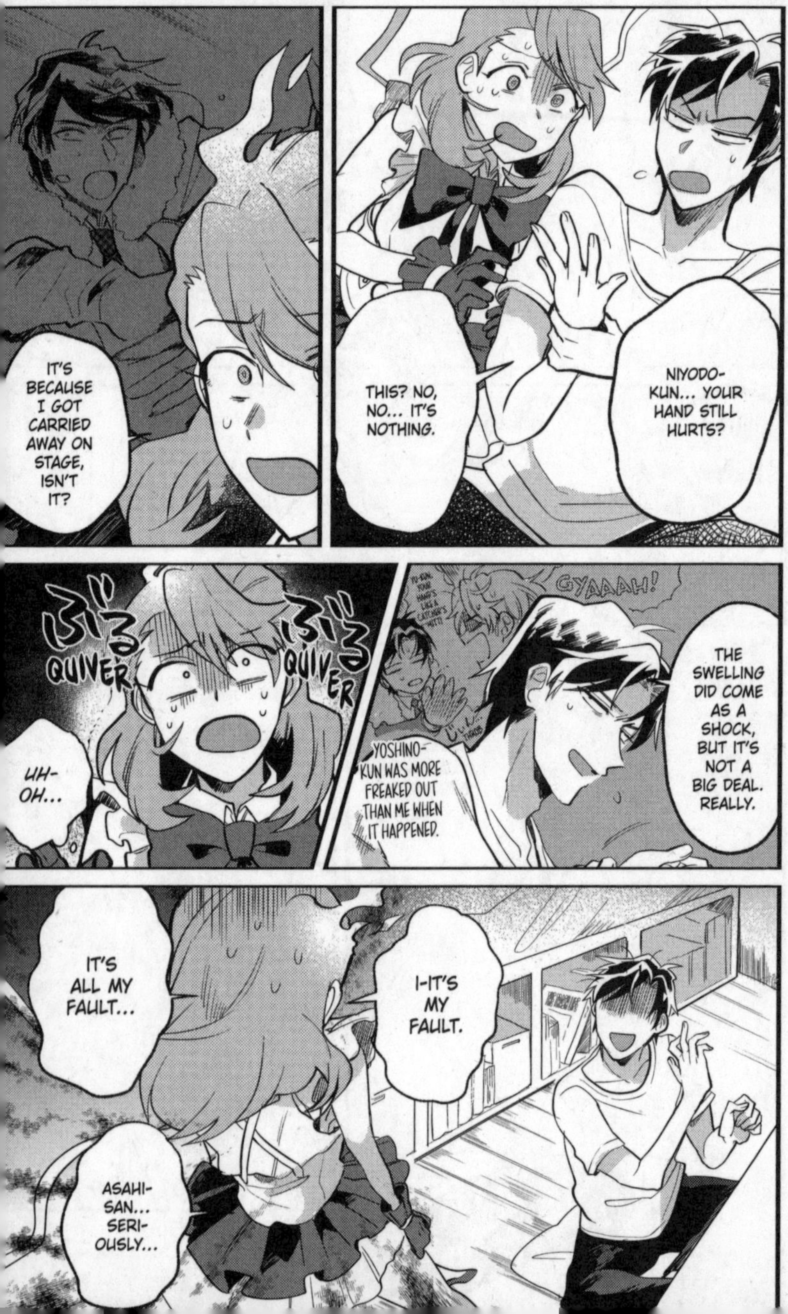
NIYODO-KUN... YOUR HAND STILL HURTS?
THIS? NO, NO... IT'S NOTHING.
IT'S BECAUSE I GOT CARRIED AWAY ON STAGE, ISN'T IT?
GYAAAH!
YU-KUN, YOUR HAND'S LIKE A CATCHER'S MITT!
THE SWELLING DID COME AS A SHOCK, BUT IT'S NOT A BIG DEAL. REALLY.
THROB
YOSHINO-KUN WAS MORE FREAKED OUT THAN ME WHEN IT HAPPENED.
ぶる QUIVER
ぶる QUIVER
UH-OH...
I-IT'S MY FAULT.
IT'S ALL MY FAULT...
ASAHI-SAN... SERIOUSLY...

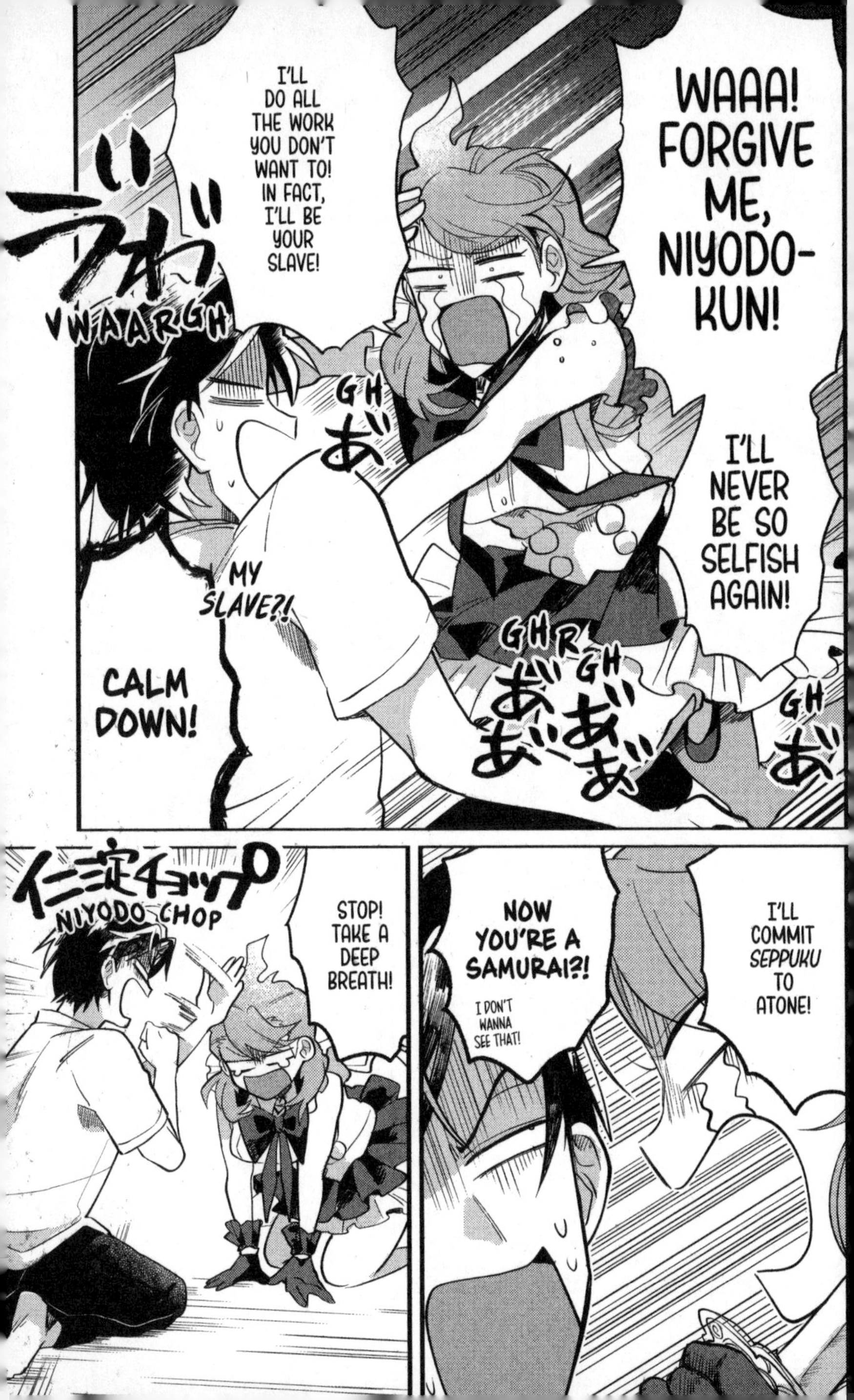
WAAA! FORGIVE ME, NIYODO-KUN!
I'LL DO ALL THE WORK YOU DON'T WANT TO! IN FACT, I'LL BE YOUR SLAVE!
WAARGH
I'LL NEVER BE SO SELFISH AGAIN!
GH
GHRGH
GH
MY SLAVE?!
CALM DOWN!
I'LL COMMIT SEPPUKU TO ATONE!
NOW YOU'RE A SAMURAI?!
I DON'T WANNA SEE THAT!
STOP! TAKE A DEEP BREATH!
NIYODO CHOP

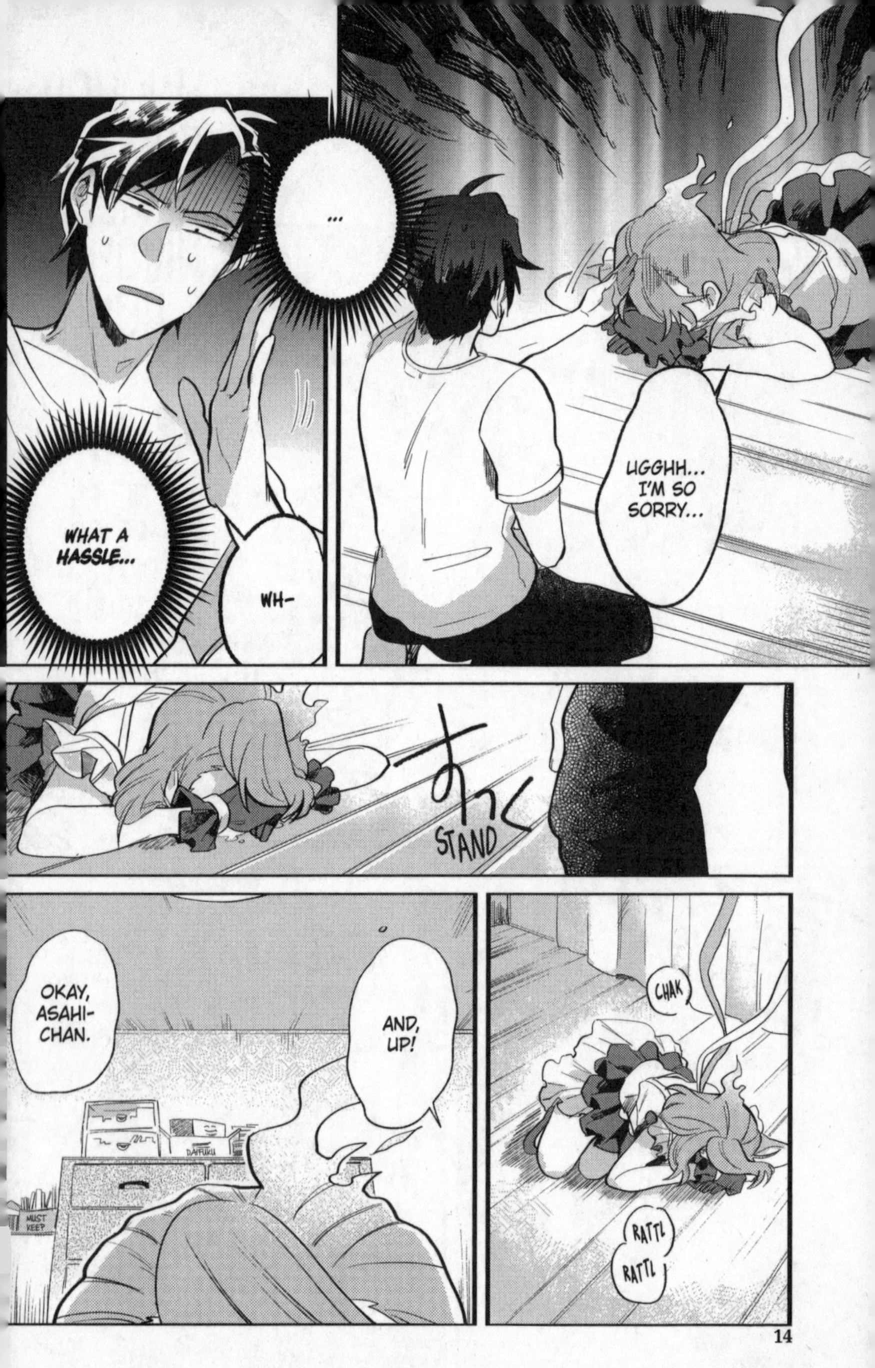
UGGHH... I'M SO SORRY...
...
WHAT A HASSLE...
WH-
STAND
CHAK
RATTL
RATTL
AND, UP!
OKAY, ASAHI-CHAN.
DAIFUKU
MUST KEEP

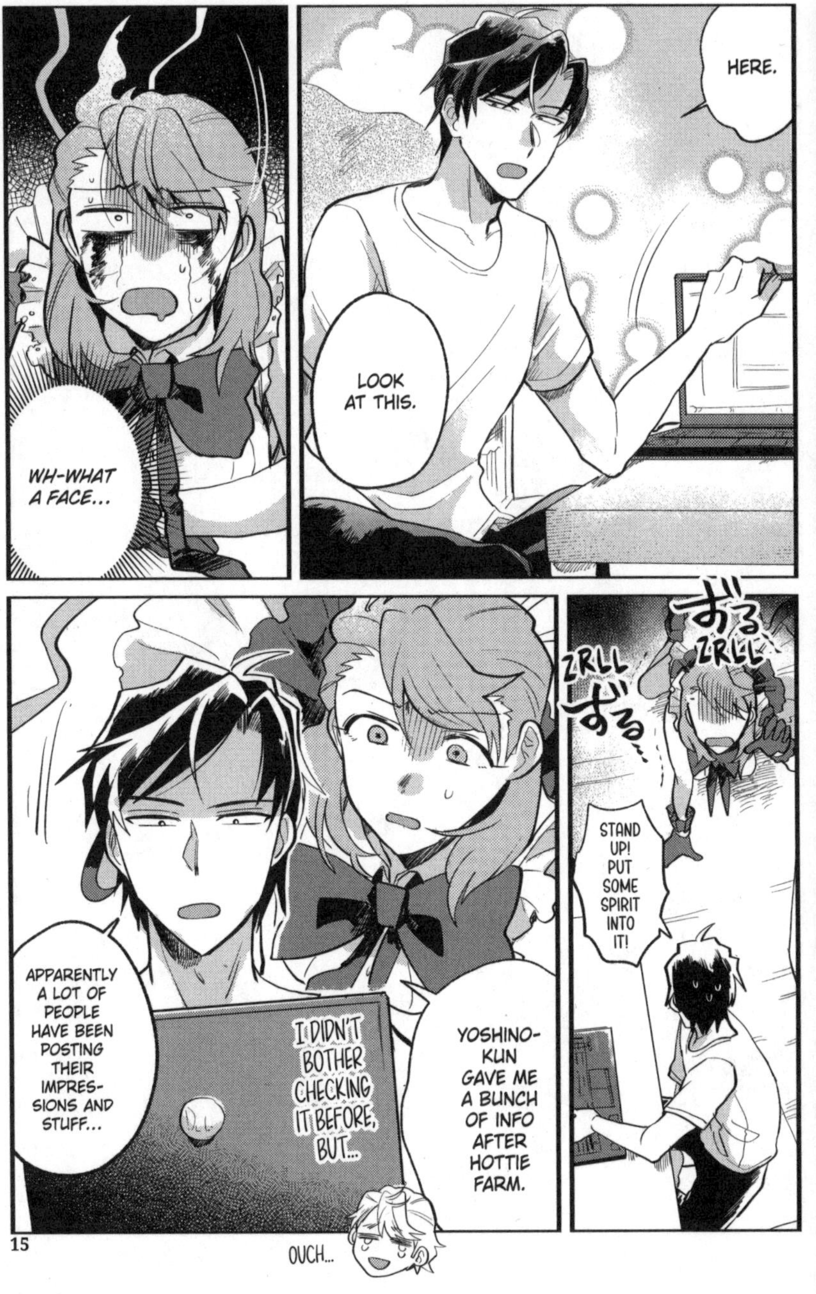
HERE.
LOOK AT THIS.
WH-WHAT A FACE...
おる ZRLL
ZRLL ずる...
STAND UP! PUT SOME SPIRIT INTO IT!
YOSHINO-KUN GAVE ME A BUNCH OF INFO AFTER HOTTIE FARM.
I DIDN'T BOTHER CHECKING IT BEFORE, BUT...
APPARENTLY A LOT OF PEOPLE HAVE BEEN POSTING THEIR IMPRES-SIONS AND STUFF...
OUCH...

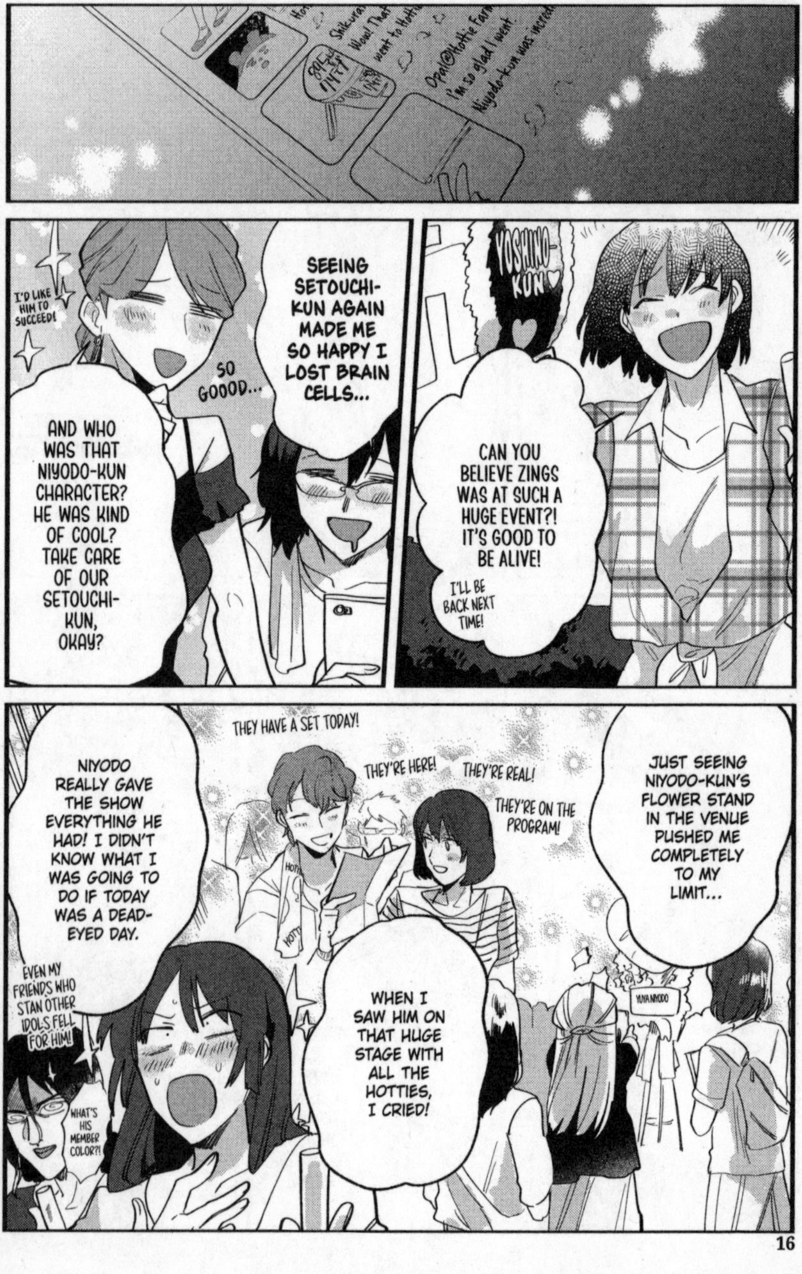
I'm so glad I went.
YOSHINO-KUN♥
CAN YOU BELIEVE ZINGS WAS AT SUCH A HUGE EVENT?! IT'S GOOD TO BE ALIVE!
I'LL BE BACK NEXT TIME!
SEEING SETOUCHI-KUN AGAIN MADE ME SO HAPPY I LOST BRAIN CELLS...
SO GOOOD...
I'D LIKE HIM TO SUCCEED!
AND WHO WAS THAT NIYODO-KUN CHARACTER? HE WAS KIND OF COOL? TAKE CARE OF OUR SETOUCHI-KUN, OKAY?
JUST SEEING NIYODO-KUN'S FLOWER STAND IN THE VENUE PUSHED ME COMPLETELY TO MY LIMIT...
THEY'RE REAL!
THEY'RE ON THE PROGRAM!
THEY'RE HERE!
THEY HAVE A SET TODAY!
NIYODO REALLY GAVE THE SHOW EVERYTHING HE HAD! I DIDN'T KNOW WHAT I WAS GOING TO DO IF TODAY WAS A DEAD-EYED DAY.
WHEN I SAW HIM ON THAT HUGE STAGE WITH ALL THE HOTTIES, I CRIED!
YUYA NIYODO
EVEN MY FRIENDS WHO STAN OTHER IDOLS FELL FOR HIM!
WHAT'S HIS MEMBER COLOR?!

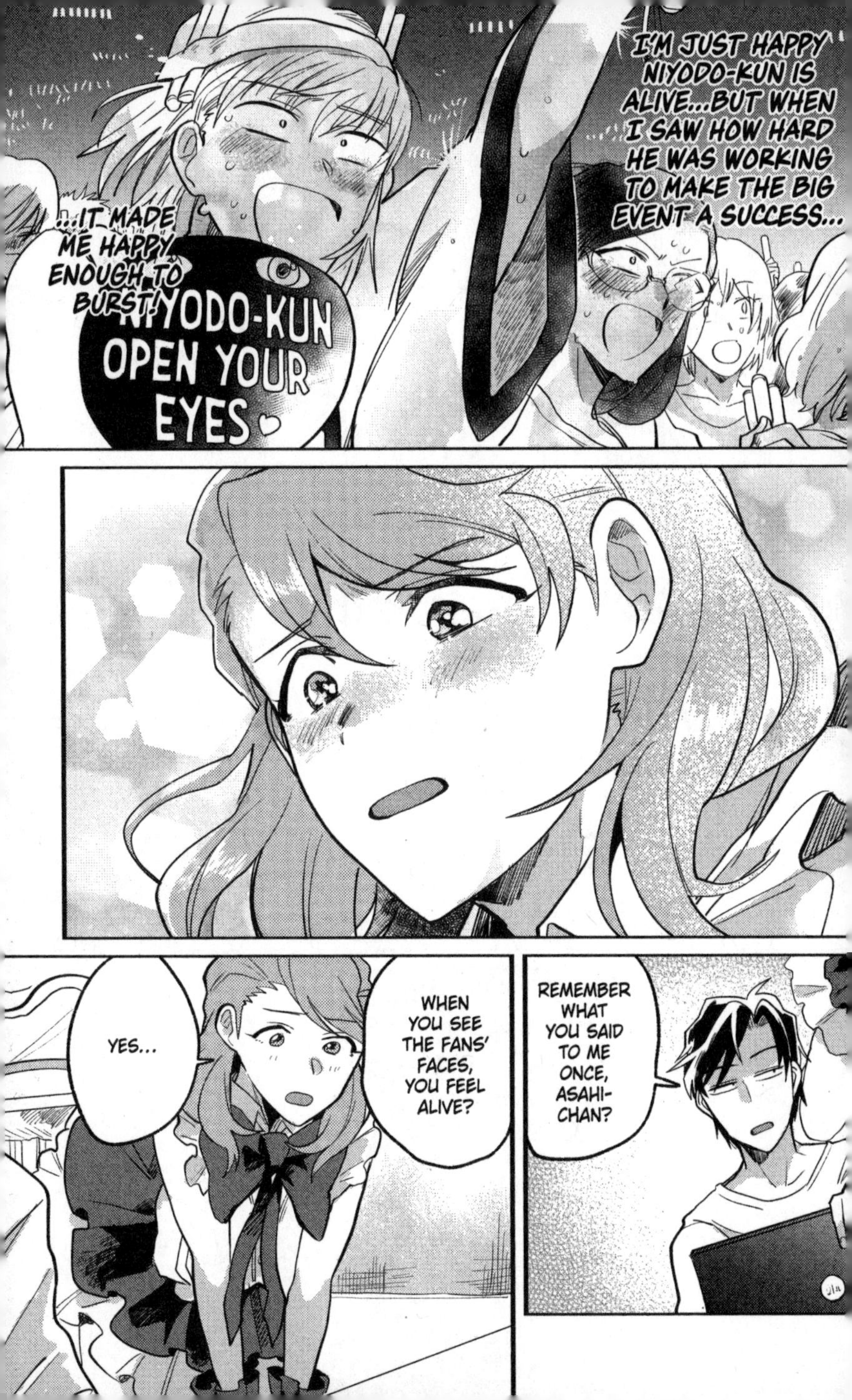
I'M JUST HAPPY NIYODO-KUN IS ALIVE...BUT WHEN I SAW HOW HARD HE WAS WORKING TO MAKE THE BIG EVENT A SUCCESS...
...IT MADE ME HAPPY ENOUGH TO BURST!
NIYODO-KUN OPEN YOUR EYES
REMEMBER WHAT YOU SAID TO ME ONCE, ASAHI-CHAN?
WHEN YOU SEE THE FANS' FACES, YOU FEEL ALIVE?
YES...

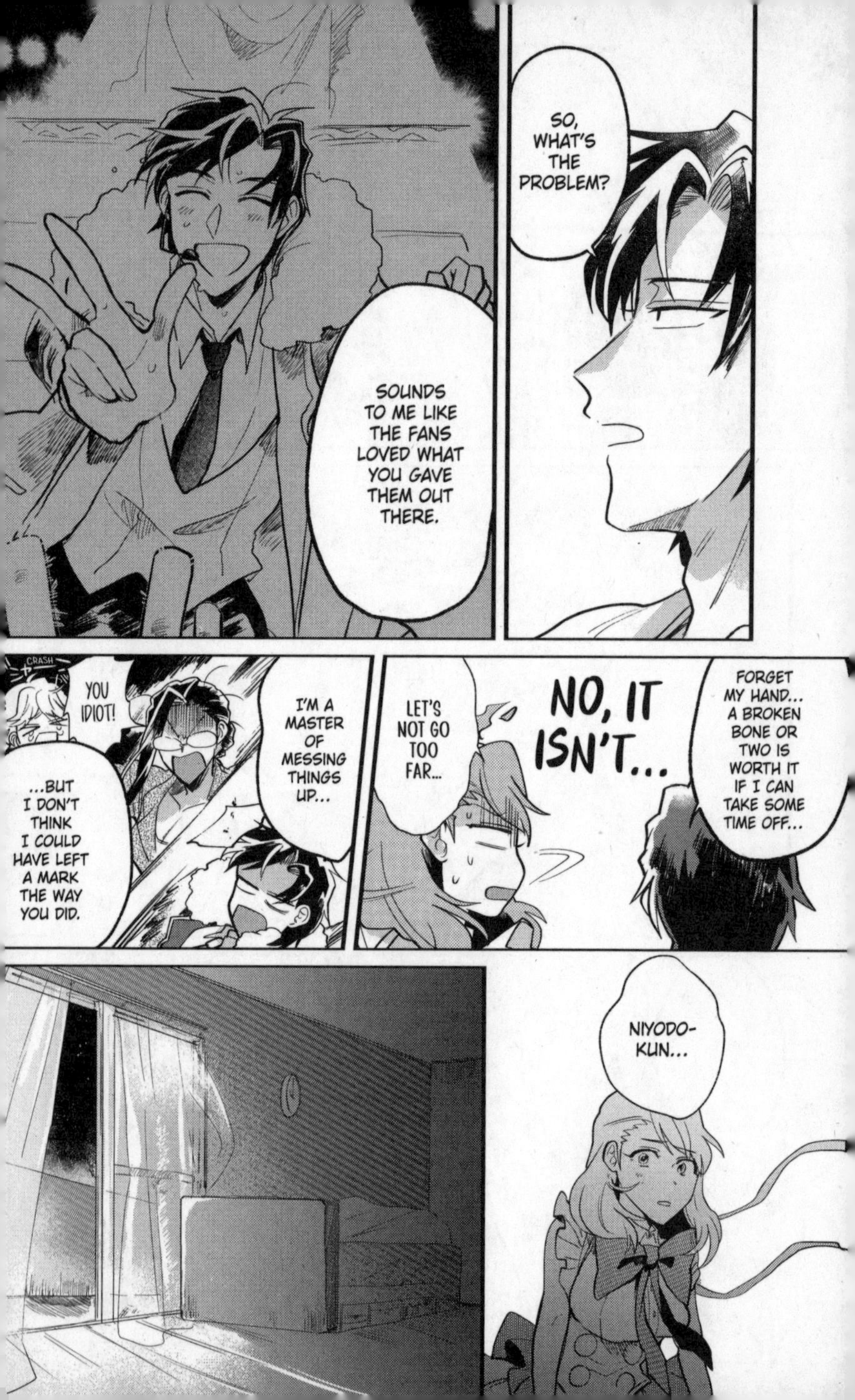
SO, WHAT'S THE PROBLEM?
SOUNDS TO ME LIKE THE FANS LOVED WHAT YOU GAVE THEM OUT THERE.
FORGET MY HAND... A BROKEN BONE OR TWO IS WORTH IT IF I CAN TAKE SOME TIME OFF...
NO, IT ISN'T...
LET'S NOT GO TOO FAR...
I'M A MASTER OF MESSING THINGS UP...
YOU IDIOT!
CRASH
...BUT I DON'T THINK I COULD HAVE LEFT A MARK THE WAY YOU DID.
NIYODO-KUN...

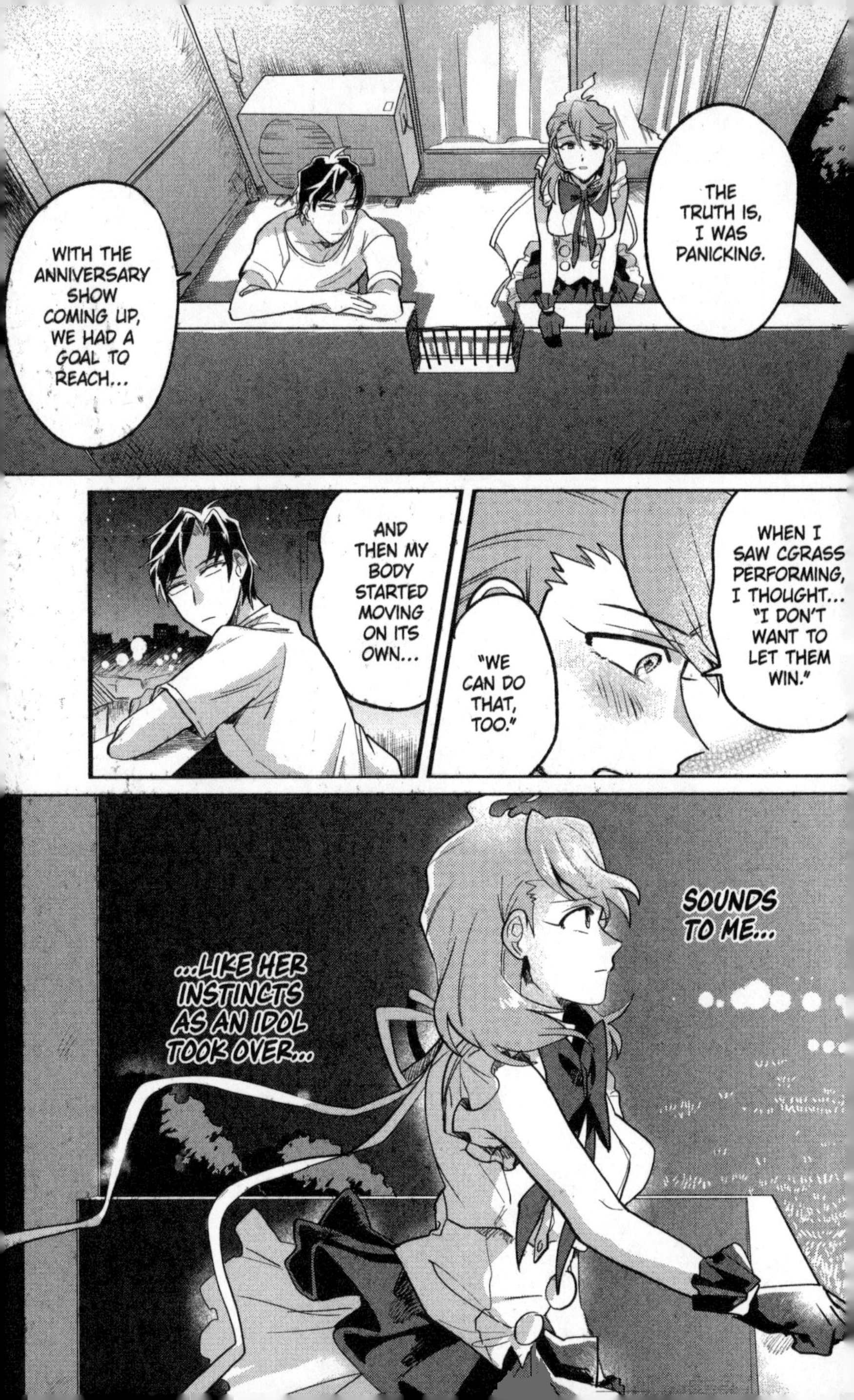
THE TRUTH IS, I WAS PANICKING.
WITH THE ANNIVERSARY SHOW COMING UP, WE HAD A GOAL TO REACH...
WHEN I SAW CGRASS PERFORMING, I THOUGHT... "I DON'T WANT TO LET THEM WIN."
"WE CAN DO THAT, TOO."
AND THEN MY BODY STARTED MOVING ON ITS OWN...
SOUNDS TO ME...
...LIKE HER INSTINCTS AS AN IDOL TOOK OVER...

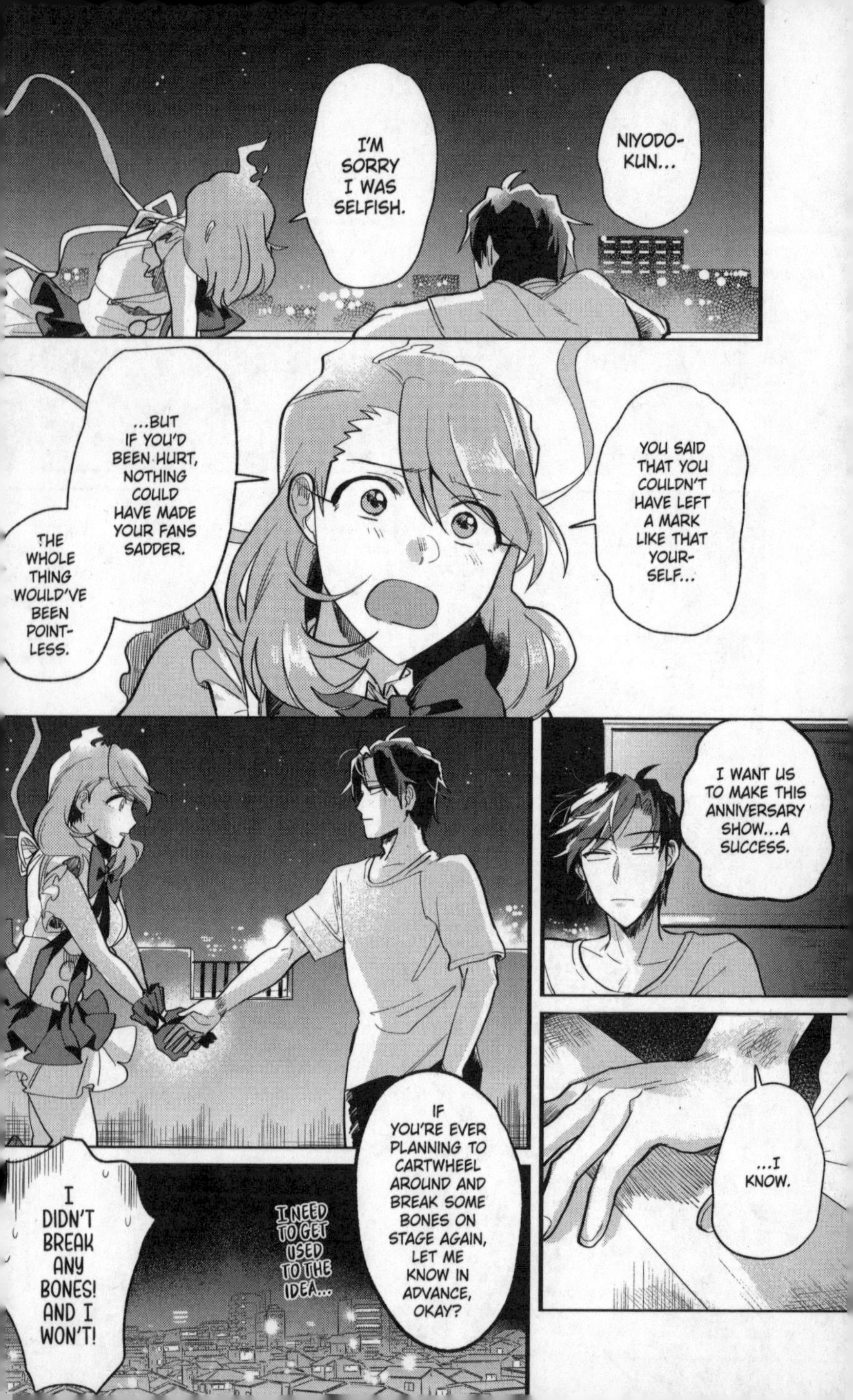
NIYODO-KUN...
I'M SORRY I WAS SELFISH.
YOU SAID THAT YOU COULDN'T HAVE LEFT A MARK LIKE THAT YOURSELF...
...BUT IF YOU'D BEEN HURT, NOTHING COULD HAVE MADE YOUR FANS SADDER.
THE WHOLE THING WOULD'VE BEEN POINTLESS.
I WANT US TO MAKE THIS ANNIVERSARY SHOW...A SUCCESS.
...I KNOW.
IF YOU'RE EVER PLANNING TO CARTWHEEL AROUND AND BREAK SOME BONES ON STAGE AGAIN, LET ME KNOW IN ADVANCE, OKAY?
I NEED TO GET USED TO THE IDEA...
I DIDN'T BREAK ANY BONES! AND I WON'T!

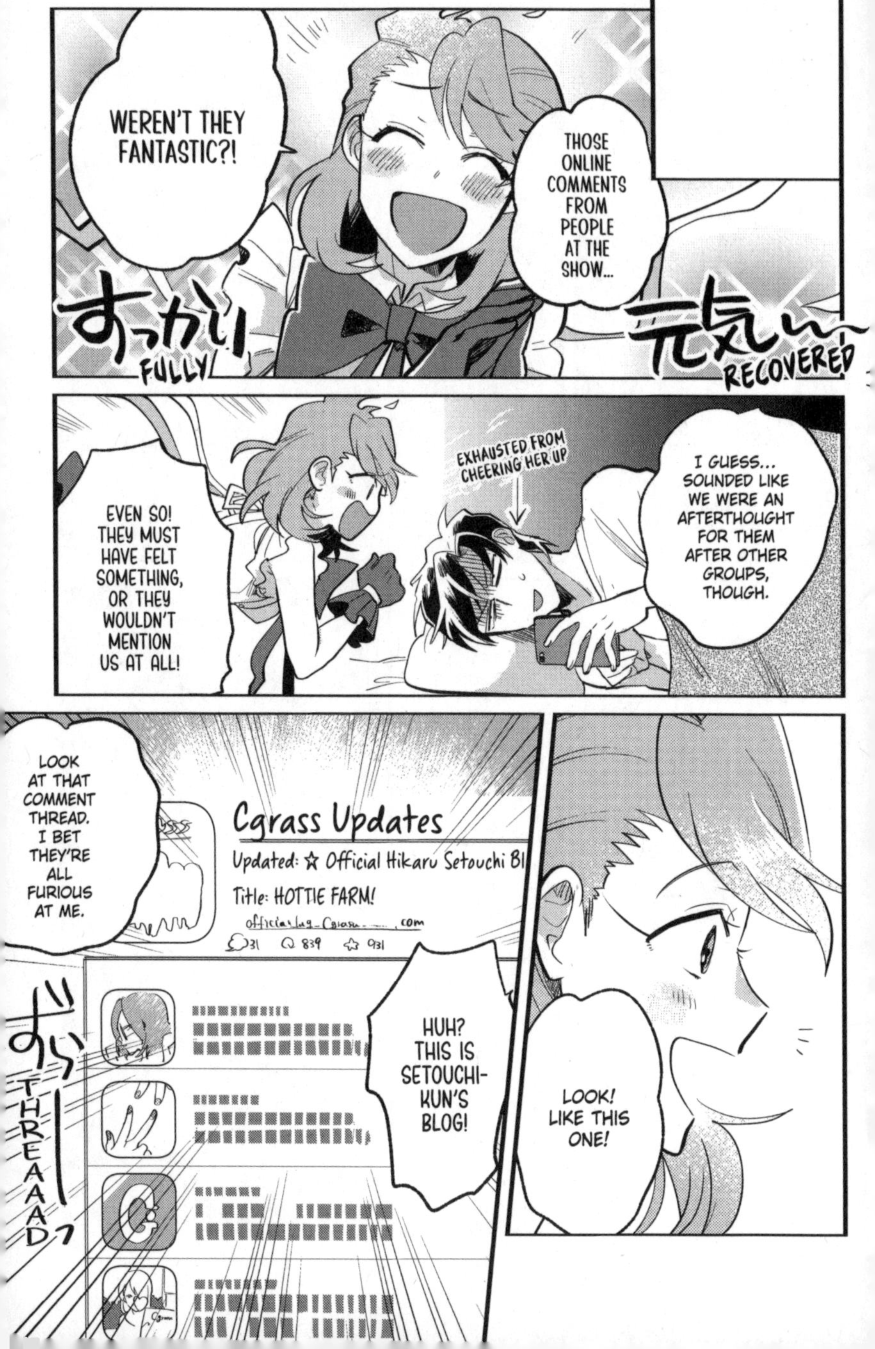
THOSE ONLINE COMMENTS FROM PEOPLE AT THE SHOW...
WEREN'T THEY FANTASTIC?!
元気
RECOVERED
すっかり
FULLY
I GUESS... SOUNDED LIKE WE WERE AN AFTERTHOUGHT FOR THEM AFTER OTHER GROUPS, THOUGH.
EXHAUSTED FROM CHEERING HER UP
EVEN SO! THEY MUST HAVE FELT SOMETHING, OR THEY WOULDN'T MENTION US AT ALL!
LOOK! LIKE THIS ONE!
Cgrass Updates
Updated: ☆ Official Hikaru Setouchi Bl
Title: HOTTIE FARM!
31 839 931
HUH? THIS IS SETOUCHI-KUN'S BLOG!
LOOK AT THAT COMMENT THREAD. I BET THEY'RE ALL FURIOUS AT ME.
ずらー
THREAAAD

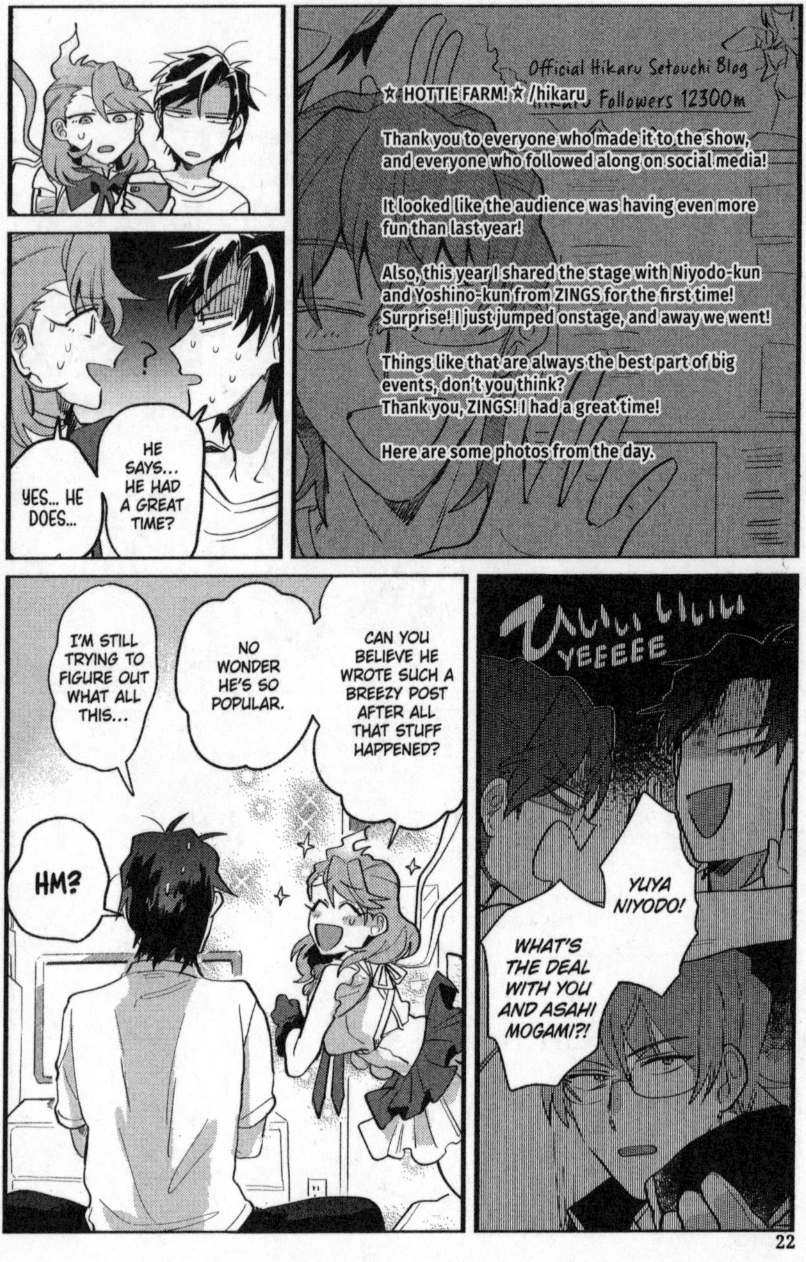
Official Hikaru Setouchi Blog
☆ HOTTIE FARM! ☆ /hikaru
Followers 12300m
Thank you to everyone who made it to the show, and everyone who followed along on social media!
It looked like the audience was having even more fun than last year!
Also, this year I shared the stage with Niyodo-kun and Yoshino-kun from ZINGS for the first time! Surprise! I just jumped onstage, and away we went!
Things like that are always the best part of big events, don't you think?
Thank you, ZINGS! I had a great time!
Here are some photos from the day.
HE SAYS... HE HAD A GREAT TIME?
YES... HE DOES...
YEEEEE
YUYA NIYODO!
WHAT'S THE DEAL WITH YOU AND ASAHI MOGAMI?!
CAN YOU BELIEVE HE WROTE SUCH A BREEZY POST AFTER ALL THAT STUFF HAPPENED?
NO WONDER HE'S SO POPULAR.
I'M STILL TRYING TO FIGURE OUT WHAT ALL THIS...
HM?

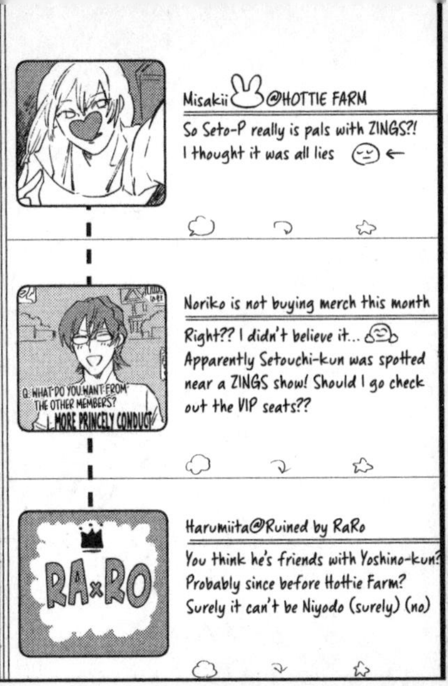
Misakii @HOTTIE FARM
So Seto-P really is pals with ZINGS?! I thought it was all lies
Noriko is not buying merch this month
Q. WHAT DO YOU WANT FROM THE OTHER MEMBERS?
MORE PRINCELY CONDUCT
Right?? I didn't believe it... Apparently Setouchi-kun was spotted near a ZINGS show! Should I go check out the VIP seats??
Harumiita@Ruined by RaRo
RA×RO
You think he's friends with Yoshino-kun? Probably since before Hottie Farm? Surely it can't be Niyodo (surely) (no)
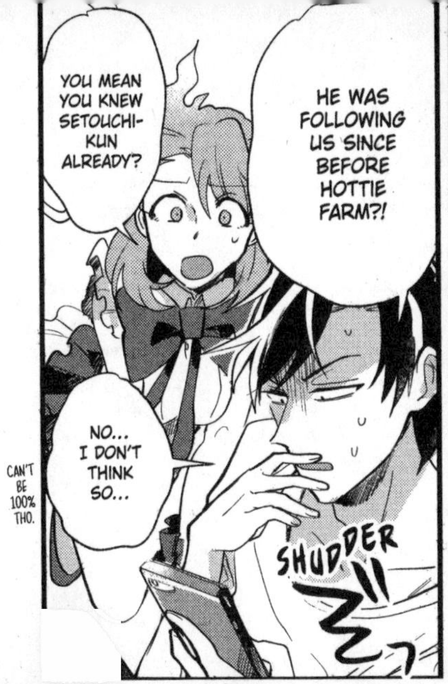
HE WAS FOLLOWING US SINCE BEFORE HOTTIE FARM?!
YOU MEAN YOU KNEW SETOUCHI-KUN ALREADY?
NO... I DON'T THINK SO...
CAN'T BE 100% THO.
SHUDDER
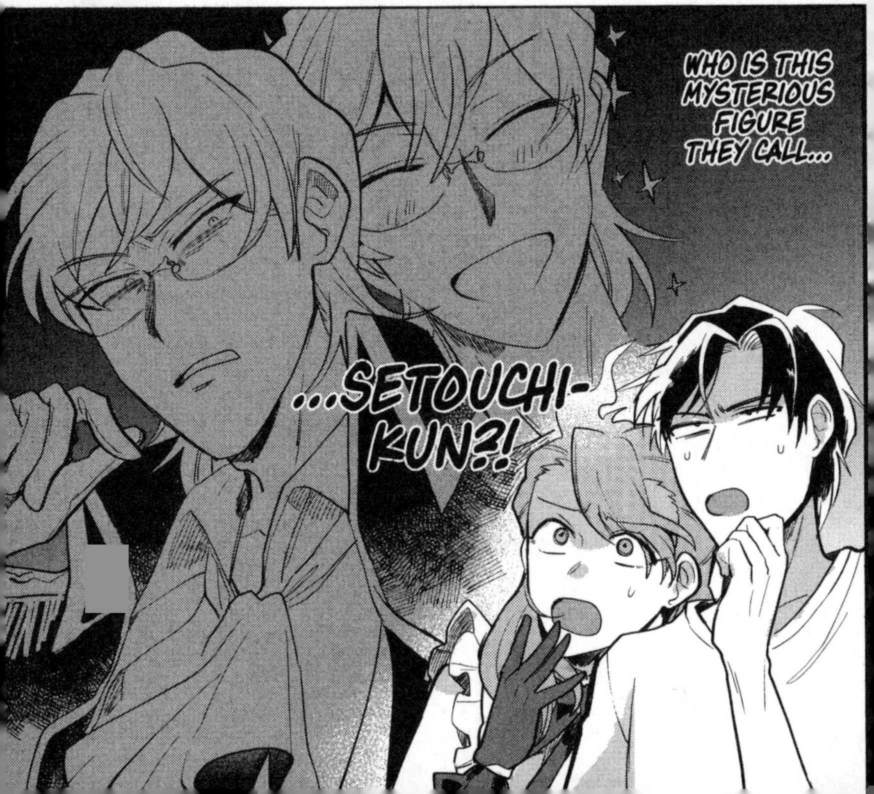
WHO IS THIS MYSTERIOUS FIGURE THEY CALL...
...SETOUCHI-KUN?!

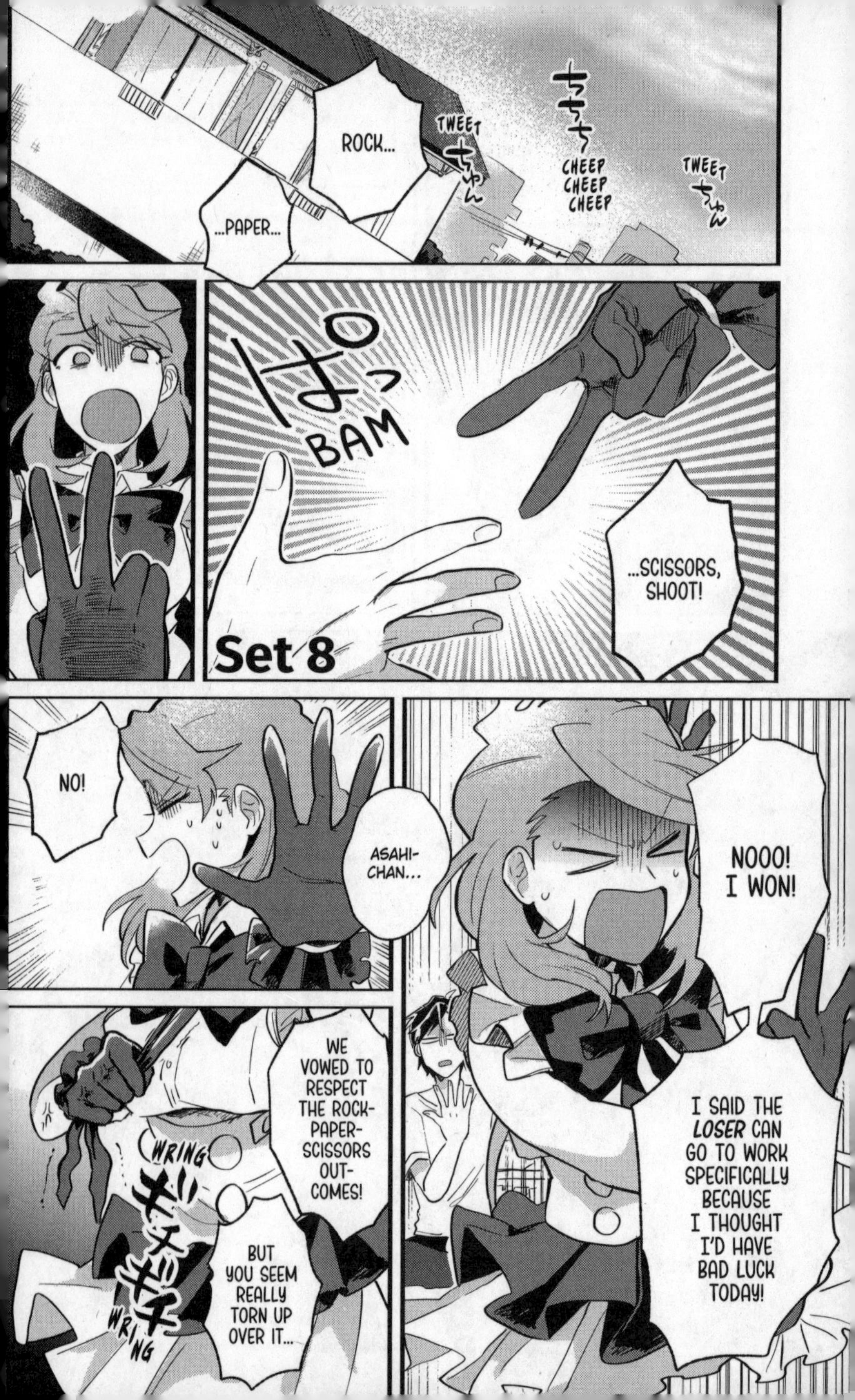
TWEET ちゅん
ちちち CHEEP CHEEP CHEEP
TWEET ちゅん
ROCK...
...PAPER...
...SCISSORS, SHOOT!
ぱっ BAM
Set 8
NOOO! I WON!
ASAHI-CHAN...
NO!
I SAID THE *LOSER* CAN GO TO WORK SPECIFICALLY BECAUSE I THOUGHT I'D HAVE BAD LUCK TODAY!
WE VOWED TO RESPECT THE ROCK-PAPER-SCISSORS OUT-COMES!
BUT YOU SEEM REALLY TORN UP OVER IT...
WRING ギチギチ WRING

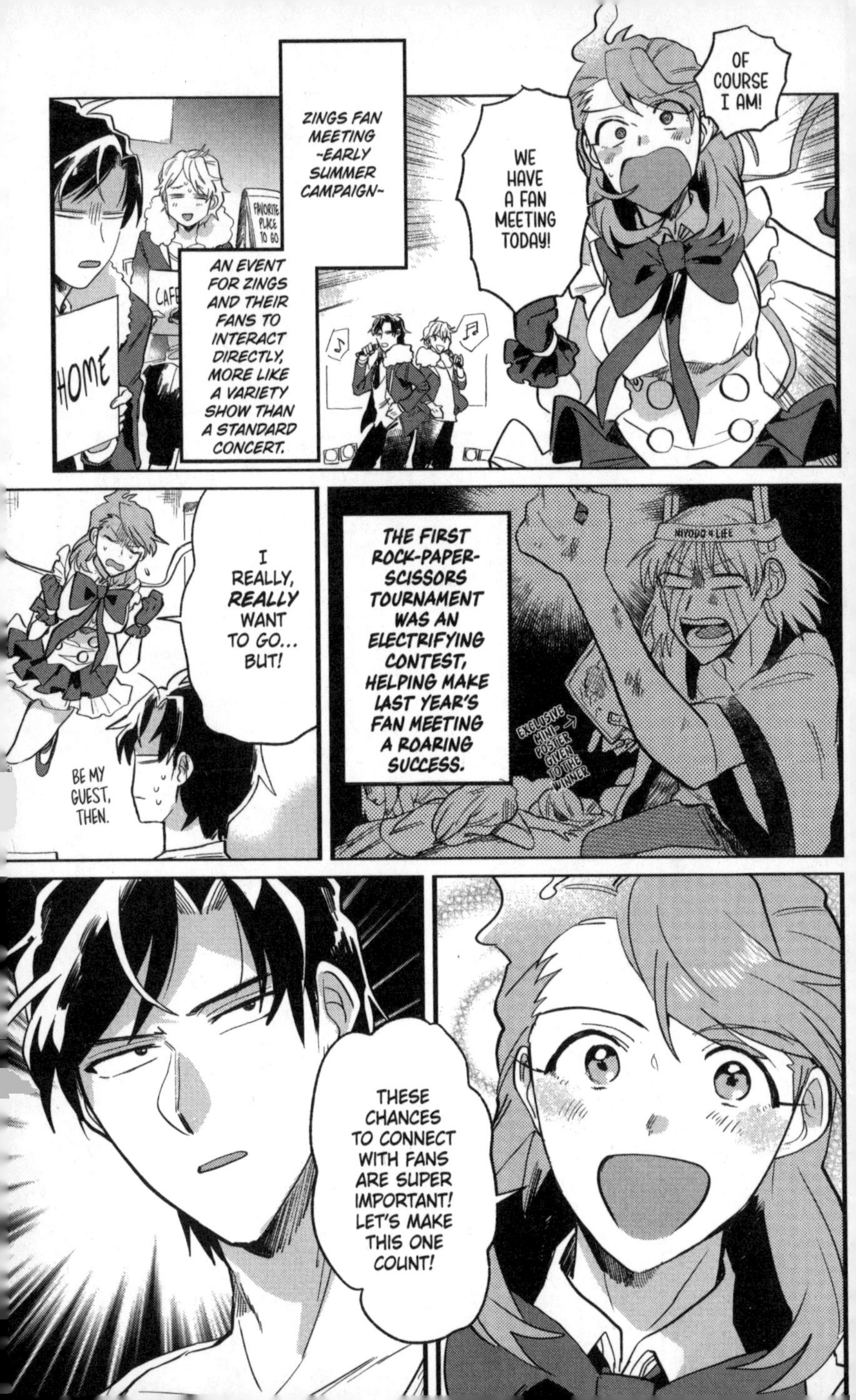
OF COURSE I AM!
WE HAVE A FAN MEETING TODAY!
ZINGS FAN MEETING ~EARLY SUMMER CAMPAIGN~
AN EVENT FOR ZINGS AND THEIR FANS TO INTERACT DIRECTLY, MORE LIKE A VARIETY SHOW THAN A STANDARD CONCERT.
FAVORITE PLACE TO GO
CAFE
HOME
THE FIRST ROCK-PAPER-SCISSORS TOURNAMENT WAS AN ELECTRIFYING CONTEST, HELPING MAKE LAST YEAR'S FAN MEETING A ROARING SUCCESS.
NIYODO 4 LIFE
EXCLUSIVE MINI-POSTER GIVEN TO THE WINNER
I REALLY, REALLY WANT TO GO... BUT!
BE MY GUEST, THEN.
THESE CHANCES TO CONNECT WITH FANS ARE SUPER IMPORTANT! LET'S MAKE THIS ONE COUNT!

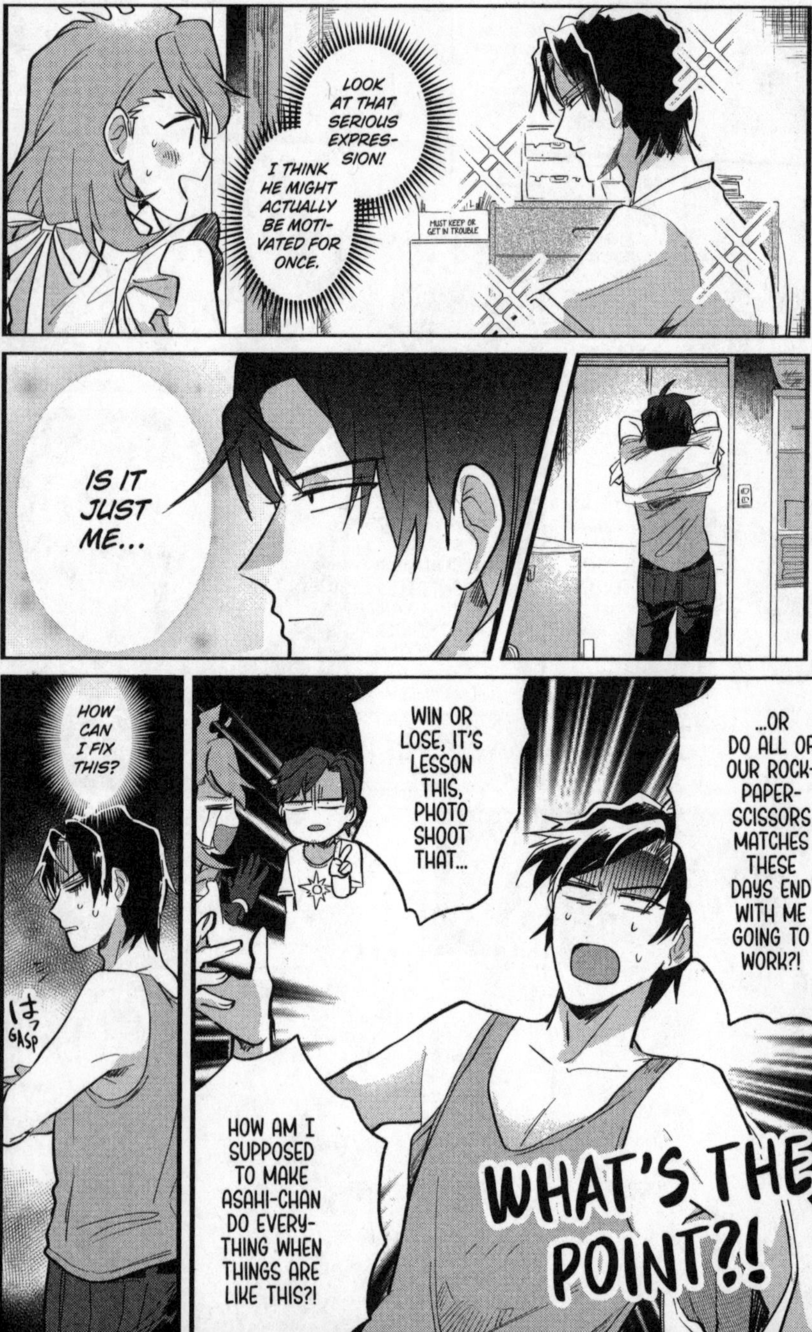
LOOK AT THAT SERIOUS EXPRESSION!
I THINK HE MIGHT ACTUALLY BE MOTIVATED FOR ONCE.
MUST KEEP OR GET IN TROUBLE
IS IT JUST ME...
...OR DO ALL OF OUR ROCK-PAPER-SCISSORS MATCHES THESE DAYS END WITH ME GOING TO WORK?!
WIN OR LOSE, IT'S LESSON THIS, PHOTO SHOOT THAT...
WHAT'S THE POINT?!
HOW AM I SUPPOSED TO MAKE ASAHI-CHAN DO EVERYTHING WHEN THINGS ARE LIKE THIS?!
HOW CAN I FIX THIS?
はっ
GASP

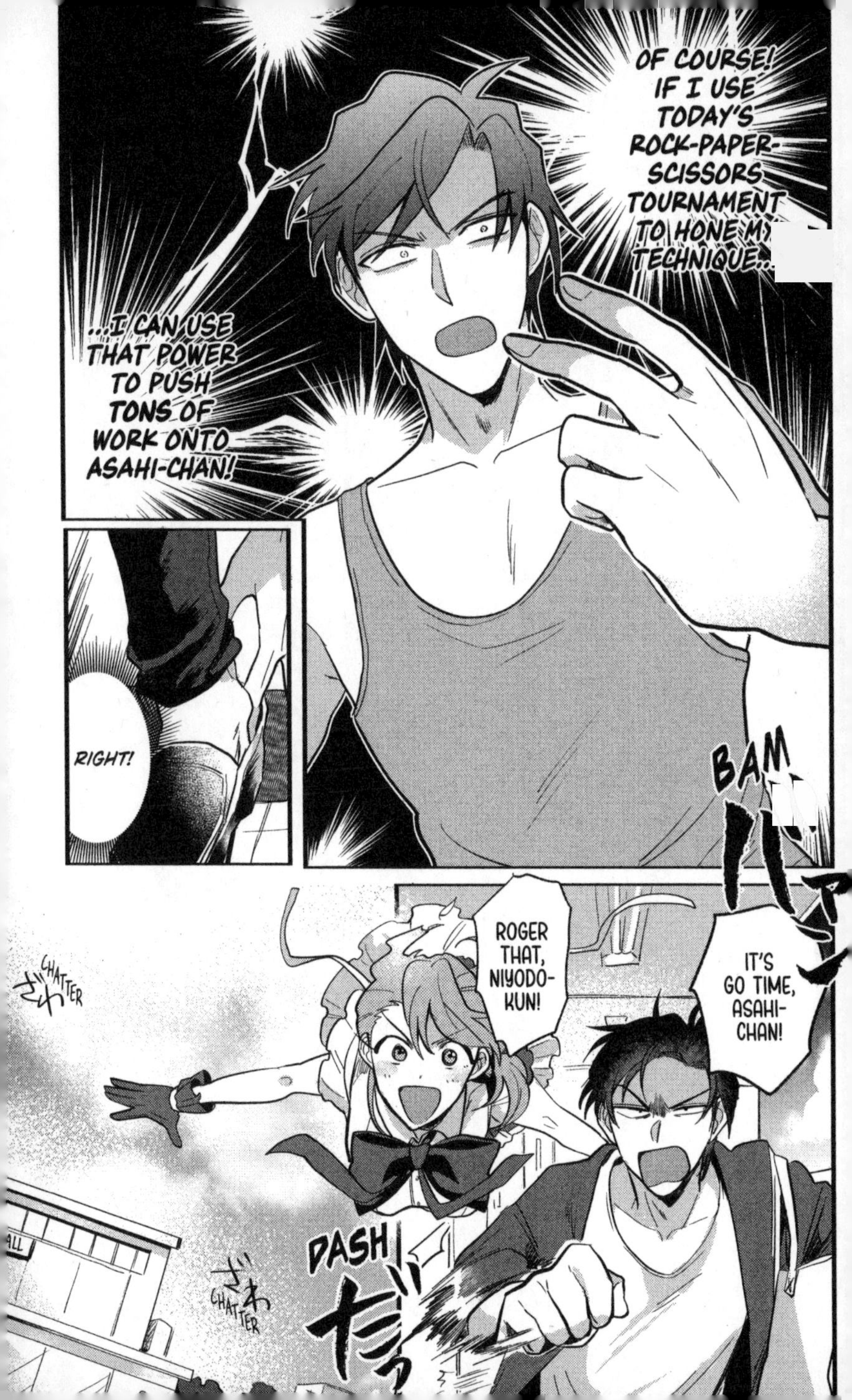
OF COURSE! IF I USE TODAY'S ROCK-PAPER-SCISSORS TOURNAMENT TO HONE MY TECHNIQUE...
...I CAN USE THAT POWER TO PUSH TONS OF WORK ONTO ASAHI-CHAN!
BAM
RIGHT!
IT'S GO TIME, ASAHI-CHAN!
ROGER THAT, NIYODO-KUN!
CHATTER
DASH
CHATTER

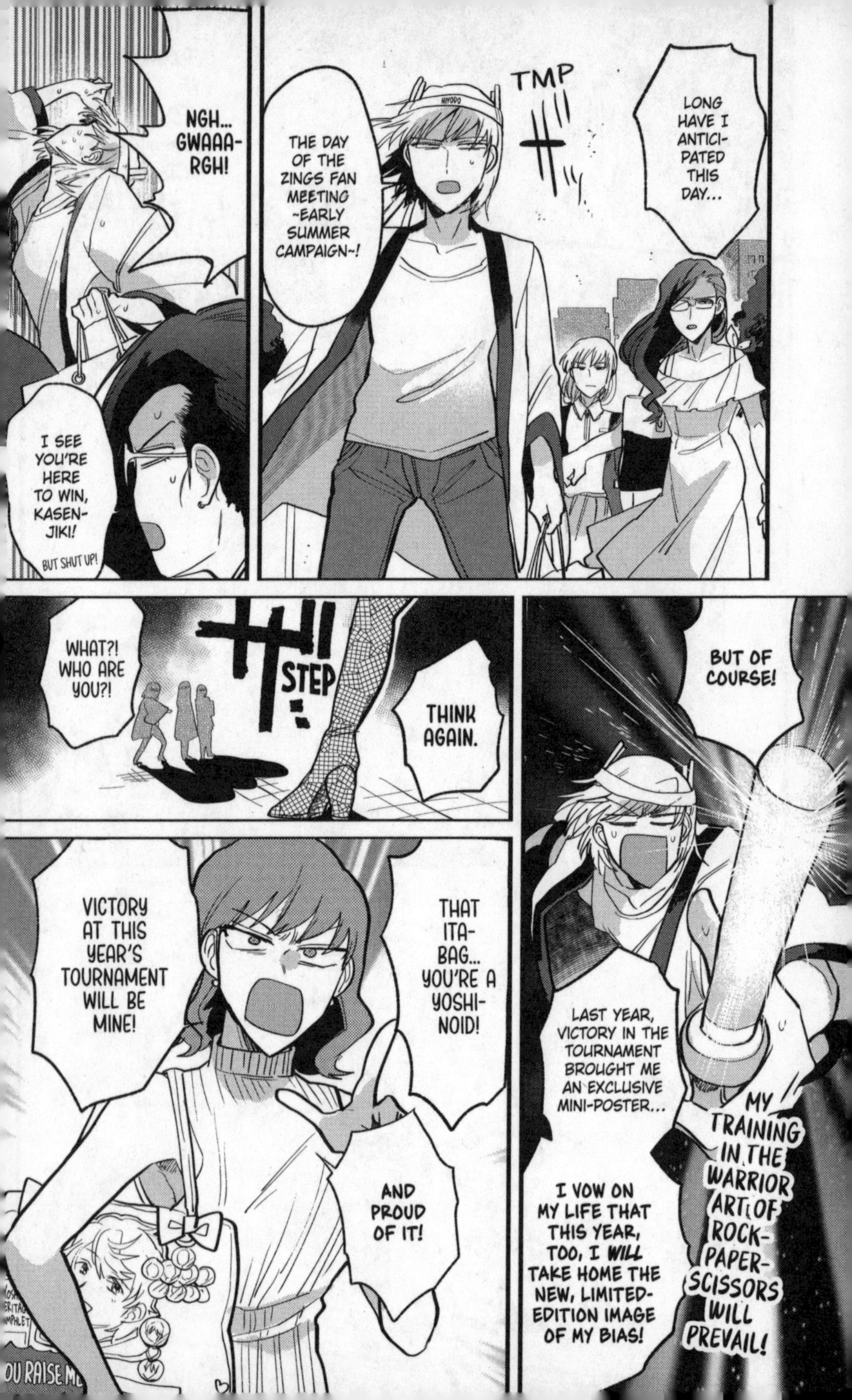
TMP
LONG HAVE I ANTICI-PATED THIS DAY...
NIYODO
THE DAY OF THE ZINGS FAN MEETING ~EARLY SUMMER CAMPAIGN~!
NGH... GWAAA-RGH!
I SEE YOU'RE HERE TO WIN, KASEN-JIKI!
BUT SHUT UP!
BUT OF COURSE!
LAST YEAR, VICTORY IN THE TOURNAMENT BROUGHT ME AN EXCLUSIVE MINI-POSTER...
MY TRAINING IN THE WARRIOR ART OF ROCK-PAPER-SCISSORS WILL PREVAIL!
I VOW ON MY LIFE THAT THIS YEAR, TOO, I WILL TAKE HOME THE NEW, LIMITED-EDITION IMAGE OF MY BIAS!
STEP
THINK AGAIN.
WHAT?! WHO ARE YOU?!
THAT ITA-BAG... YOU'RE A YOSHI-NOID!
VICTORY AT THIS YEAR'S TOURNAMENT WILL BE MINE!
AND PROUD OF IT!

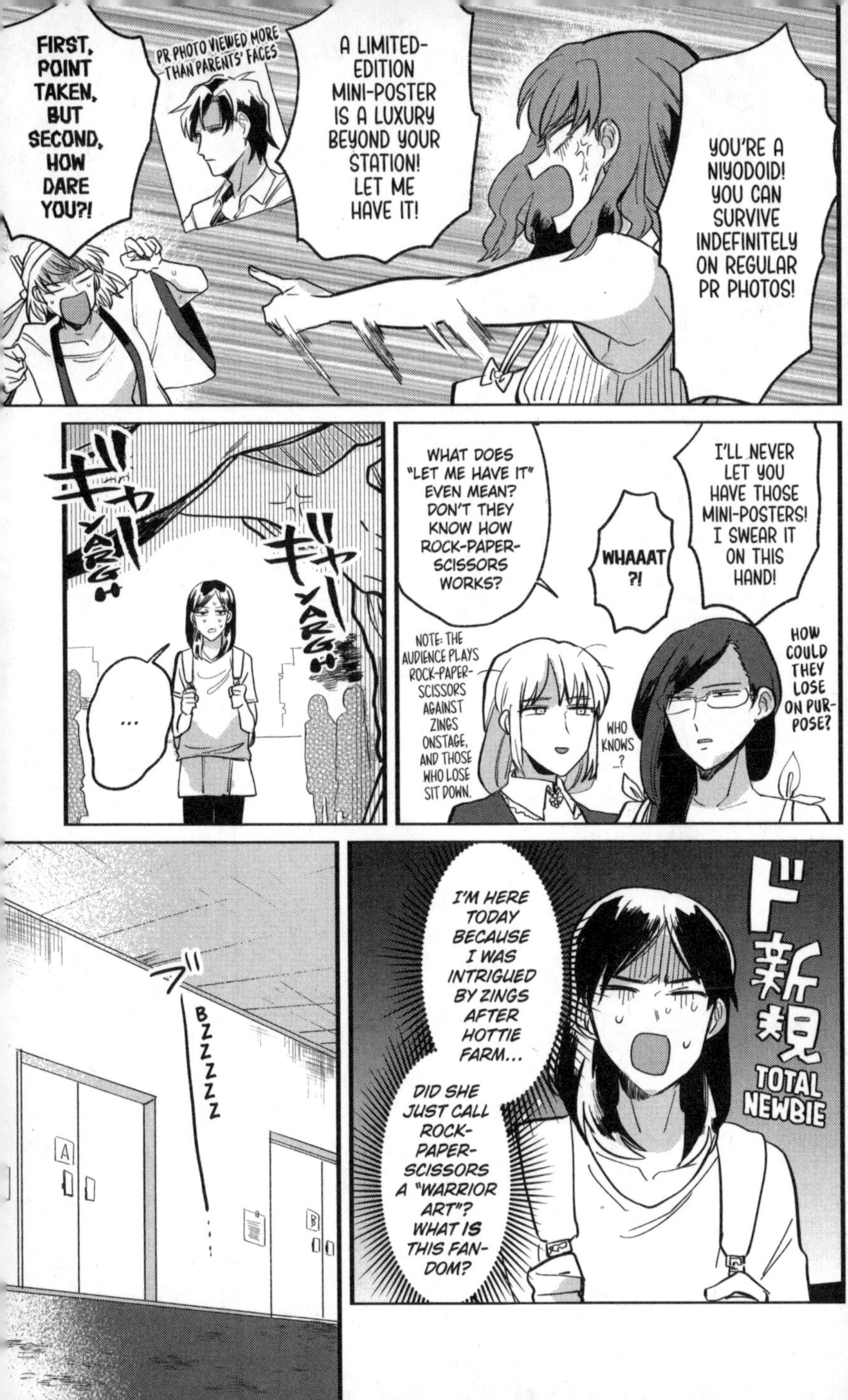

YOU'RE A NIYODOID! YOU CAN SURVIVE INDEFINITELY ON REGULAR PR PHOTOS!
A LIMITED-EDITION MINI-POSTER IS A LUXURY BEYOND YOUR STATION! LET ME HAVE IT!
PR PHOTO VIEWED MORE THAN PARENTS' FACES
FIRST, POINT TAKEN, BUT SECOND, HOW DARE YOU?!
I'LL NEVER LET YOU HAVE THOSE MINI-POSTERS! I SWEAR IT ON THIS HAND!
WHAAAT?!
WHAT DOES "LET ME HAVE IT" EVEN MEAN? DON'T THEY KNOW HOW ROCK-PAPER-SCISSORS WORKS?
HOW COULD THEY LOSE ON PURPOSE?
WHO KNOWS...?
NOTE: THE AUDIENCE PLAYS ROCK-PAPER-SCISSORS AGAINST ZINGS ONSTAGE, AND THOSE WHO LOSE SIT DOWN.
ギャー
ARGH
ギャー
ARGH
...
ド新規
TOTAL NEWBIE
I'M HERE TODAY BECAUSE I WAS INTRIGUED BY ZINGS AFTER HOTTIE FARM...
DID SHE JUST CALL ROCK-PAPER-SCISSORS A "WARRIOR ART"? WHAT IS THIS FANDOM?
ブ
BZZZZZZ...
A
B

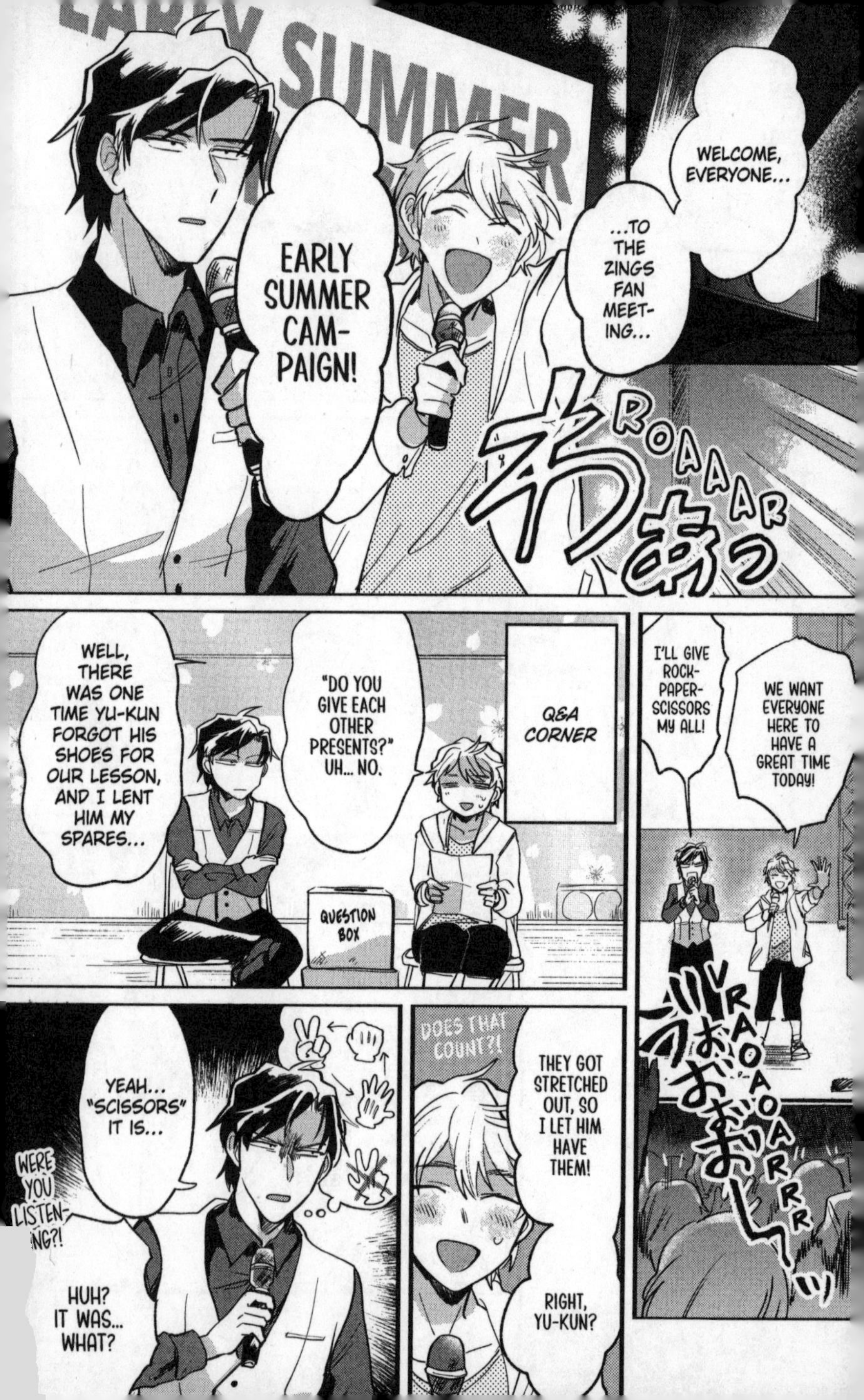
WELCOME, EVERYONE...
...TO THE ZINGS FAN MEETING...
EARLY SUMMER CAMPAIGN!
ROAAAAR
WE WANT EVERYONE HERE TO HAVE A GREAT TIME TODAY!
I'LL GIVE ROCK-PAPER-SCISSORS MY ALL!
VRAOOAARRR
Q&A CORNER
"DO YOU GIVE EACH OTHER PRESENTS?" UH... NO.
WELL, THERE WAS ONE TIME YU-KUN FORGOT HIS SHOES FOR OUR LESSON, AND I LENT HIM MY SPARES...
QUESTION BOX
THEY GOT STRETCHED OUT, SO I LET HIM HAVE THEM!
DOES THAT COUNT?!
RIGHT, YU-KUN?
YEAH... "SCISSORS" IT IS...
WERE YOU LISTENING?!
HUH? IT WAS... WHAT?

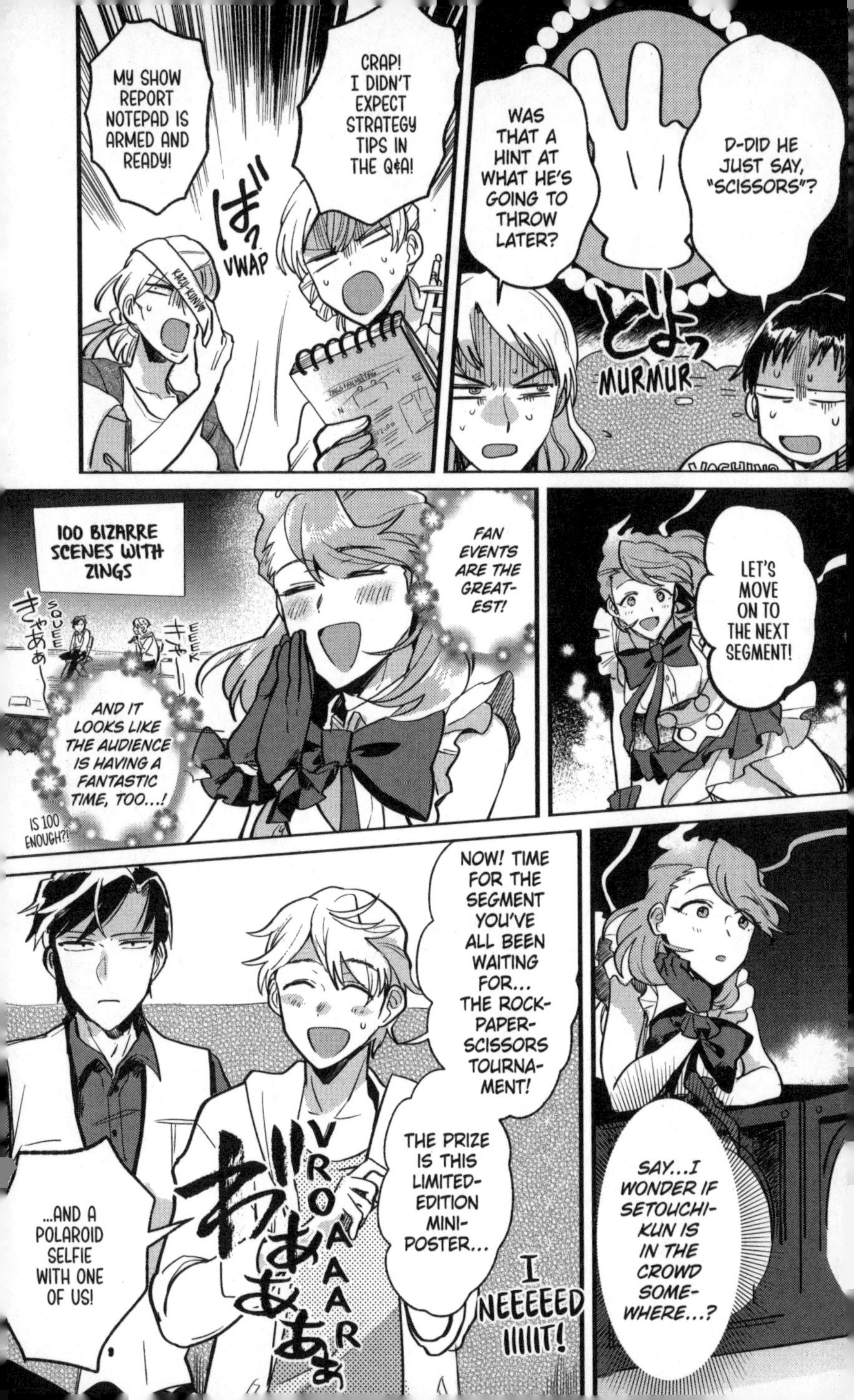
D-DID HE JUST SAY, "SCISSORS"?
WAS THAT A HINT AT WHAT HE'S GOING TO THROW LATER?
MURMUR
CRAP! I DIDN'T EXPECT STRATEGY TIPS IN THE Q&A!
MY SHOW REPORT NOTEPAD IS ARMED AND READY!
VWAP
LET'S MOVE ON TO THE NEXT SEGMENT!
FAN EVENTS ARE THE GREATEST!
100 BIZARRE SCENES WITH ZINGS
EEEK
SQUEE
AND IT LOOKS LIKE THE AUDIENCE IS HAVING A FANTASTIC TIME, TOO...!
IS 100 ENOUGH?!
SAY...I WONDER IF SETOUCHI-KUN IS IN THE CROWD SOMEWHERE...?
NOW! TIME FOR THE SEGMENT YOU'VE ALL BEEN WAITING FOR... THE ROCK-PAPER-SCISSORS TOURNAMENT!
THE PRIZE IS THIS LIMITED-EDITION MINI-POSTER...
...AND A POLAROID SELFIE WITH ONE OF US!
VROAAAR
I NEEEEED IIIIIIT!

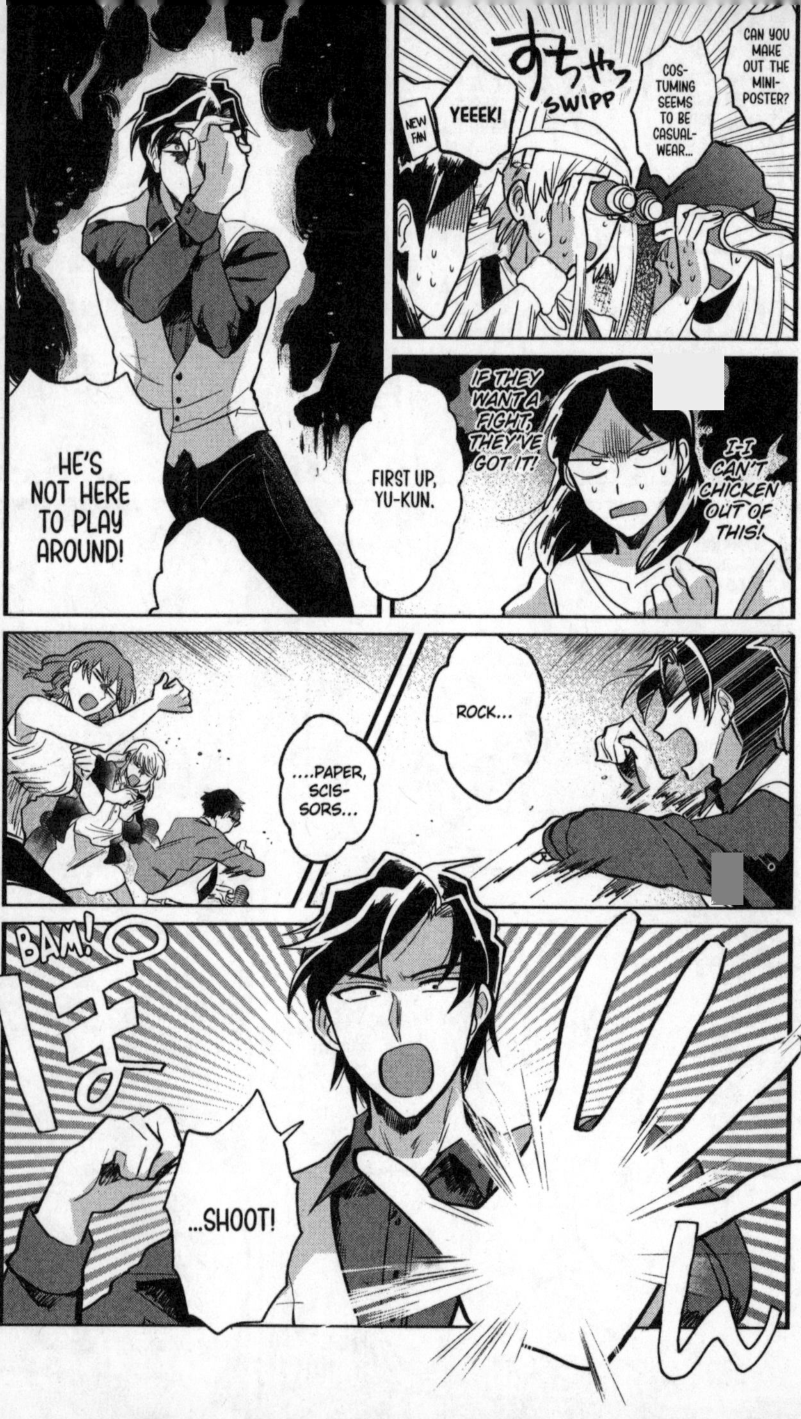

CAN YOU MAKE OUT THE MINI-POSTER?
COS-TUMING SEEMS TO BE CASUAL-WEAR...
すちゃっ
SWIPP
YEEEK!
NEW FAN
I-I CAN'T CHICKEN OUT OF THIS!
IF THEY WANT A FIGHT, THEY'VE GOT IT!
FIRST UP, YU-KUN.
HE'S NOT HERE TO PLAY AROUND!
ROCK...
....PAPER, SCIS-SORS...
ぽん
BAM!
...SHOOT!

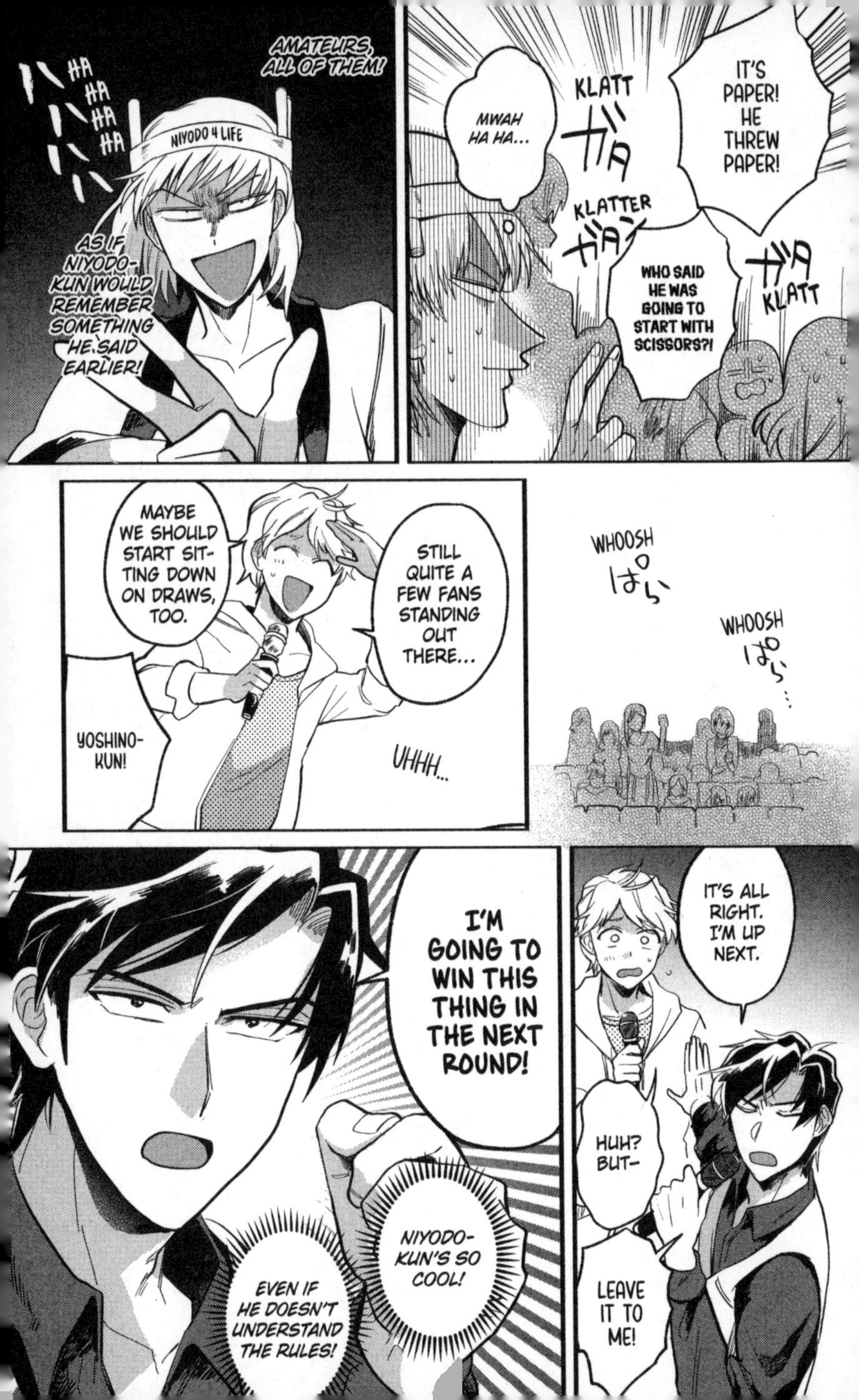
IT'S PAPER! HE THREW PAPER!
KLATT
ガタ
MWAH HA HA...
KLATTER
ガタン
WHO SAID HE WAS GOING TO START WITH SCISSORS?!
ガタ
KLATT
AMATEURS, ALL OF THEM!
HA HA HA HA
ハハハハ
NIYODO 4 LIFE
AS IF NIYODO-KUN WOULD REMEMBER SOMETHING HE SAID EARLIER!
WHOOSH
ぱら
WHOOSH
ぱら...
STILL QUITE A FEW FANS STANDING OUT THERE...
MAYBE WE SHOULD START SITTING DOWN ON DRAWS, TOO.
UHHH...
YOSHINO-KUN!
IT'S ALL RIGHT. I'M UP NEXT.
HUH? BUT-
LEAVE IT TO ME!
I'M GOING TO WIN THIS THING IN THE NEXT ROUND!
NIYODO-KUN'S SO COOL!
EVEN IF HE DOESN'T UNDERSTAND THE RULES!

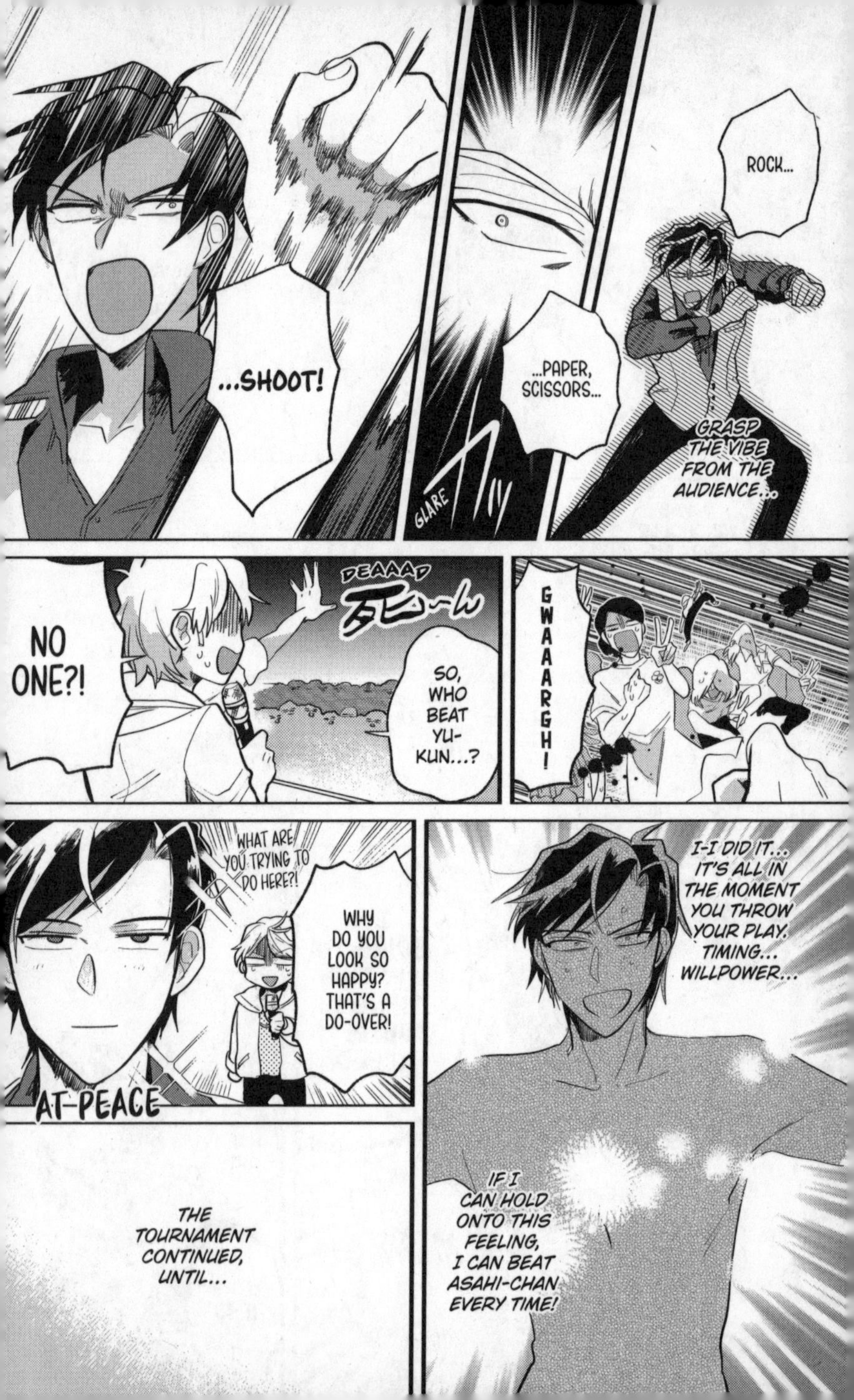
ROCK...
GRASP THE VIBE FROM THE AUDIENCE...
...PAPER, SCISSORS...
GLARE
...SHOOT!
GWAAAARGH!
DEAAAD
SO, WHO BEAT YU-KUN...?
NO ONE?!
I-I DID IT... IT'S ALL IN THE MOMENT YOU THROW YOUR PLAY. TIMING... WILLPOWER...
IF I CAN HOLD ONTO THIS FEELING, I CAN BEAT ASAHI-CHAN EVERY TIME!
WHAT ARE YOU TRYING TO DO HERE?!
WHY DO YOU LOOK SO HAPPY? THAT'S A DO-OVER!
AT-PEACE
THE TOURNAMENT CONTINUED, UNTIL...

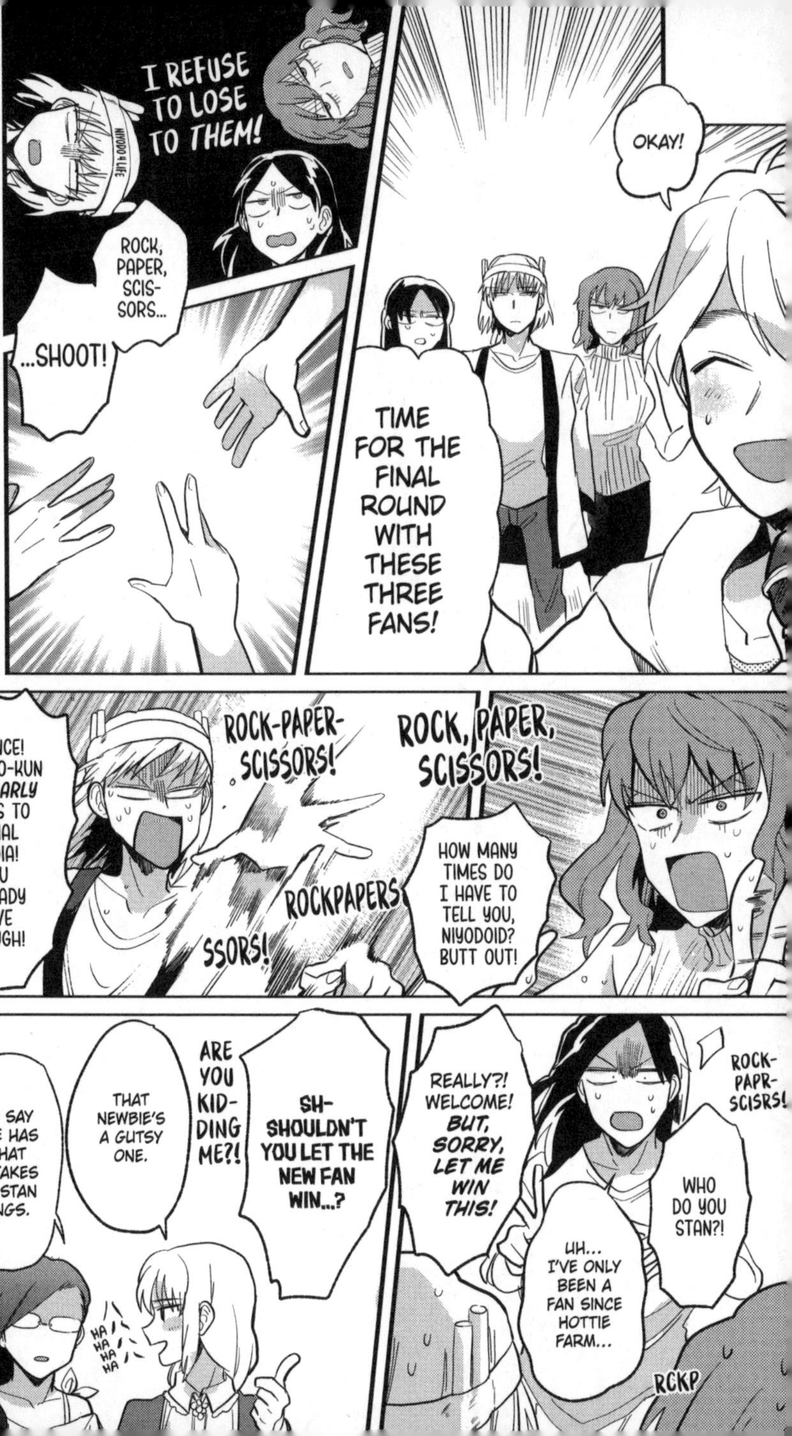
OKAY!
TIME FOR THE FINAL ROUND WITH THESE THREE FANS!
I REFUSE TO LOSE TO THEM!
NIYODO 4 LIFE
ROCK, PAPER, SCISSORS...
...SHOOT!
ROCK, PAPER, SCISSORS!
HOW MANY TIMES DO I HAVE TO TELL YOU, NIYODOID? BUTT OUT!
ROCK-PAPER-SCISSORS!
ROCKPAPERS
SSORS!
SILENCE! YOSHINO-KUN ***REGULARLY*** POSTS TO SOCIAL MEDIA! YOU ALREADY HAVE ENOUGH!
ROCK-PAPR-SCISRS!
WHO DO YOU STAN?!
REALLY?! WELCOME! ***BUT, SORRY, LET ME WIN THIS!***
UH... I'VE ONLY BEEN A FAN SINCE HOTTIE FARM...
RCKP
SH-SHOULDN'T YOU LET THE NEW FAN WIN...?
ARE YOU KIDDING ME?!
THAT NEWBIE'S A GUTSY ONE.
I'D SAY SHE HAS WHAT IT TAKES TO STAN ZINGS.
HA HA HA HA

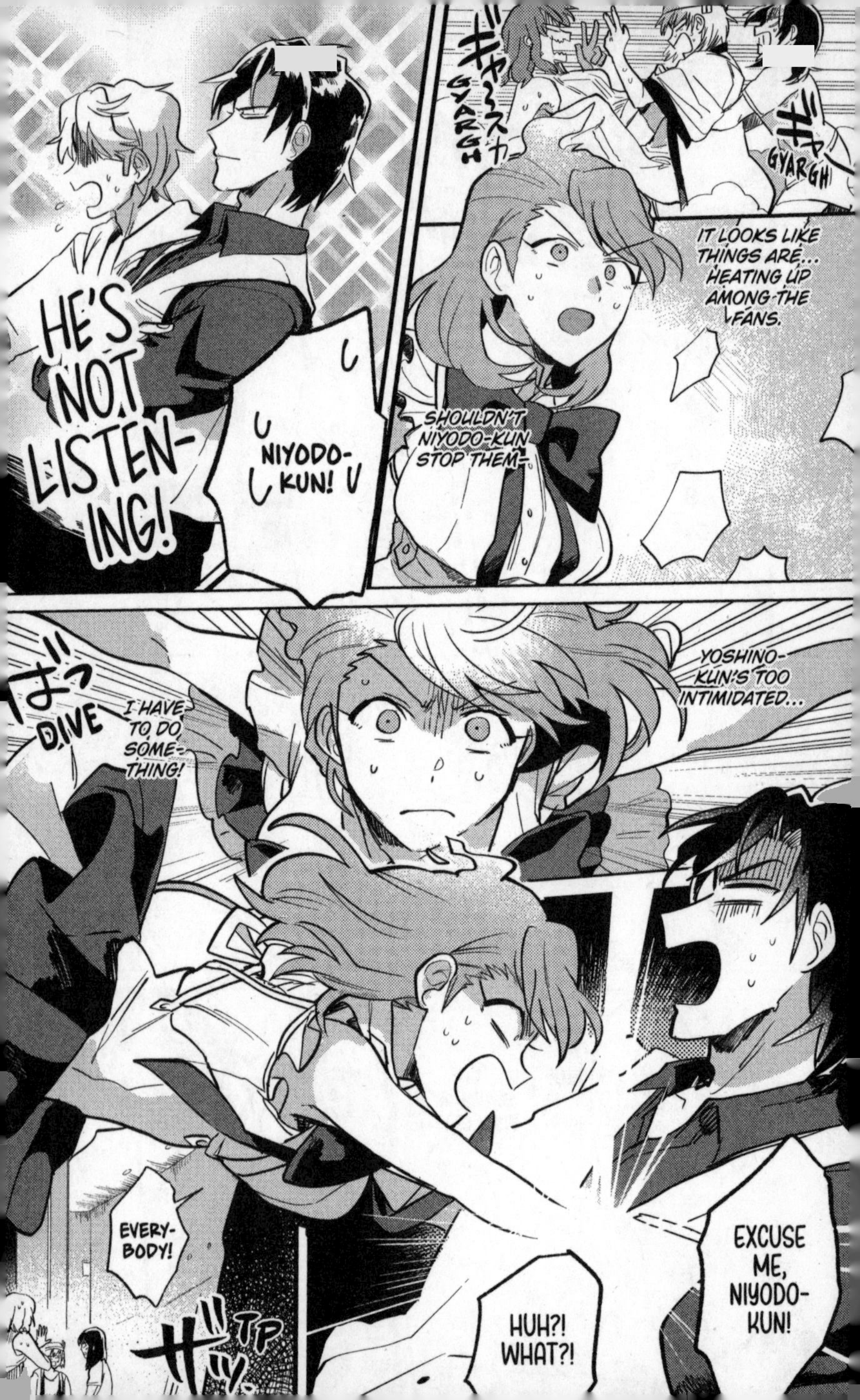
ギャ〜スカ
GYARGH
ギャ
GYARGH
IT LOOKS LIKE THINGS ARE... HEATING UP AMONG THE FANS.
SHOULDN'T NIYODO-KUN STOP THEM-
NIYODO-KUN!
HE'S NOT LISTENING!
YOSHINO-KUN'S TOO INTIMIDATED...
I HAVE TO DO SOMETHING!
ばっ
DIVE
EXCUSE ME, NIYODO-KUN!
HUH?! WHAT?!
EVERYBODY!
ザッ
TP

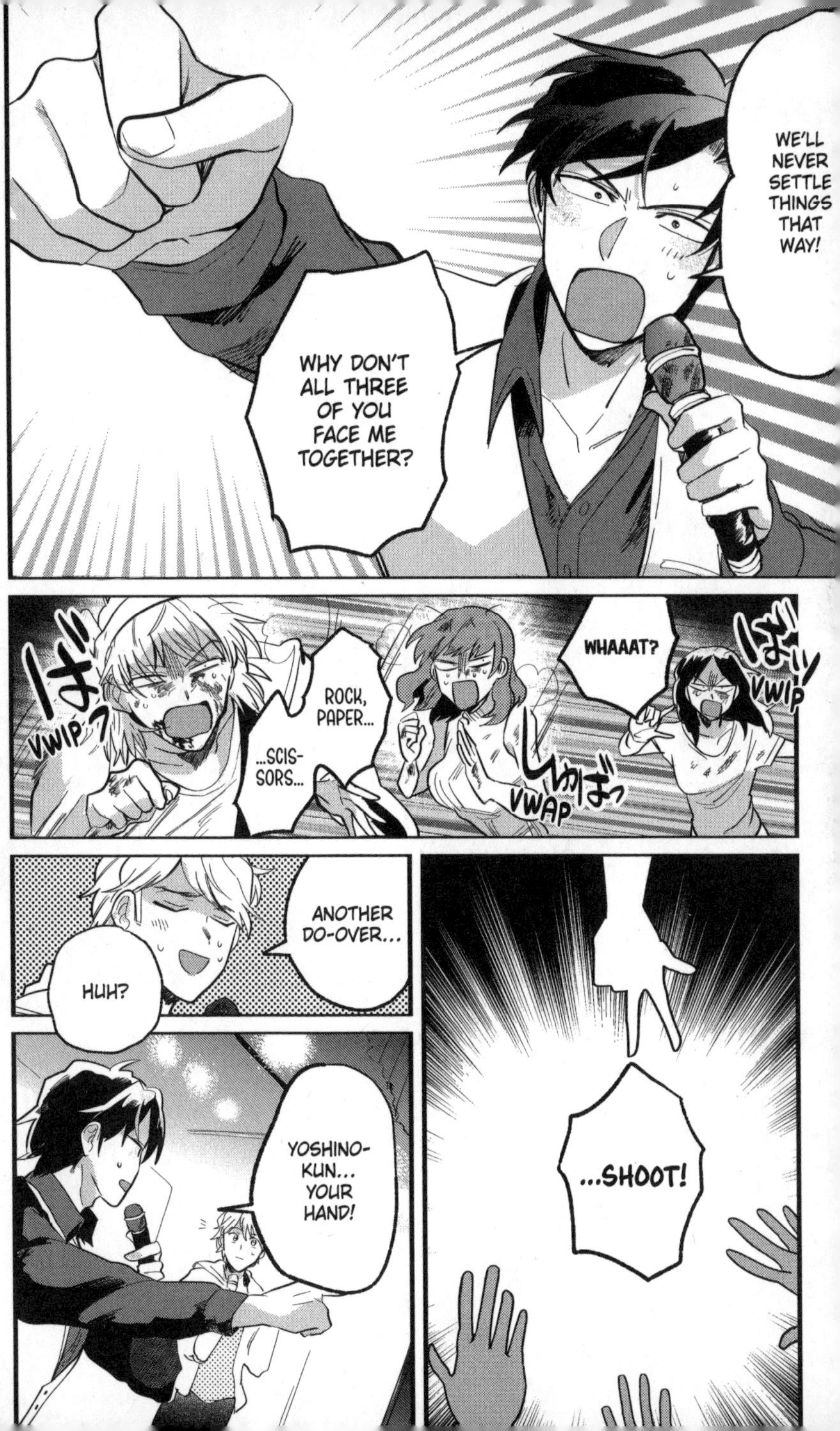
WE'LL NEVER SETTLE THINGS THAT WAY!
WHY DON'T ALL THREE OF YOU FACE ME TOGETHER?
ばっ VWIP
WHAAAT?
しゅばっ VWAP
ROCK, PAPER...
...SCIS-SORS...
ばっ VWIP
...SHOOT!
ANOTHER DO-OVER...
HUH?
YOSHINO-KUN... YOUR HAND!

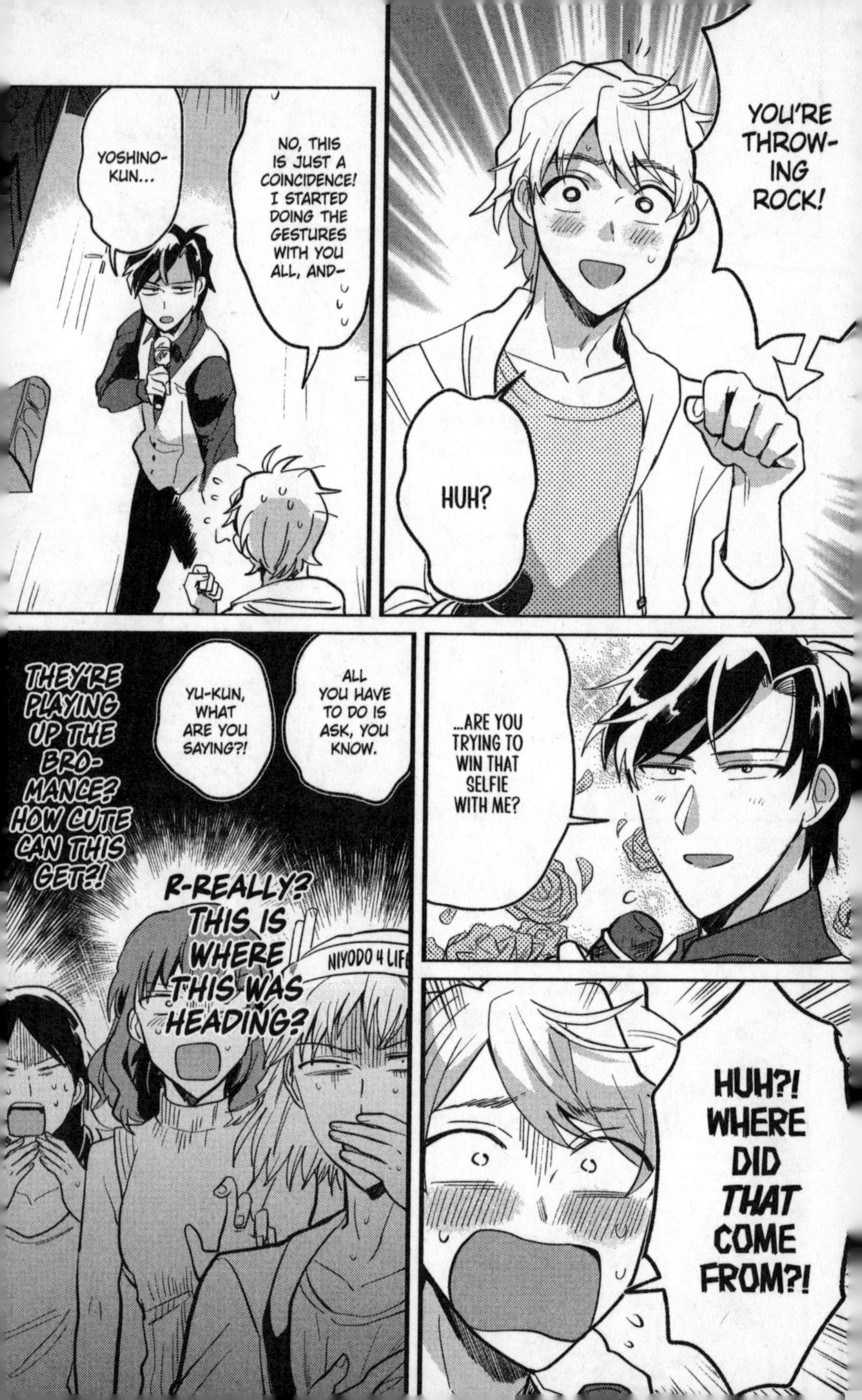
YOU'RE THROWING-ING ROCK!
HUH?
NO, THIS IS JUST A COINCIDENCE! I STARTED DOING THE GESTURES WITH YOU ALL, AND—
YOSHINO-KUN...
...ARE YOU TRYING TO WIN THAT SELFIE WITH ME?
HUH?! WHERE DID *THAT* COME FROM?!
ALL YOU HAVE TO DO IS ASK, YOU KNOW.
YU-KUN, WHAT ARE YOU SAYING?!
THEY'RE PLAYING UP THE BRO-MANCE? HOW CUTE CAN THIS GET?!
R-REALLY? THIS IS WHERE THIS WAS HEADING?
NIYODO 4 LIF

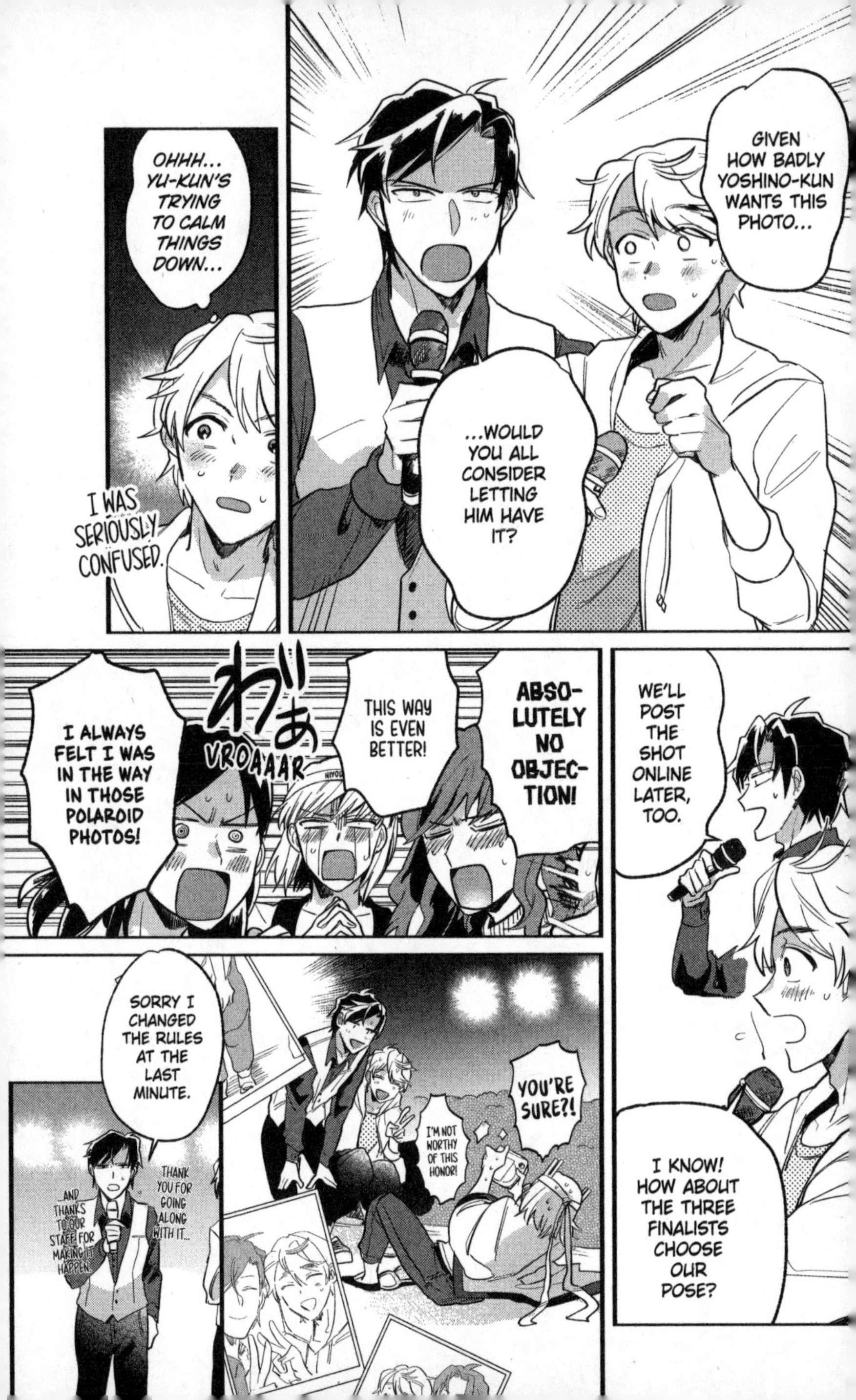
GIVEN HOW BADLY YOSHINO-KUN WANTS THIS PHOTO...
...WOULD YOU ALL CONSIDER LETTING HIM HAVE IT?
OHHH... YU-KUN'S TRYING TO CALM THINGS DOWN...
I WAS SERIOUSLY CONFUSED.
WE'LL POST THE SHOT ONLINE LATER, TOO.
I KNOW! HOW ABOUT THE THREE FINALISTS CHOOSE OUR POSE?
ABSOLUTELY NO OBJECTION!
THIS WAY IS EVEN BETTER!
わあ
VROAAAR
I ALWAYS FELT I WAS IN THE WAY IN THOSE POLAROID PHOTOS!
SORRY I CHANGED THE RULES AT THE LAST MINUTE.
YOU'RE SURE?!
I'M NOT WORTHY OF THIS HONOR!
THANK YOU FOR GOING ALONG WITH IT...
...AND THANKS TO OUR STAFF FOR MAKING IT HAPPEN.

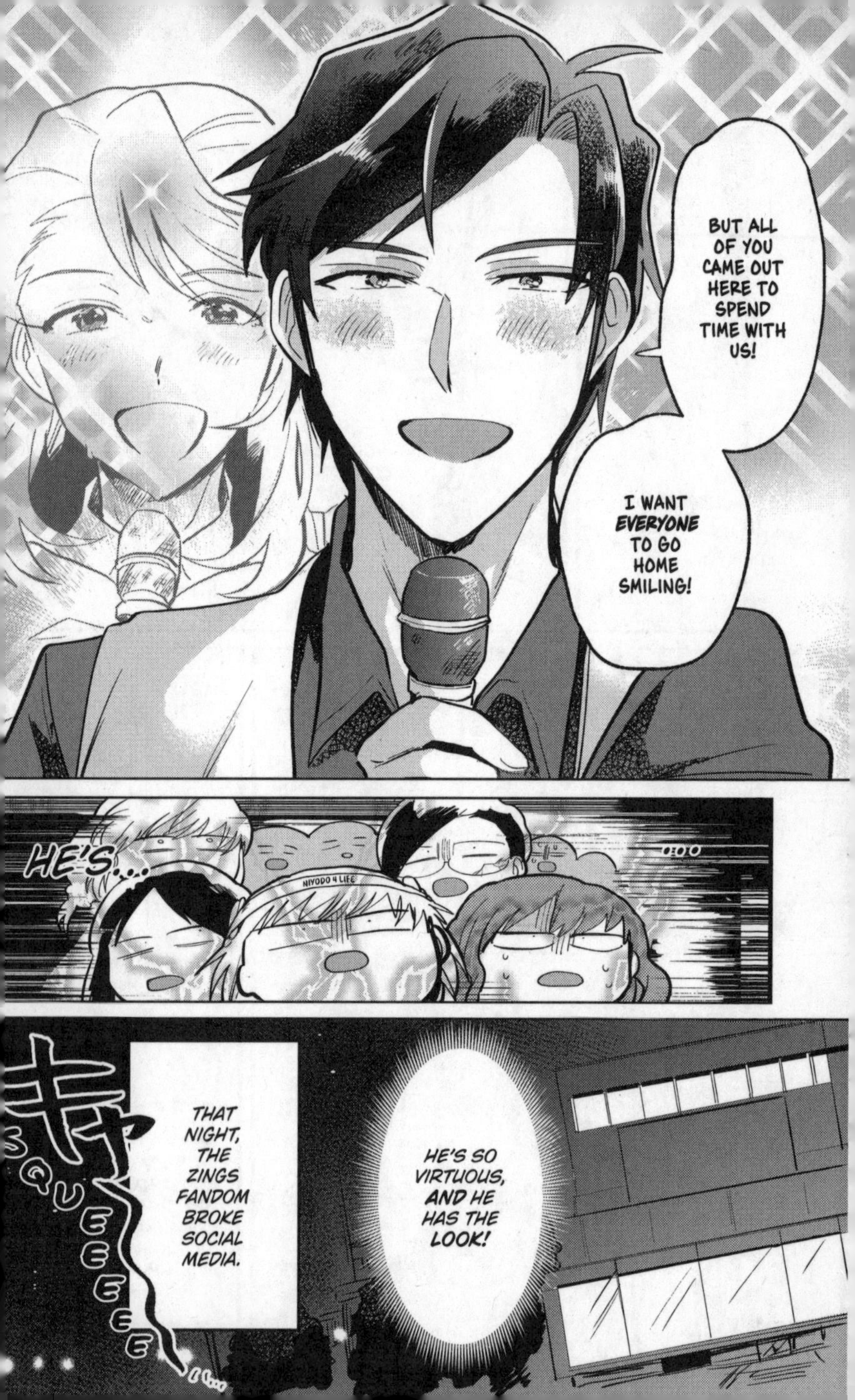
BUT ALL OF YOU CAME OUT HERE TO SPEND TIME WITH US!
I WANT EVERYONE TO GO HOME SMILING!
NIYODO 4 LIFE
HE'S...
HE'S SO VIRTUOUS, AND HE HAS THE LOOK!
THAT NIGHT, THE ZINGS FANDOM BROKE SOCIAL MEDIA.
キャ
SQUEEEEEEE

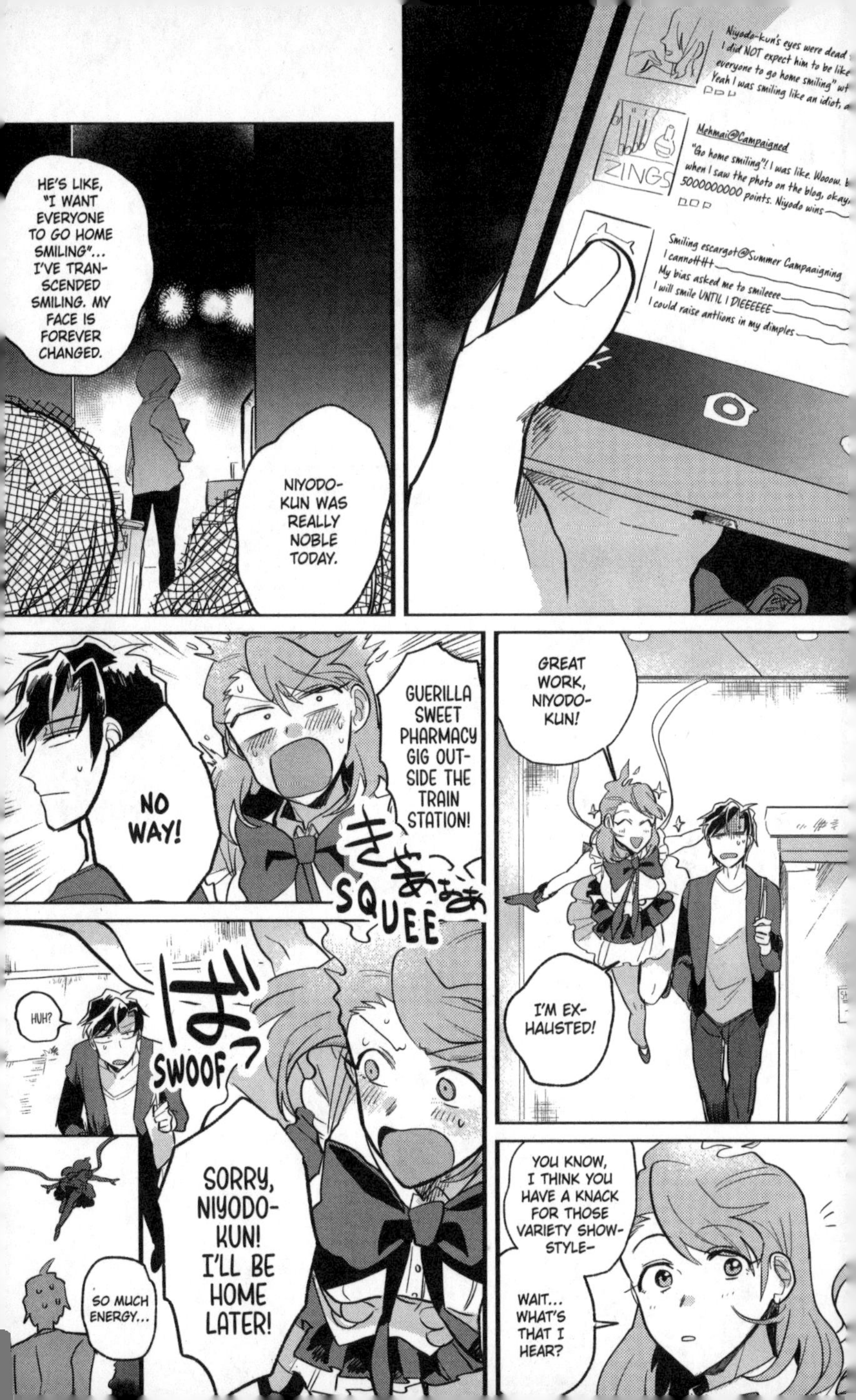

Niyodo-kun's eyes were dead
I did NOT expect him to be like
everyone to go home smiling" wt
Yeah I was smiling like an idiot, a
Mehmai@Campaigned
"Go home smiling"! I was like. Wooow.
when I saw the photo on the blog, okay,
5000000000 points. Niyodo wins
ZINGS
Smiling escargot@Summer Campaaigning
I cannottttt
My bias asked me to smileeee
I will smile UNTIL I DIEEEEEE
I could raise antlions in my dimples
HE'S LIKE, "I WANT EVERYONE TO GO HOME SMILING"... I'VE TRANSCENDED SMILING. MY FACE IS FOREVER CHANGED.
NIYODO-KUN WAS REALLY NOBLE TODAY.
GREAT WORK, NIYODO-KUN!
I'M EXHAUSTED!
YOU KNOW, I THINK YOU HAVE A KNACK FOR THOSE VARIETY SHOW-STYLE-
WAIT... WHAT'S THAT I HEAR?
GUERILLA SWEET PHARMACY GIG OUTSIDE THE TRAIN STATION!
NO WAY!
きゃあぁあ
SQUEE
HUH?
ばっ
SWOOF
SORRY, NIYODO-KUN! I'LL BE HOME LATER!
SO MUCH ENERGY...

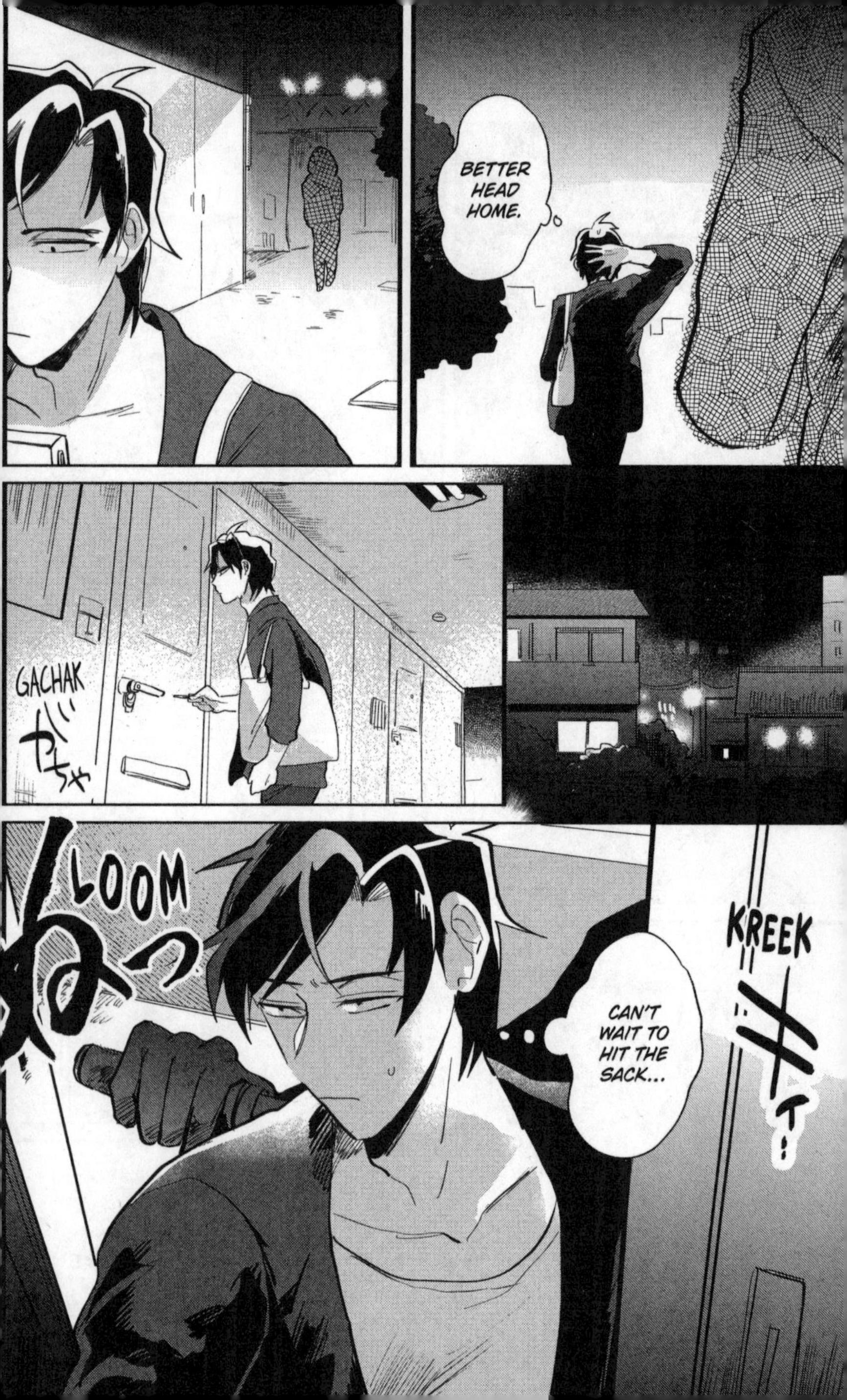
BETTER HEAD HOME.
GACHAK
がちゃ
KREEK
CAN'T WAIT TO HIT THE SACK...
LOOM
ぬっ

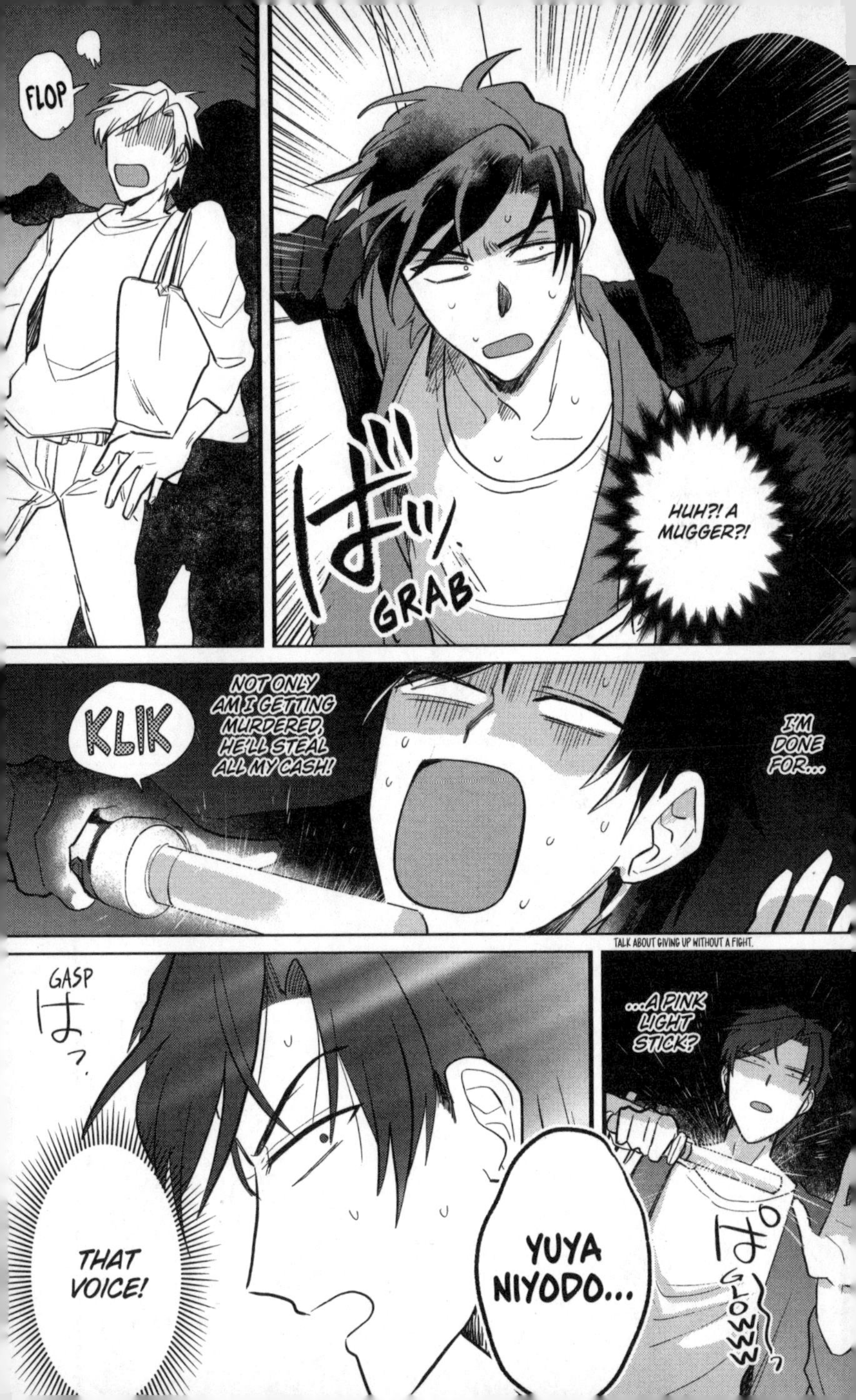

ばッ
GRAB
HUH?! A MUGGER?!
FLOP
I'M DONE FOR...
NOT ONLY AM I GETTING MURDERED, HE'LL STEAL ALL MY CASH!
KLIK
TALK ABOUT GIVING UP WITHOUT A FIGHT.
...A PINK LIGHT STICK?
ぽ
GLOWWW~
YUYA NIYODO...
GASP
はっ
THAT VOICE!

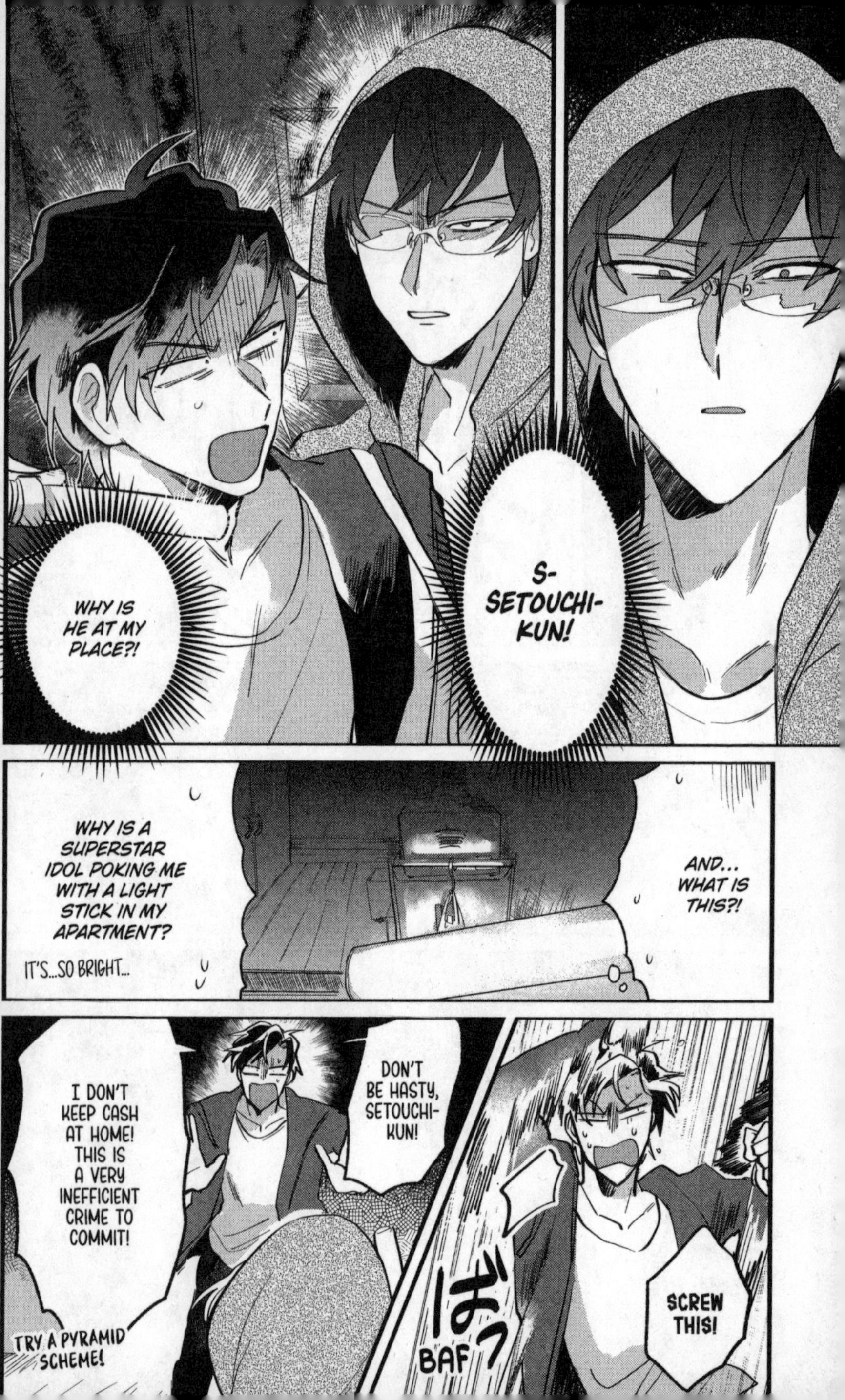
S-SETOUCHI-KUN!
WHY IS HE AT MY PLACE?!
AND... WHAT IS THIS?!
WHY IS A SUPERSTAR IDOL POKING ME WITH A LIGHT STICK IN MY APARTMENT?
IT'S...SO BRIGHT...
SCREW THIS!
ぼっ
BAF
DON'T BE HASTY, SETOUCHI-KUN!
I DON'T KEEP CASH AT HOME! THIS IS A VERY INEFFICIENT CRIME TO COMMIT!
TRY A PYRAMID SCHEME!

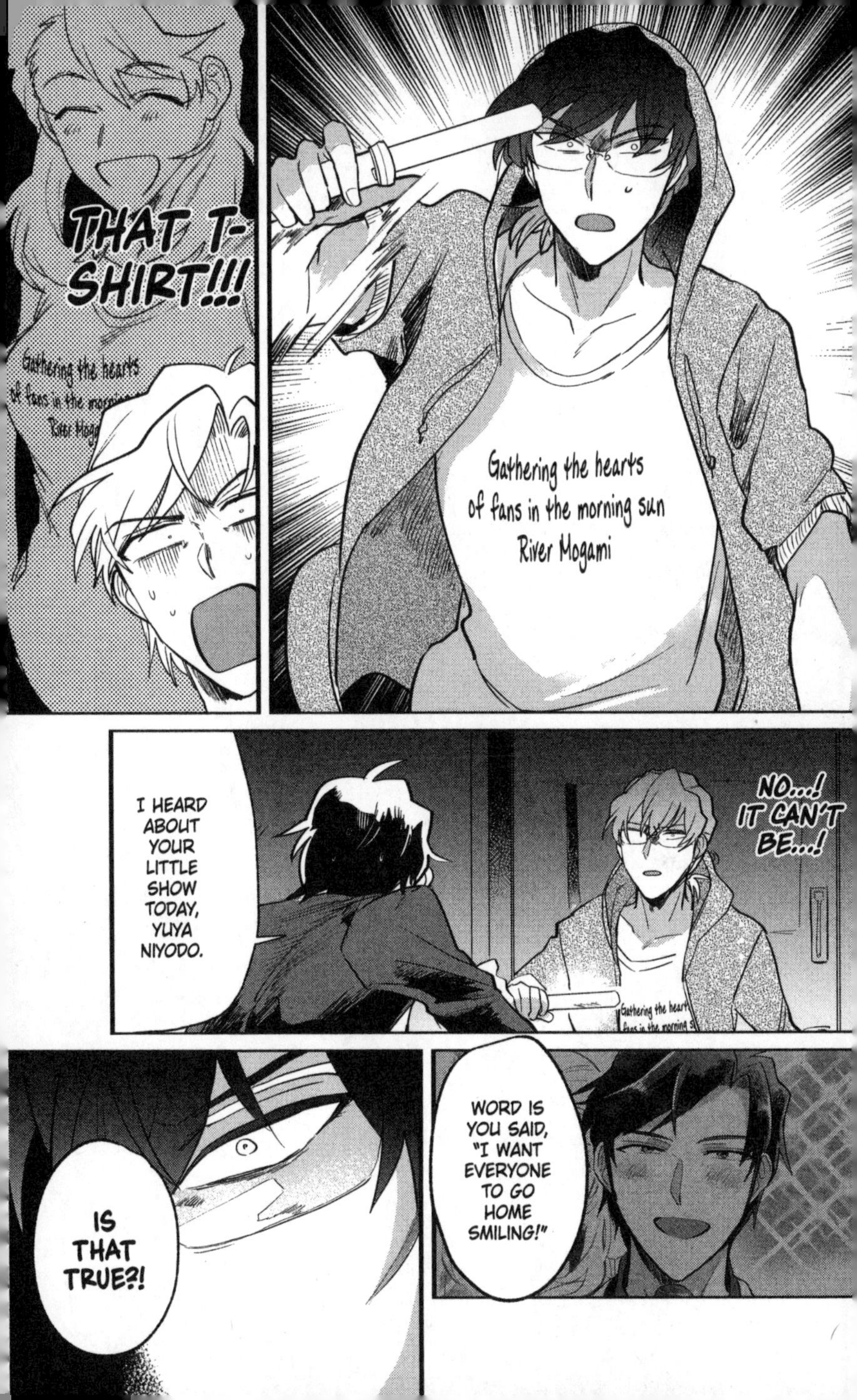
Gathering the hearts
of fans in the morning sun
River Mogami
THAT T-SHIRT!!!
NO...! IT CAN'T BE...!
I HEARD ABOUT YOUR LITTLE SHOW TODAY, YUYA NIYODO.
WORD IS YOU SAID, "I WANT EVERYONE TO GO HOME SMILING!"
IS THAT TRUE?!

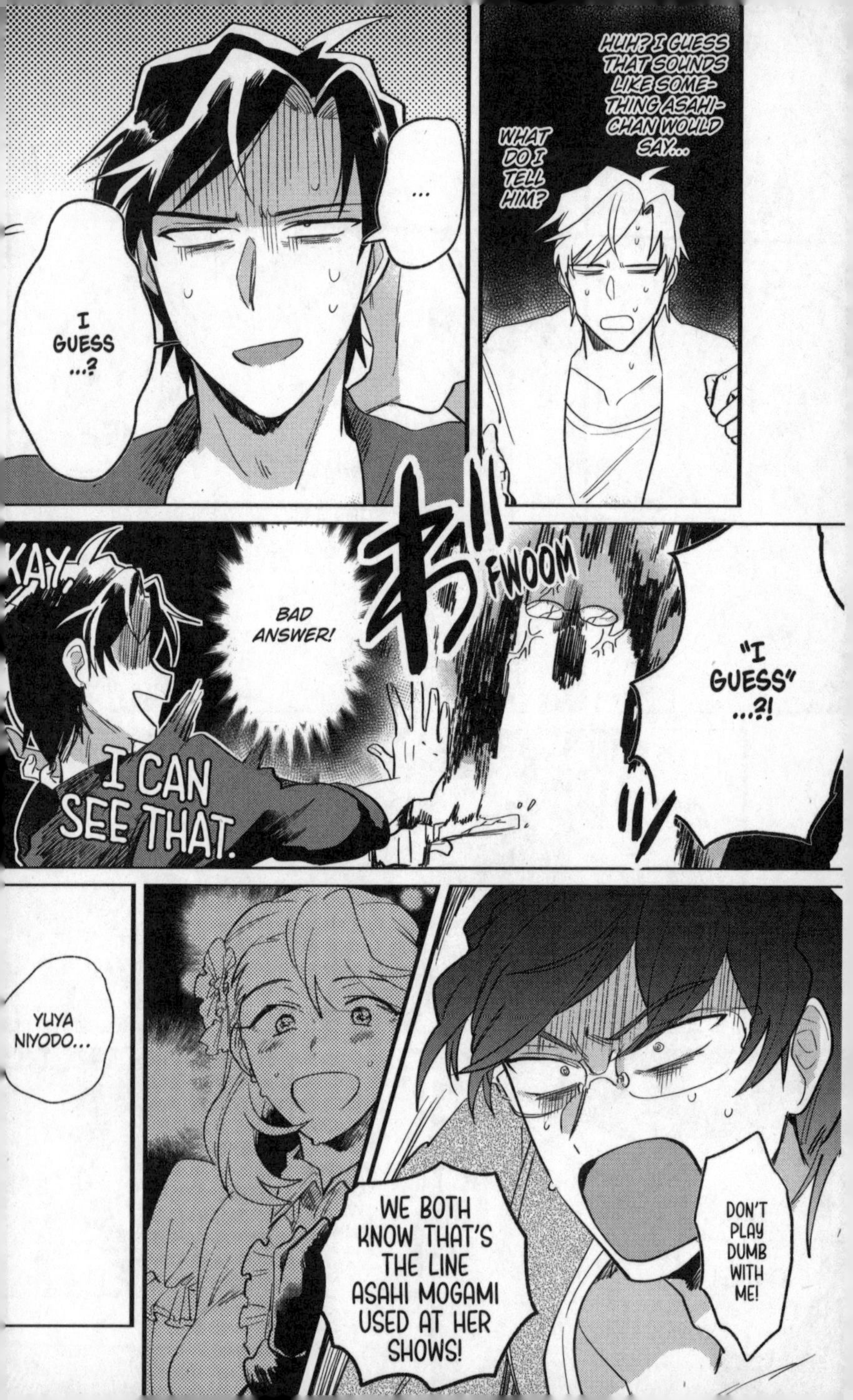
HUH? I GUESS THAT SOUNDS LIKE SOME-THING ASAHI-CHAN WOULD SAY...
WHAT DO I TELL HIM?
...
I GUESS ...?
"I GUESS" ...?!
FWOOM
BAD ANSWER!
I CAN SEE THAT.
DON'T PLAY DUMB WITH ME!
WE BOTH KNOW THAT'S THE LINE ASAHI MOGAMI USED AT HER SHOWS!
YUYA NIYODO...

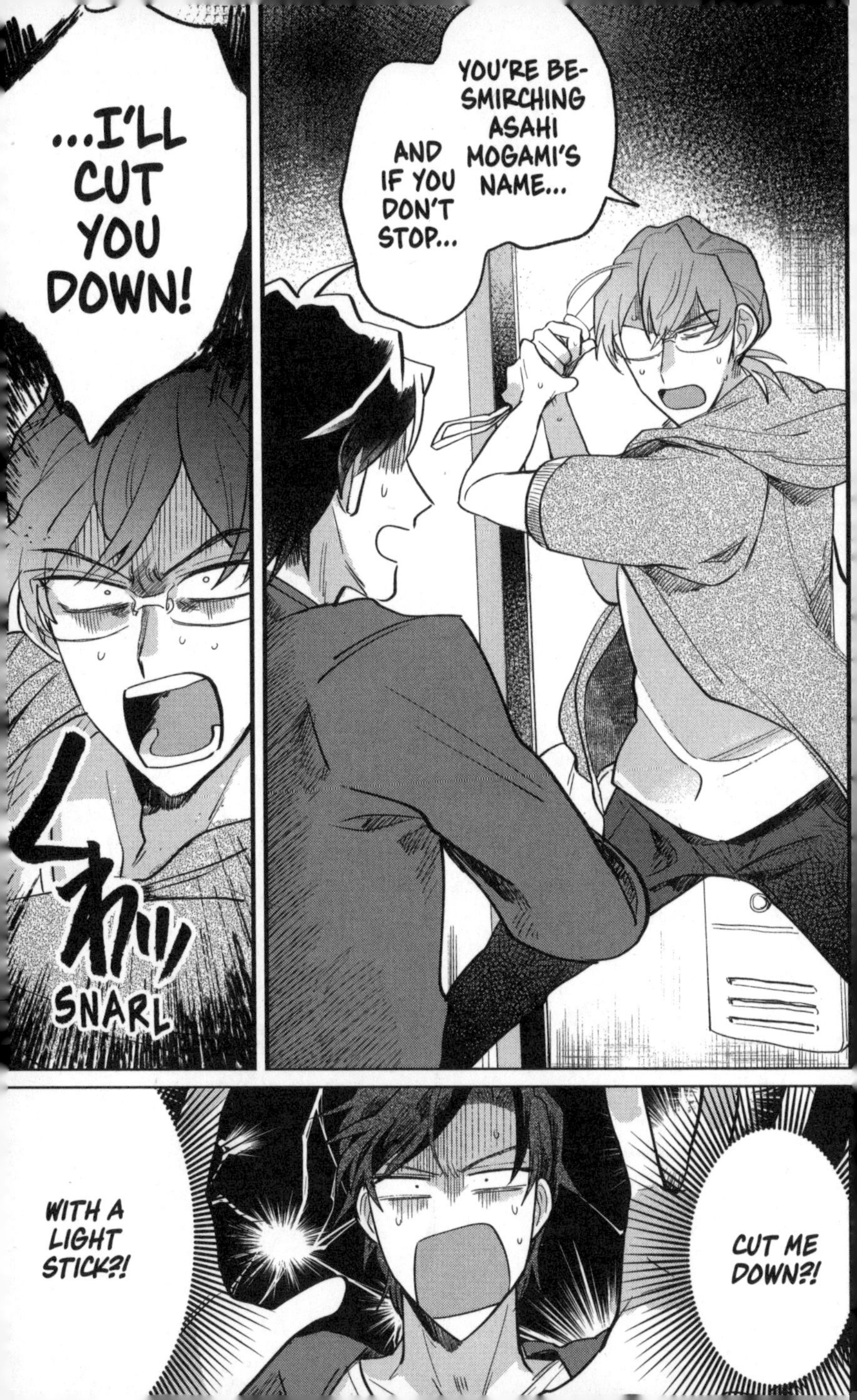
YOU'RE BE-SMIRCHING ASAHI MOGAMI'S NAME...
AND IF YOU DON'T STOP...
...I'LL CUT YOU DOWN!
くわっ!!
SNARL
CUT ME DOWN?!
WITH A LIGHT STICK?!

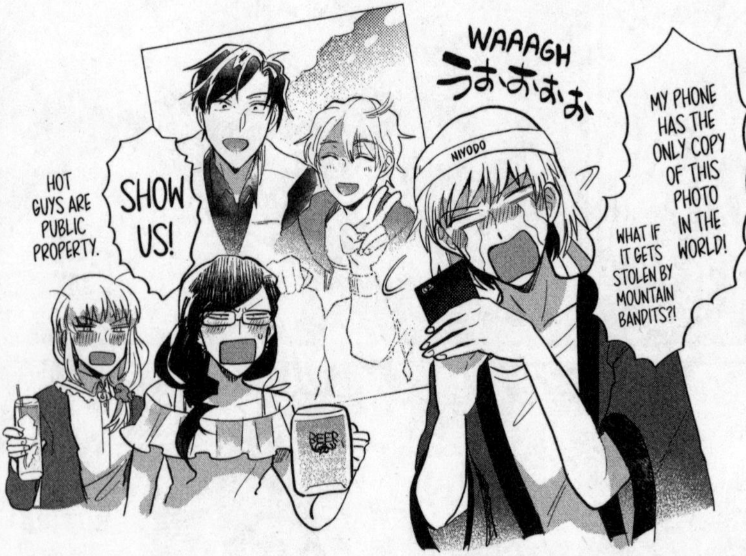
WAAAGH
うおおおお
MY PHONE HAS THE ONLY COPY OF THIS PHOTO IN THE WORLD!
WHAT IF IT GETS STOLEN BY MOUNTAIN BANDITS?!
NIYODO
SHOW US!
HOT GUYS ARE PUBLIC PROPERTY.
BEER

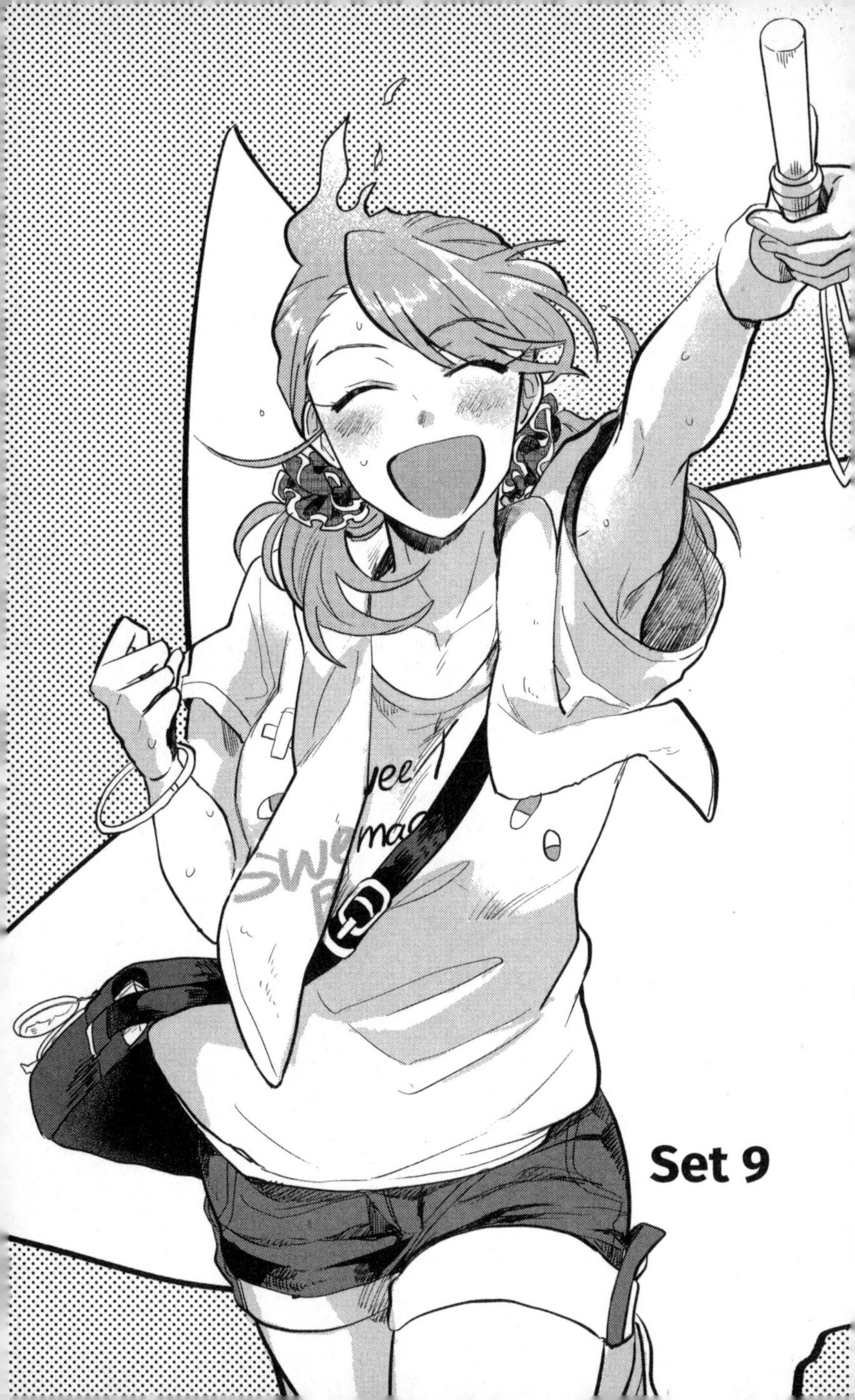

Set 9

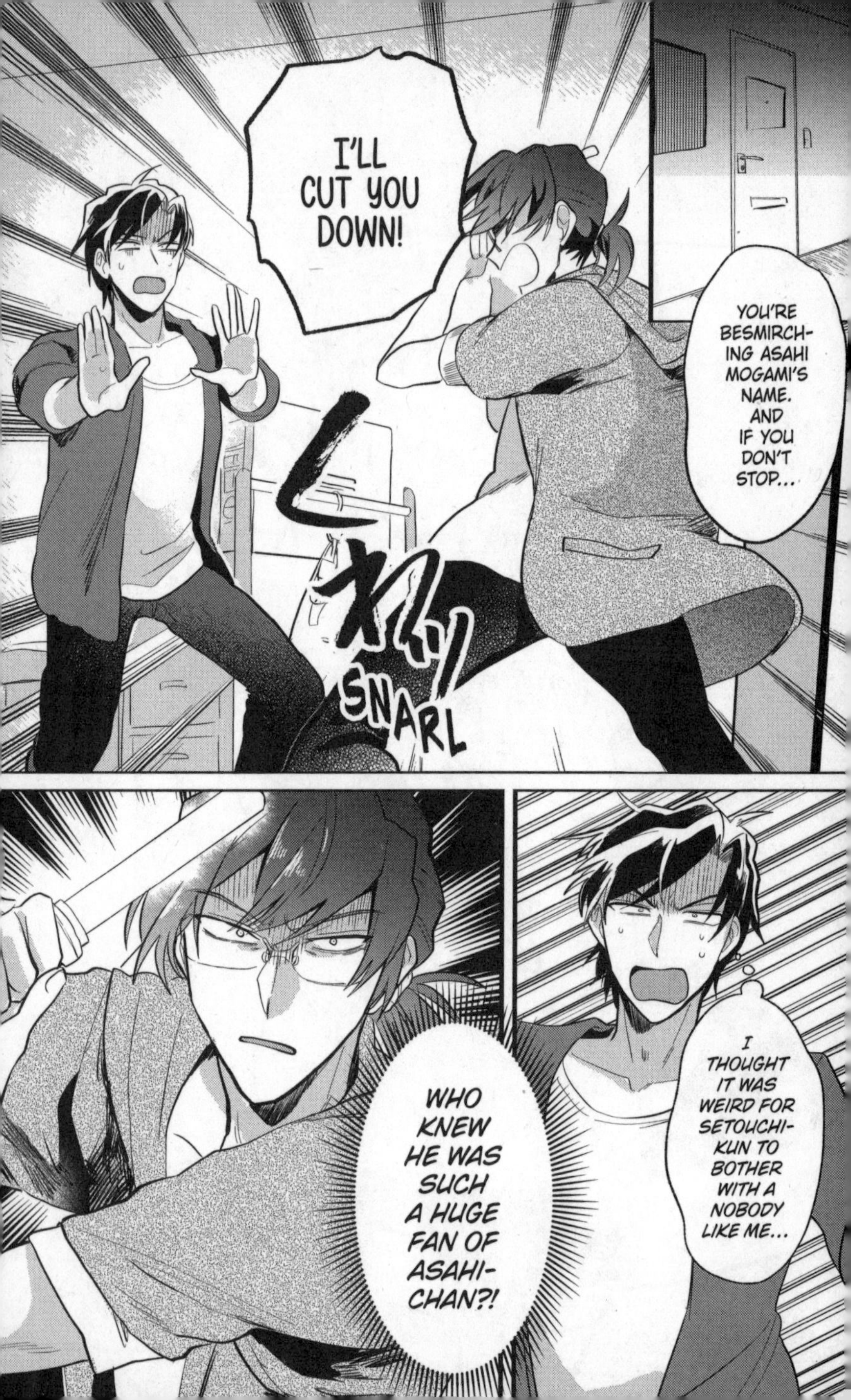
YOU'RE BESMIRCHING ASAHI MOGAMI'S NAME. AND IF YOU DON'T STOP...
I'LL CUT YOU DOWN!
SNARL
I THOUGHT IT WAS WEIRD FOR SETOUCHI-KUN TO BOTHER WITH A NOBODY LIKE ME...
WHO KNEW HE WAS SUCH A HUGE FAN OF ASAHI-CHAN?!

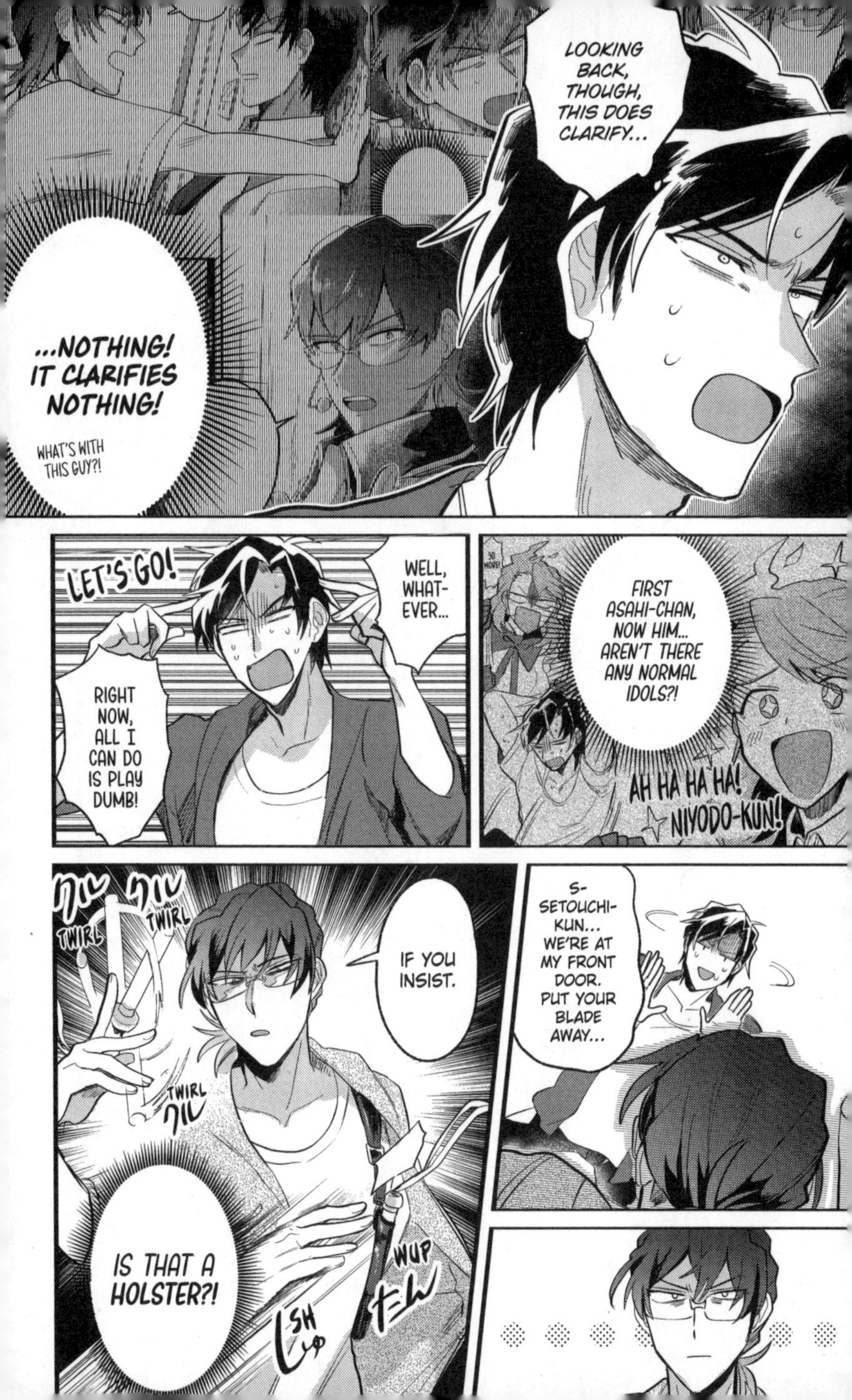
LOOKING BACK, THOUGH, THIS DOES CLARIFY...
...NOTHING! IT CLARIFIES NOTHING!
WHAT'S WITH THIS GUY?!
FIRST ASAHI-CHAN, NOW HIM... AREN'T THERE ANY NORMAL IDOLS?!
AH HA HA HA! NIYODO-KUN!
WELL, WHATEVER...
LET'S GO!
RIGHT NOW, ALL I CAN DO IS PLAY DUMB!
S-SETOUCHI-KUN... WE'RE AT MY FRONT DOOR. PUT YOUR BLADE AWAY...
IF YOU INSIST.
TWIRL TWIRL
TWIRL
IS THAT A HOLSTER?!
WUP
SH

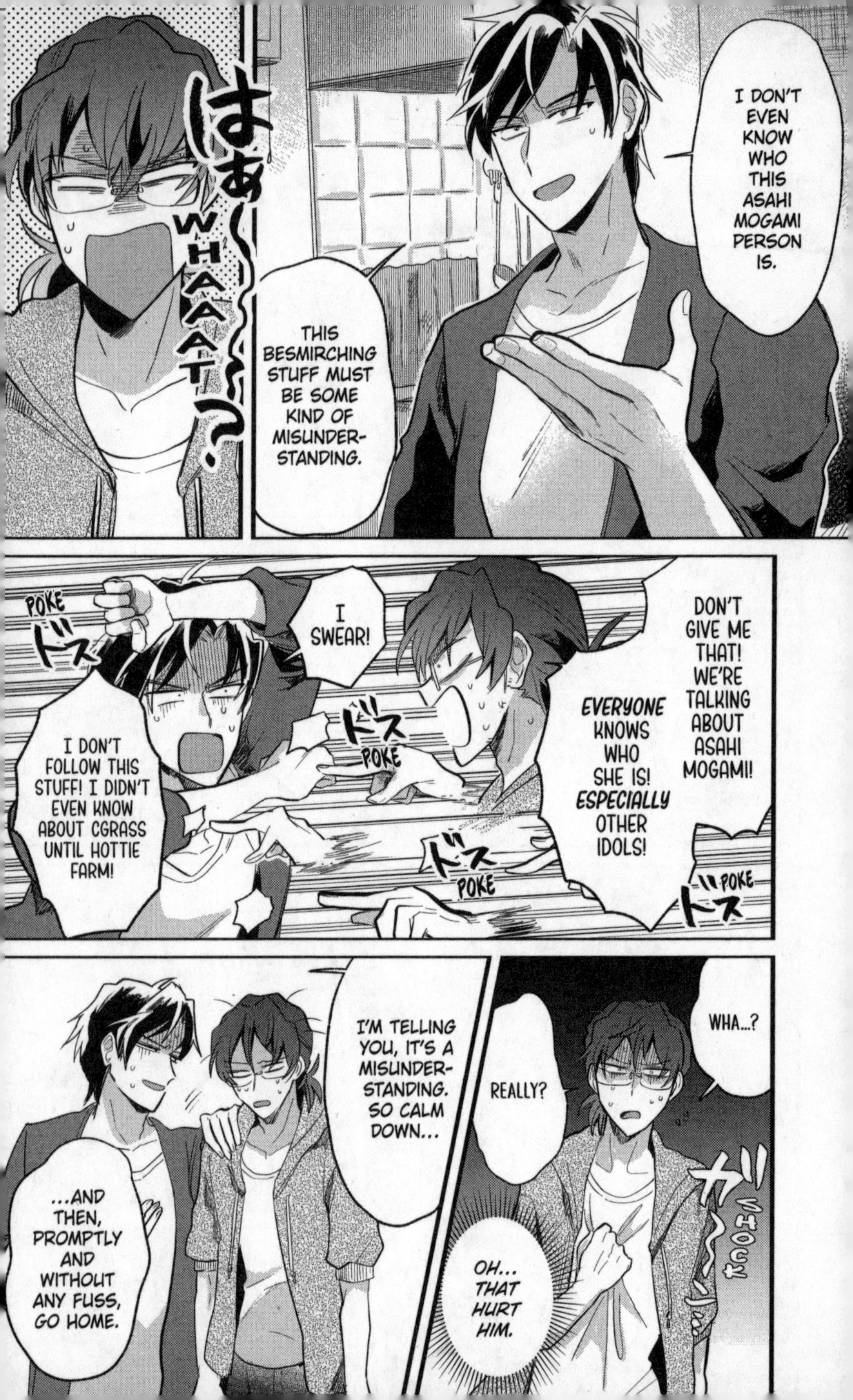
I DON'T EVEN KNOW WHO THIS ASAHI MOGAMI PERSON IS.
THIS BESMIRCHING STUFF MUST BE SOME KIND OF MISUNDERSTANDING.
はあ～～？
WHAAAT?
DON'T GIVE ME THAT! WE'RE TALKING ABOUT ASAHI MOGAMI!
EVERYONE KNOWS WHO SHE IS! ESPECIALLY OTHER IDOLS!
ドス POKE
ドス POKE
ドス POKE
I SWEAR!
ドス POKE
I DON'T FOLLOW THIS STUFF! I DIDN'T EVEN KNOW ABOUT CGRASS UNTIL HOTTIE FARM!
WHA...?
REALLY?
ガーン SHOCK
OH... THAT HURT HIM.
I'M TELLING YOU, IT'S A MISUNDERSTANDING. SO CALM DOWN...
...AND THEN, PROMPTLY AND WITHOUT ANY FUSS, GO HOME.

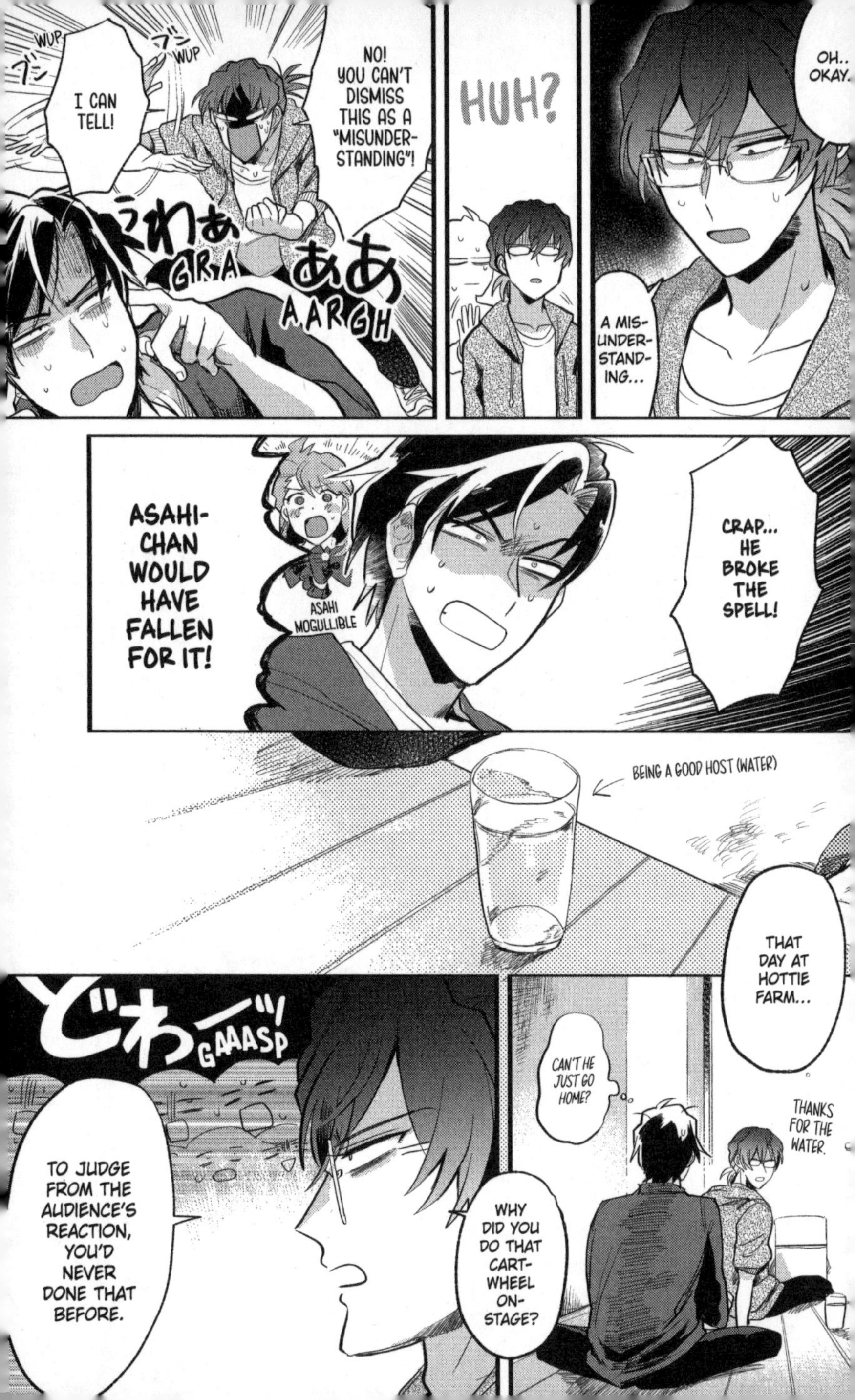
OH.. OKAY.
A MIS-UNDER-STAND-ING...
HUH?
NO! YOU CAN'T DISMISS THIS AS A "MISUNDER-STANDING"!
I CAN TELL!
ブン WUP
ブン WUP
うわあ GRA
ああ AARGH
CRAP... HE BROKE THE SPELL!
ASAHI-CHAN WOULD HAVE FALLEN FOR IT!
ASAHI MOGULLIBLE
BEING A GOOD HOST (WATER)
THAT DAY AT HOTTIE FARM...
THANKS FOR THE WATER.
CAN'T HE JUST GO HOME?
WHY DID YOU DO THAT CART-WHEEL ON-STAGE?
どわーッ GAAASP
TO JUDGE FROM THE AUDIENCE'S REACTION, YOU'D NEVER DONE THAT BEFORE.

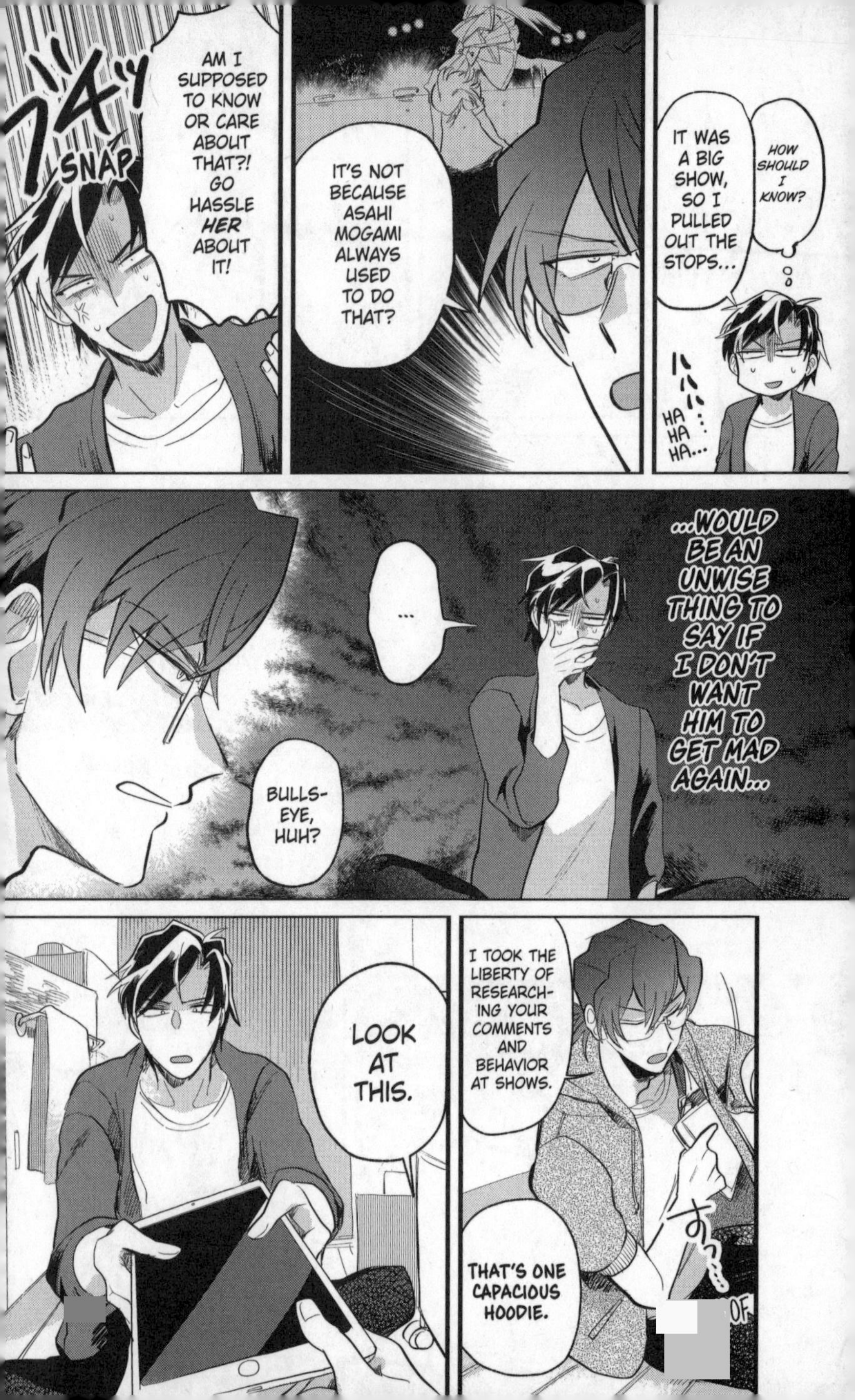
IT WAS A BIG SHOW, SO I PULLED OUT THE STOPS...
HOW SHOULD I KNOW?
HA HA HA...
IT'S NOT BECAUSE ASAHI MOGAMI ALWAYS USED TO DO THAT?
SNAP
AM I SUPPOSED TO KNOW OR CARE ABOUT THAT?! GO HASSLE HER ABOUT IT!
...WOULD BE AN UNWISE THING TO SAY IF I DON'T WANT HIM TO GET MAD AGAIN...
...
BULLS-EYE, HUH?
I TOOK THE LIBERTY OF RESEARCHING YOUR COMMENTS AND BEHAVIOR AT SHOWS.
THAT'S ONE CAPACIOUS HOODIE.
LOOK AT THIS.

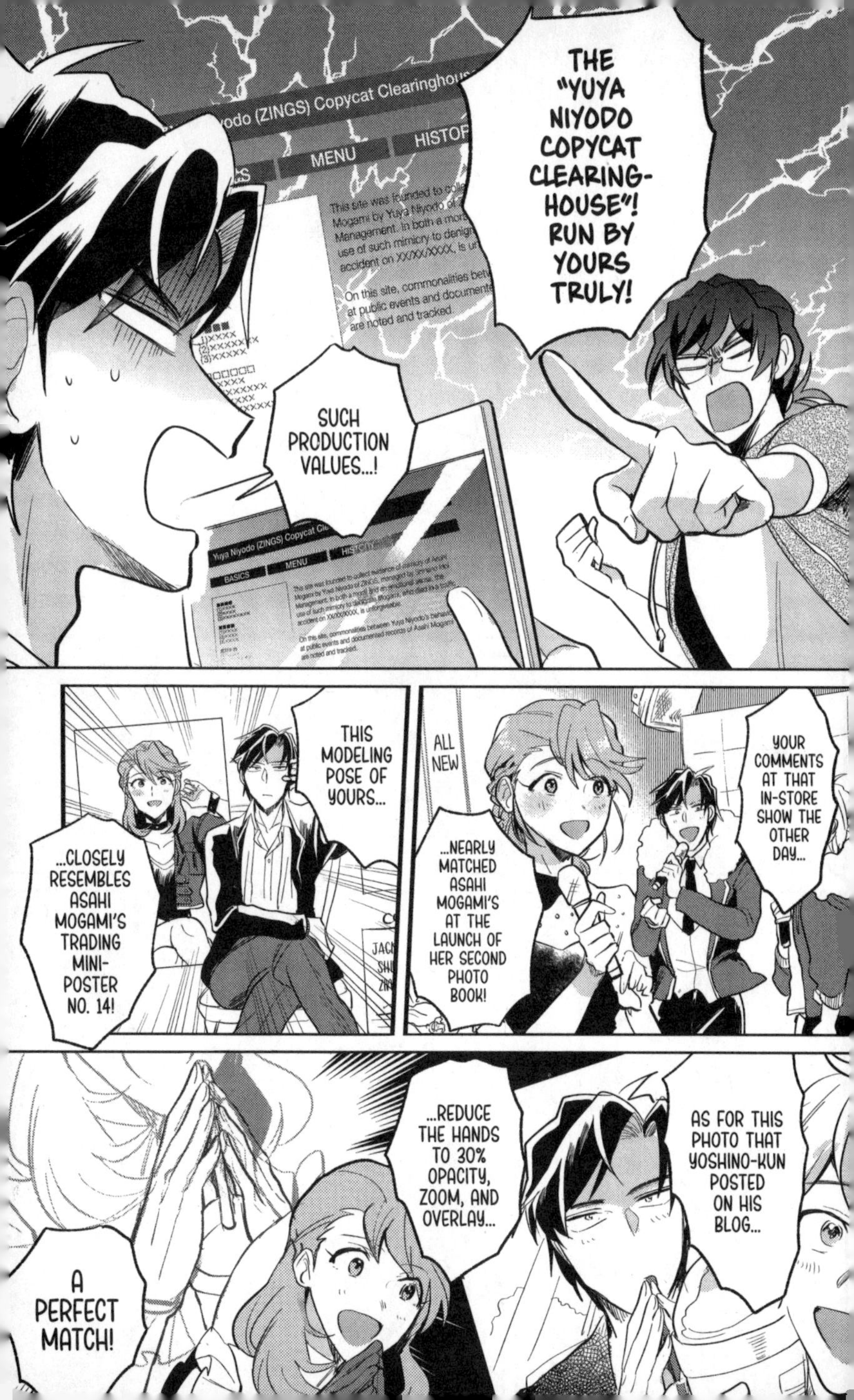
THE "YUYA NIYODO COPYCAT CLEARING-HOUSE"! RUN BY YOURS TRULY!
SUCH PRODUCTION VALUES...!
YOUR COMMENTS AT THAT IN-STORE SHOW THE OTHER DAY...
ALL NEW
...NEARLY MATCHED ASAHI MOGAMI'S AT THE LAUNCH OF HER SECOND PHOTO BOOK!
THIS MODELING POSE OF YOURS...
...CLOSELY RESEMBLES ASAHI MOGAMI'S TRADING MINI-POSTER NO. 14!
AS FOR THIS PHOTO THAT YOSHINO-KUN POSTED ON HIS BLOG...
...REDUCE THE HANDS TO 30% OPACITY, ZOOM, AND OVERLAY...
A PERFECT MATCH!

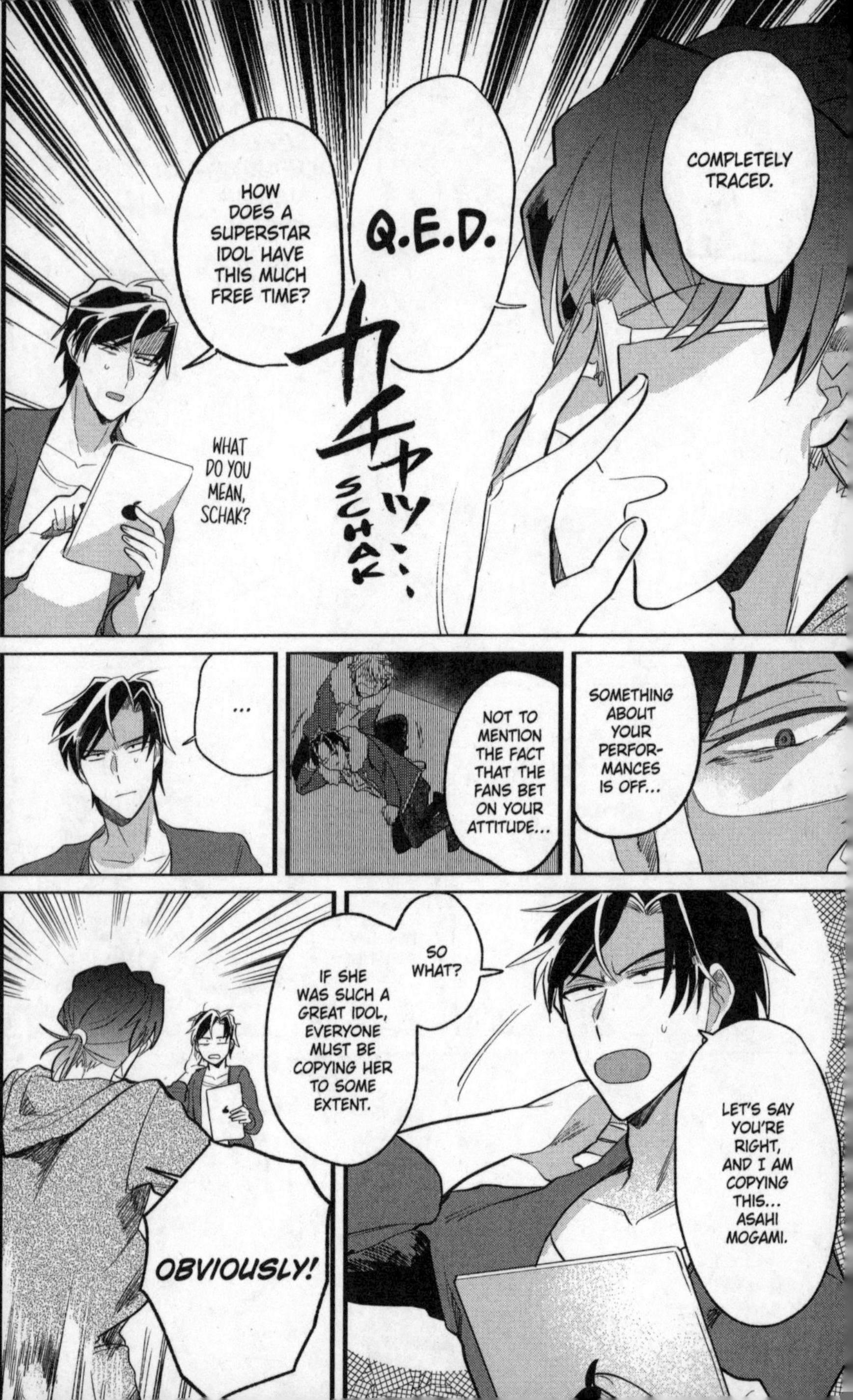
COMPLETELY TRACED.
Q.E.D.
HOW DOES A SUPERSTAR IDOL HAVE THIS MUCH FREE TIME?
カチャッ
SCHAK
WHAT DO YOU MEAN, SCHAK?
SOMETHING ABOUT YOUR PERFORMANCES IS OFF...
NOT TO MENTION THE FACT THAT THE FANS BET ON YOUR ATTITUDE...
...
LET'S SAY YOU'RE RIGHT, AND I AM COPYING THIS... ASAHI MOGAMI.
SO WHAT?
IF SHE WAS SUCH A GREAT IDOL, EVERYONE MUST BE COPYING HER TO SOME EXTENT.
OBVIOUSLY!

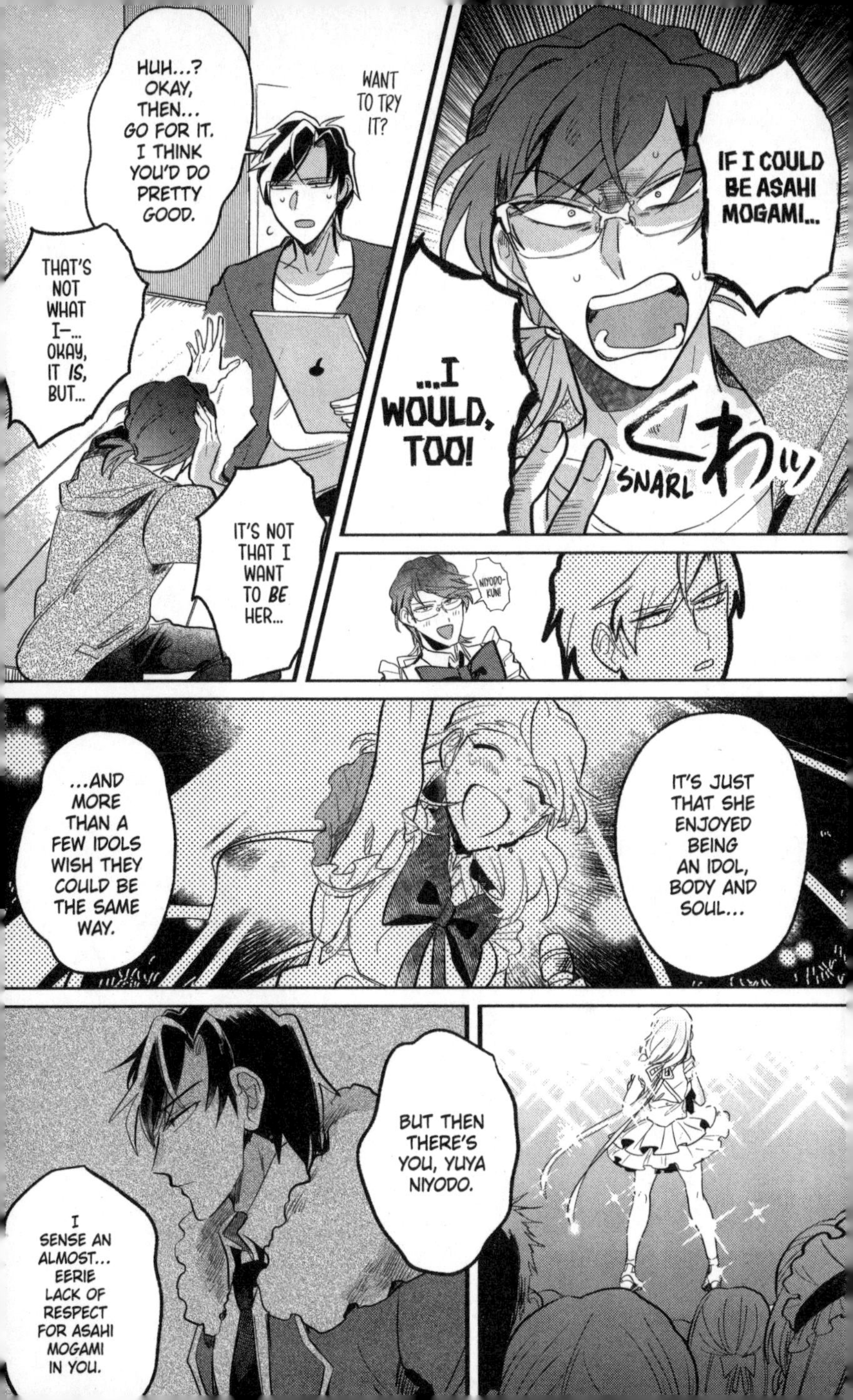
IF I COULD BE ASAHI MOGAMI...
...I WOULD, TOO!
SNARL
くわッ
NIYODO-KUN!
WANT TO TRY IT?
HUH...? OKAY, THEN... GO FOR IT. I THINK YOU'D DO PRETTY GOOD.
THAT'S NOT WHAT I—... OKAY, IT *IS*, BUT...
IT'S NOT THAT I WANT TO *BE* HER...
IT'S JUST THAT SHE ENJOYED BEING AN IDOL, BODY AND SOUL...
...AND MORE THAN A FEW IDOLS WISH THEY COULD BE THE SAME WAY.
BUT THEN THERE'S YOU, YUYA NIYODO.
I SENSE AN ALMOST... EERIE LACK OF RESPECT FOR ASAHI MOGAMI IN YOU.

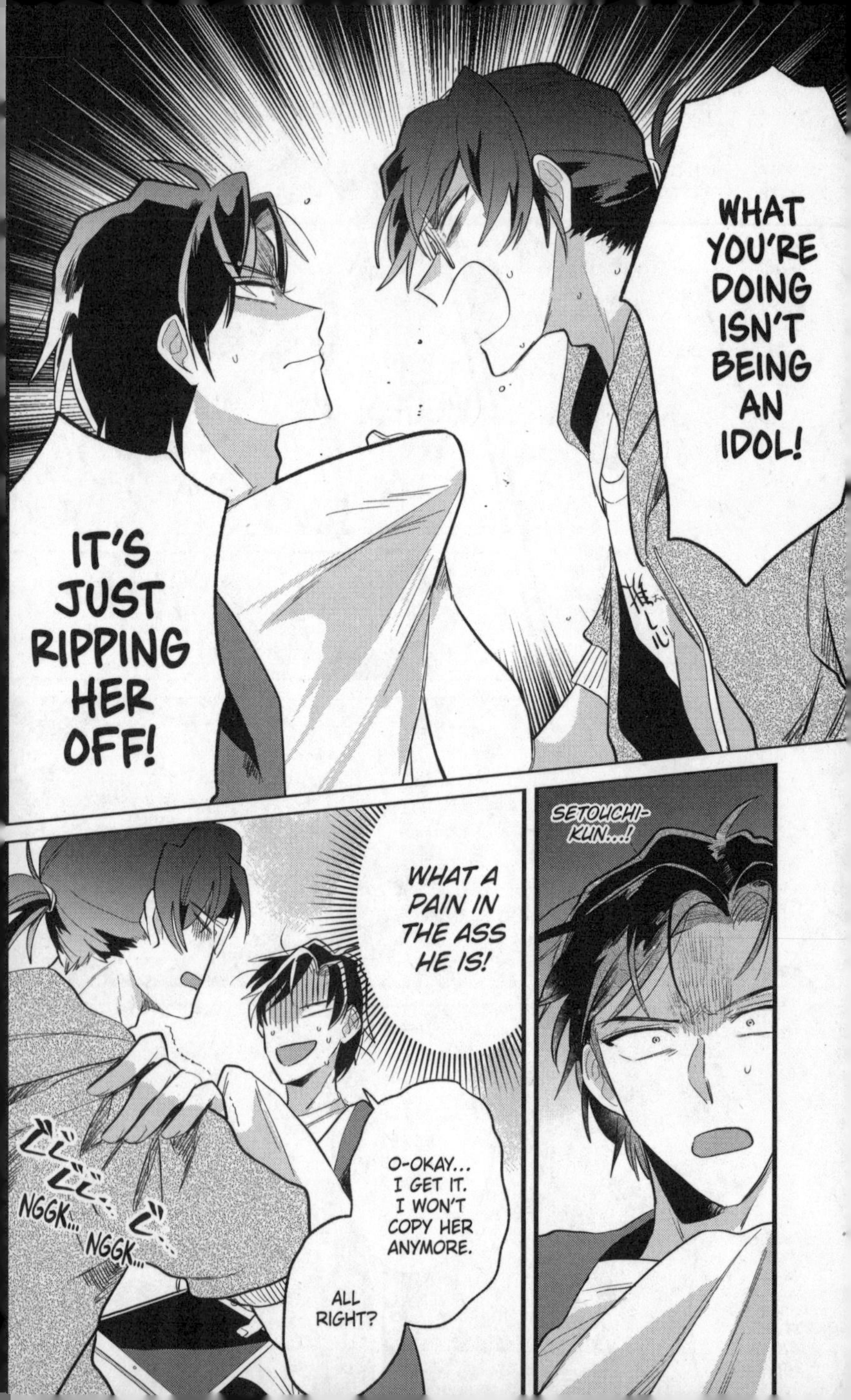
WHAT YOU'RE DOING ISN'T BEING AN IDOL!
IT'S JUST RIPPING HER OFF!
SETOUCHI-KUN...!
WHAT A PAIN IN THE ASS HE IS!
O-OKAY... I GET IT. I WON'T COPY HER ANYMORE.
ALL RIGHT?
ぐぐ… ぐぐ… ぐ…
NGGK... NGGK...

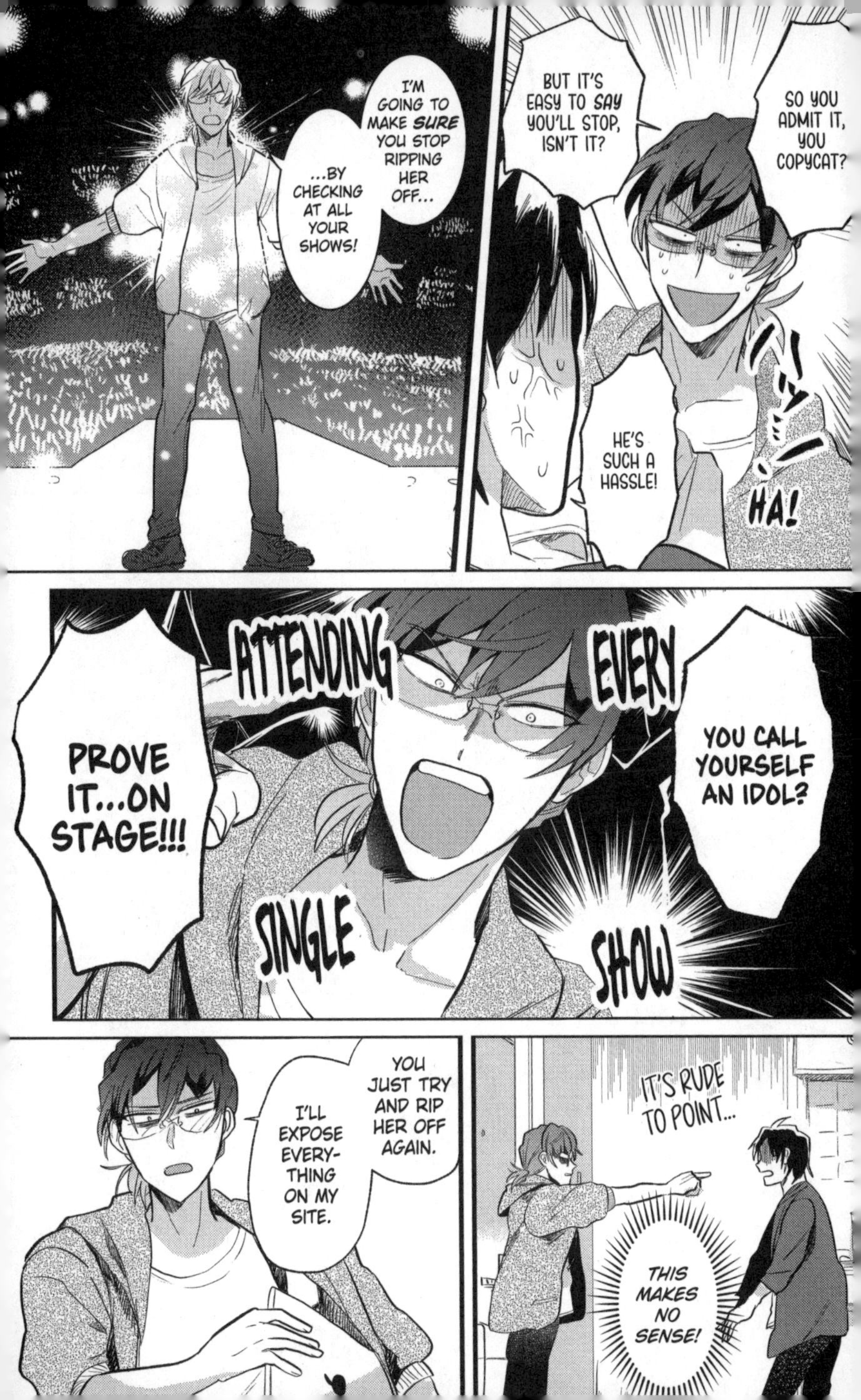
SO YOU ADMIT IT, YOU COPYCAT?
BUT IT'S EASY TO SAY YOU'LL STOP, ISN'T IT?
HA!
HE'S SUCH A HASSLE!
I'M GOING TO MAKE SURE YOU STOP RIPPING HER OFF...
...BY CHECKING AT ALL YOUR SHOWS!
YOU CALL YOURSELF AN IDOL?
ATTENDING
EVERY
SINGLE
SHOW
PROVE IT...ON STAGE!!!
IT'S RUDE TO POINT...
THIS MAKES NO SENSE!
YOU JUST TRY AND RIP HER OFF AGAIN.
I'LL EXPOSE EVERY-THING ON MY SITE.

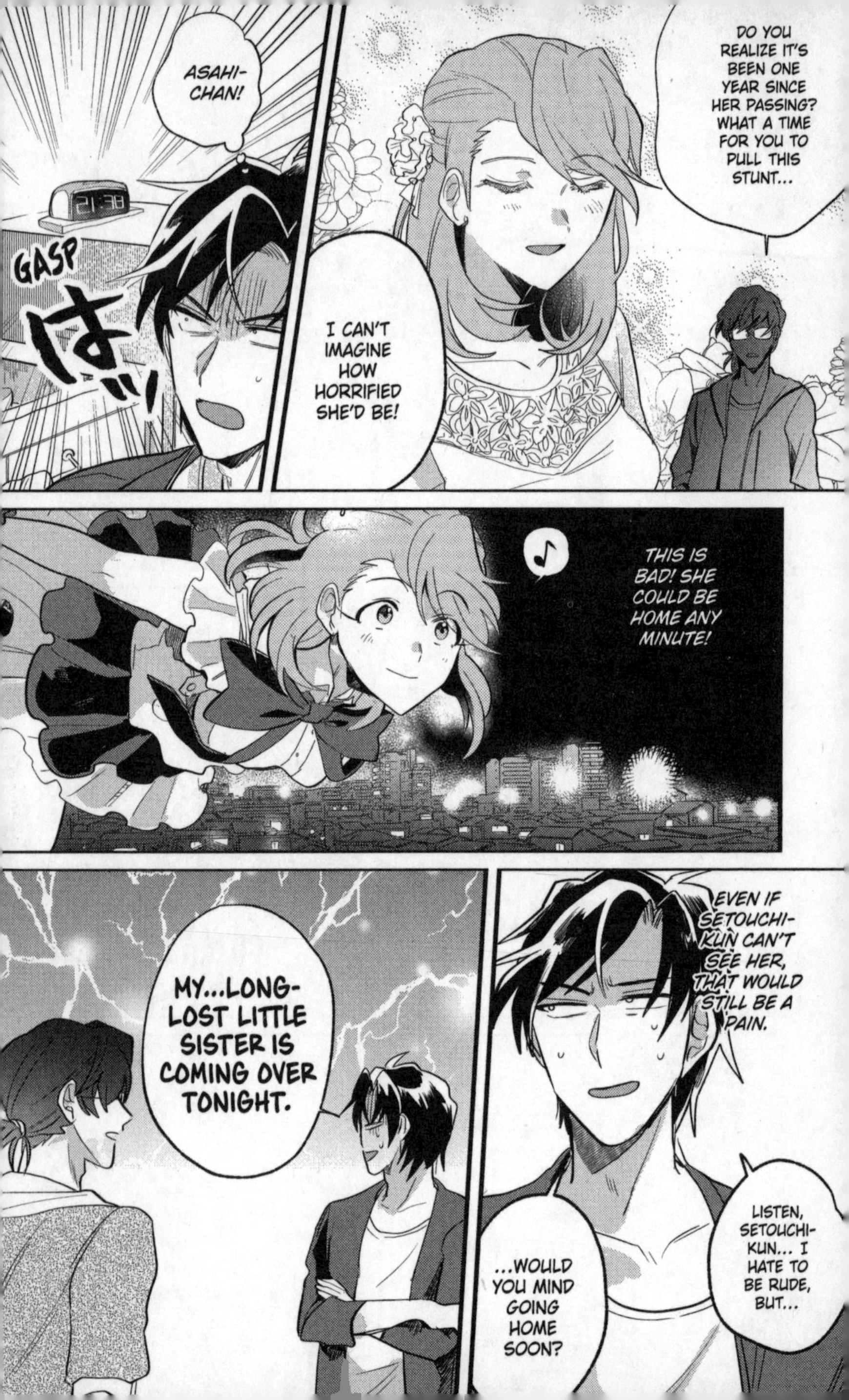
DO YOU REALIZE IT'S BEEN ONE YEAR SINCE HER PASSING? WHAT A TIME FOR YOU TO PULL THIS STUNT...
I CAN'T IMAGINE HOW HORRIFIED SHE'D BE!
ASAHI-CHAN!
GASP
THIS IS BAD! SHE COULD BE HOME ANY MINUTE!
EVEN IF SETOUCHI-KUN CAN'T SEE HER, THAT WOULD STILL BE A PAIN.
LISTEN, SETOUCHI-KUN... I HATE TO BE RUDE, BUT...
...WOULD YOU MIND GOING HOME SOON?
MY...LONG-LOST LITTLE SISTER IS COMING OVER TONIGHT.

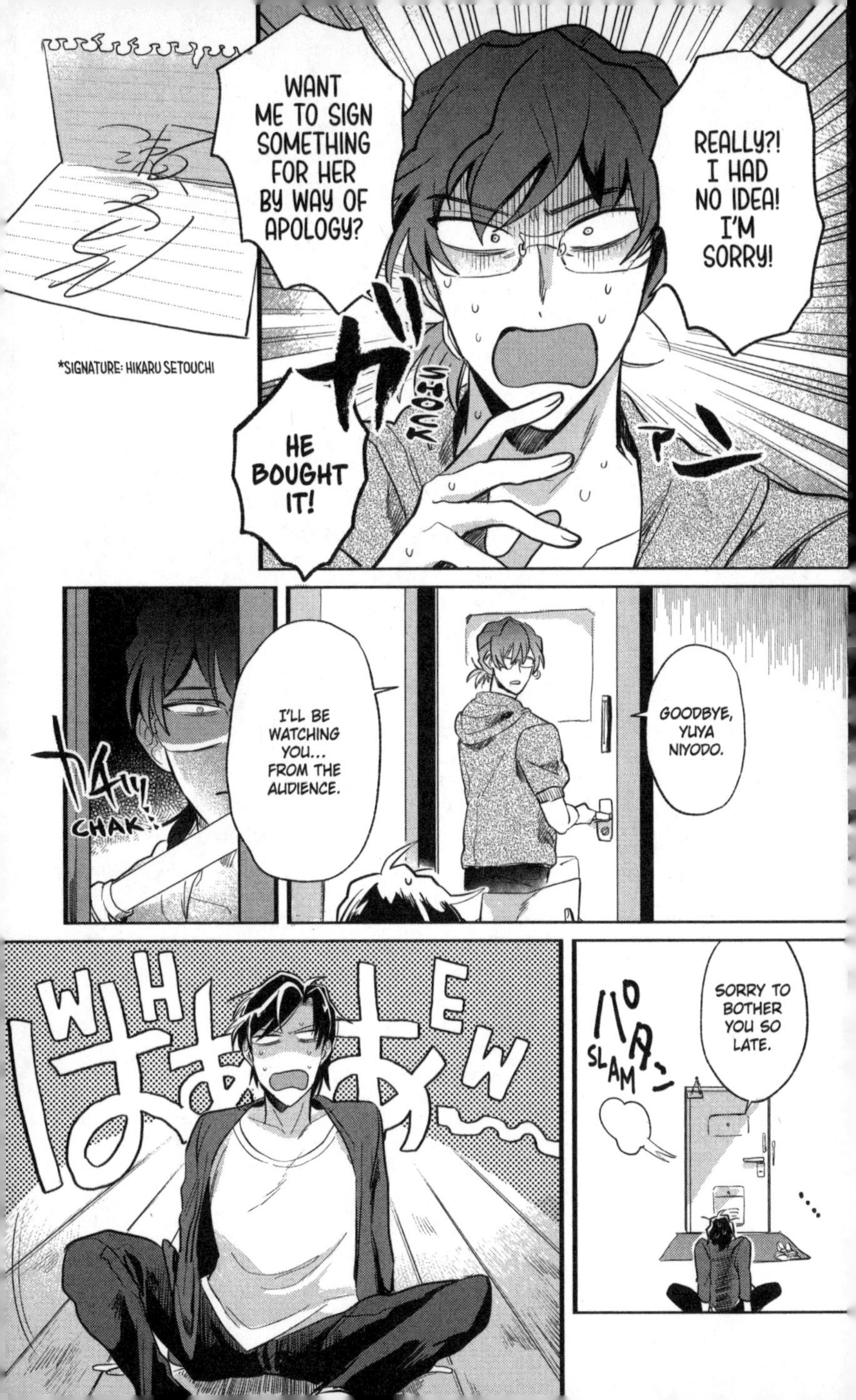
REALLY?! I HAD NO IDEA! I'M SORRY!
WANT ME TO SIGN SOMETHING FOR HER BY WAY OF APOLOGY?
SHOCK
HE BOUGHT IT!
*SIGNATURE: HIKARU SETOUCHI
GOODBYE, YUYA NIYODO.
I'LL BE WATCHING YOU... FROM THE AUDIENCE.
CHAK!
SORRY TO BOTHER YOU SO LATE.
SLAM
....
WHEW

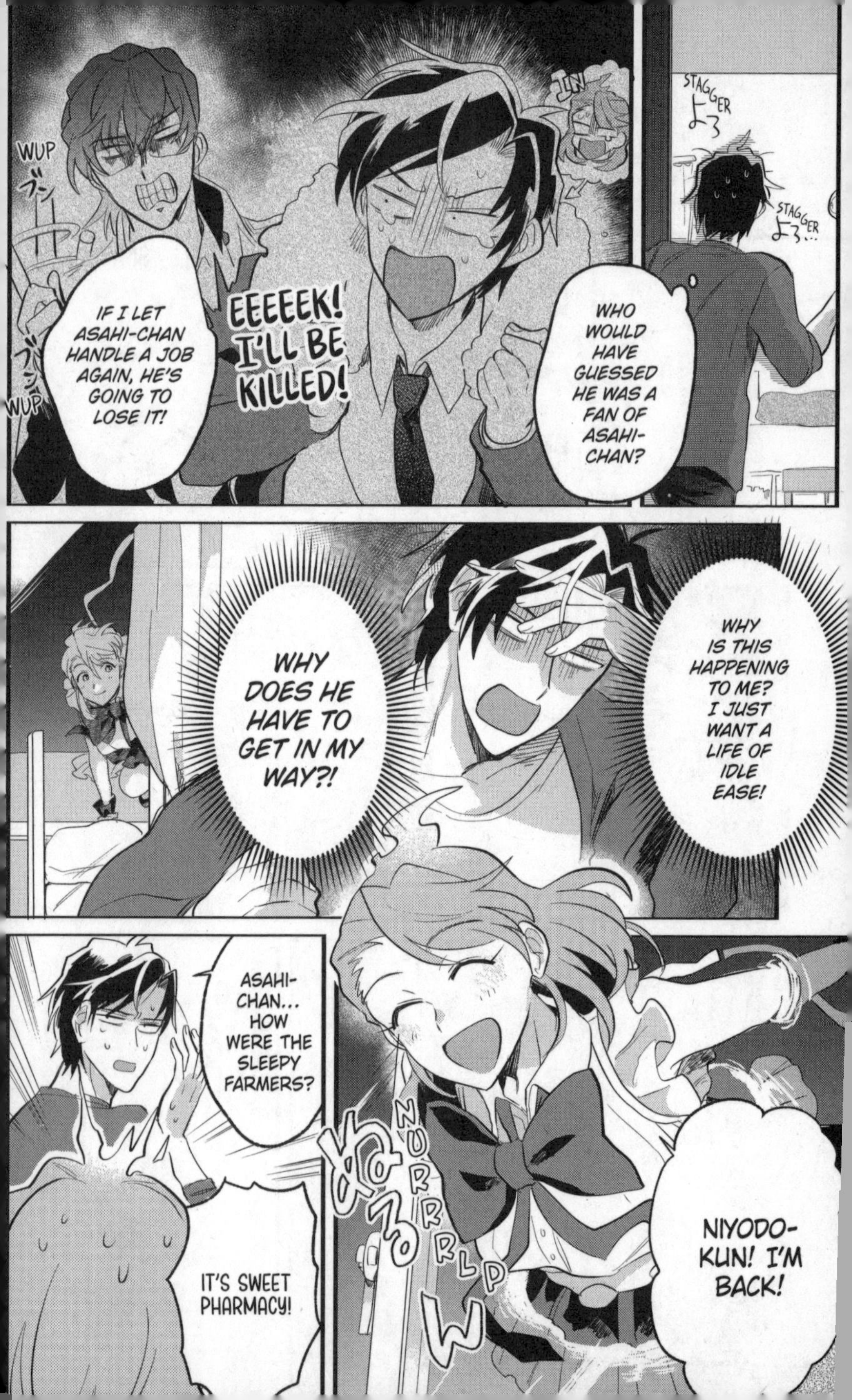

STAGGER
よろ
STAGGER
よろ…
WHO WOULD HAVE GUESSED HE WAS A FAN OF ASAHI-CHAN?
EEEEEK! I'LL BE KILLED!
IF I LET ASAHI-CHAN HANDLE A JOB AGAIN, HE'S GOING TO LOSE IT!
WUP
ブン
ブン
WUP
WHY IS THIS HAPPENING TO ME? I JUST WANT A LIFE OF IDLE EASE!
WHY DOES HE HAVE TO GET IN MY WAY?!
NIYODO-KUN! I'M BACK!
NURRRLP
ぬるっ
ASAHI-CHAN... HOW WERE THE SLEEPY FARMERS?
IT'S SWEET PHARMACY!

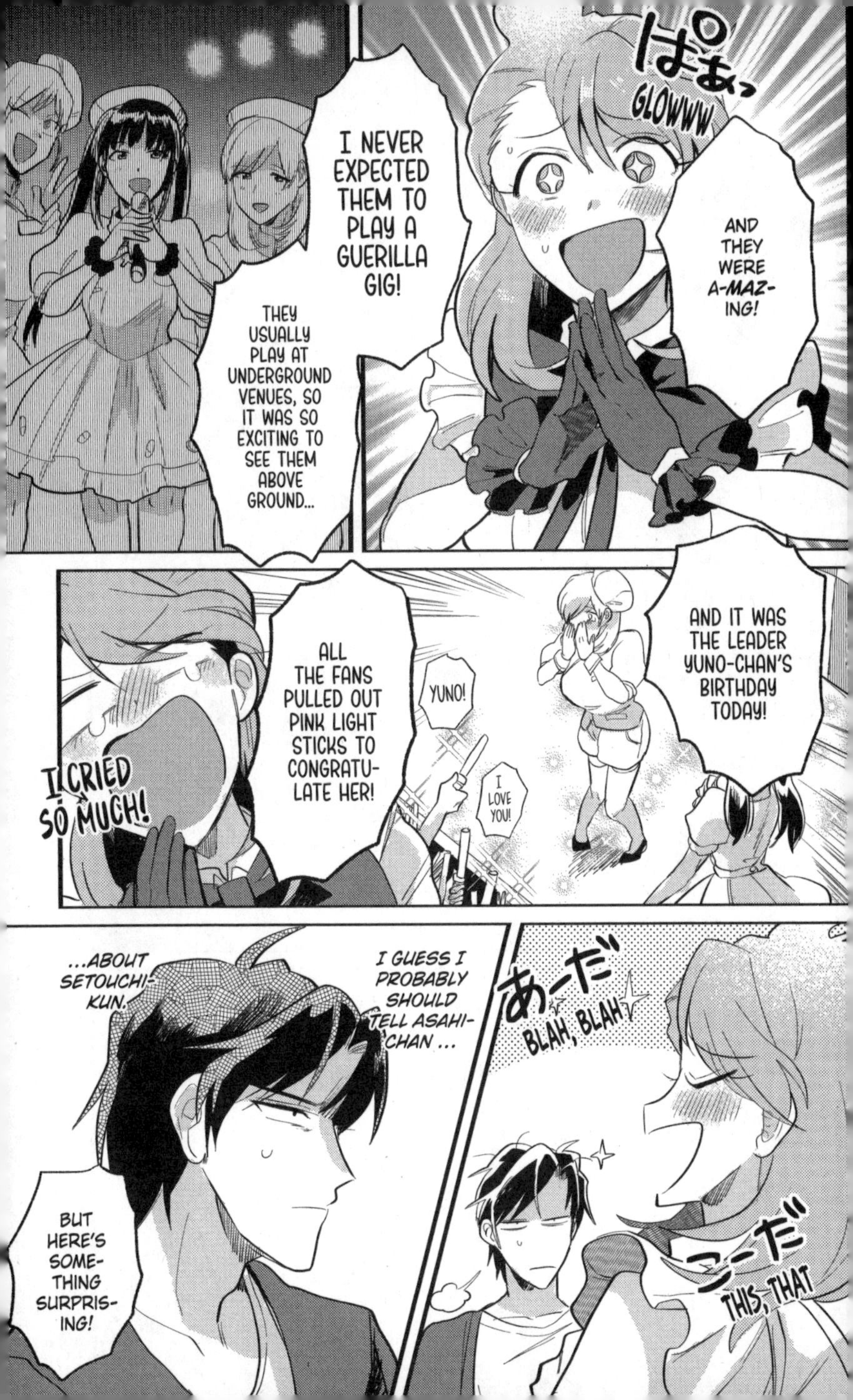
ぱあっ
GLOWWW
I NEVER EXPECTED THEM TO PLAY A GUERILLA GIG!
THEY USUALLY PLAY AT UNDERGROUND VENUES, SO IT WAS SO EXCITING TO SEE THEM ABOVE GROUND...
AND THEY WERE A-MAZ-ING!
AND IT WAS THE LEADER YUNO-CHAN'S BIRTHDAY TODAY!
I LOVE YOU!
YUNO!
ALL THE FANS PULLED OUT PINK LIGHT STICKS TO CONGRATU-LATE HER!
I CRIED SO MUCH!
あーだ
BLAH, BLAH
こーだ
THIS, THAT
I GUESS I PROBABLY SHOULD TELL ASAHI-CHAN ...
...ABOUT SETOUCHI-KUN.
BUT HERE'S SOME-THING SURPRIS-ING!

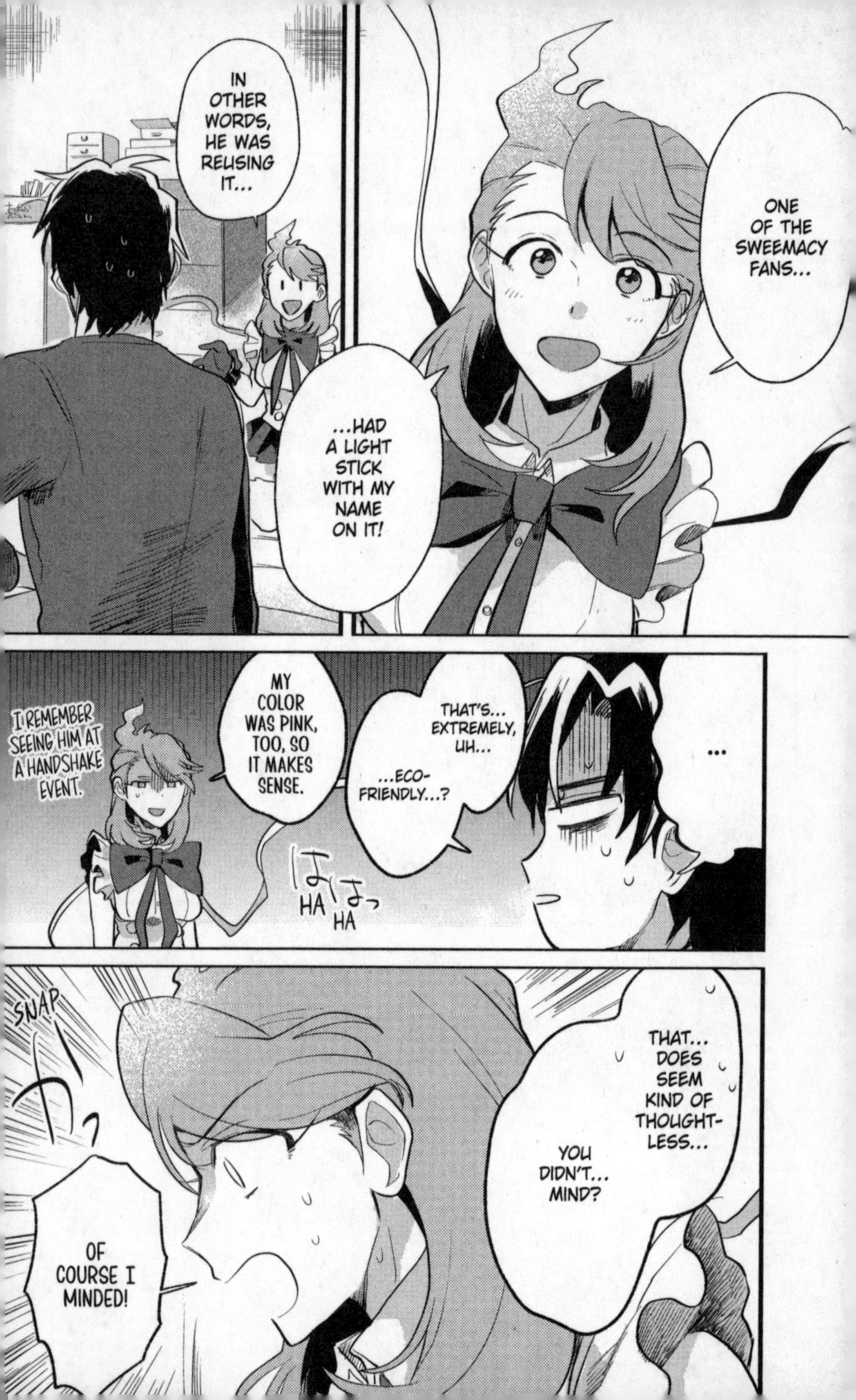
ONE OF THE SWEEMACY FANS...
...HAD A LIGHT STICK WITH MY NAME ON IT!
IN OTHER WORDS, HE WAS REUSING IT...
...
THAT'S... EXTREMELY, UH...
...ECO-FRIENDLY...?
MY COLOR WAS PINK, TOO, SO IT MAKES SENSE.
HA HA
I REMEMBER SEEING HIM AT A HANDSHAKE EVENT.
THAT... DOES SEEM KIND OF THOUGHT-LESS...
YOU DIDN'T... MIND?
SNAP
OF COURSE I MINDED!

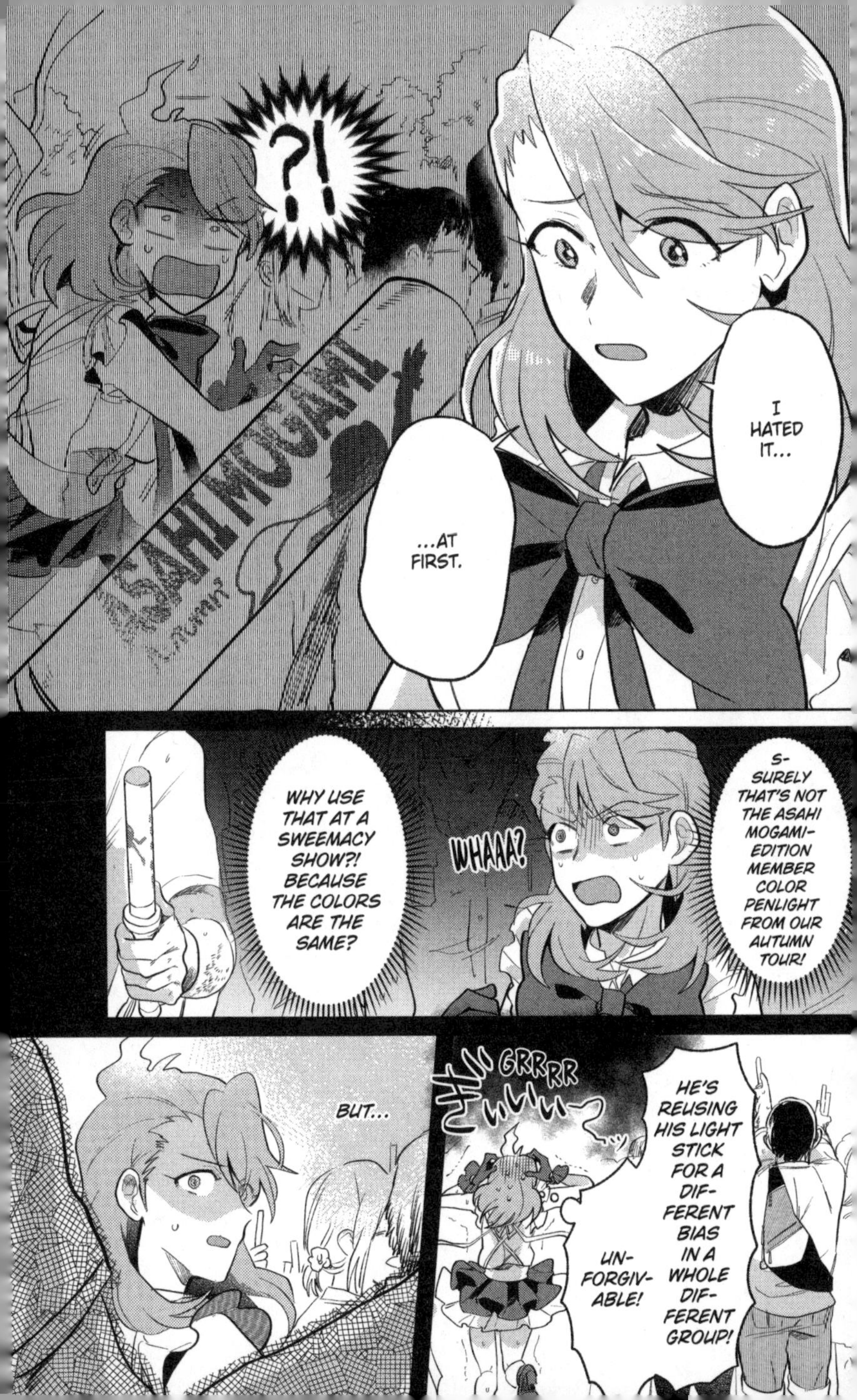
?!
I HATED IT…
…AT FIRST.
S-SURELY THAT'S NOT THE ASAHI MOGAMI-EDITION MEMBER COLOR PENLIGHT FROM OUR AUTUMN TOUR!
WHAAA?
WHY USE THAT AT A SWEEMACY SHOW?! BECAUSE THE COLORS ARE THE SAME?
HE'S REUSING HIS LIGHT STICK FOR A DIFFERENT BIAS IN A WHOLE DIFFERENT GROUP!
GRRRR
UNFORGIVABLE!
BUT…

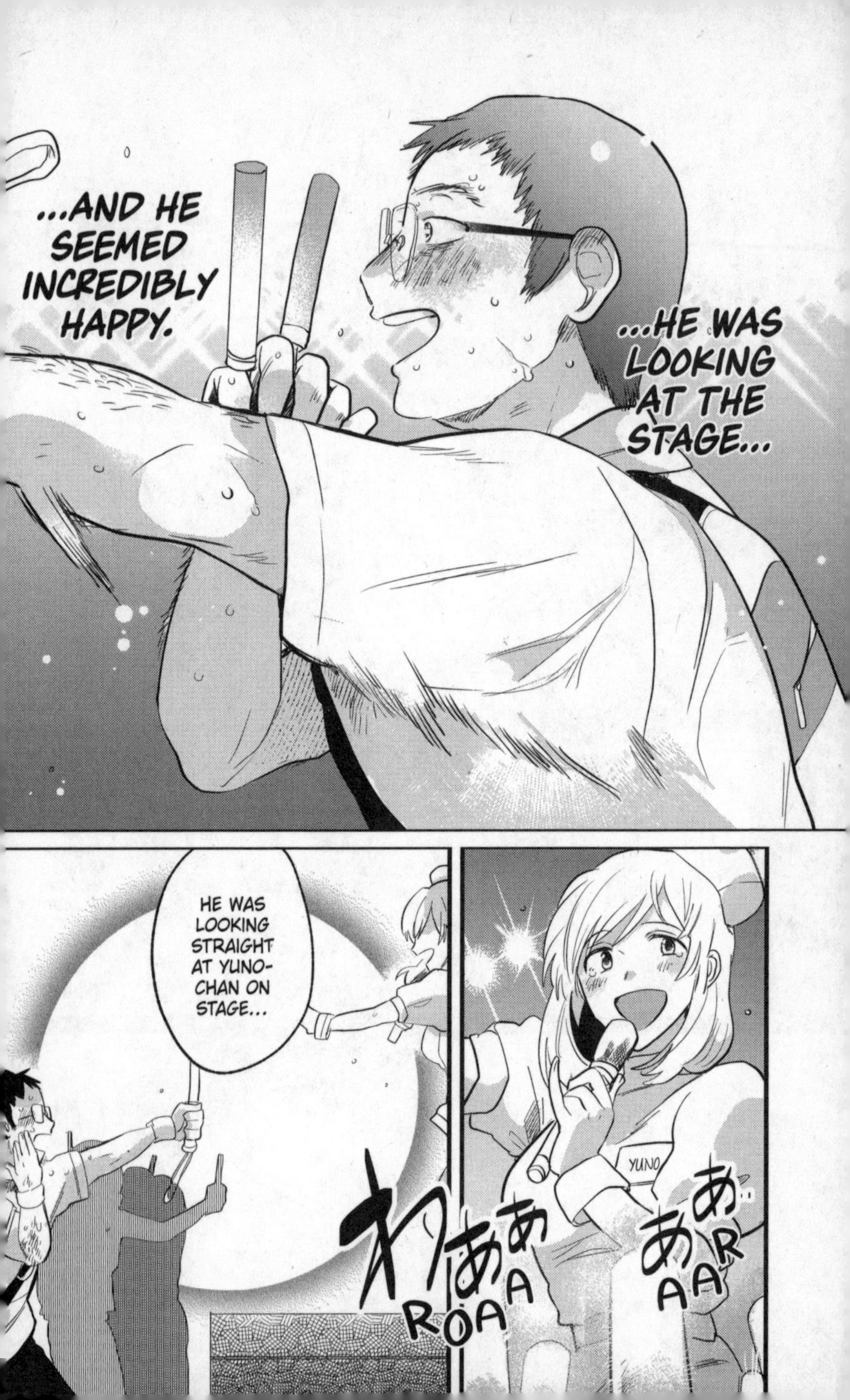
...HE WAS LOOKING AT THE STAGE...
...AND HE SEEMED INCREDIBLY HAPPY.
YUNO
わあああ
ROAA
ああ..
AAR
HE WAS LOOKING STRAIGHT AT YUNO-CHAN ON STAGE...

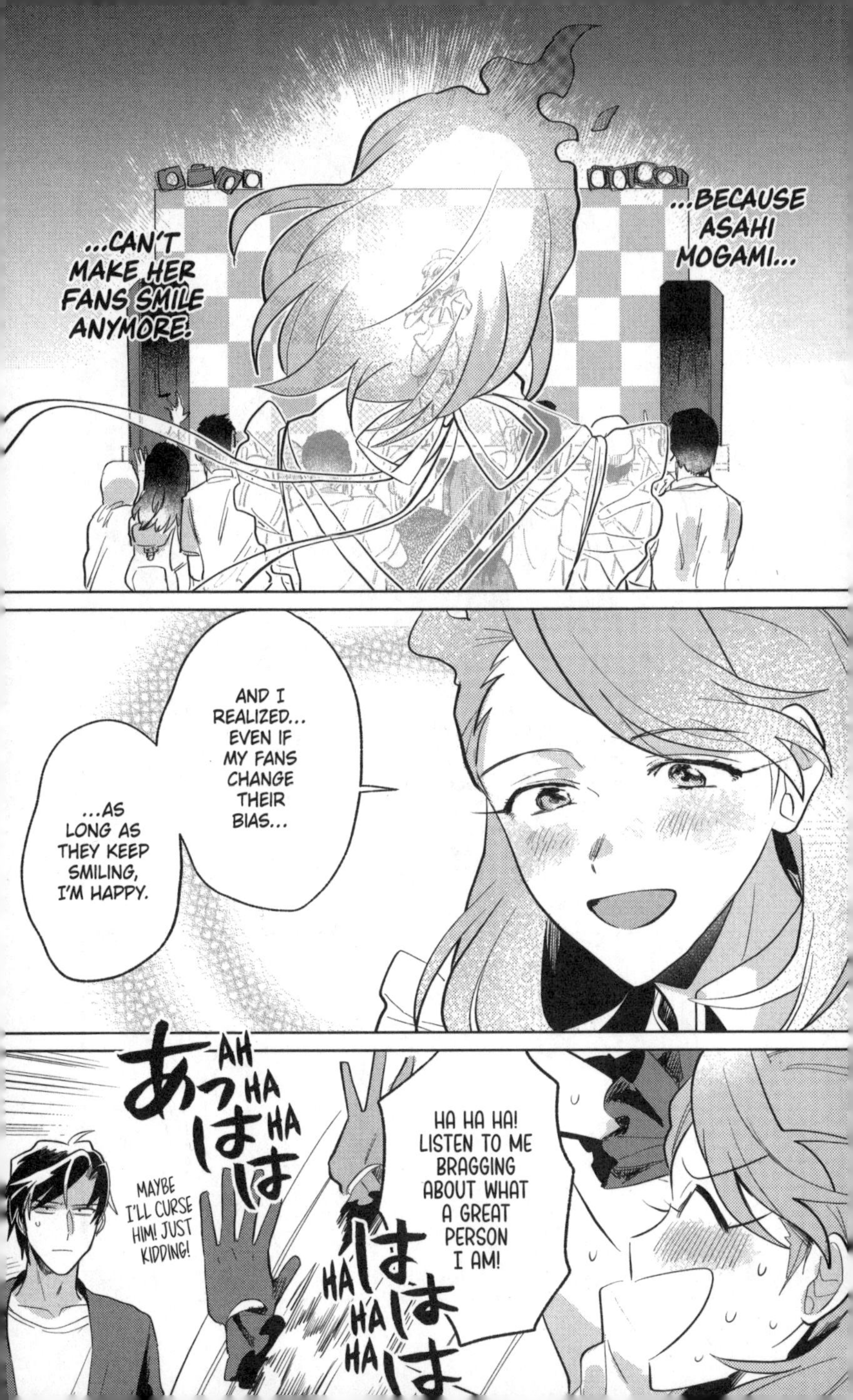
...BECAUSE ASAHI MOGAMI...
...CAN'T MAKE HER FANS SMILE ANYMORE.
AND I REALIZED... EVEN IF MY FANS CHANGE THEIR BIAS...
...AS LONG AS THEY KEEP SMILING, I'M HAPPY.
HA HA HA! LISTEN TO ME BRAGGING ABOUT WHAT A GREAT PERSON I AM!
あっはは AH HA HA HA
はははは HA HA HA HA
MAYBE I'LL CURSE HIM! JUST KIDDING!

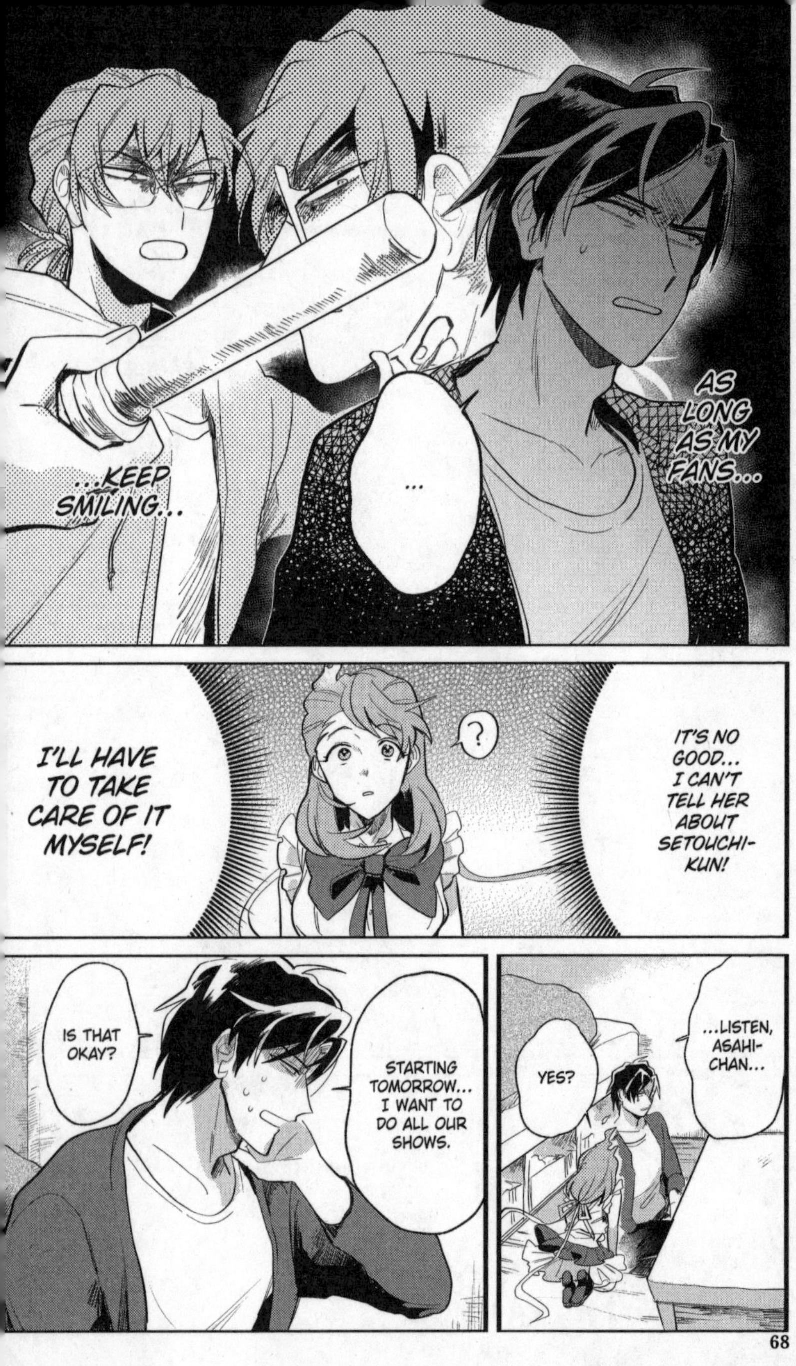
AS LONG AS MY FANS...
...
...KEEP SMILING...
IT'S NO GOOD... I CAN'T TELL HER ABOUT SETOUCHI-KUN!
?
I'LL HAVE TO TAKE CARE OF IT MYSELF!
...LISTEN, ASAHI-CHAN...
YES?
STARTING TOMORROW... I WANT TO DO ALL OUR SHOWS.
IS THAT OKAY?

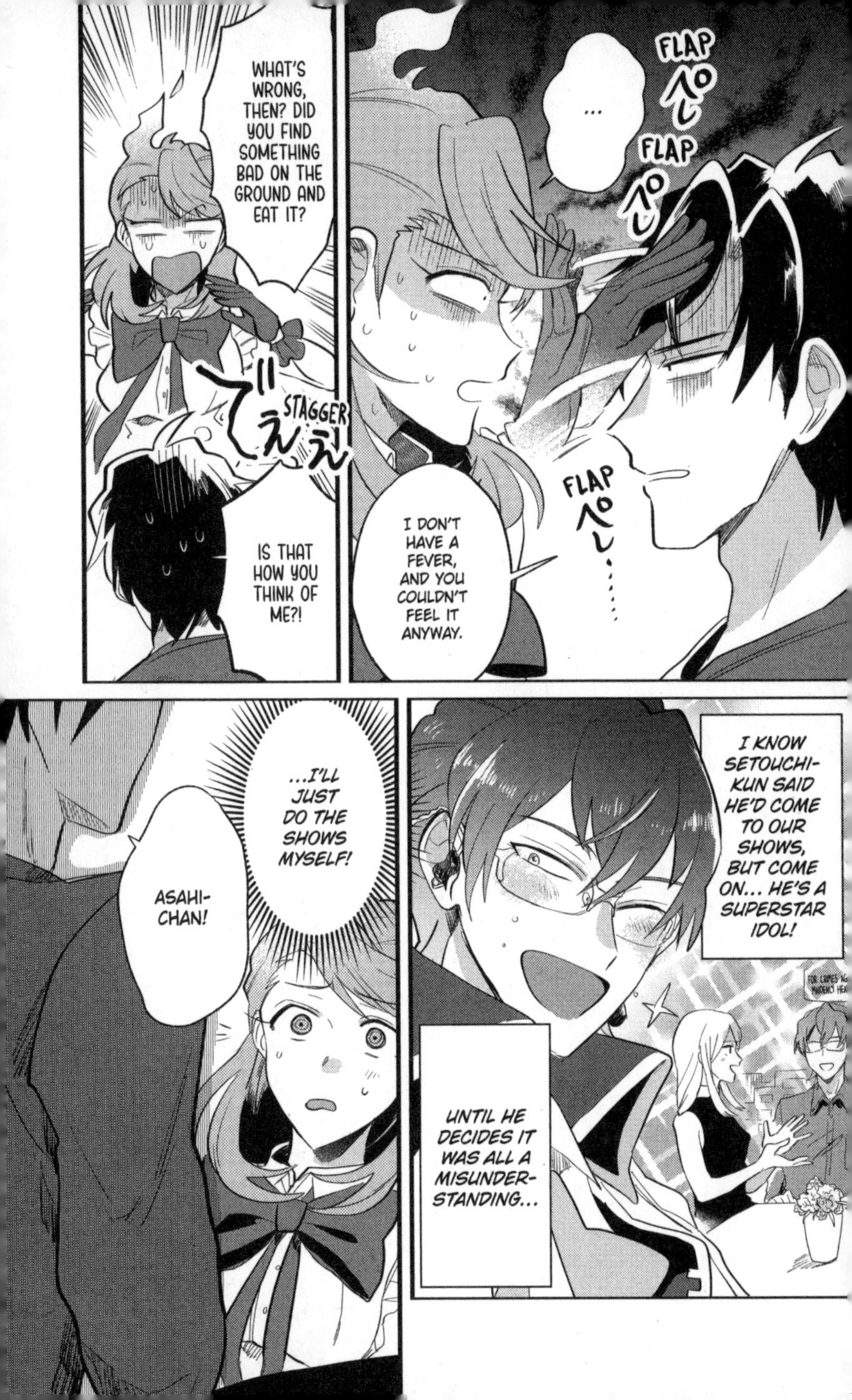
...
FLAP ぺし
FLAP ぺし
FLAP ぺし......
I DON'T HAVE A FEVER, AND YOU COULDN'T FEEL IT ANYWAY.
WHAT'S WRONG, THEN? DID YOU FIND SOMETHING BAD ON THE GROUND AND EAT IT?
STAGGER でぇぇ
IS THAT HOW YOU THINK OF ME?!
I KNOW SETOUCHI-KUN SAID HE'D COME TO OUR SHOWS, BUT COME ON... HE'S A SUPERSTAR IDOL!
UNTIL HE DECIDES IT WAS ALL A MISUNDERSTANDING...
...I'LL JUST DO THE SHOWS MYSELF!
ASAHI-CHAN!

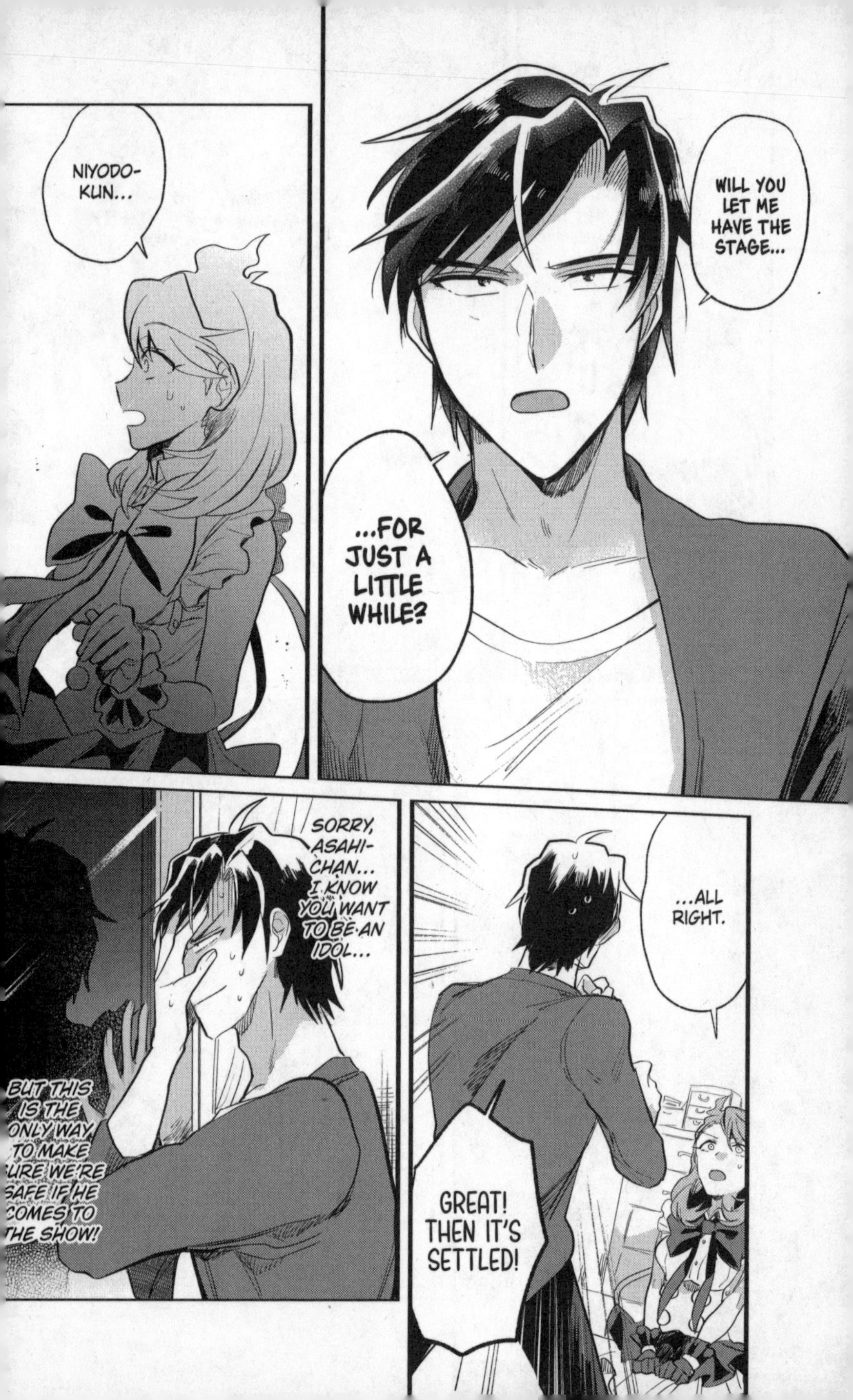
WILL YOU LET ME HAVE THE STAGE...
...FOR JUST A LITTLE WHILE?
NIYODO-KUN...
...ALL RIGHT.
GREAT! THEN IT'S SETTLED!
SORRY, ASAHI-CHAN... I KNOW YOU WANT TO BE AN IDOL...
BUT THIS IS THE ONLY WAY TO MAKE SURE WE'RE SAFE IF HE COMES TO THE SHOW!

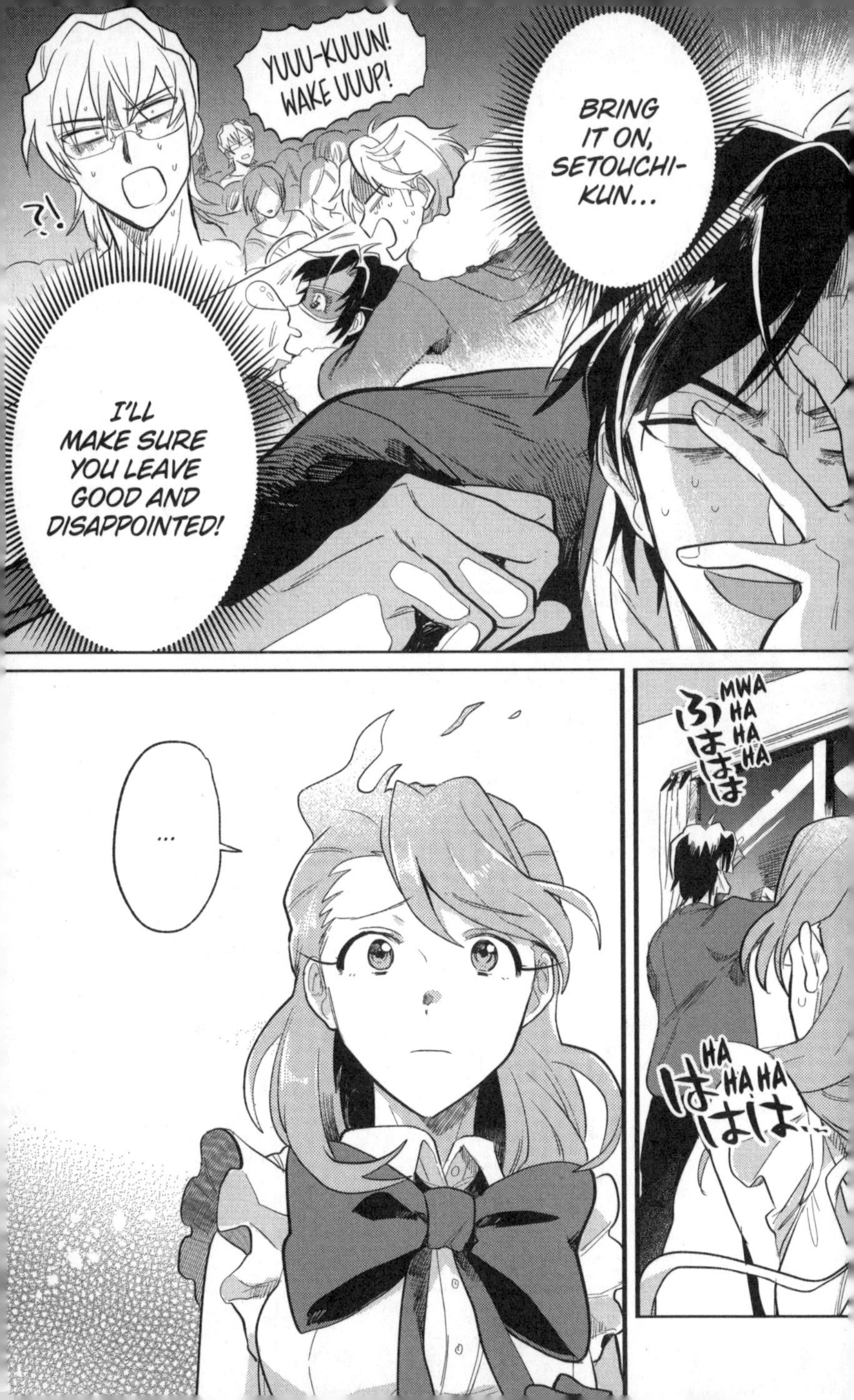
BRING IT ON, SETOUCHI-KUN...
YUUU-KUUUN! WAKE UUUP!
?!
I'LL MAKE SURE YOU LEAVE GOOD AND DISAPPOINTED!
ふははは MWA HA HA HA
ははは HA HA HA
...

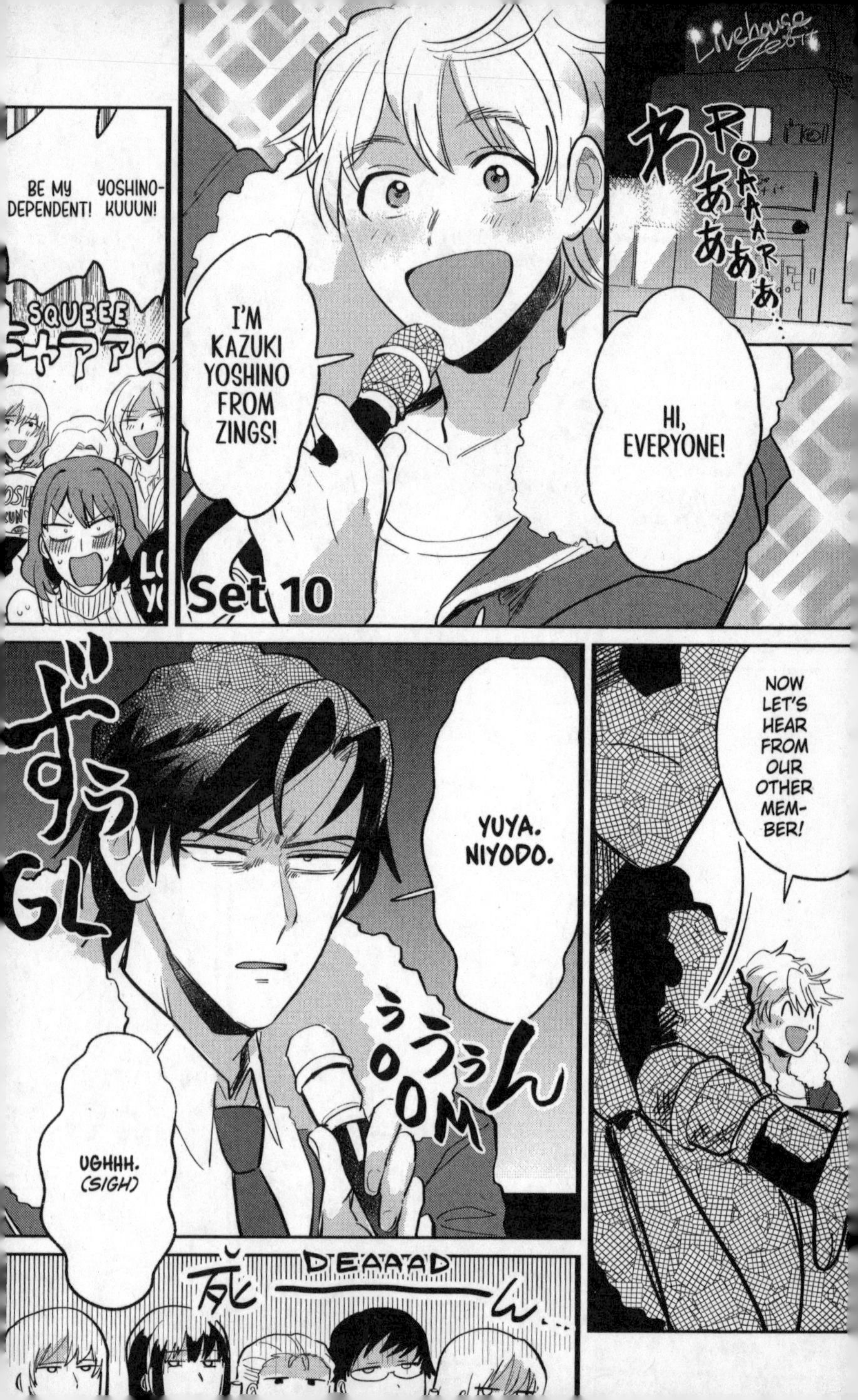
Livehouse Gett
ROAAAR
HI, EVERYONE!
I'M KAZUKI YOSHINO FROM ZINGS!
Set 10
YOSHINO-KUUUN!
BE MY DEPENDENT!
SQUEEE
NOW LET'S HEAR FROM OUR OTHER MEMBER!
GL
YUYA. NIYODO.
OOM
UGHHH. (SIGH)
DEAAAD

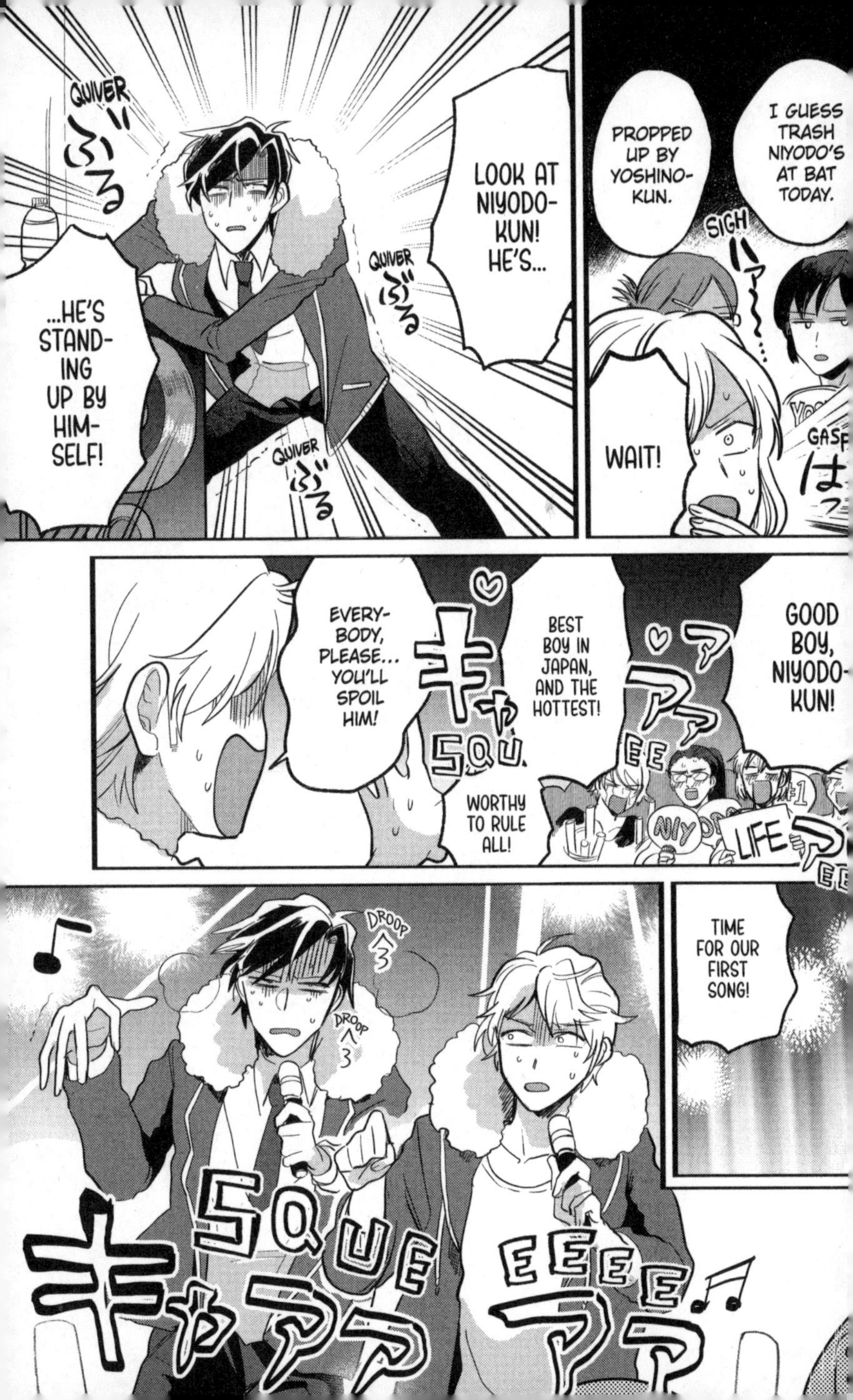
I GUESS TRASH NIYODO'S AT BAT TODAY.
PROPPED UP BY YOSHINO-KUN.
SIGH
ハァ~…
GASP
はっ
WAIT!
LOOK AT NIYODO-KUN! HE'S...
QUIVER
ぶる
QUIVER
ぷる
QUIVER
ぷる
...HE'S STANDING UP BY HIMSELF!
GOOD BOY, NIYODO-KUN!
BEST BOY IN JAPAN, AND THE HOTTEST!
WORTHY TO RULE ALL!
SQUEE
キャアア
EVERYBODY, PLEASE... YOU'LL SPOIL HIM!
NIY
LIFE
#1
TIME FOR OUR FIRST SONG!
DROOP
DROOP
SQUEEEEE.
キャアアアア

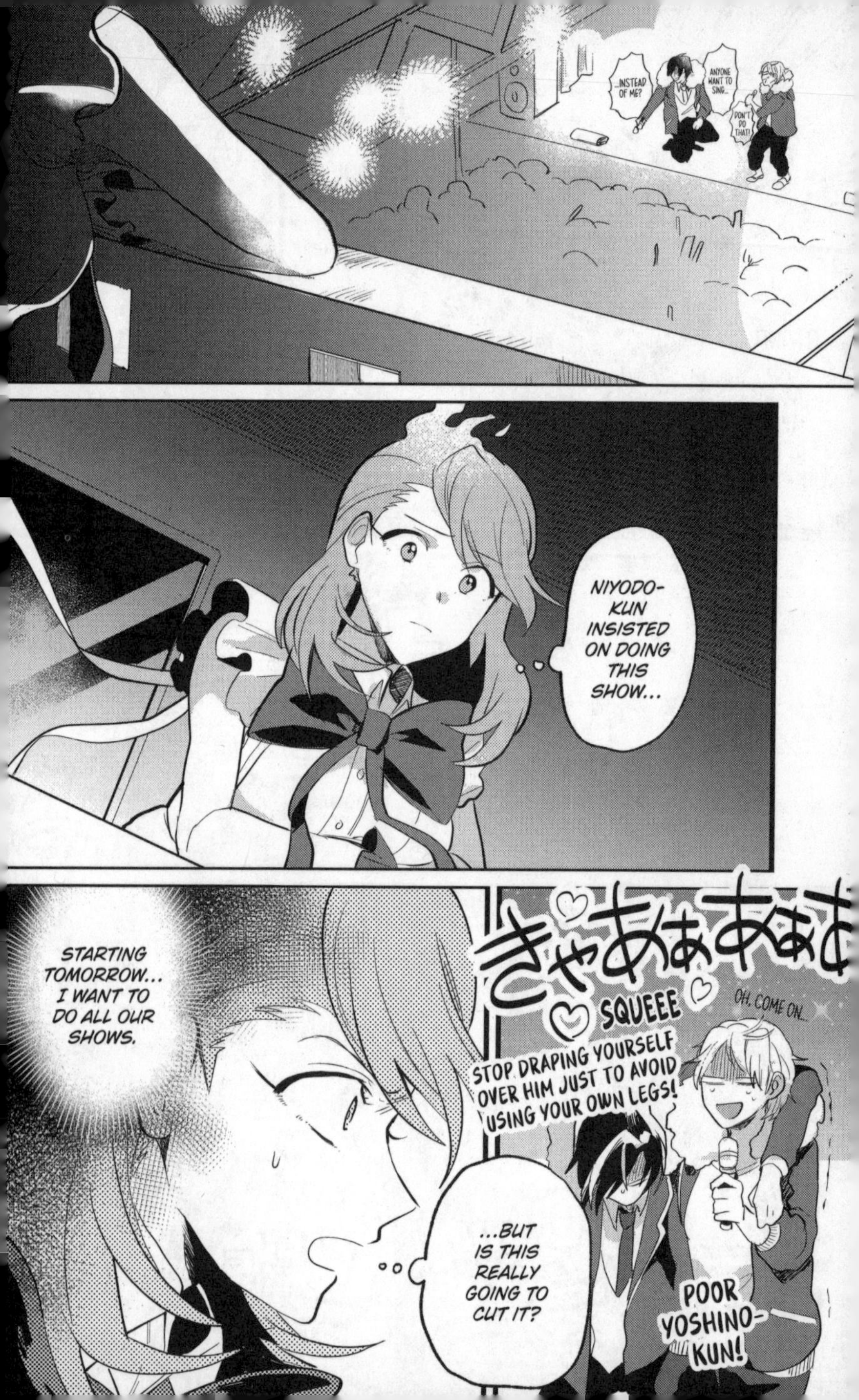
ANYONE WANT TO SING...
...INSTEAD OF ME?
DON'T DO THAT!
NIYODO-KUN INSISTED ON DOING THIS SHOW...
SQUEEE
OH, COME ON...
STOP DRAPING YOURSELF OVER HIM JUST TO AVOID USING YOUR OWN LEGS!
POOR YOSHINO-KUN!
STARTING TOMORROW... I WANT TO DO ALL OUR SHOWS.
...BUT IS THIS REALLY GOING TO CUT IT?

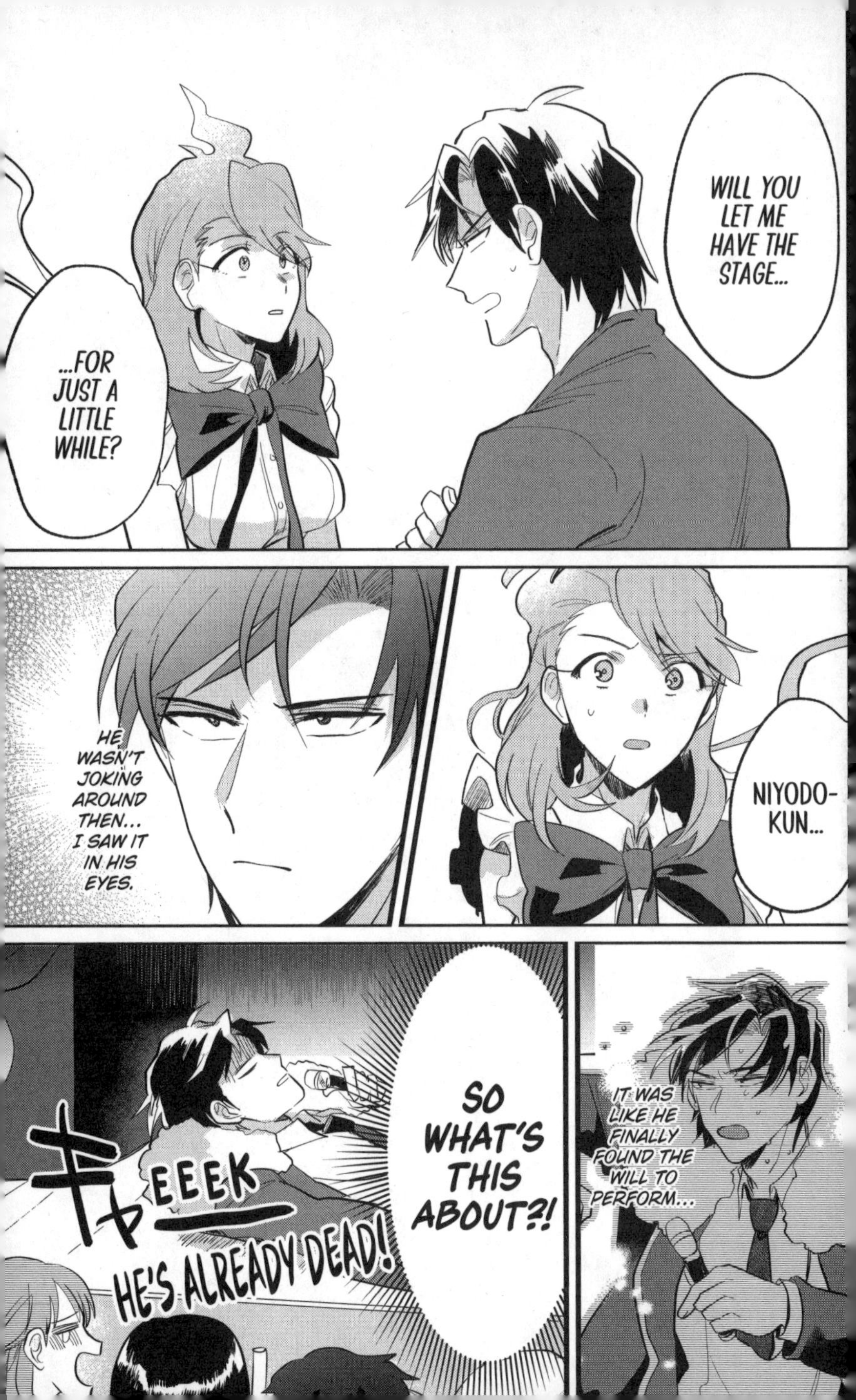
WILL YOU LET ME HAVE THE STAGE...
...FOR JUST A LITTLE WHILE?
NIYODO-KUN...
HE WASN'T JOKING AROUND THEN... I SAW IT IN HIS EYES.
IT WAS LIKE HE FINALLY FOUND THE WILL TO PERFORM...
SO WHAT'S THIS ABOUT?!
キャEEEK
HE'S ALREADY DEAD!

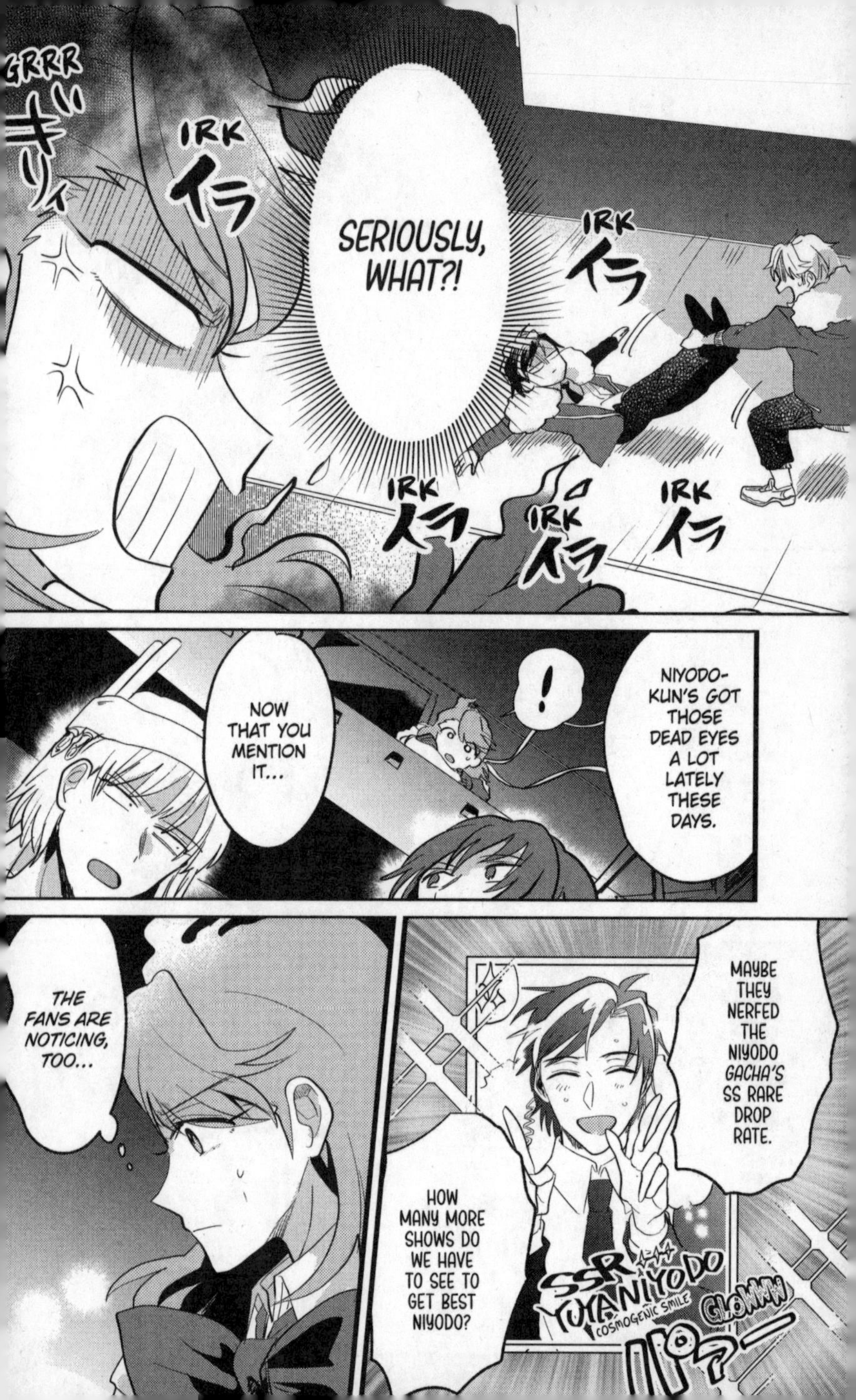
IRK
イラ
SERIOUSLY, WHAT?!
IRK
イラ
GRRR
ギリィ
IRK
イラ
IRK
イラ
IRK
イラ
NIYODO-KUN'S GOT THOSE DEAD EYES A LOT LATELY THESE DAYS.
!
NOW THAT YOU MENTION IT...
MAYBE THEY NERFED THE NIYODO GACHA'S SS RARE DROP RATE.
HOW MANY MORE SHOWS DO WE HAVE TO SEE TO GET BEST NIYODO?
SSR YUYA NIYODO
COSMOGENIC SMILE
GLOWWW
パァー
THE FANS ARE NOTICING, TOO...

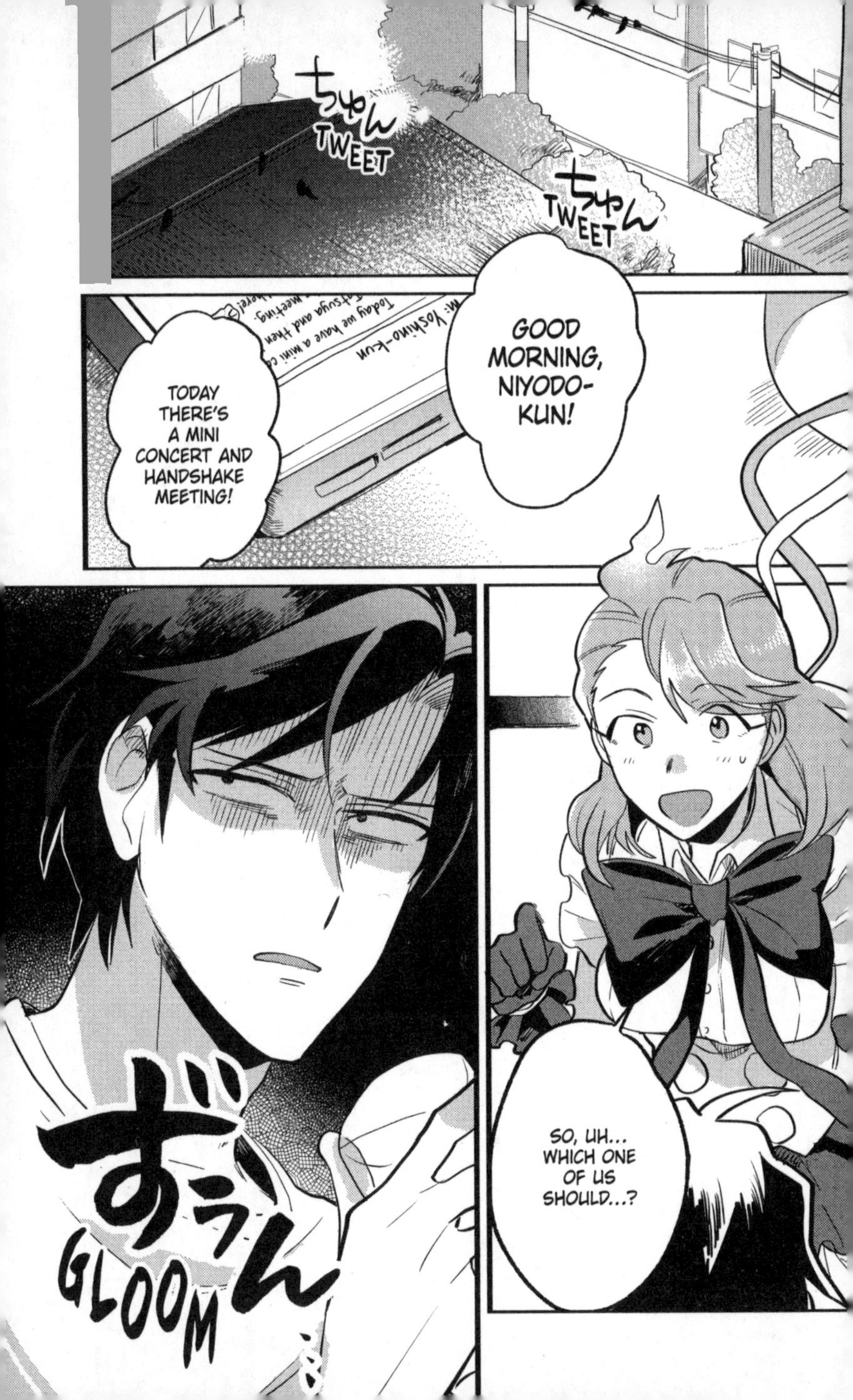

ちゅん
TWEET
ちゅん
TWEET
GOOD MORNING, NIYODO-KUN!
TODAY THERE'S A MINI CONCERT AND HANDSHAKE MEETING!
SO, UH... WHICH ONE OF US SHOULD...?
ずぅん
GLOOM

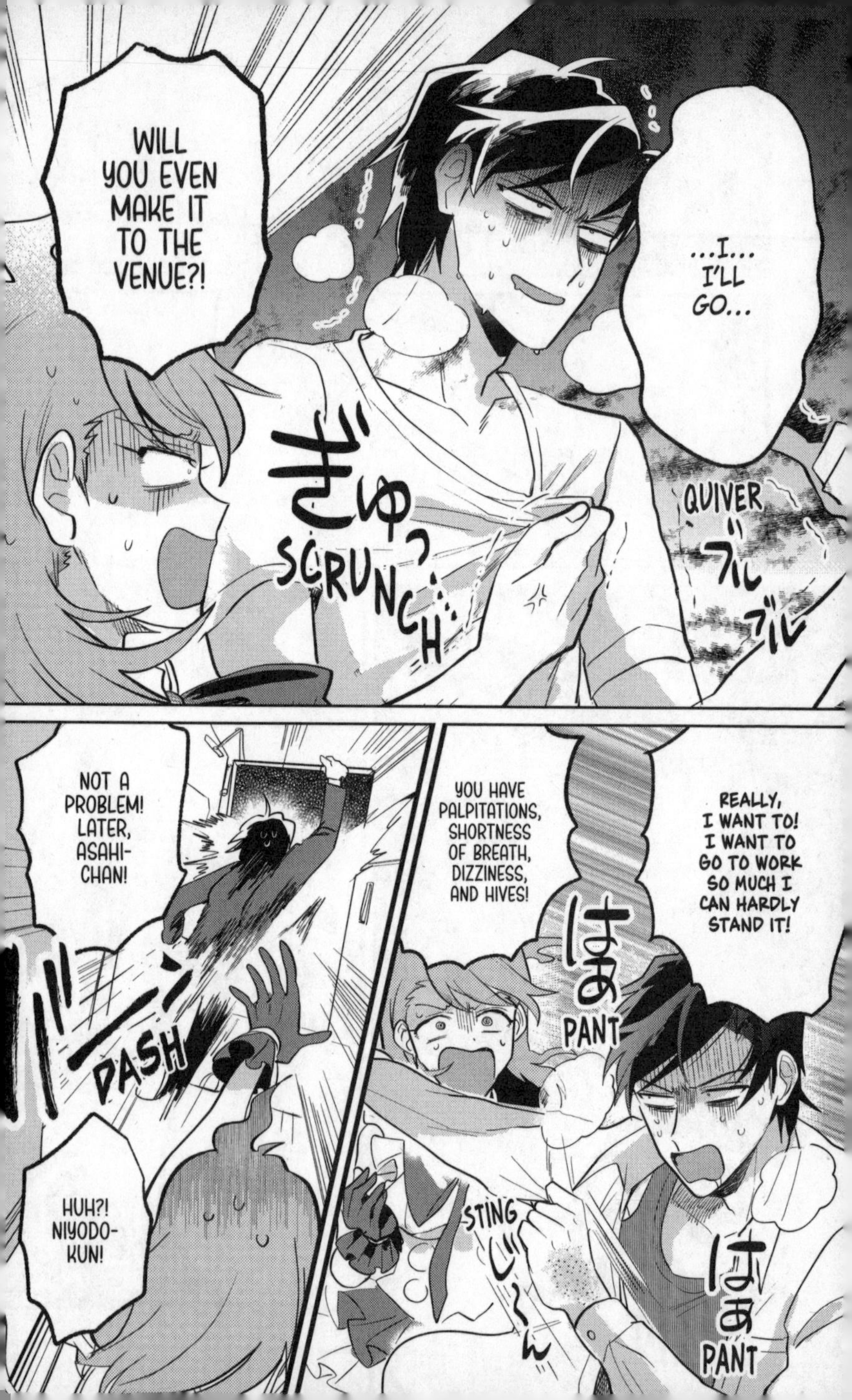
...I... I'LL GO...
WILL YOU EVEN MAKE IT TO THE VENUE?!
ブルブル QUIVER
ぎゅっ SCRUNCH
REALLY, I WANT TO! I WANT TO GO TO WORK SO MUCH I CAN HARDLY STAND IT!
はあ PANT
はあ PANT
YOU HAVE PALPITATIONS, SHORTNESS OF BREATH, DIZZINESS, AND HIVES!
じ〜ん STING
NOT A PROBLEM! LATER, ASAHI-CHAN!
ダッ DASH
HUH?! NIYODO-KUN!

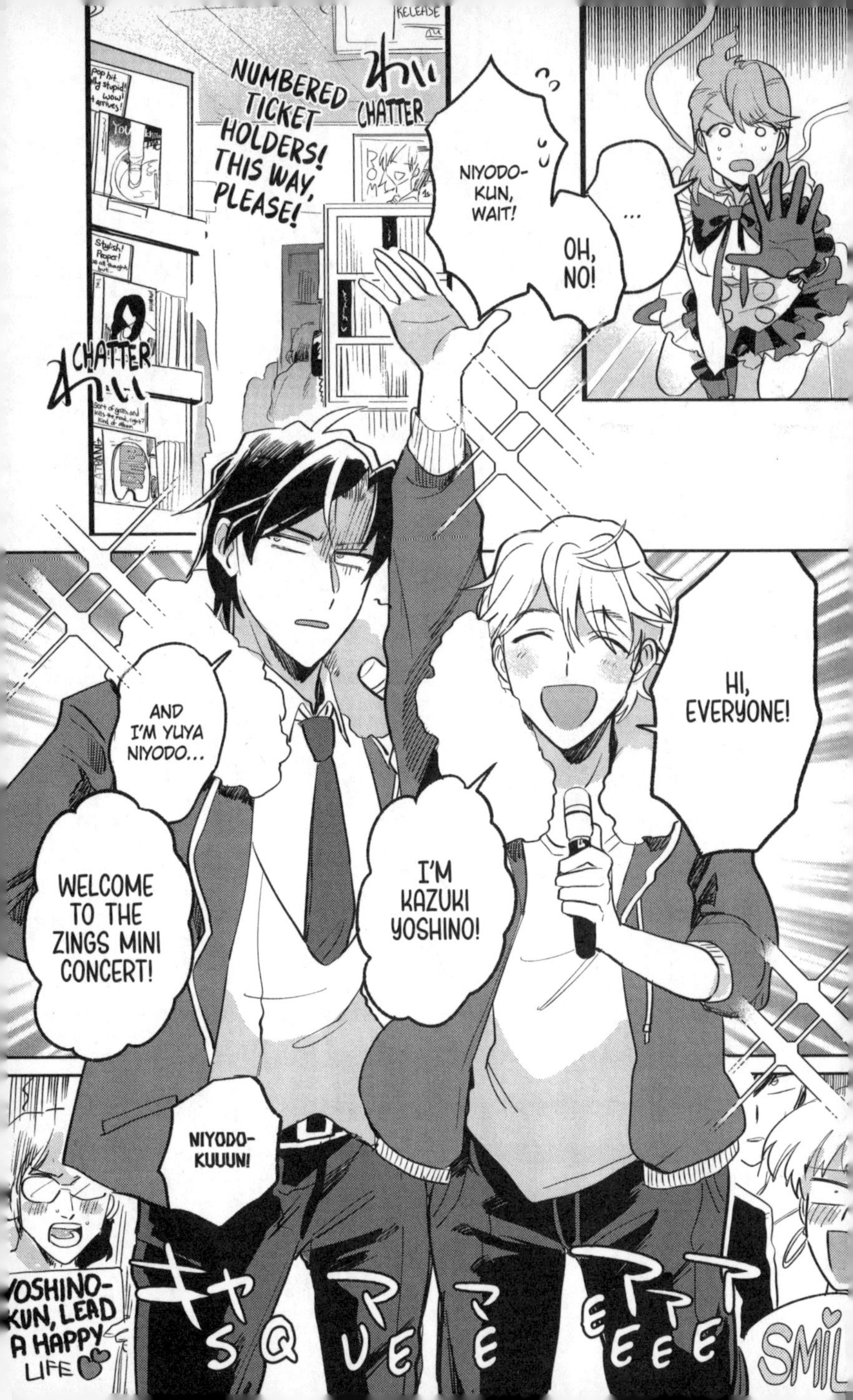

...
OH, NO!
NIYODO-KUN, WAIT!
NUMBERED TICKET HOLDERS! THIS WAY, PLEASE!
CHATTER
CHATTER
HI, EVERYONE!
I'M KAZUKI YOSHINO!
AND I'M YUYA NIYODO...
WELCOME TO THE ZINGS MINI CONCERT!
NIYODO-KUUUN!
SQUEEEEE
SMIL
YOSHINO-KUN, LEAD A HAPPY LIFE

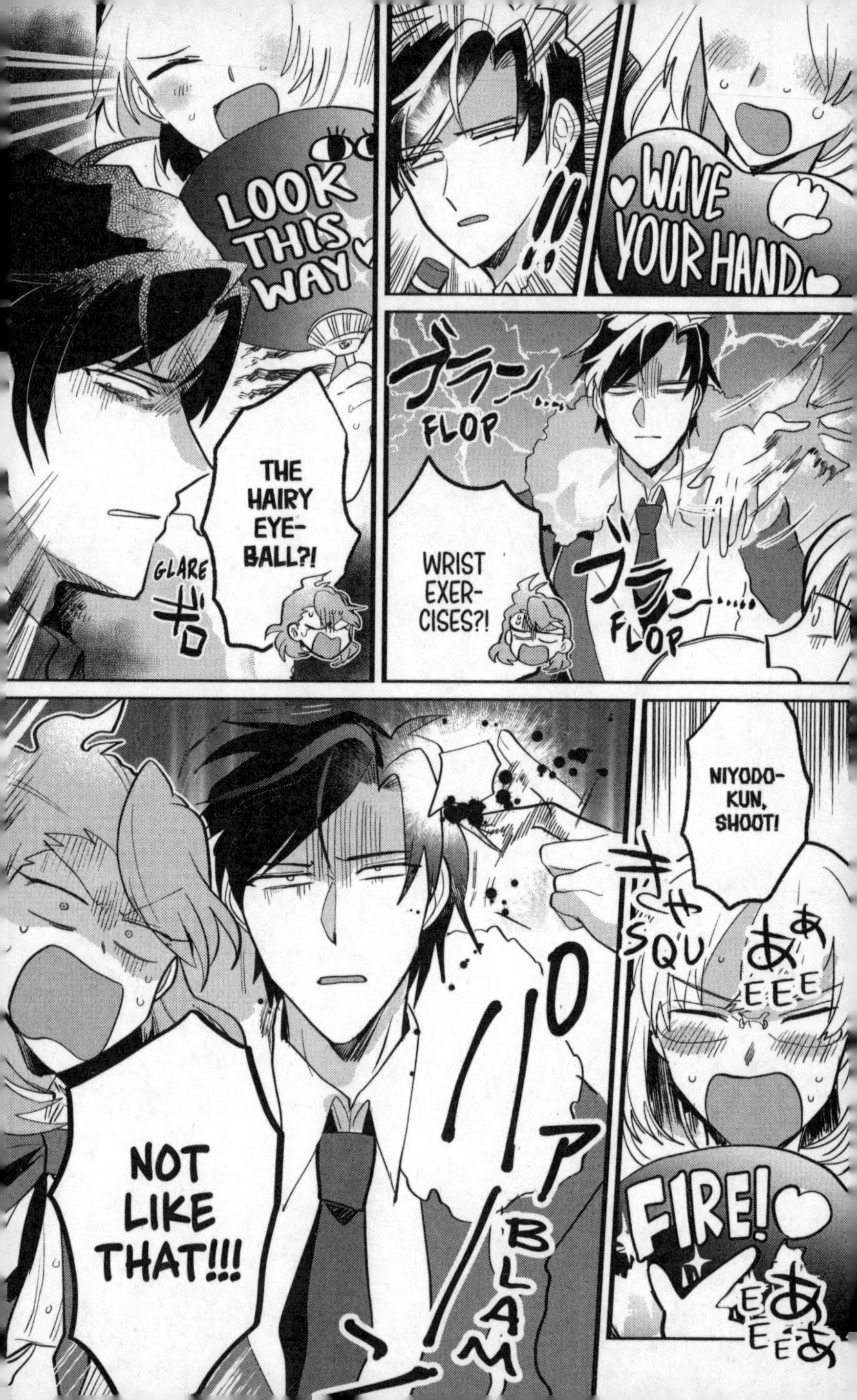
WAVE YOUR HAND
!!
ブラーン…
FLOP
WRIST EXER-CISES?!
ブラーン…
FLOP
LOOK THIS WAY
THE HAIRY EYE-BALL?!
ギロ
GLARE
NIYODO-KUN, SHOOT!
きゃ
SQU
ああ
EEE
FIRE!
ああ
EEEE
BLAM
NOT LIKE THAT!!!

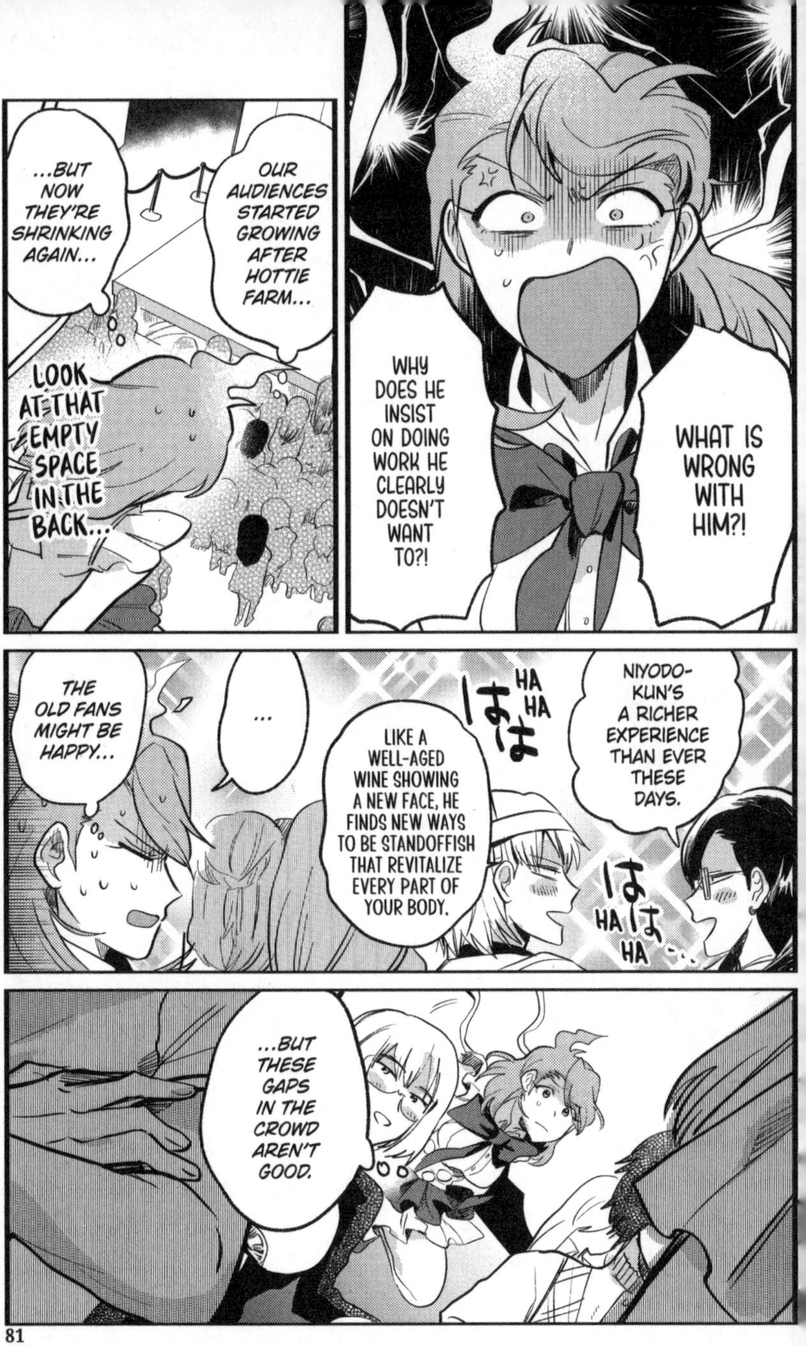
WHAT IS WRONG WITH HIM?!
WHY DOES HE INSIST ON DOING WORK HE CLEARLY DOESN'T WANT TO?!
OUR AUDIENCES STARTED GROWING AFTER HOTTIE FARM...
...BUT NOW THEY'RE SHRINKING AGAIN...
LOOK AT THAT EMPTY SPACE IN THE BACK...
NIYODO-KUN'S A RICHER EXPERIENCE THAN EVER THESE DAYS.
はは HA HA
LIKE A WELL-AGED WINE SHOWING A NEW FACE, HE FINDS NEW WAYS TO BE STANDOFFISH THAT REVITALIZE EVERY PART OF YOUR BODY.
はは HA HA
...
THE OLD FANS MIGHT BE HAPPY...
...BUT THESE GAPS IN THE CROWD AREN'T GOOD.

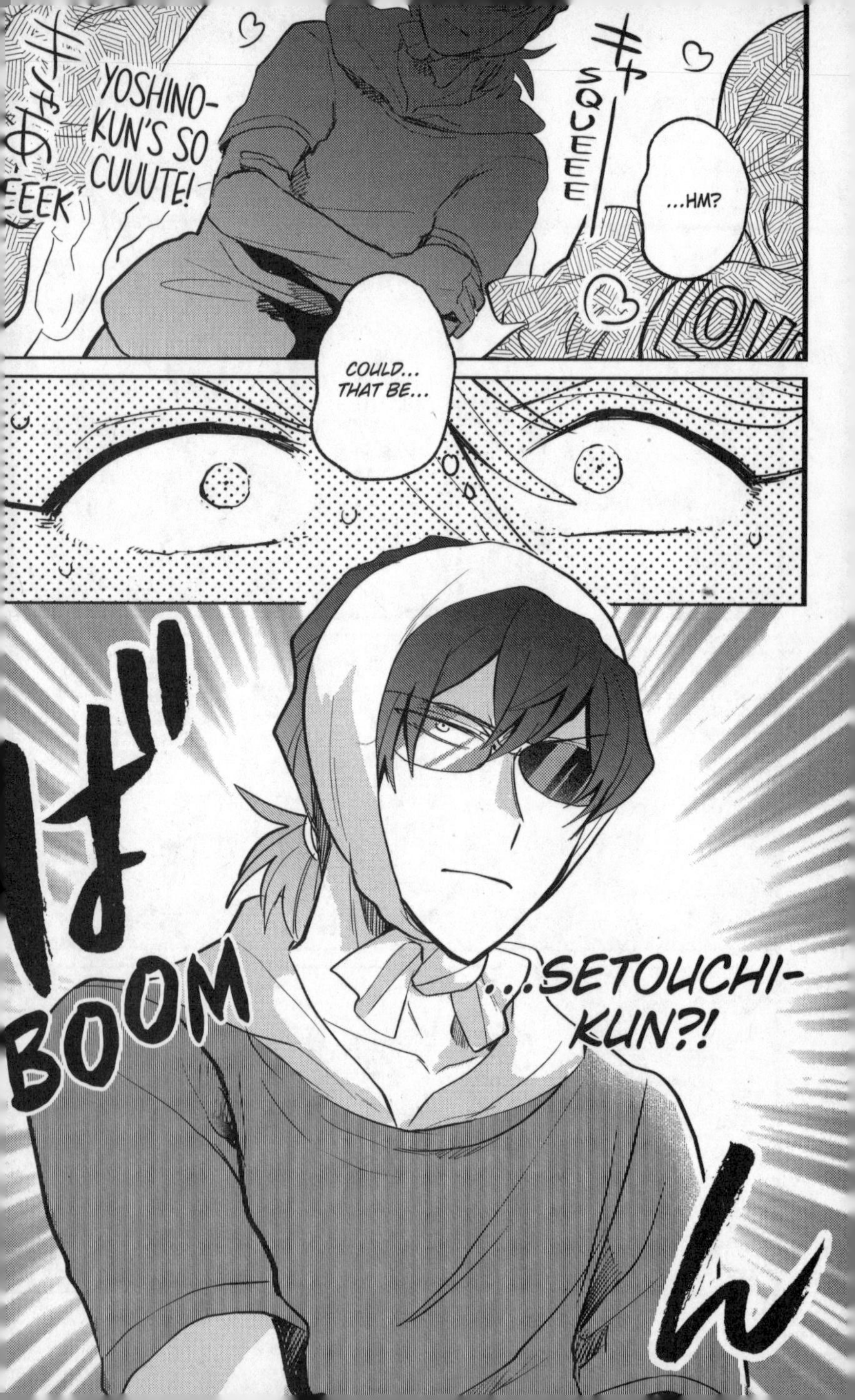
SQUEEEE
...HM?
YOSHINO-KUN'S SO CUUUTE!
EEEK
LOV
COULD... THAT BE...
...SETOUCHI-KUN?!
BOOM

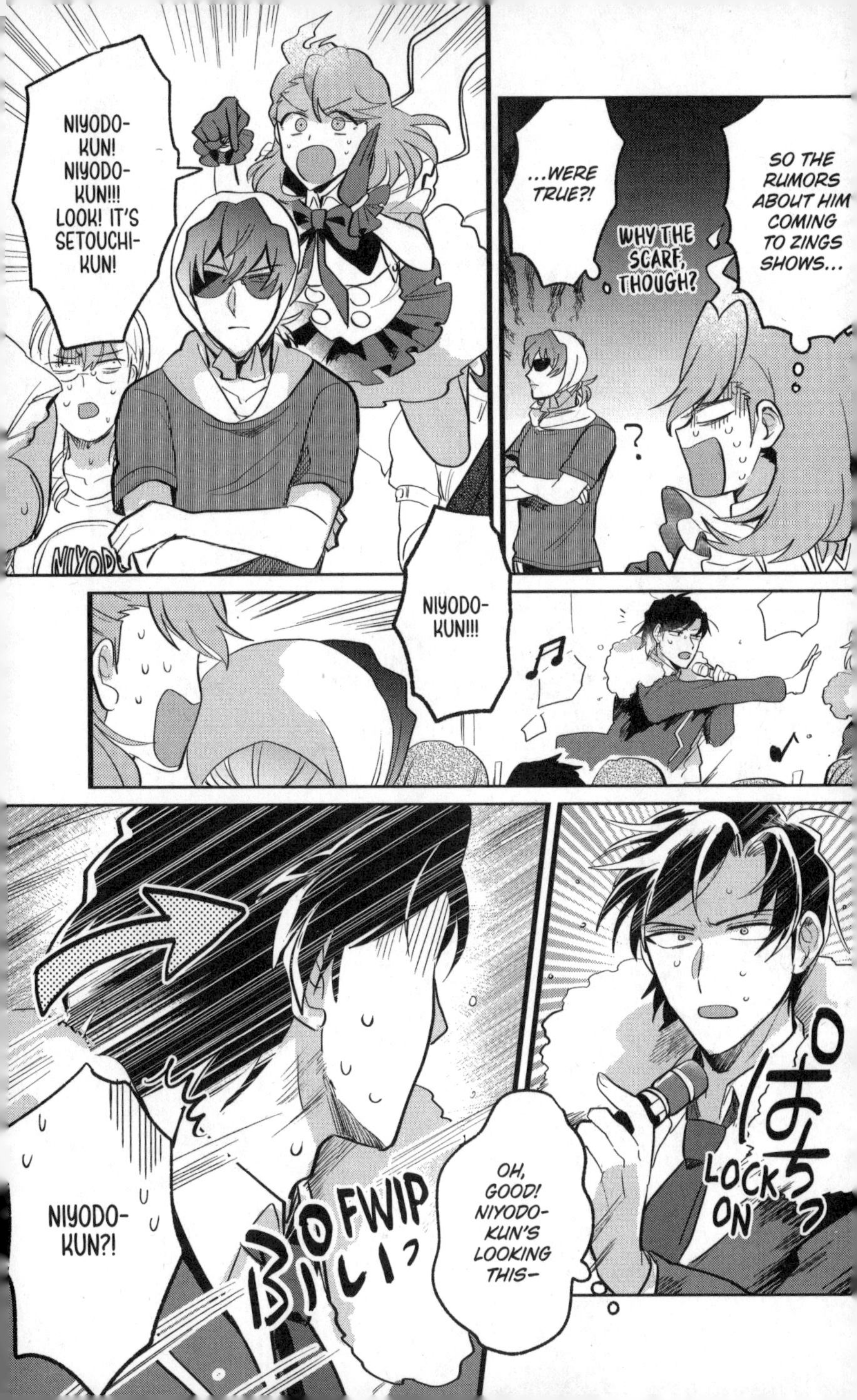
SO THE RUMORS ABOUT HIM COMING TO ZINGS SHOWS...
...WERE TRUE?!
WHY THE SCARF, THOUGH?
NIYODO-KUN! NIYODO-KUN!!! LOOK! IT'S SETOUCHI-KUN!
NIYODO-KUN!!!
ぱちっ
LOCK ON
OH, GOOD! NIYODO-KUN'S LOOKING THIS-
BOFWIP
ビリっ
NIYODO-KUN?!

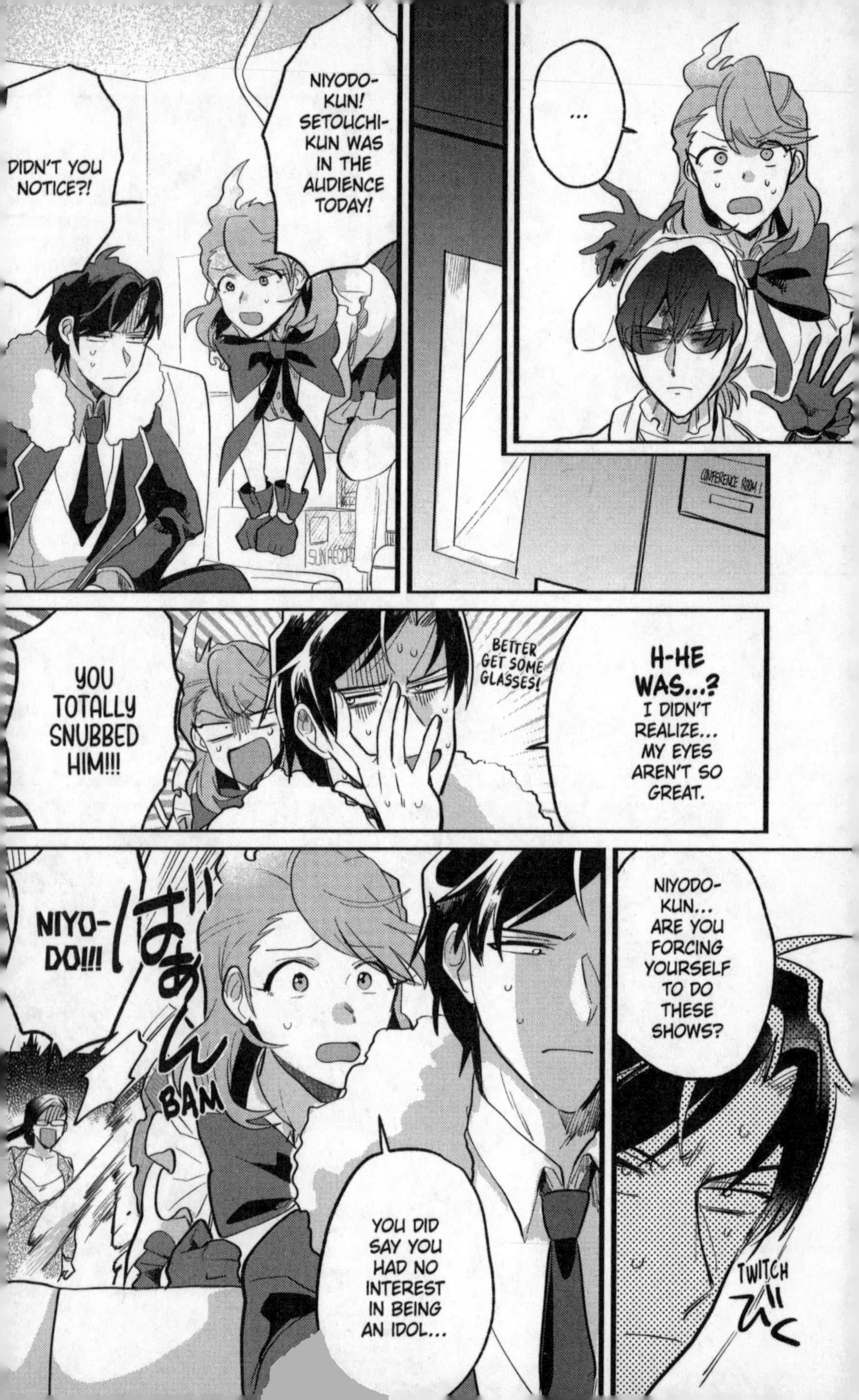
...
CONFERENCE ROOM 1
NIYODO-KUN! SETOUCHI-KUN WAS IN THE AUDIENCE TODAY!
DIDN'T YOU NOTICE?!
SUN RECORD
H-HE WAS...? I DIDN'T REALIZE... MY EYES AREN'T SO GREAT.
BETTER GET SOME GLASSES!
YOU TOTALLY SNUBBED HIM!!!
NIYODO-KUN... ARE YOU FORCING YOURSELF TO DO THESE SHOWS?
TWITCH
びく
NIYO-DO!!!
ばあん
BAM
YOU DID SAY YOU HAD NO INTEREST IN BEING AN IDOL...

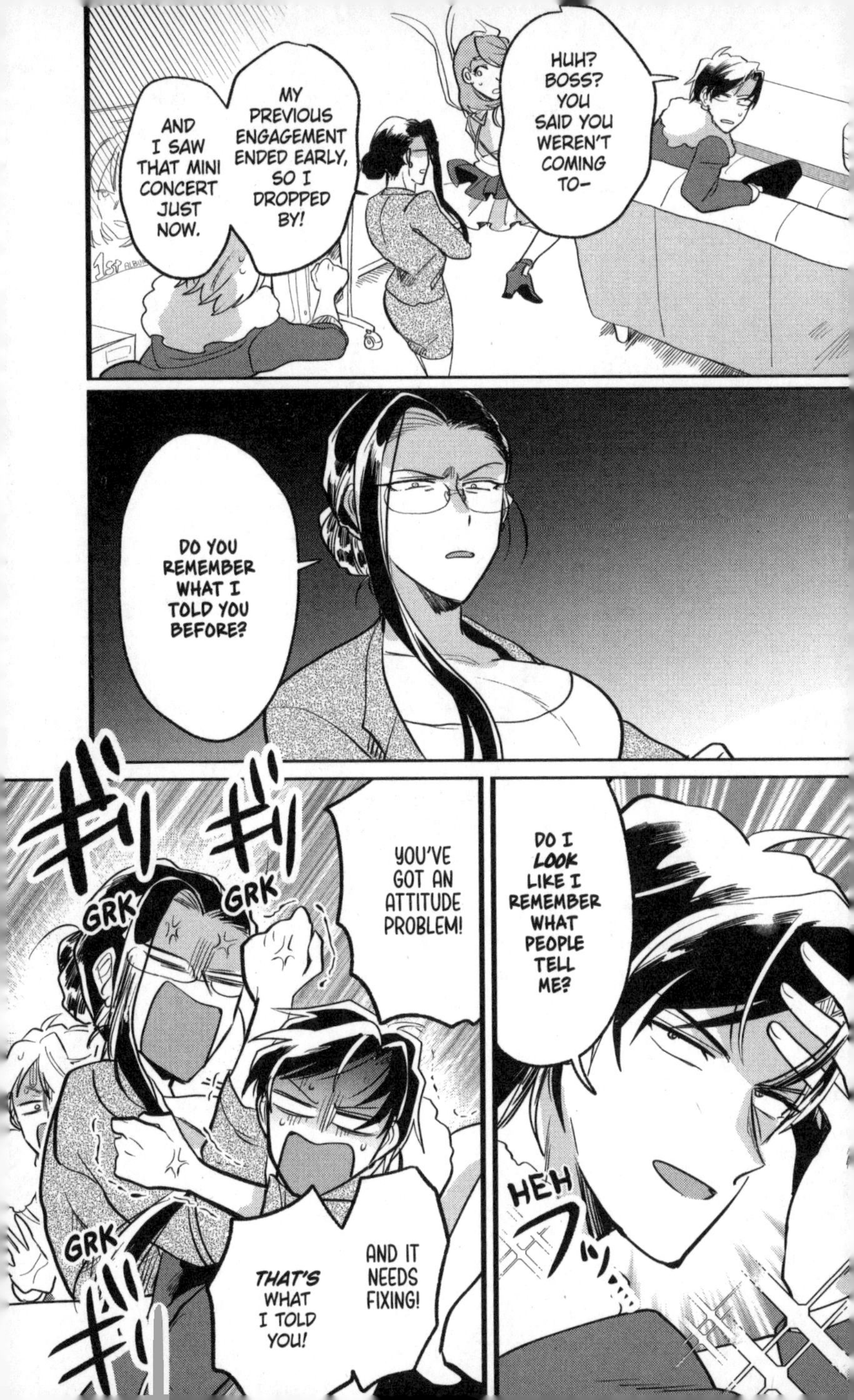
HUH? BOSS? YOU SAID YOU WEREN'T COMING TO–
MY PREVIOUS ENGAGEMENT ENDED EARLY, SO I DROPPED BY!
AND I SAW THAT MINI CONCERT JUST NOW.
DO YOU REMEMBER WHAT I TOLD YOU BEFORE?
DO I *LOOK* LIKE I REMEMBER WHAT PEOPLE TELL ME?
HEH
フッ
YOU'VE GOT AN ATTITUDE PROBLEM!
ギリ
GRK
ギリ
GRK
GRK
ギリ
AND IT NEEDS FIXING!
THAT'S WHAT I TOLD YOU!

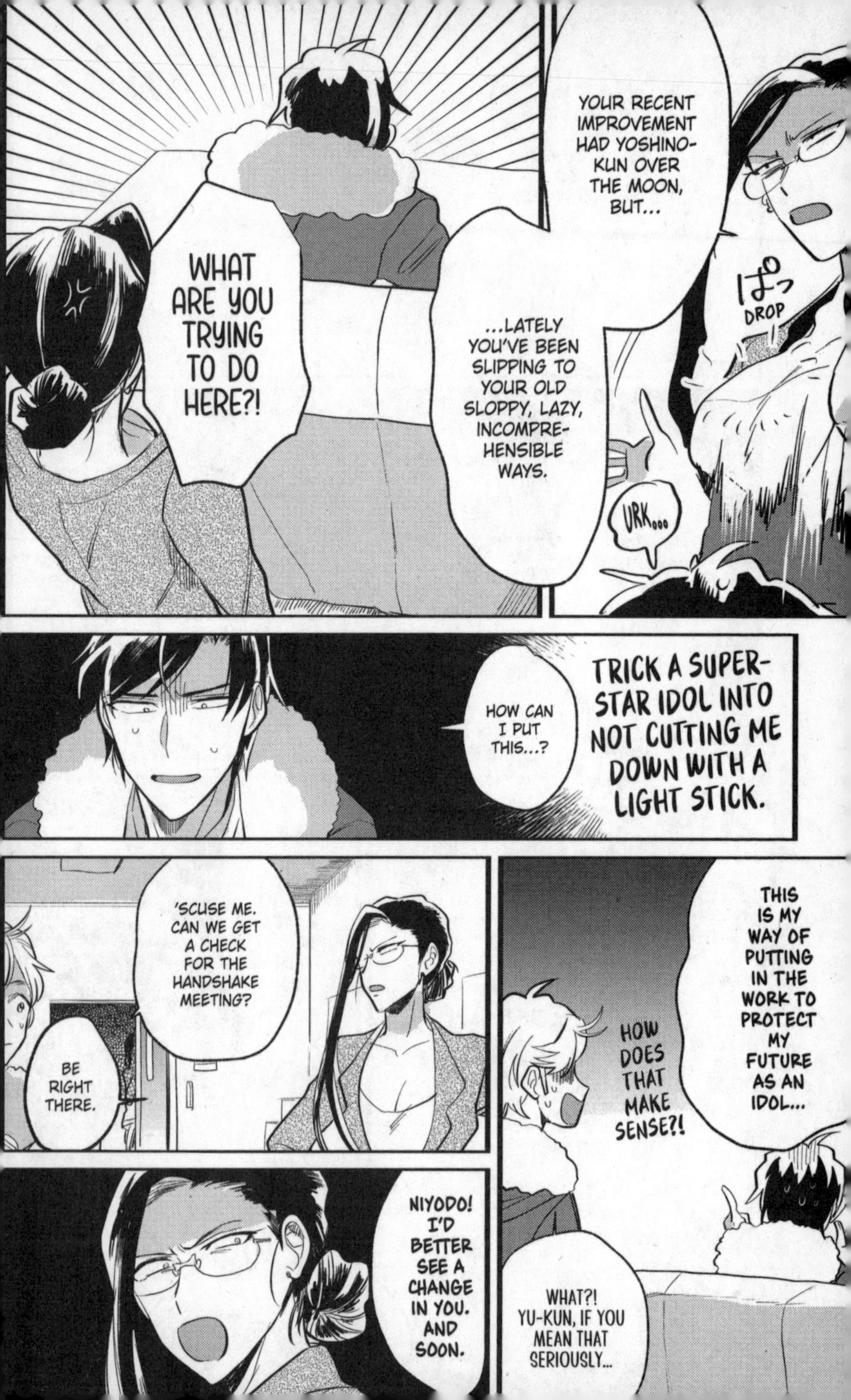
YOUR RECENT IMPROVEMENT HAD YOSHINO-KUN OVER THE MOON, BUT...
ぱっ
DROP
...LATELY YOU'VE BEEN SLIPPING TO YOUR OLD SLOPPY, LAZY, INCOMPRE-HENSIBLE WAYS.
URK...
WHAT ARE YOU TRYING TO DO HERE?!
TRICK A SUPER-STAR IDOL INTO NOT CUTTING ME DOWN WITH A LIGHT STICK.
HOW CAN I PUT THIS...?
THIS IS MY WAY OF PUTTING IN THE WORK TO PROTECT MY FUTURE AS AN IDOL...
HOW DOES THAT MAKE SENSE?!
WHAT?! YU-KUN, IF YOU MEAN THAT SERIOUSLY...
'SCUSE ME. CAN WE GET A CHECK FOR THE HANDSHAKE MEETING?
BE RIGHT THERE.
NIYODO! I'D BETTER SEE A CHANGE IN YOU. AND SOON.

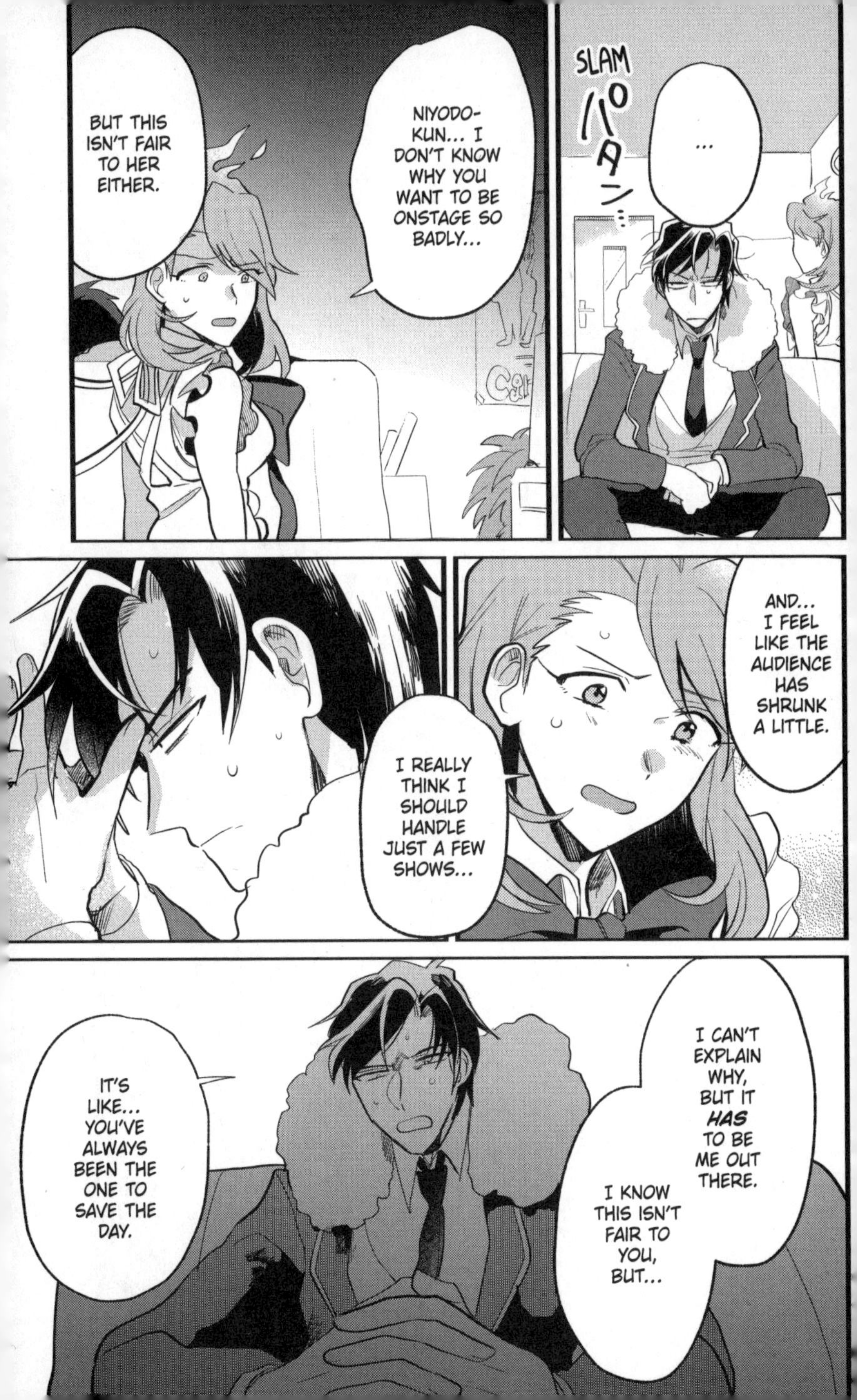
SLAM
パタン
...
NIYODO-KUN... I DON'T KNOW WHY YOU WANT TO BE ONSTAGE SO BADLY...
BUT THIS ISN'T FAIR TO HER EITHER.
AND... I FEEL LIKE THE AUDIENCE HAS SHRUNK A LITTLE.
I REALLY THINK I SHOULD HANDLE JUST A FEW SHOWS...
I CAN'T EXPLAIN WHY, BUT IT ***HAS*** TO BE ME OUT THERE.
I KNOW THIS ISN'T FAIR TO YOU, BUT...
IT'S LIKE... YOU'VE ALWAYS BEEN THE ONE TO SAVE THE DAY.

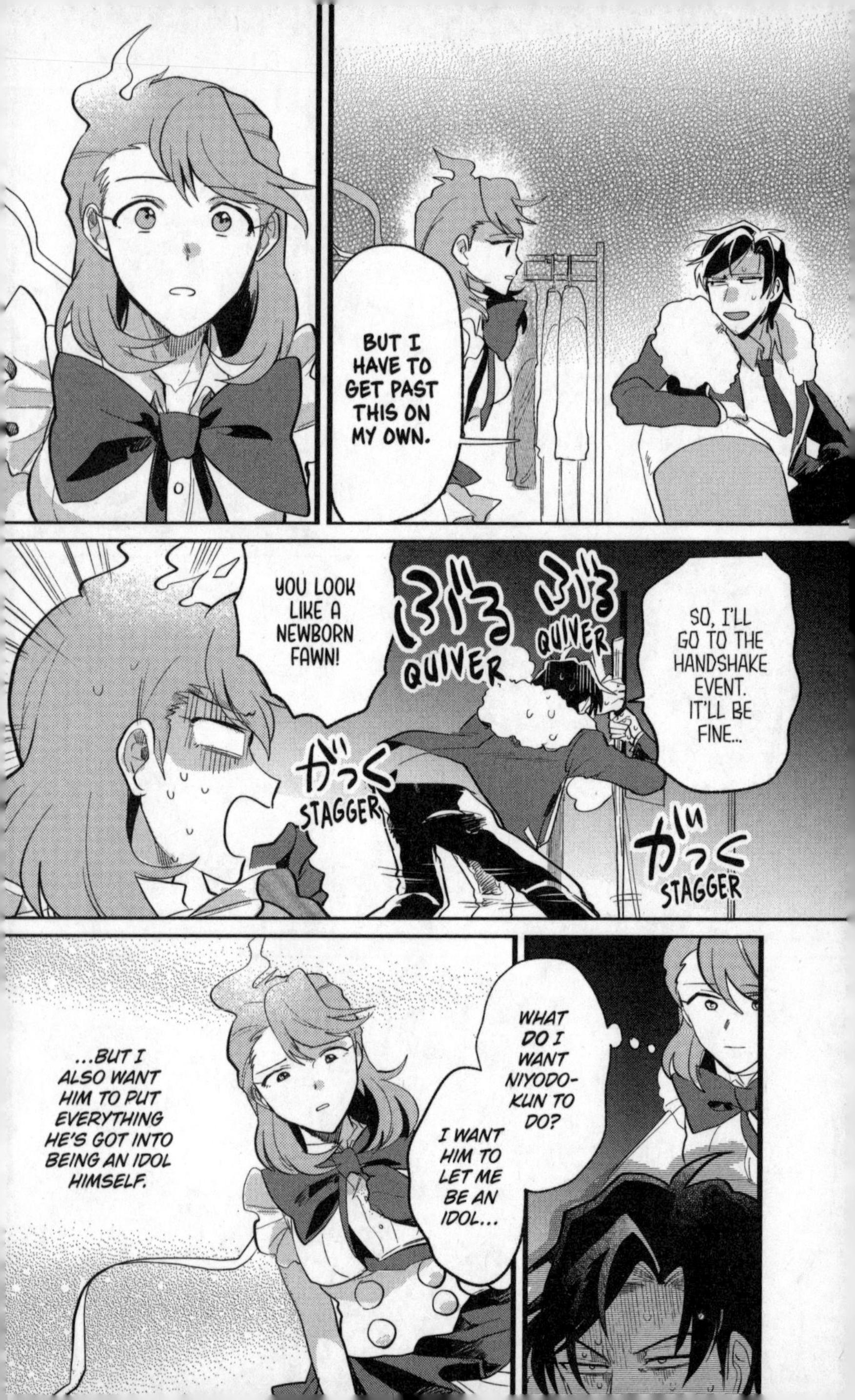
BUT I HAVE TO GET PAST THIS ON MY OWN.
SO, I'LL GO TO THE HANDSHAKE EVENT. IT'LL BE FINE...
QUIVER
QUIVER
STAGGER
STAGGER
YOU LOOK LIKE A NEWBORN FAWN!
WHAT DO I WANT NIYODO-KUN TO DO?
I WANT HIM TO LET ME BE AN IDOL...
...BUT I ALSO WANT HIM TO PUT EVERYTHING HE'S GOT INTO BEING AN IDOL HIMSELF.

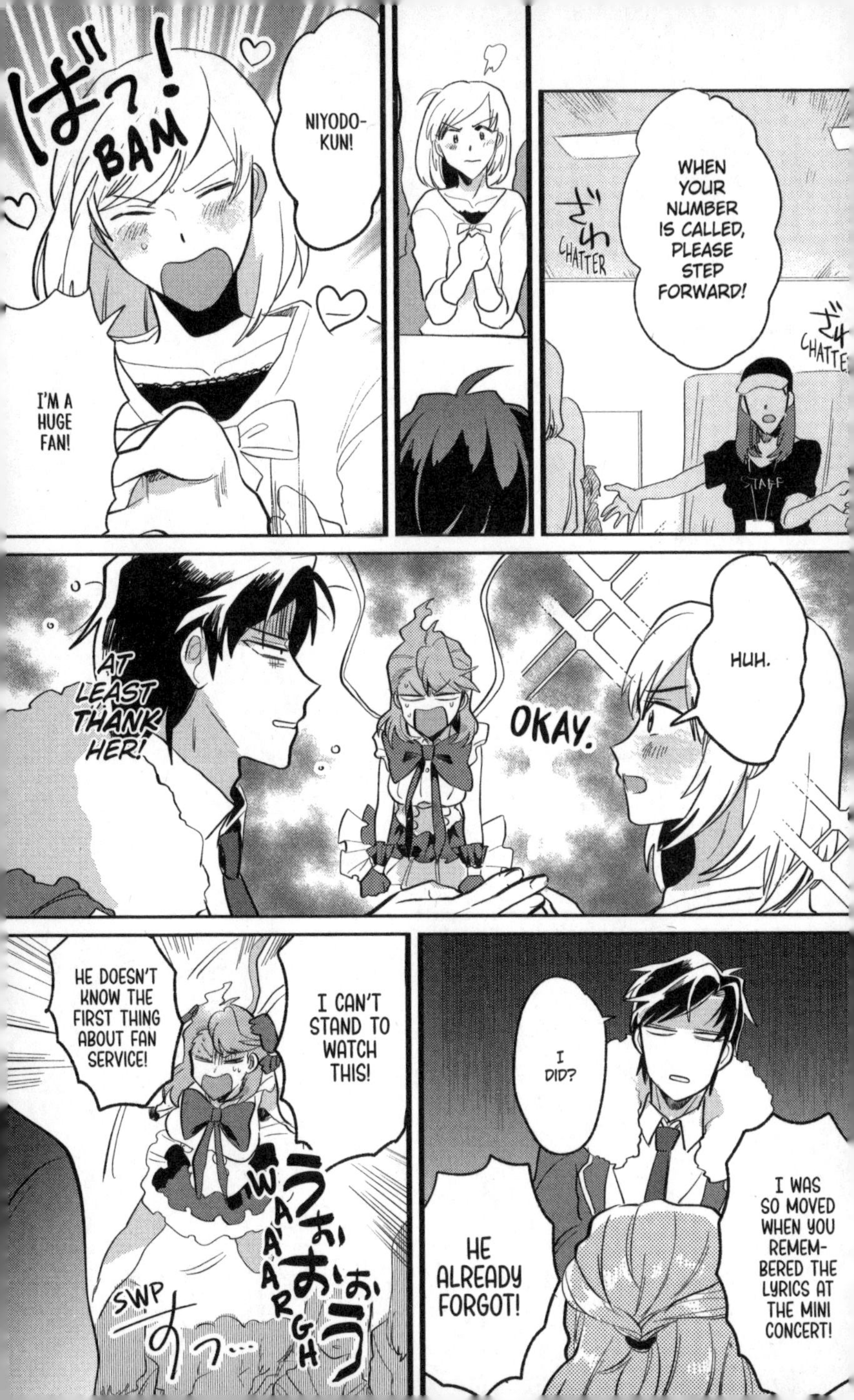
WHEN YOUR NUMBER IS CALLED, PLEASE STEP FORWARD!
ざわ
CHATTER
ざわ
CHATTER
ばっ!
BAM
NIYODO-KUN!
I'M A HUGE FAN!
HUH.
OKAY.
AT LEAST THANK HER!
I WAS SO MOVED WHEN YOU REMEMBERED THE LYRICS AT THE MINI CONCERT!
I DID?
HE ALREADY FORGOT!
I CAN'T STAND TO WATCH THIS!
HE DOESN'T KNOW THE FIRST THING ABOUT FAN SERVICE!
うおおおう
WAAARGH
すっ…
SWP

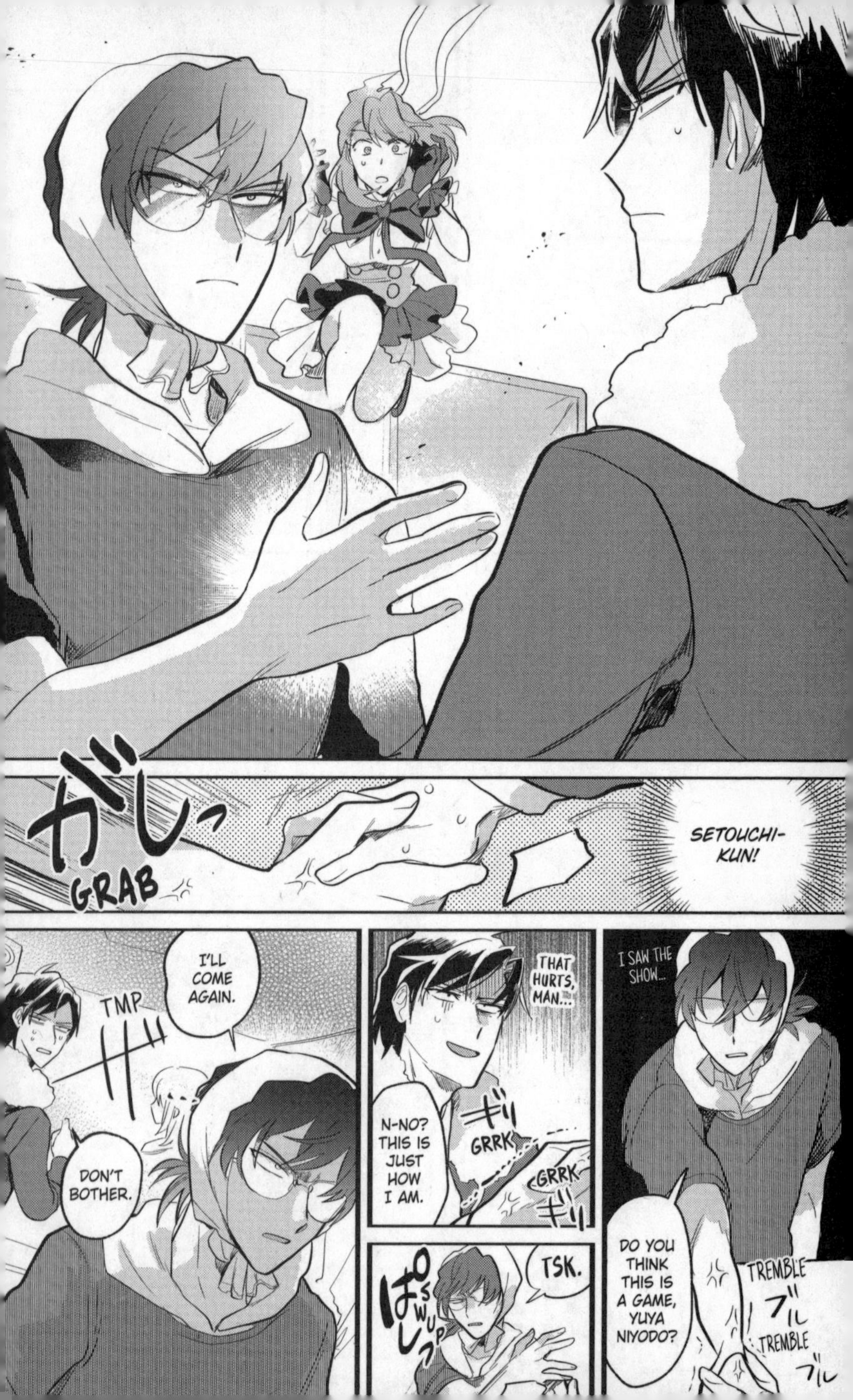
SETOUCHI-KUN!
がしっ
GRAB
I SAW THE SHOW...
DO YOU THINK THIS IS A GAME, YUYA NIYODO?
TREMBLE
ブル
TREMBLE
ブル
THAT HURTS, MAN...
N-NO? THIS IS JUST HOW I AM.
ギリ
GRRK
GRRK
ギリ
TSK.
ぱしっ
SWUP
I'LL COME AGAIN.
TMP
DON'T BOTHER.

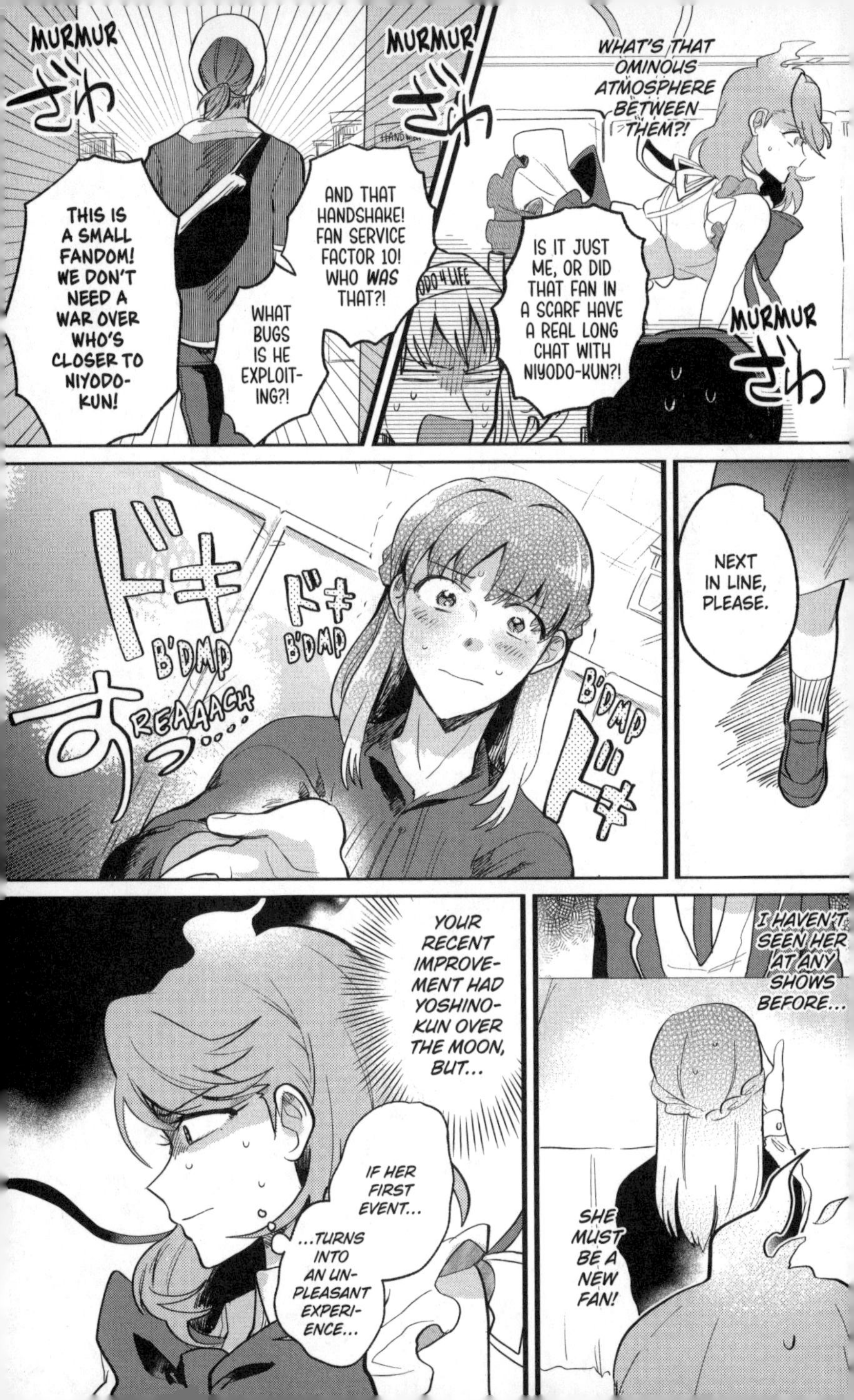
WHAT'S THAT OMINOUS ATMOSPHERE BETWEEN THEM?!
IS IT JUST ME, OR DID THAT FAN IN A SCARF HAVE A REAL LONG CHAT WITH NIYODO-KUN?!
MURMUR
ざわ
MURMUR
ざわ
AND THAT HANDSHAKE! FAN SERVICE FACTOR 10! WHO WAS THAT?!
WHAT BUGS IS HE EXPLOIT-ING?!
MURMUR
ざわ
THIS IS A SMALL FANDOM! WE DON'T NEED A WAR OVER WHO'S CLOSER TO NIYODO-KUN!
NEXT IN LINE, PLEASE.
ドキ
B'DMP
ドキ
B'DMP
ドキ
B'DMP
すっ…
REAAACH
I HAVEN'T SEEN HER AT ANY SHOWS BEFORE…
SHE MUST BE A NEW FAN!
YOUR RECENT IMPROVE-MENT HAD YOSHINO-KUN OVER THE MOON, BUT…
IF HER FIRST EVENT…
…TURNS INTO AN UN-PLEASANT EXPERI-ENCE…

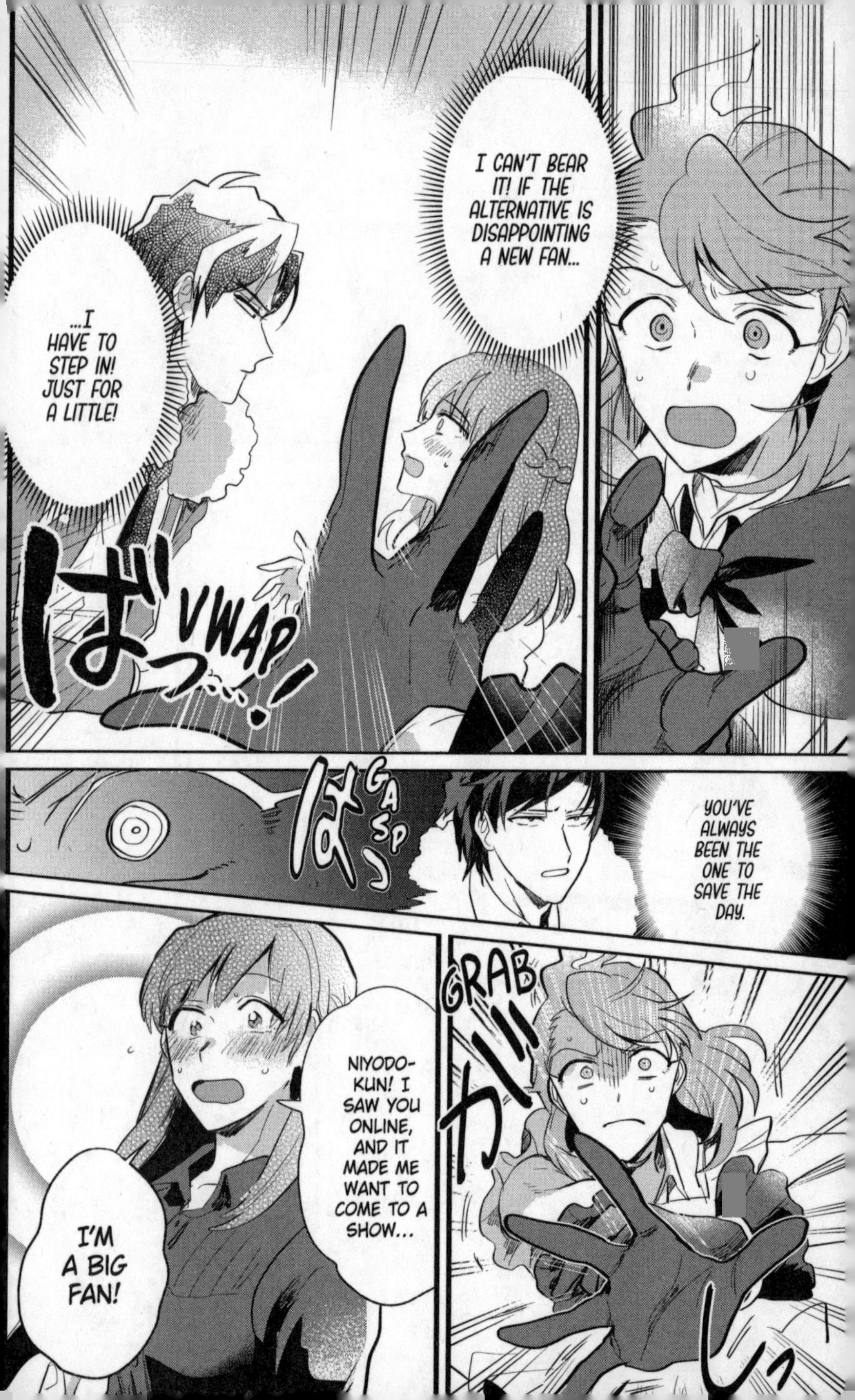
I CAN'T BEAR IT! IF THE ALTERNATIVE IS DISAPPOINTING A NEW FAN...
...I HAVE TO STEP IN! JUST FOR A LITTLE!
ばっ
VWAP!
YOU'VE ALWAYS BEEN THE ONE TO SAVE THE DAY.
はっ
GASP
GRAB
ガッ
NIYODO-KUN! I SAW YOU ONLINE, AND IT MADE ME WANT TO COME TO A SHOW...
I'M A BIG FAN!

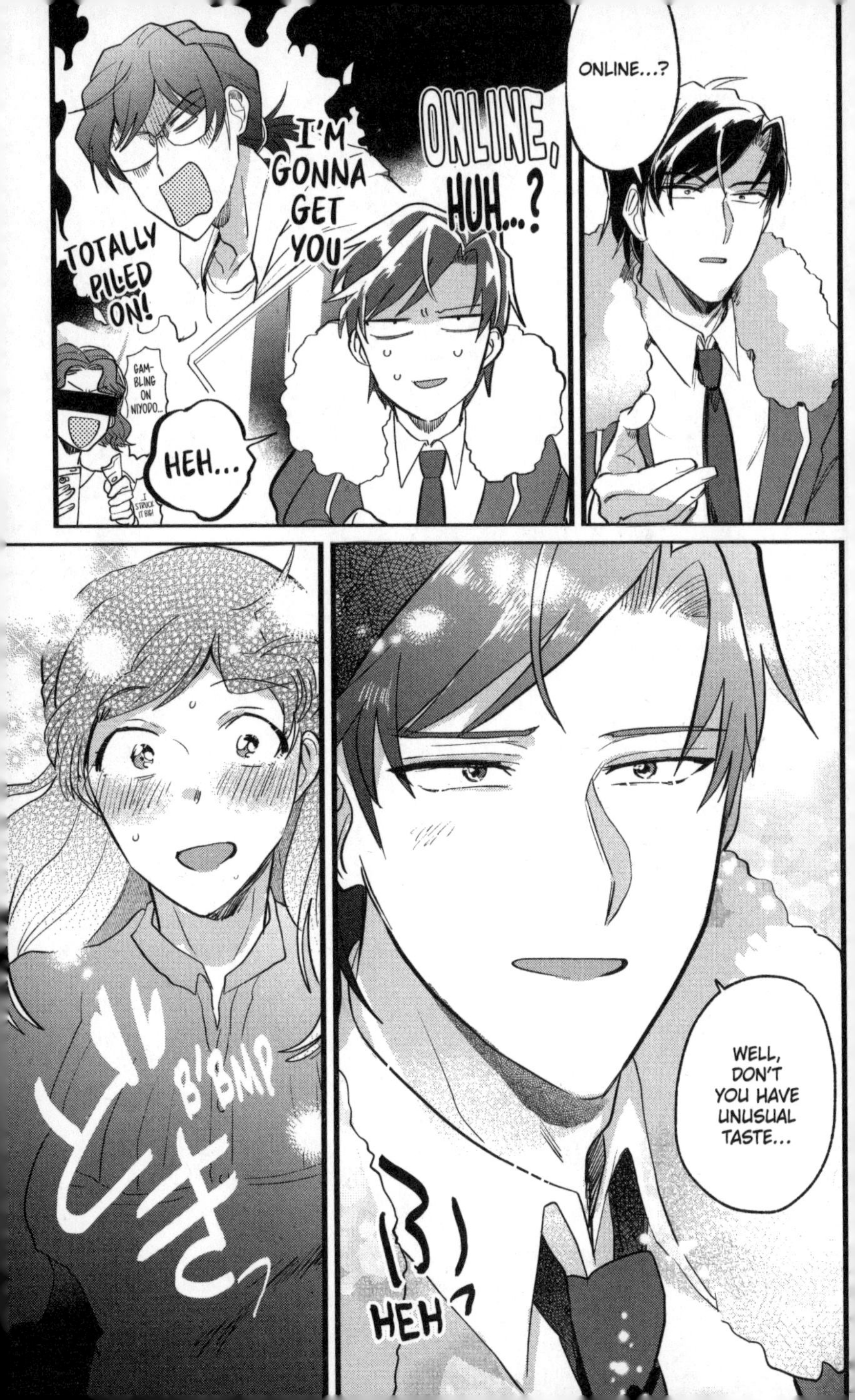

ONLINE...?
ONLINE, HUH...?
I'M GONNA GET YOU
TOTALLY PILED ON!
GAMBLING ON NIYODO...
HEH...
I STRUCK IT BIG!
WELL, DON'T YOU HAVE UNUSUAL TASTE...
HEH
B'BMP

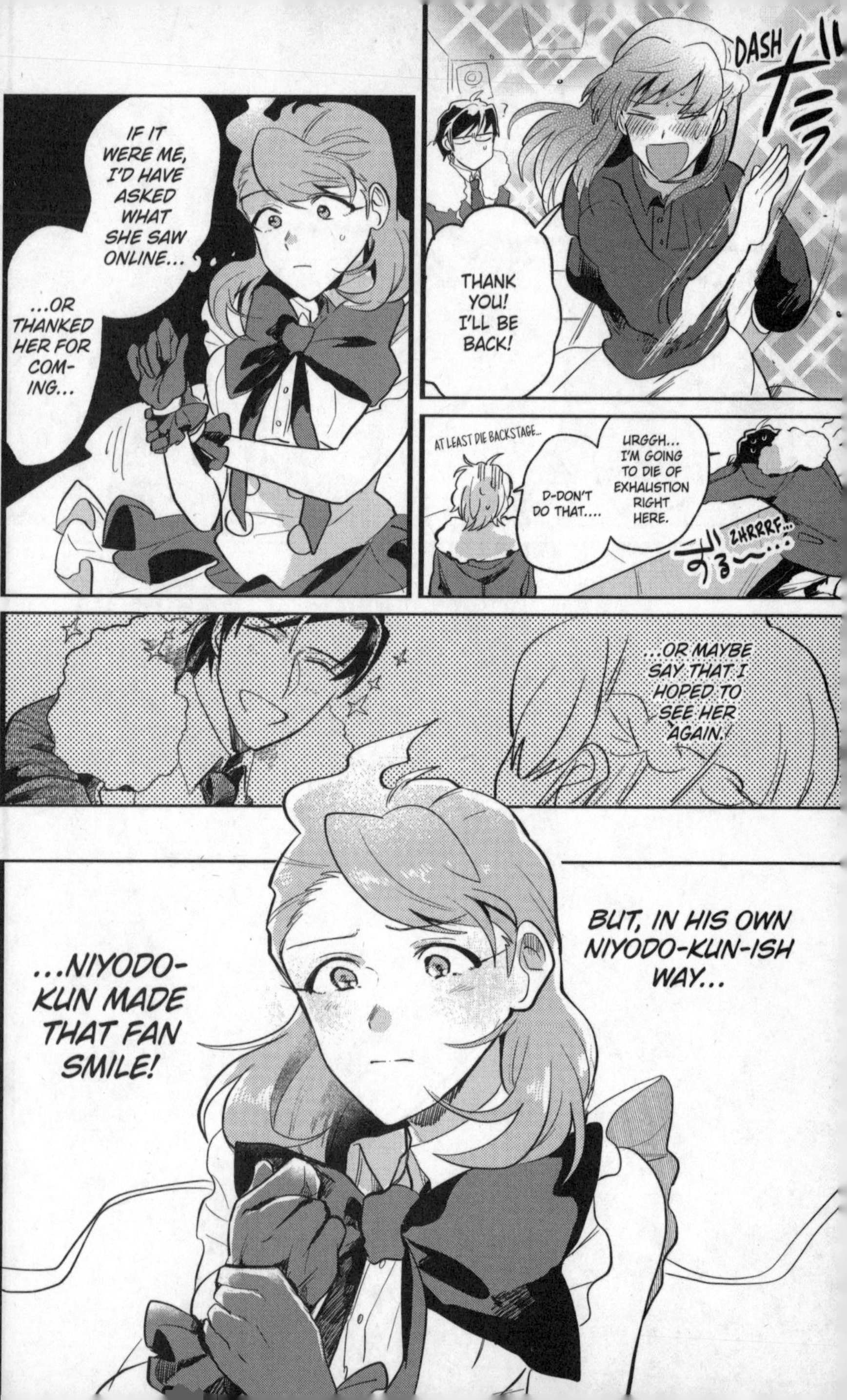
DASH
THANK YOU! I'LL BE BACK!
URGGH... I'M GOING TO DIE OF EXHAUSTION RIGHT HERE.
D-DON'T DO THAT....
AT LEAST DIE BACKSTAGE...
ZHRRRF...
IF IT WERE ME, I'D HAVE ASKED WHAT SHE SAW ONLINE...
...OR THANKED HER FOR COMING...
...OR MAYBE SAY THAT I HOPED TO SEE HER AGAIN.
BUT, IN HIS OWN NIYODO-KUN-ISH WAY...
...NIYODO-KUN MADE THAT FAN SMILE!

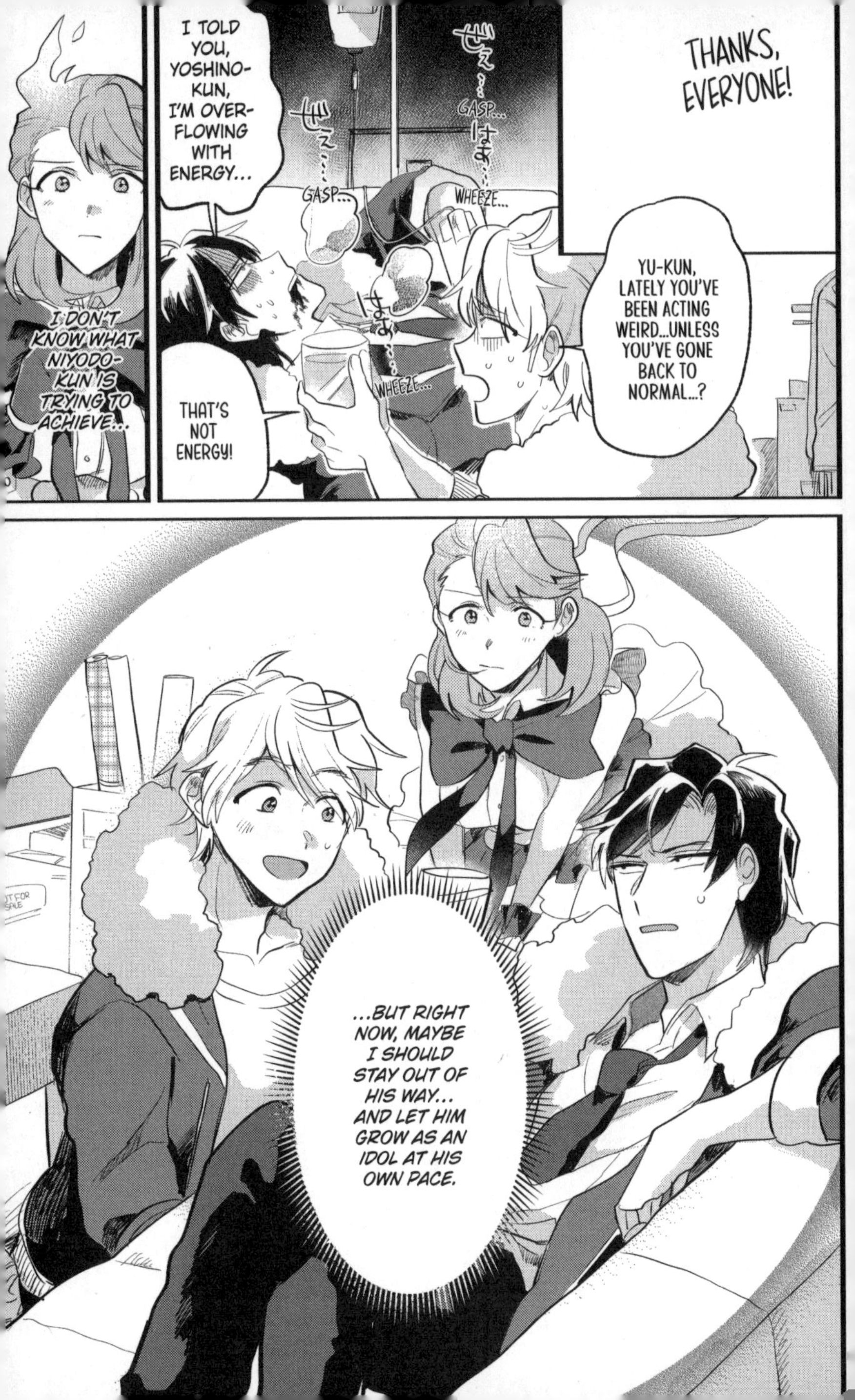
THANKS, EVERYONE!
YU-KUN, LATELY YOU'VE BEEN ACTING WEIRD...UNLESS YOU'VE GONE BACK TO NORMAL...?
ぜぇ… GASP… はぁ… WHEEZE…
ぜぇ… GASP… はぁ… WHEEZE…
I TOLD YOU, YOSHINO-KUN, I'M OVER-FLOWING WITH ENERGY...
THAT'S NOT ENERGY!
I DON'T KNOW WHAT NIYODO-KUN IS TRYING TO ACHIEVE...
...BUT RIGHT NOW, MAYBE I SHOULD STAY OUT OF HIS WAY... AND LET HIM GROW AS AN IDOL AT HIS OWN PACE.

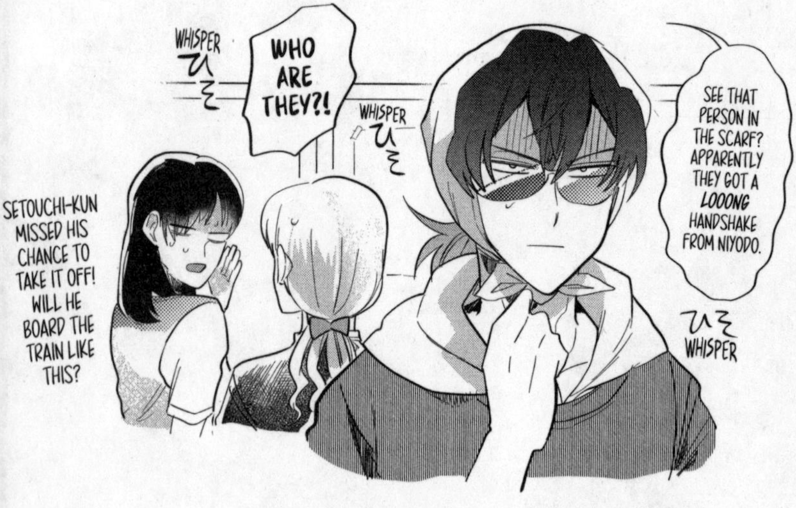
SEE THAT PERSON IN THE SCARF? APPARENTLY THEY GOT A LOOONG HANDSHAKE FROM NIYODO.
ひそ WHISPER
WHISPER ひそ
WHO ARE THEY?!
WHISPER ひそ
SETOUCHI-KUN MISSED HIS CHANCE TO TAKE IT OFF! WILL HE BOARD THE TRAIN LIKE THIS?

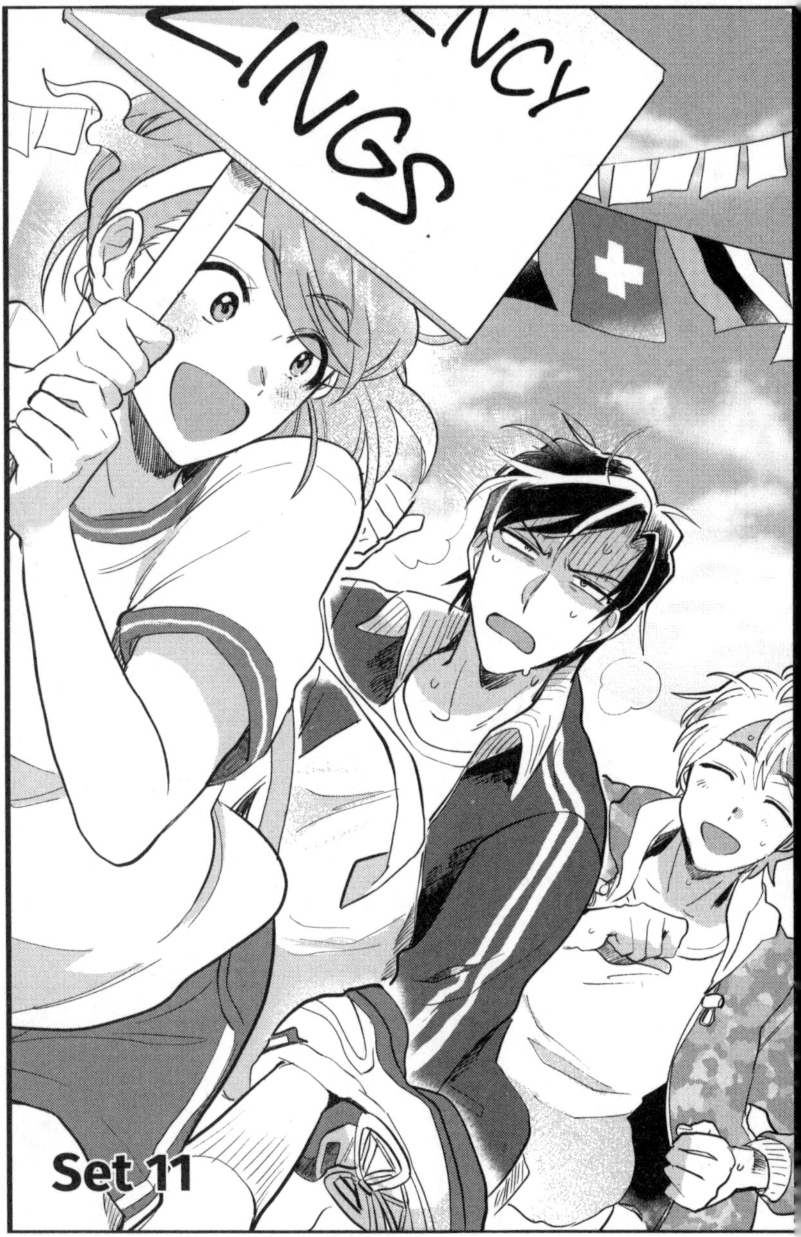

...NCY
...INGS

Set 11

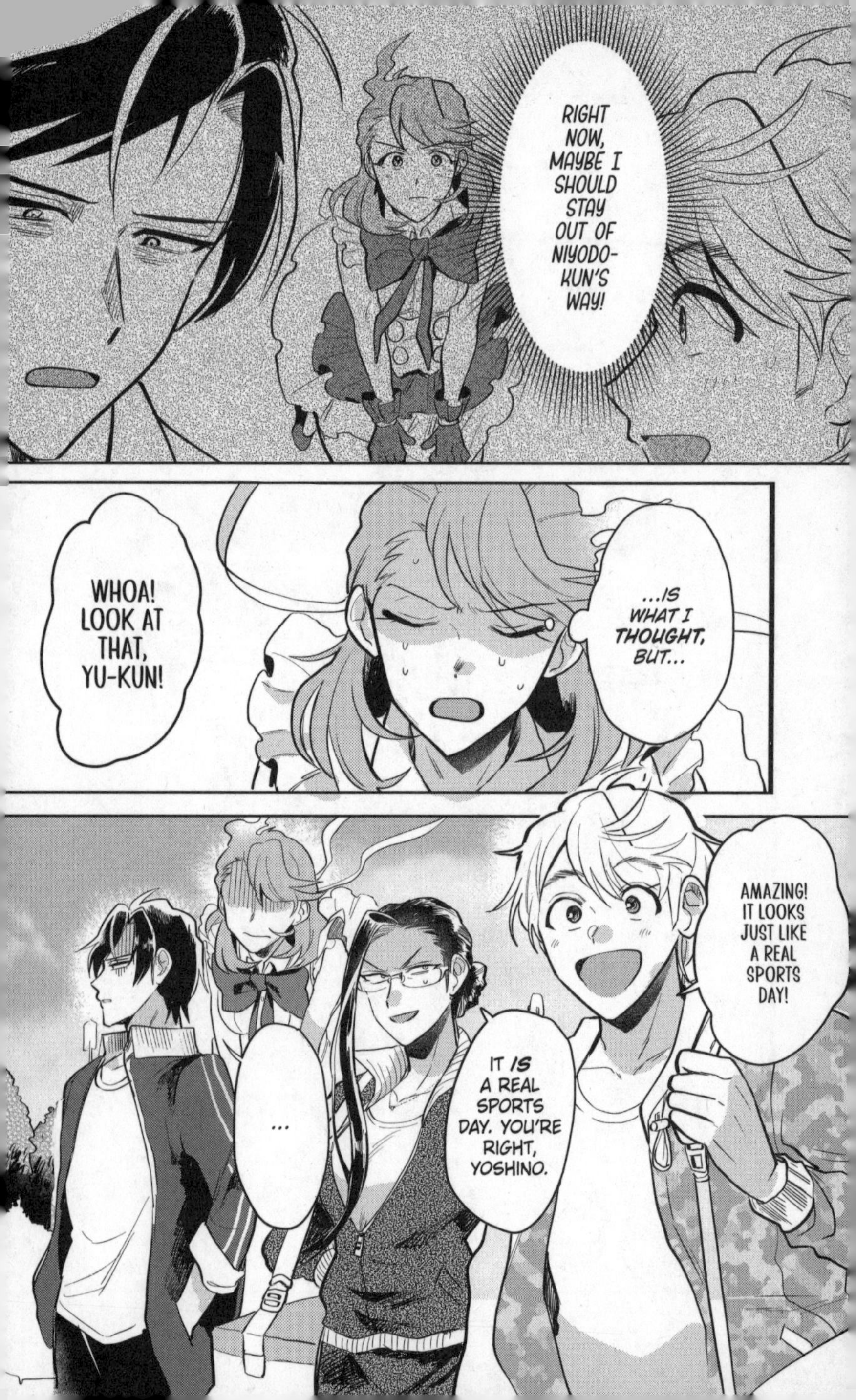
RIGHT NOW, MAYBE I SHOULD STAY OUT OF NIYODO-KUN'S WAY!
...IS WHAT I *THOUGHT*, BUT...
WHOA! LOOK AT THAT, YU-KUN!
AMAZING! IT LOOKS JUST LIKE A REAL SPORTS DAY!
IT *IS* A REAL SPORTS DAY. YOU'RE RIGHT, YOSHINO.
...

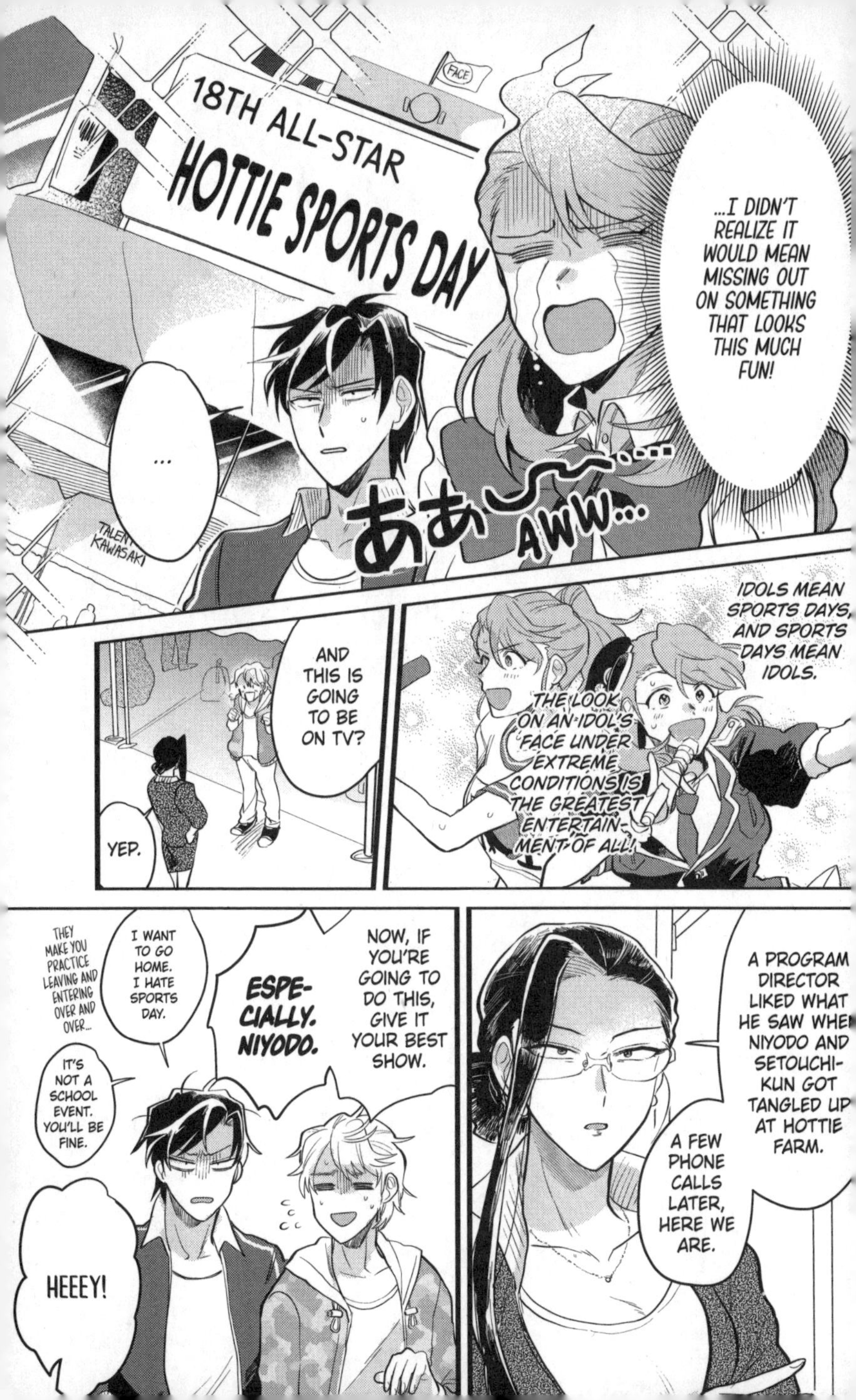
...I DIDN'T REALIZE IT WOULD MEAN MISSING OUT ON SOMETHING THAT LOOKS THIS MUCH FUN!
FACE
18TH ALL-STAR HOTTIE SPORTS DAY
ああ～…
AWW...
...
TALENT KAWASAKI
IDOLS MEAN SPORTS DAYS, AND SPORTS DAYS MEAN IDOLS.
THE LOOK ON AN IDOL'S FACE UNDER EXTREME CONDITIONS IS THE GREATEST ENTERTAIN-MENT OF ALL!
AND THIS IS GOING TO BE ON TV?
YEP.
A PROGRAM DIRECTOR LIKED WHAT HE SAW WHE NIYODO AND SETOUCHI-KUN GOT TANGLED UP AT HOTTIE FARM.
A FEW PHONE CALLS LATER, HERE WE ARE.
NOW, IF YOU'RE GOING TO DO THIS, GIVE IT YOUR BEST SHOW.
ESPE-CIALLY. NIYODO.
I WANT TO GO HOME. I HATE SPORTS DAY.
THEY MAKE YOU PRACTICE LEAVING AND ENTERING OVER AND OVER...
IT'S NOT A SCHOOL EVENT. YOU'LL BE FINE.
HEEEY!

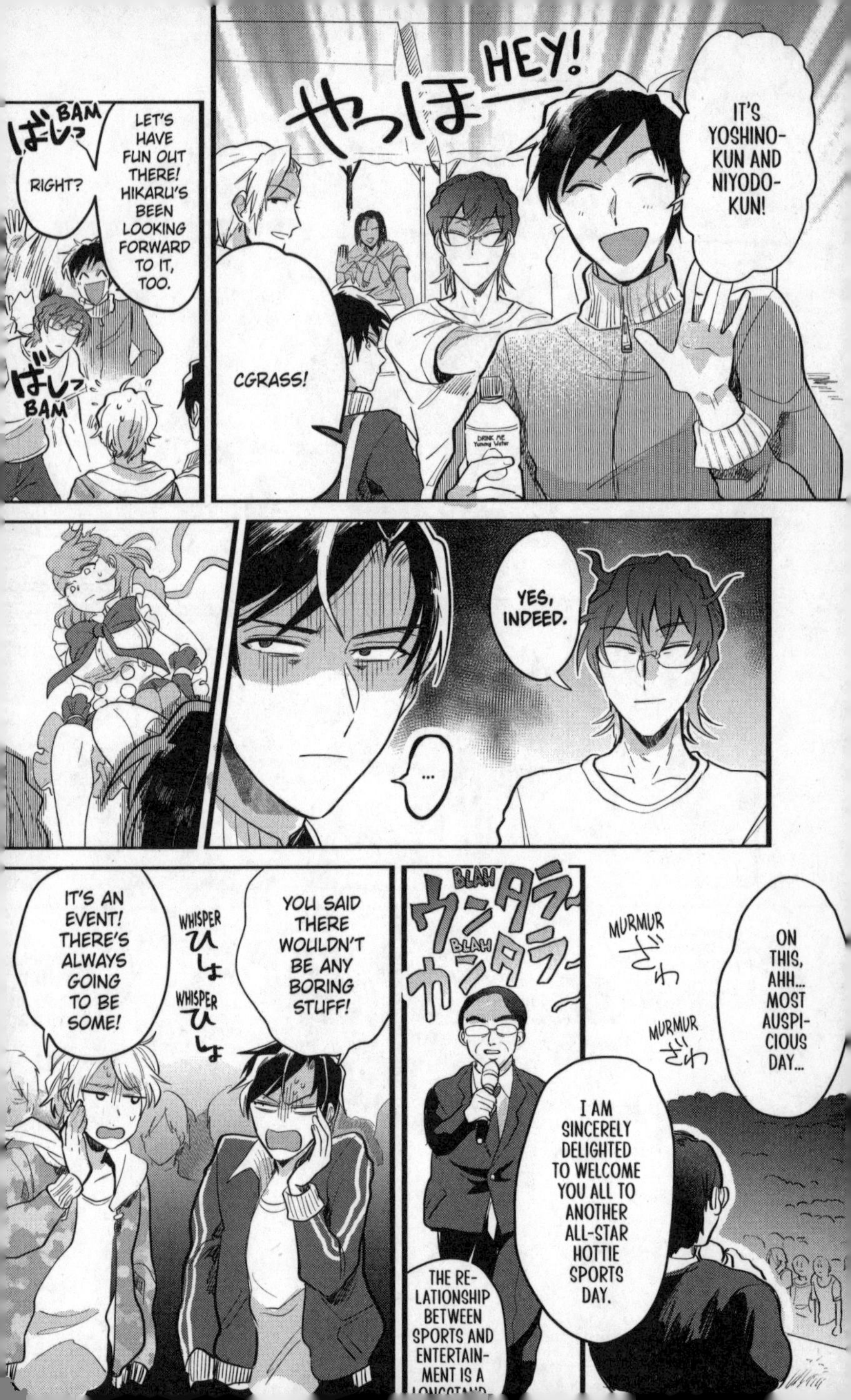
やっほー HEY!
IT'S YOSHINO-KUN AND NIYODO-KUN!
CGRASS!
LET'S HAVE FUN OUT THERE! HIKARU'S BEEN LOOKING FORWARD TO IT, TOO.
RIGHT?
ばしっ BAM
ばしっ BAM
YES, INDEED.
...
ON THIS, AHH... MOST AUSPICIOUS DAY...
ざわ MURMUR
ざわ MURMUR
ウンタラ BLAH
ウンタラ BLAH
I AM SINCERELY DELIGHTED TO WELCOME YOU ALL TO ANOTHER ALL-STAR HOTTIE SPORTS DAY.
THE RELATIONSHIP BETWEEN SPORTS AND ENTERTAINMENT IS A
YOU SAID THERE WOULDN'T BE ANY BORING STUFF!
ひしょ WHISPER
ひしょ WHISPER
IT'S AN EVENT! THERE'S ALWAYS GOING TO BE SOME!

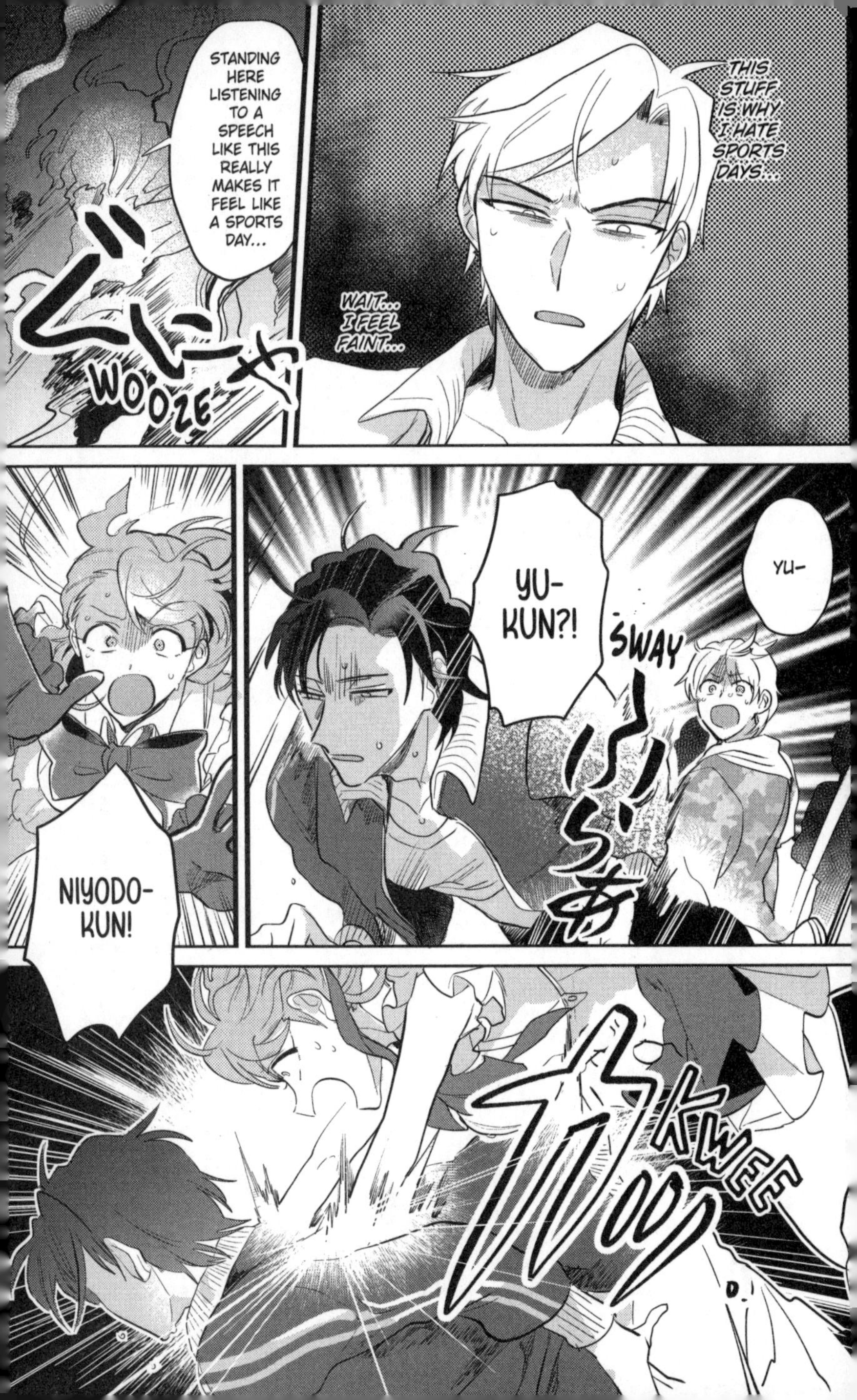

THIS STUFF IS WHY I HATE SPORTS DAYS...
WAIT... I FEEL FAINT...
STANDING HERE LISTENING TO A SPEECH LIKE THIS REALLY MAKES IT FEEL LIKE A SPORTS DAY...
WOOZE
YU-
YU-KUN?!
SWAY
NIYODO-KUN!
KWEE

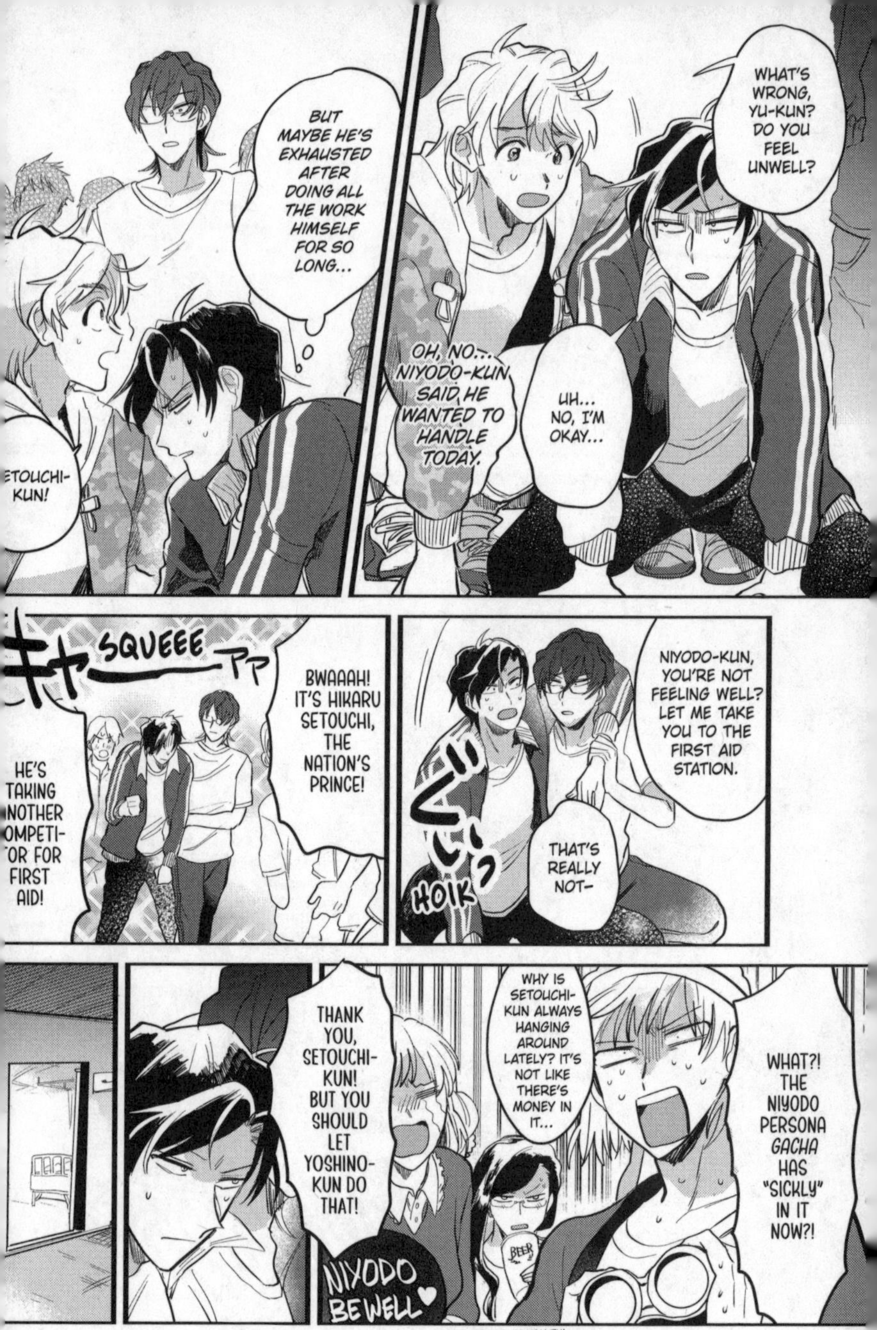
WHAT'S WRONG, YU-KUN? DO YOU FEEL UNWELL?
UH... NO, I'M OKAY...
OH, NO... NIYODO-KUN SAID HE WANTED TO HANDLE TODAY.
BUT MAYBE HE'S EXHAUSTED AFTER DOING ALL THE WORK HIMSELF FOR SO LONG...
ETOUCHI-KUN!
NIYODO-KUN, YOU'RE NOT FEELING WELL? LET ME TAKE YOU TO THE FIRST AID STATION.
THAT'S REALLY NOT-
HOIK
SQUEEE
BWAAAH! IT'S HIKARU SETOUCHI, THE NATION'S PRINCE!
HE'S TAKING NOTHER OMPETI-OR FOR FIRST AID!
WHAT?! THE NIYODO PERSONA GACHA HAS "SICKLY" IN IT NOW?!
WHY IS SETOUCHI-KUN ALWAYS HANGING AROUND LATELY? IT'S NOT LIKE THERE'S MONEY IN IT...
THANK YOU, SETOUCHI-KUN! BUT YOU SHOULD LET YOSHINO-KUN DO THAT!
NIYODO BE WELL
BEER

WORRY ABOUT HIS HEALTH!

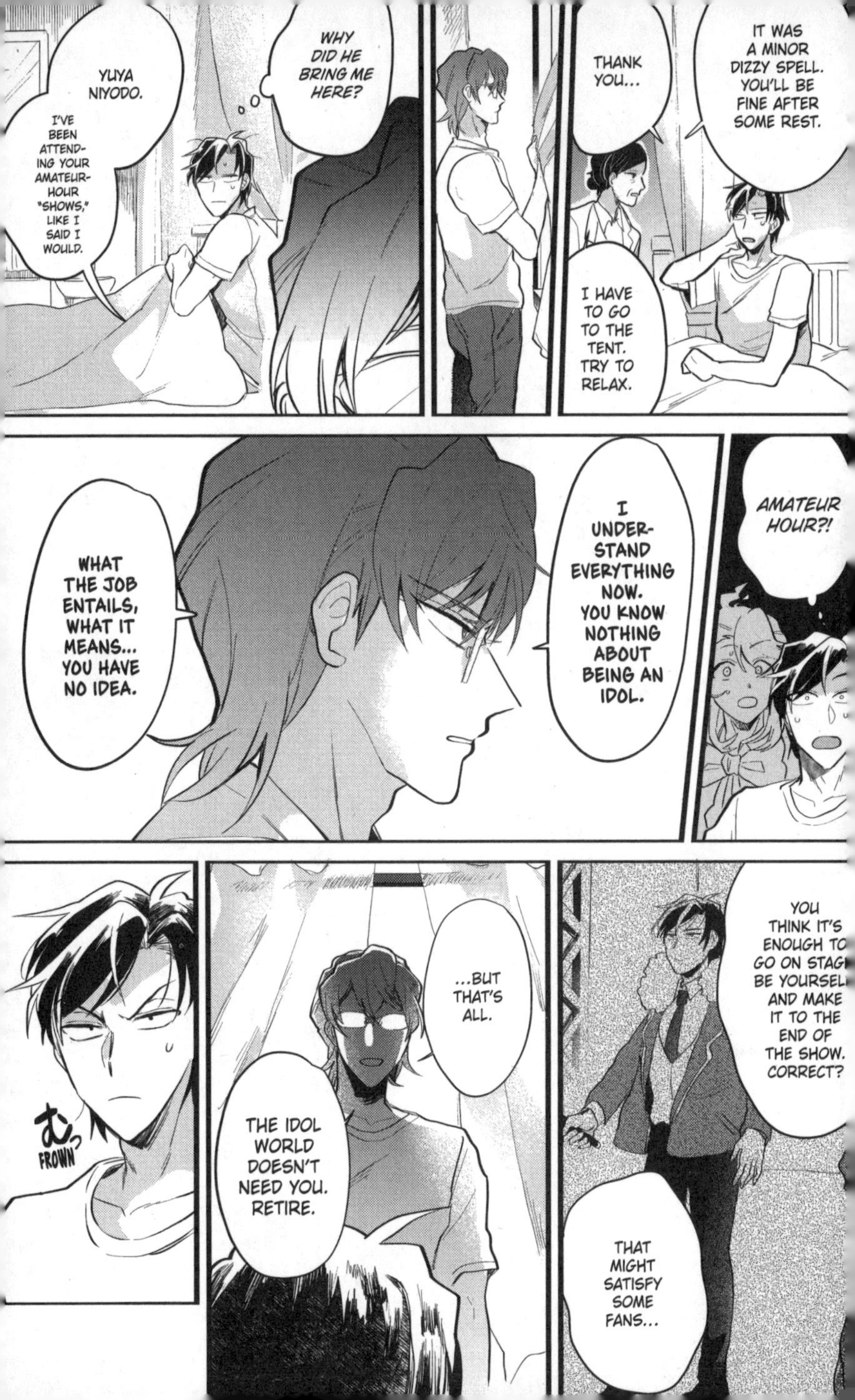
IT WAS A MINOR DIZZY SPELL. YOU'LL BE FINE AFTER SOME REST.
THANK YOU...
I HAVE TO GO TO THE TENT. TRY TO RELAX.
WHY DID HE BRING ME HERE?
YUYA NIYODO.
I'VE BEEN ATTENDING YOUR AMATEUR-HOUR "SHOWS," LIKE I SAID I WOULD.
AMATEUR HOUR?!
I UNDERSTAND EVERYTHING NOW. YOU KNOW NOTHING ABOUT BEING AN IDOL.
WHAT THE JOB ENTAILS, WHAT IT MEANS... YOU HAVE NO IDEA.
YOU THINK IT'S ENOUGH TO GO ON STAG BE YOURSEL AND MAKE IT TO THE END OF THE SHOW. CORRECT?
THAT MIGHT SATISFY SOME FANS...
...BUT THAT'S ALL.
THE IDOL WORLD DOESN'T NEED YOU. RETIRE.
む
FROWN

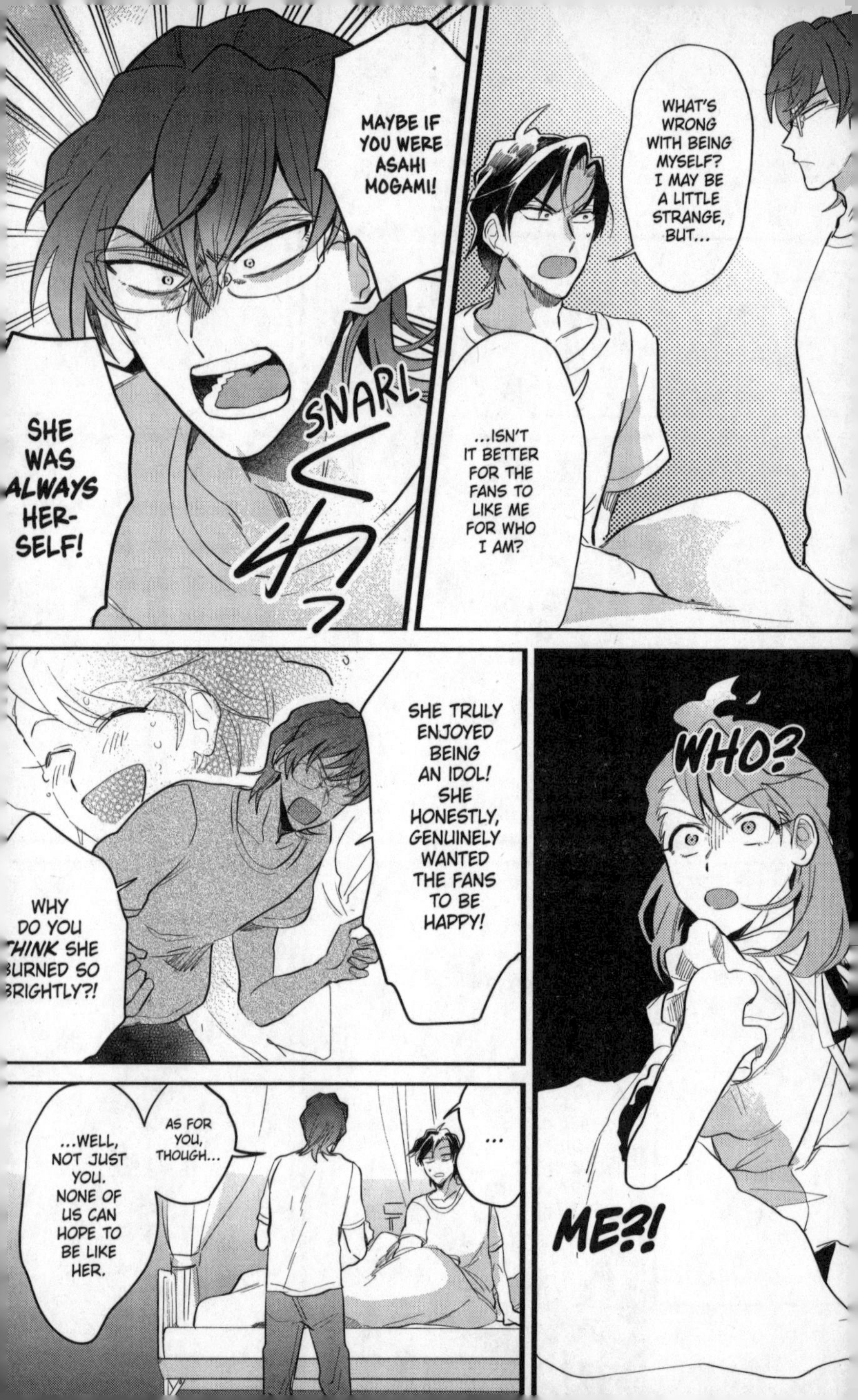
WHAT'S WRONG WITH BEING MYSELF? I MAY BE A LITTLE STRANGE, BUT...
...ISN'T IT BETTER FOR THE FANS TO LIKE ME FOR WHO I AM?
MAYBE IF YOU WERE ASAHI MOGAMI!
SNARL
SHE WAS ALWAYS HER-SELF!
WHO?
ME?!
SHE TRULY ENJOYED BEING AN IDOL! SHE HONESTLY, GENUINELY WANTED THE FANS TO BE HAPPY!
WHY DO YOU THINK SHE BURNED SO BRIGHTLY?!
...
AS FOR YOU, THOUGH...
...WELL, NOT JUST YOU. NONE OF US CAN HOPE TO BE LIKE HER.

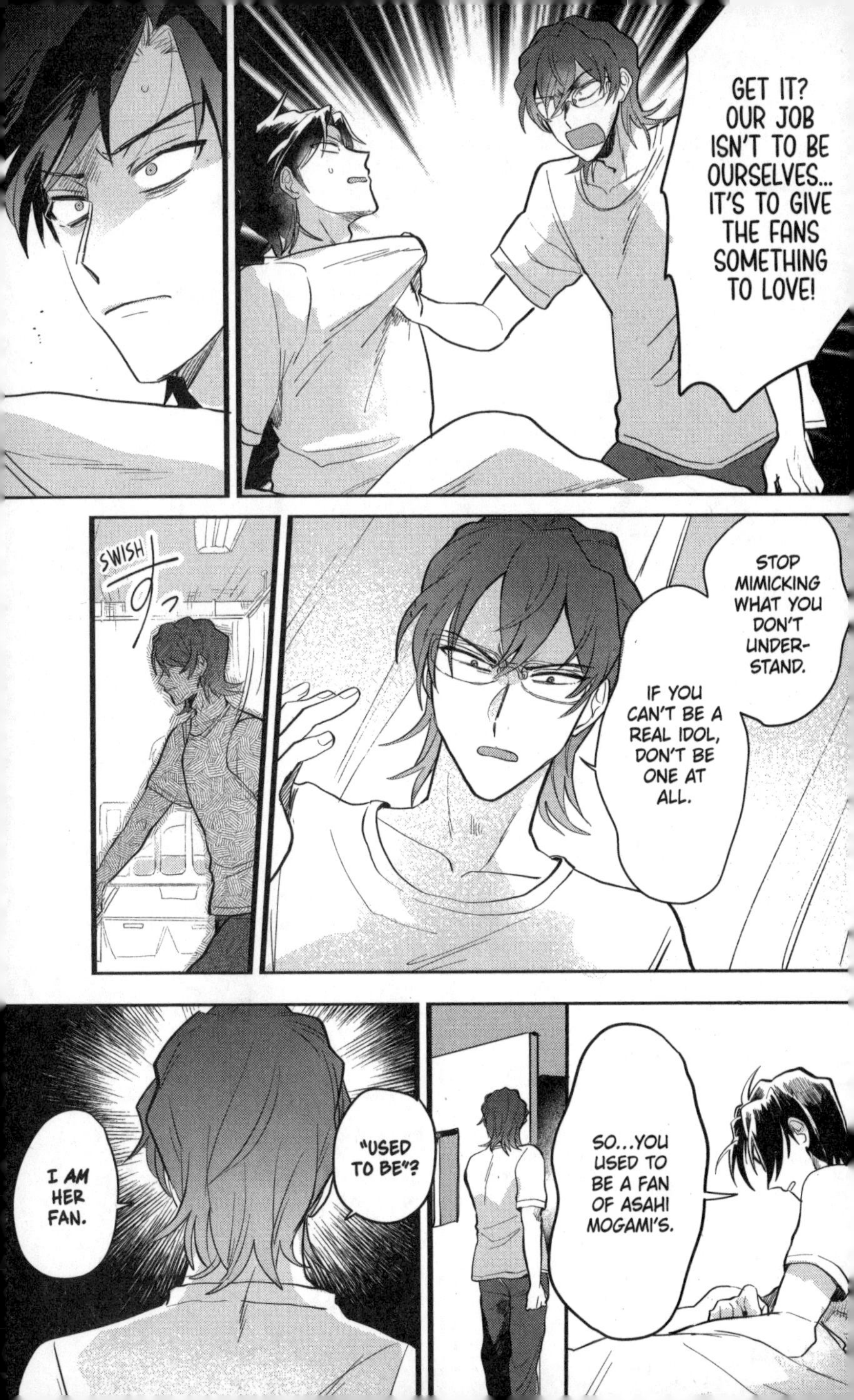
GET IT? OUR JOB ISN'T TO BE OURSELVES... IT'S TO GIVE THE FANS SOMETHING TO LOVE!
STOP MIMICKING WHAT YOU DON'T UNDER-STAND.
IF YOU CAN'T BE A REAL IDOL, DON'T BE ONE AT ALL.
SWISH
SO...YOU USED TO BE A FAN OF ASAHI MOGAMI'S.
"USED TO BE"?
I AM HER FAN.

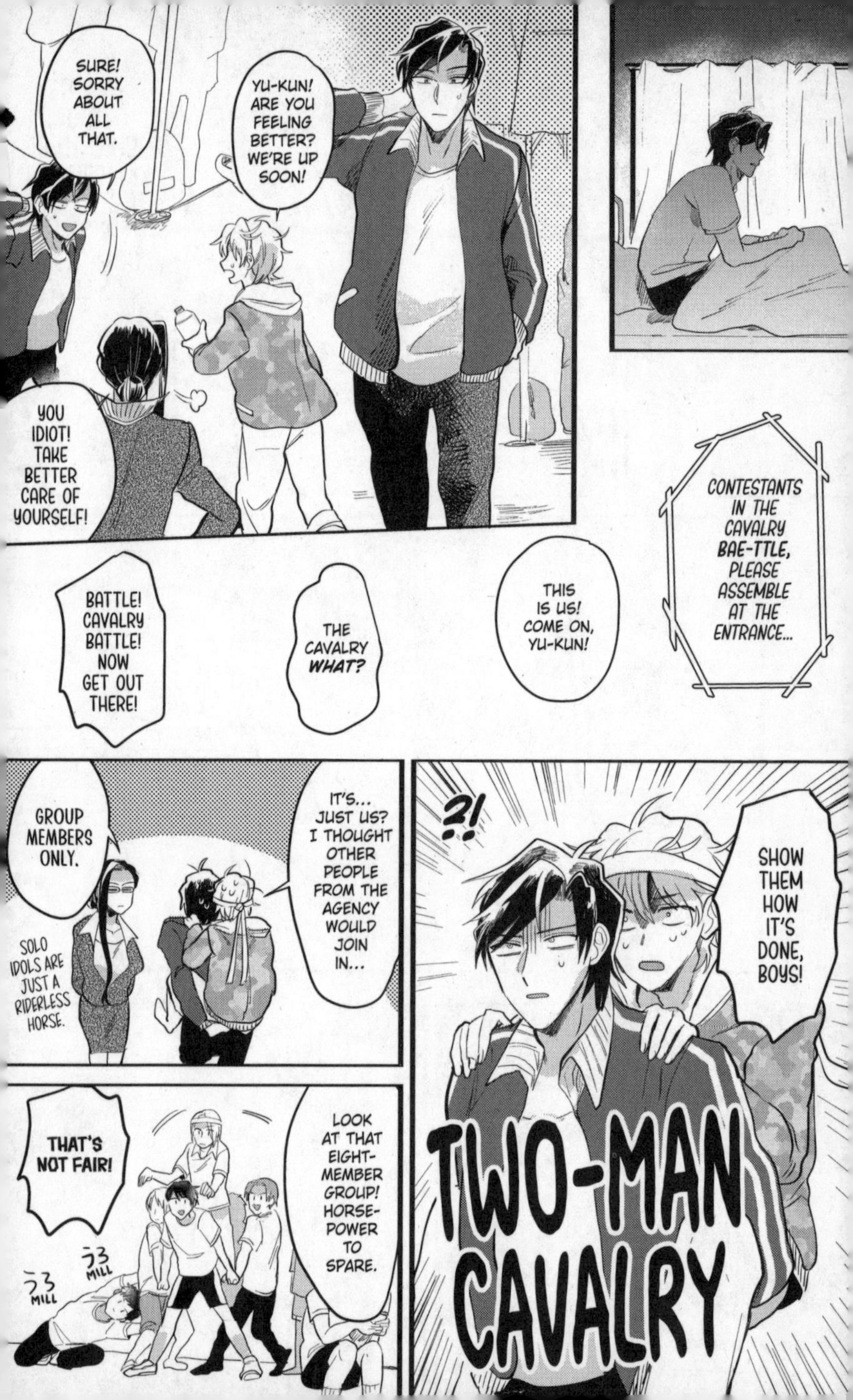
YU-KUN! ARE YOU FEELING BETTER? WE'RE UP SOON!
SURE! SORRY ABOUT ALL THAT.
YOU IDIOT! TAKE BETTER CARE OF YOURSELF!
CONTESTANTS IN THE CAVALRY BAE-TTLE, PLEASE ASSEMBLE AT THE ENTRANCE...
THIS IS US! COME ON, YU-KUN!
THE CAVALRY *WHAT?*
BATTLE! CAVALRY BATTLE! NOW GET OUT THERE!
?!
SHOW THEM HOW IT'S DONE, BOYS!
TWO-MAN CAVALRY
IT'S... JUST US? I THOUGHT OTHER PEOPLE FROM THE AGENCY WOULD JOIN IN...
GROUP MEMBERS ONLY.
SOLO IDOLS ARE JUST A RIDERLESS HORSE.
LOOK AT THAT EIGHT-MEMBER GROUP! HORSE-POWER TO SPARE.
THAT'S NOT FAIR!
うろ MILL
うろ MILL

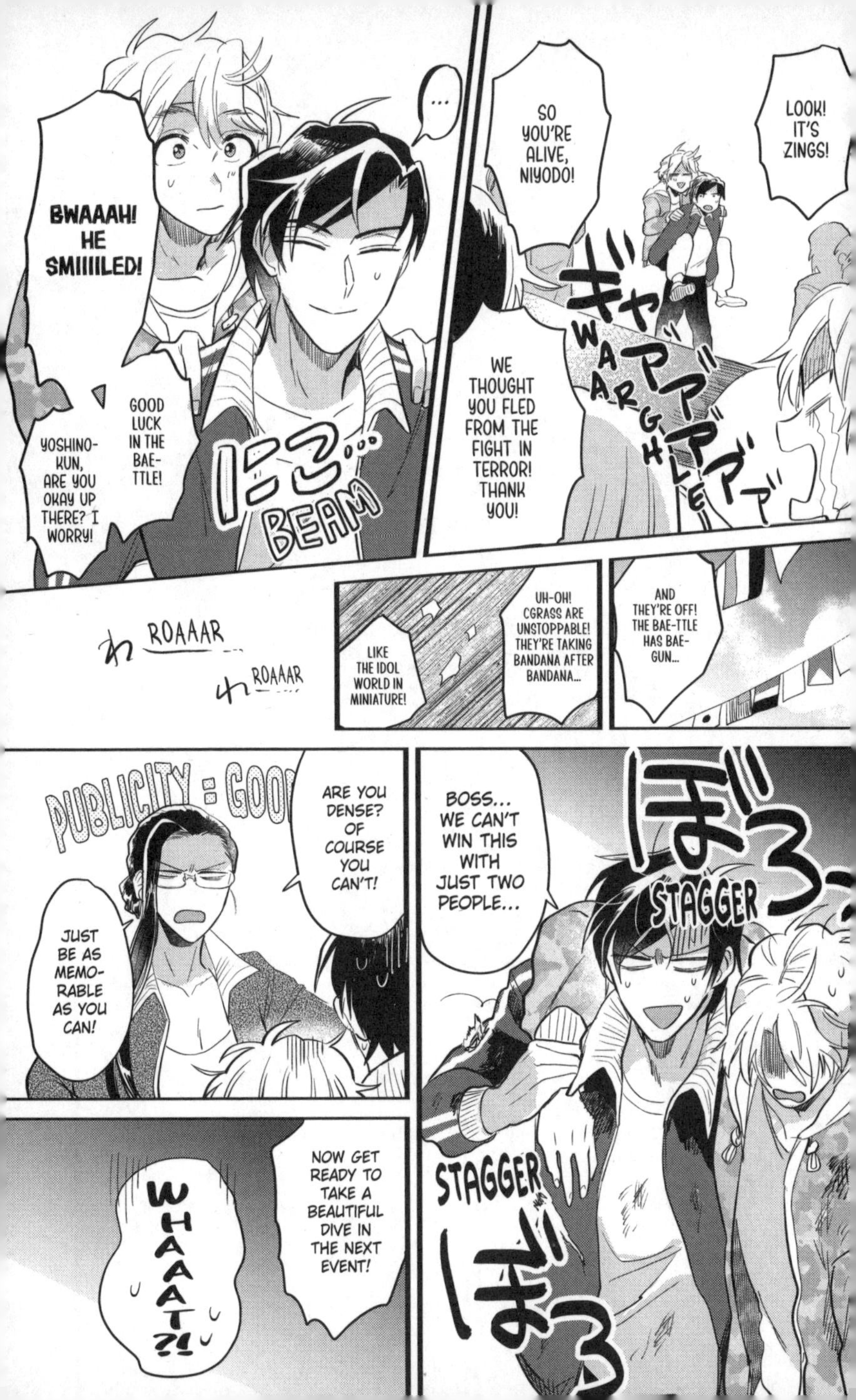
LOOK! IT'S ZINGS!
WARGHLE
SO YOU'RE ALIVE, NIYODO!
WE THOUGHT YOU FLED FROM THE FIGHT IN TERROR! THANK YOU!
...
BWAAAH! HE SMIIIILED!
BEAM
GOOD LUCK IN THE BAE-TTLE!
YOSHINO-KUN, ARE YOU OKAY UP THERE? I WORRY!
AND THEY'RE OFF! THE BAE-TTLE HAS BAE-GUN...
UH-OH! CGRASS ARE UNSTOPPABLE! THEY'RE TAKING BANDANA AFTER BANDANA...
LIKE THE IDOL WORLD IN MINIATURE!
ROAAAR
ROAAAR
STAGGER
BOSS... WE CAN'T WIN THIS WITH JUST TWO PEOPLE...
STAGGER
ARE YOU DENSE? OF COURSE YOU CAN'T!
PUBLICITY = GOOD
JUST BE AS MEMORABLE AS YOU CAN!
NOW GET READY TO TAKE A BEAUTIFUL DIVE IN THE NEXT EVENT!
WHAAAT?!

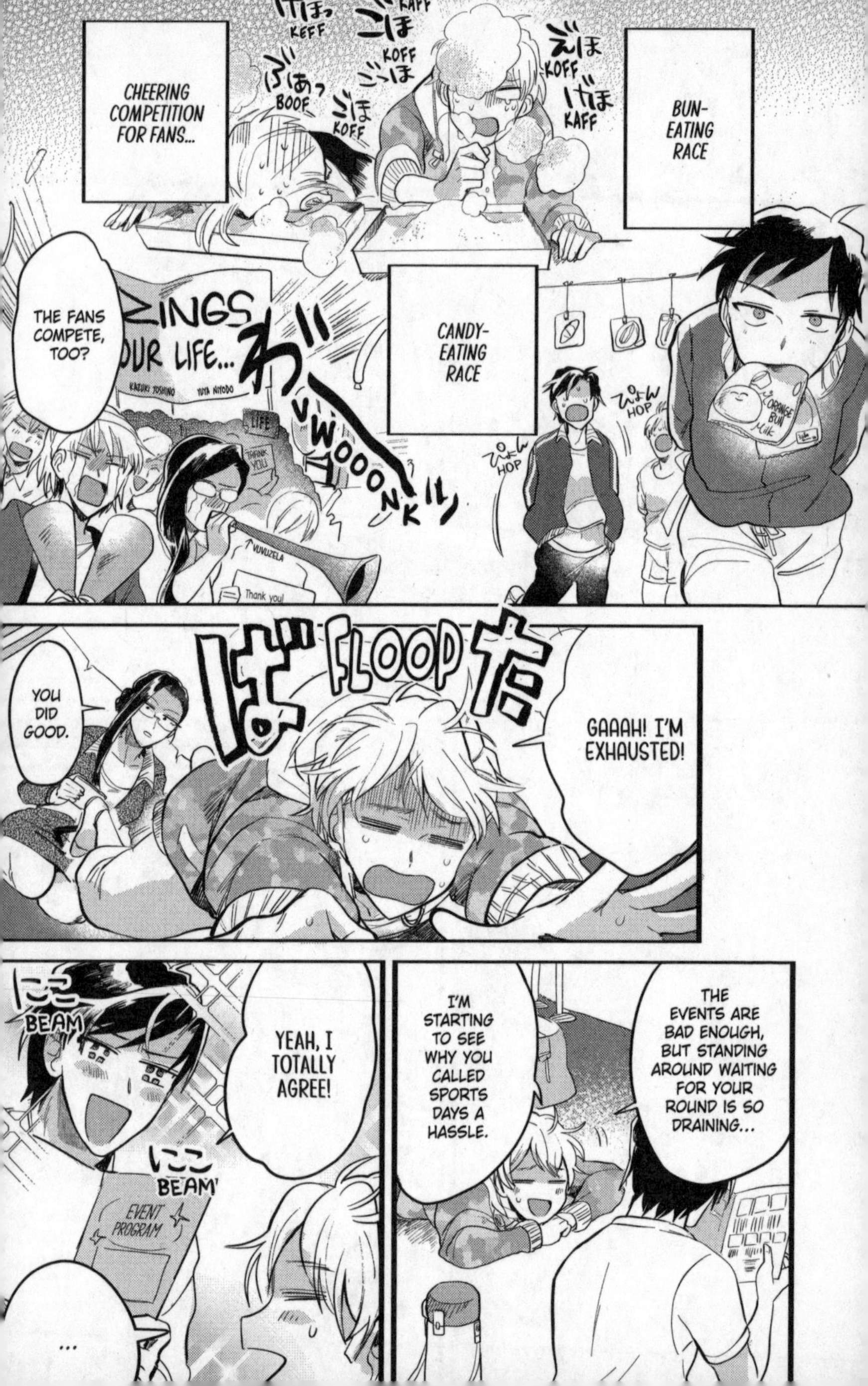
BUN-EATING RACE
えほ KOFF
げほ KAFF
ごほ KAFF
ごっほ KOFF
げほっ KEFF
ぶはっ BOOF
ごほ KOFF
CHEERING COMPETITION FOR FANS...
CANDY-EATING RACE
ORANGE BUN Milk
ぴょん HOP
ぴょん HOP
RINGS OUR LIFE...
KAZUKI YOSHINO
YUYA NIYODO
LIFE
THANK YOU
VUVUZELA
Thank you!
わ゛ー VWOOOONK
THE FANS COMPETE, TOO?
ばた FLOOP
GAAAH! I'M EXHAUSTED!
YOU DID GOOD.
THE EVENTS ARE BAD ENOUGH, BUT STANDING AROUND WAITING FOR YOUR ROUND IS SO DRAINING...
I'M STARTING TO SEE WHY YOU CALLED SPORTS DAYS A HASSLE.
YEAH, I TOTALLY AGREE!
にこ BEAM
にこ BEAM
EVENT PROGRAM
...

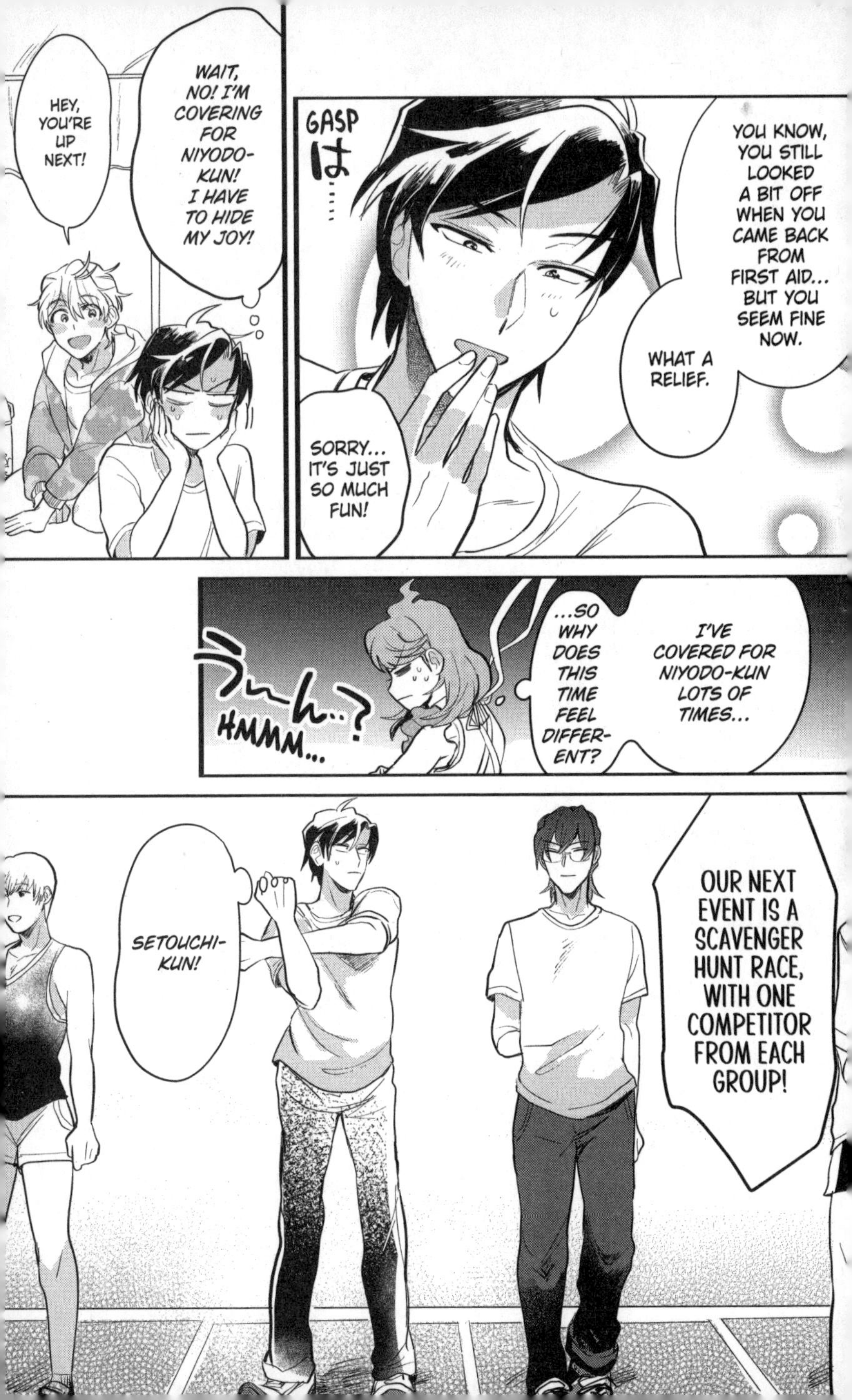
YOU KNOW, YOU STILL LOOKED A BIT OFF WHEN YOU CAME BACK FROM FIRST AID... BUT YOU SEEM FINE NOW.
WHAT A RELIEF.
GASP
は...
SORRY... IT'S JUST SO MUCH FUN!
WAIT, NO! I'M COVERING FOR NIYODO-KUN! I HAVE TO HIDE MY JOY!
HEY, YOU'RE UP NEXT!
I'VE COVERED FOR NIYODO-KUN LOTS OF TIMES...
...SO WHY DOES THIS TIME FEEL DIFFER-ENT?
うーん..?
HMMM...
OUR NEXT EVENT IS A SCAVENGER HUNT RACE, WITH ONE COMPETITOR FROM EACH GROUP!
SETOUCHI-KUN!

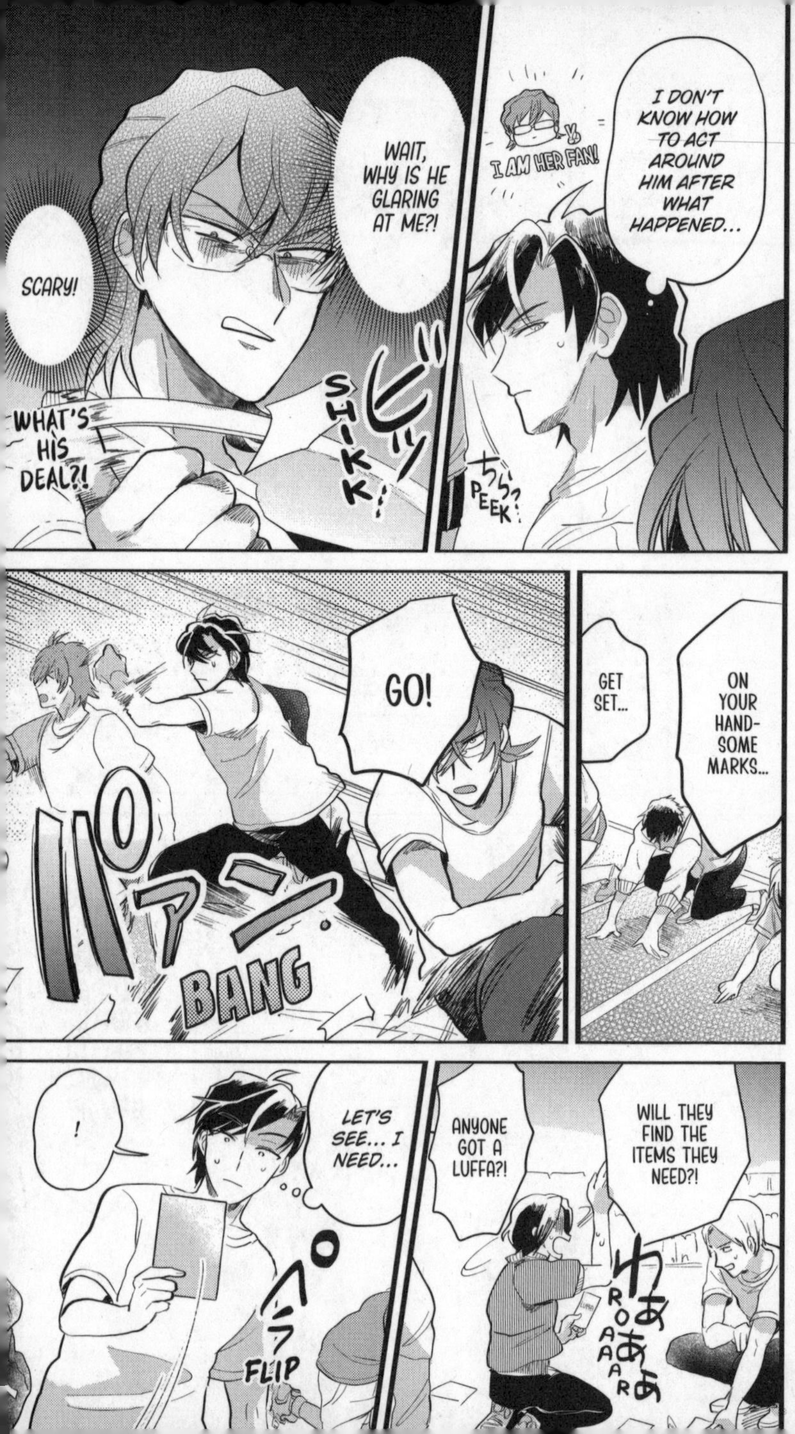
I DON'T KNOW HOW TO ACT AROUND HIM AFTER WHAT HAPPENED...
I AM HER FAN!
PEEK?
WAIT, WHY IS HE GLARING AT ME?!
SCARY!
SHIKK!
WHAT'S HIS DEAL?!
ON YOUR HAND-SOME MARKS...
GET SET...
GO!
BANG
WILL THEY FIND THE ITEMS THEY NEED?!
ANYONE GOT A LUFFA?!
ROAAAR
LET'S SEE... I NEED...
!
FLIP

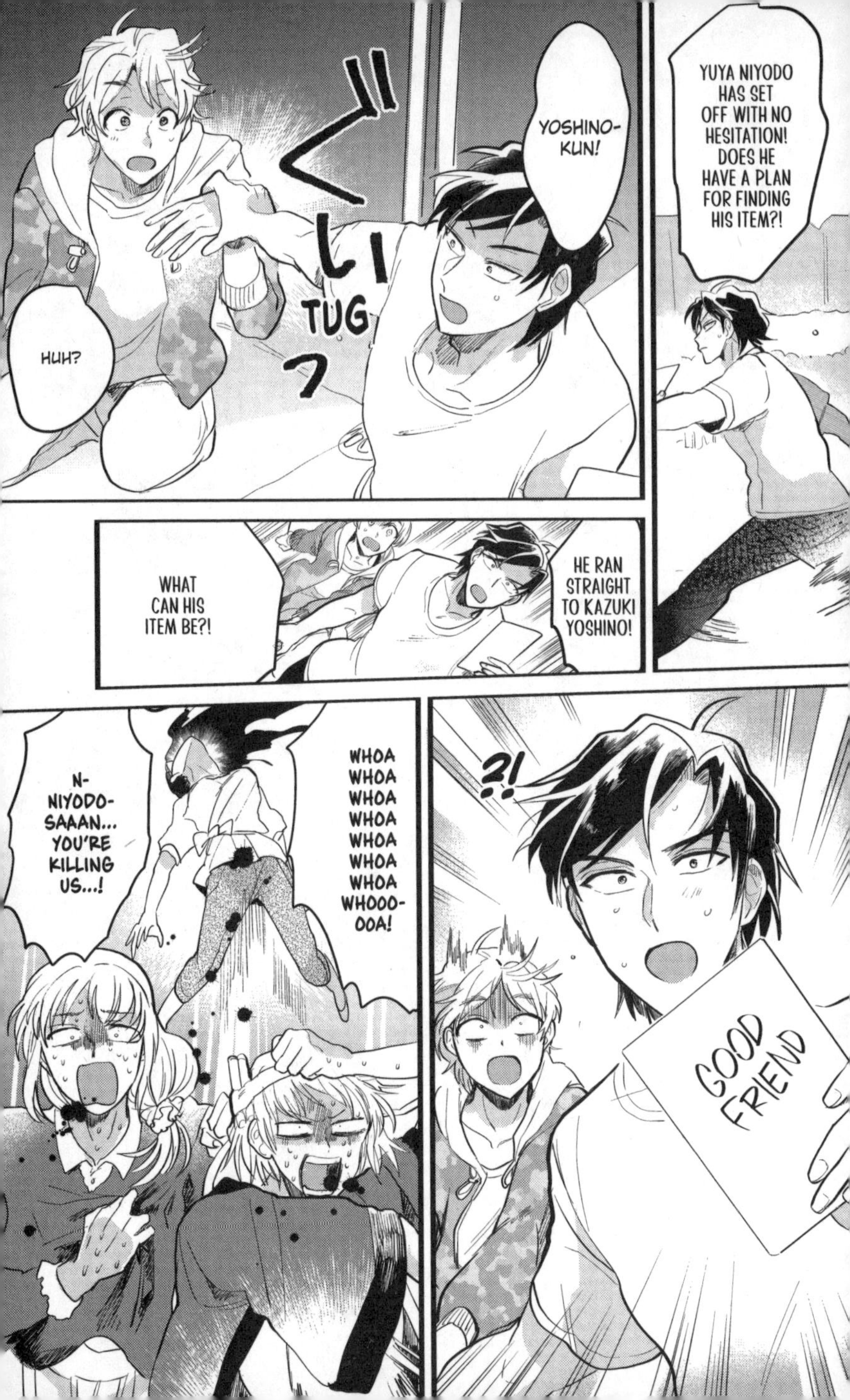
YUYA NIYODO HAS SET OFF WITH NO HESITATION! DOES HE HAVE A PLAN FOR FINDING HIS ITEM?!
YOSHINO-KUN!
TUG
HUH?
HE RAN STRAIGHT TO KAZUKI YOSHINO!
WHAT CAN HIS ITEM BE?!
?!
GOOD FRIEND
WHOA WHOA WHOA WHOA WHOA WHOA WHOA WHOOO-OOA!
N-NIYODO-SAAAN... YOU'RE KILLING US...!

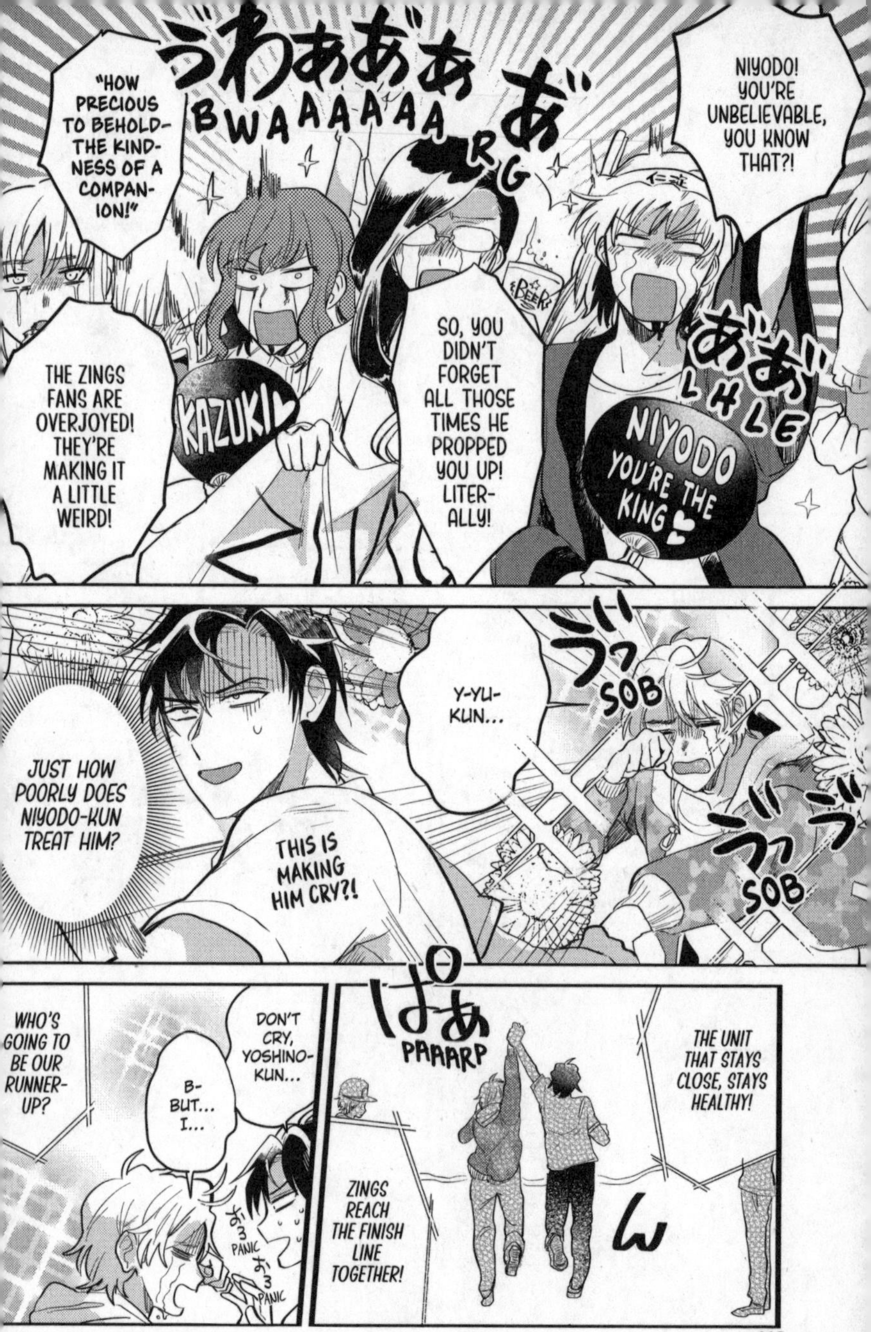
NIYODO! YOU'RE UNBELIEVABLE, YOU KNOW THAT?!
うわあああぁあ゛
BWAAAAAARG
"HOW PRECIOUS TO BEHOLD- THE KINDNESS OF A COMPANION!"
BEER
SO, YOU DIDN'T FORGET ALL THOSE TIMES HE PROPPED YOU UP! LITERALLY!
あ゛あ゛
NIYODO YOU'RE THE KING
KAZUKI
THE ZINGS FANS ARE OVERJOYED! THEY'RE MAKING IT A LITTLE WEIRD!
うっ
SOB
Y-YU-KUN...
うっ
SOB
THIS IS MAKING HIM CRY?!
JUST HOW POORLY DOES NIYODO-KUN TREAT HIM?
ぱあ
PAAARP
THE UNIT THAT STAYS CLOSE, STAYS HEALTHY!
ZINGS REACH THE FINISH LINE TOGETHER!
ん
DON'T CRY, YOSHINO-KUN...
B-BUT... I...
おろ PANIC
おろ PANIC
WHO'S GOING TO BE OUR RUNNER-UP?

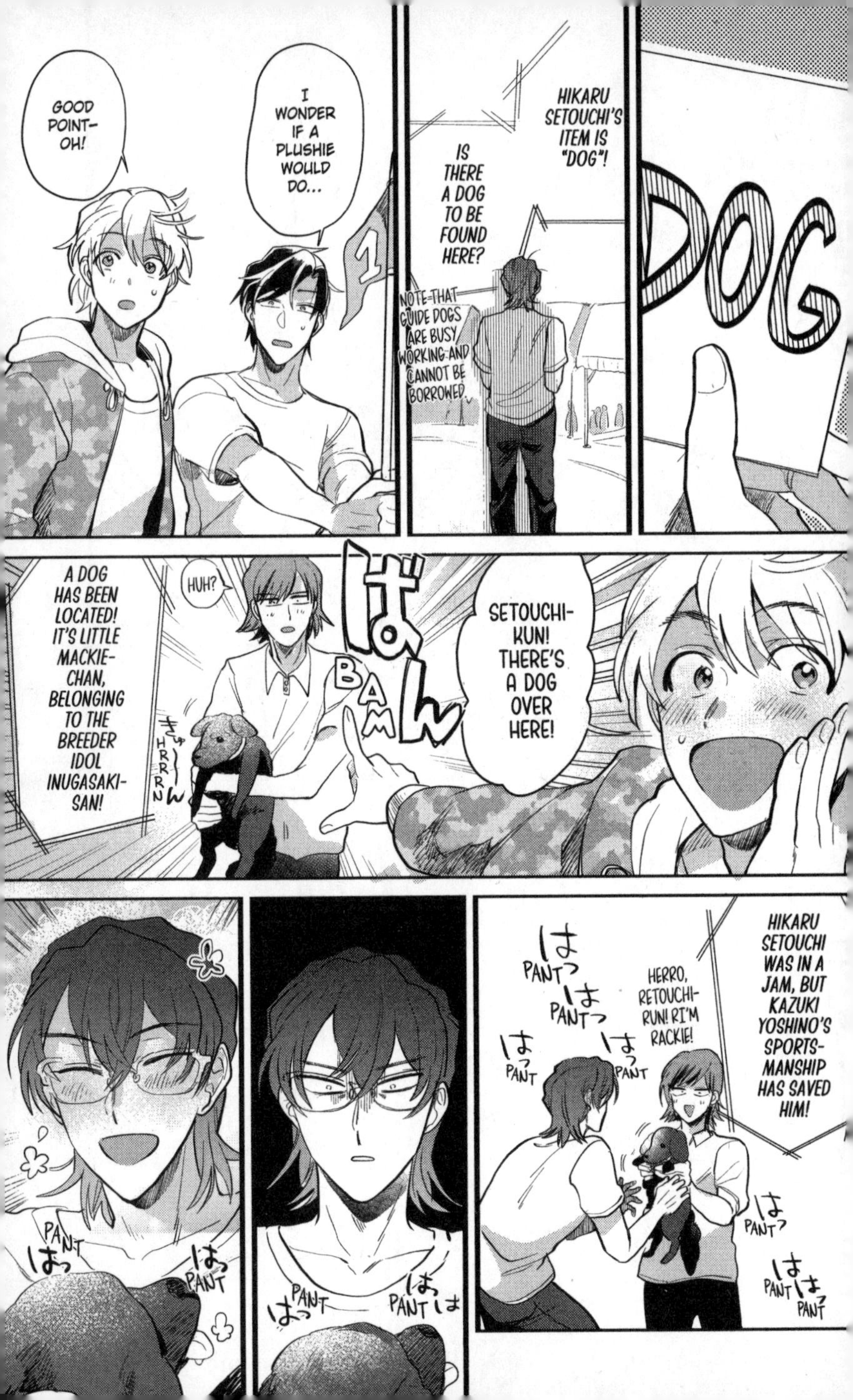
DOG
HIKARU SETOUCHI'S ITEM IS "DOG"!
IS THERE A DOG TO BE FOUND HERE?
NOTE THAT GUIDE DOGS ARE BUSY WORKING AND CANNOT BE BORROWED.
I WONDER IF A PLUSHIE WOULD DO...
GOOD POINT— OH!
SETOUCHI-KUN! THERE'S A DOG OVER HERE!
ばん BAM
HUH?
A DOG HAS BEEN LOCATED! IT'S LITTLE MACKIE-CHAN, BELONGING TO THE BREEDER IDOL INUGASAKI-SAN!
きゅ~ん HRRRN
HIKARU SETOUCHI WAS IN A JAM, BUT KAZUKI YOSHINO'S SPORTSMANSHIP HAS SAVED HIM!
HERRO, RETOUCHI-RUN! RI'M RACKIE!
はっ PANT はっ PANT はっ PANT はっ PANT
はっ PANT はっ PANT はっ PANT
はっ PANT はっ PANT
はっ PANT はっ PANT

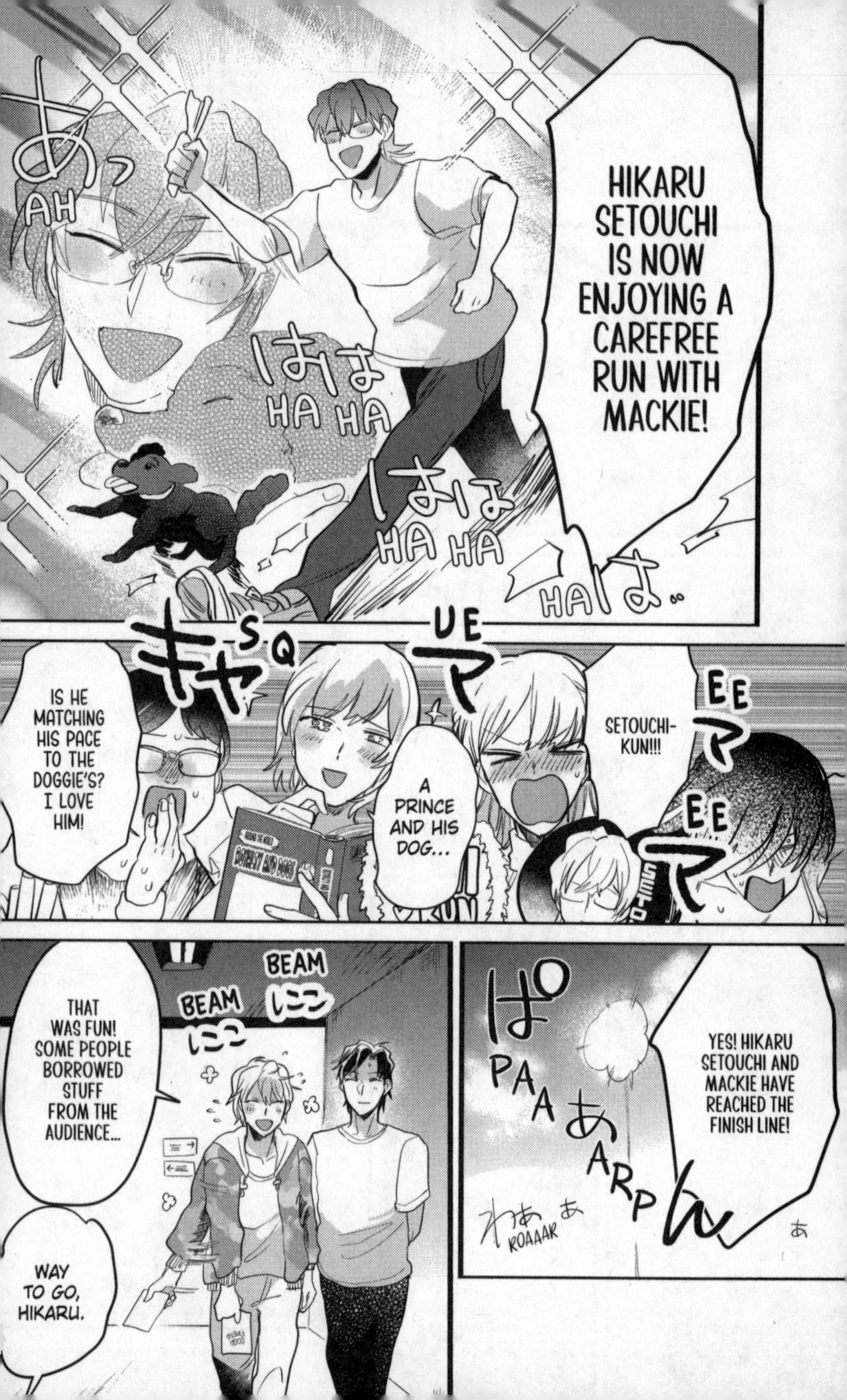
HIKARU SETOUCHI IS NOW ENJOYING A CAREFREE RUN WITH MACKIE!
AH
HA HA
HA HA
HA
SETOUCHI-KUN!!!
EE
EE
A PRINCE AND HIS DOG...
IS HE MATCHING HIS PACE TO THE DOGGIE'S? I LOVE HIM!
SQ
UE
YES! HIKARU SETOUCHI AND MACKIE HAVE REACHED THE FINISH LINE!
PAAARP
ROAAAR
BEAM
BEAM
THAT WAS FUN! SOME PEOPLE BORROWED STUFF FROM THE AUDIENCE...
WAY TO GO, HIKARU.

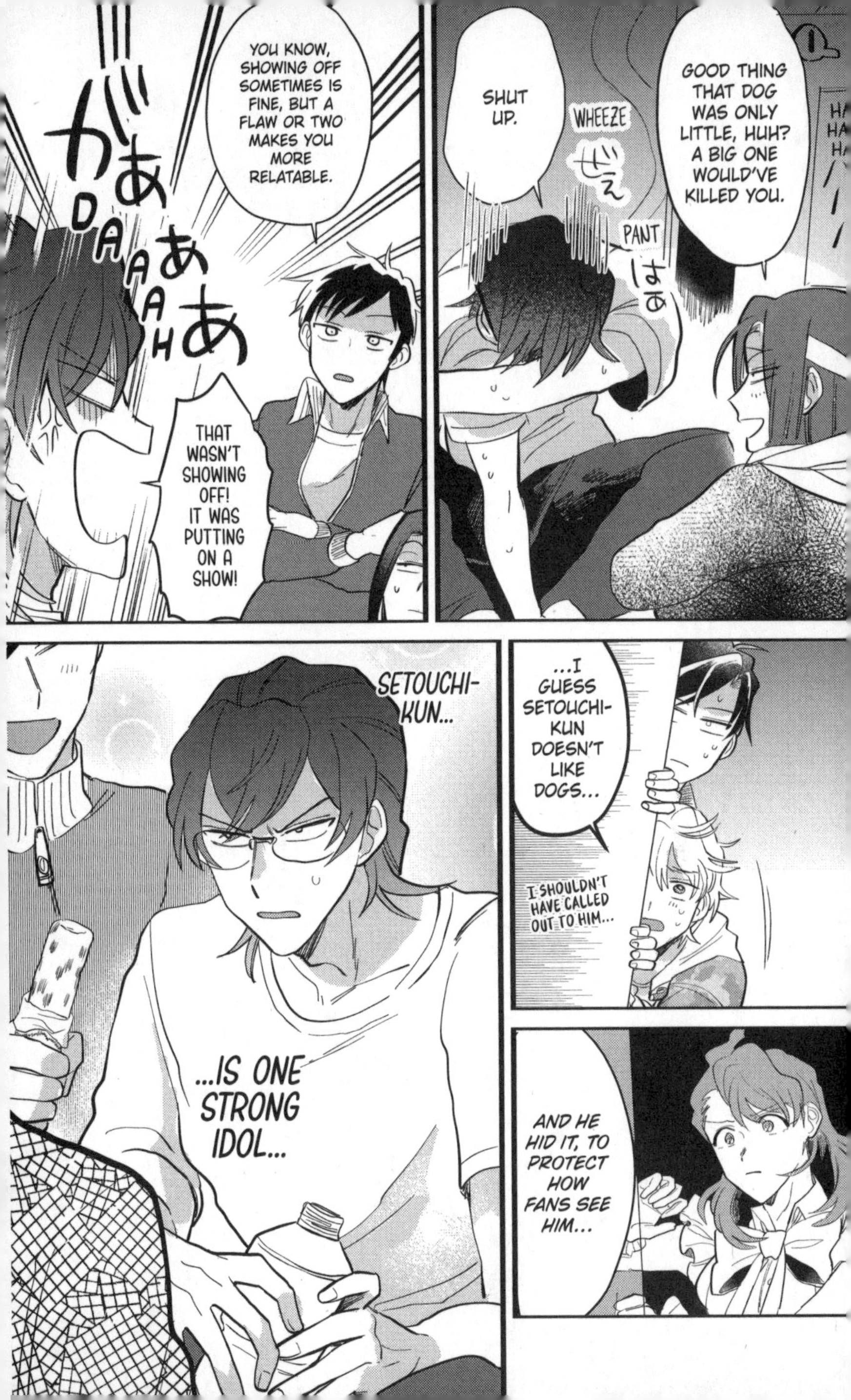
GOOD THING THAT DOG WAS ONLY LITTLE, HUH? A BIG ONE WOULD'VE KILLED YOU.
HA HA HA
SHUT UP.
WHEEZE ぜぇ
PANT はぁ
YOU KNOW, SHOWING OFF SOMETIMES IS FINE, BUT A FLAW OR TWO MAKES YOU MORE RELATABLE.
があああ DAAAAH
THAT WASN'T SHOWING OFF! IT WAS PUTTING ON A SHOW!
...I GUESS SETOUCHI-KUN DOESN'T LIKE DOGS...
I SHOULDN'T HAVE CALLED OUT TO HIM...
AND HE HID IT, TO PROTECT HOW FANS SEE HIM...
SETOUCHI-KUN...
...IS ONE STRONG IDOL...

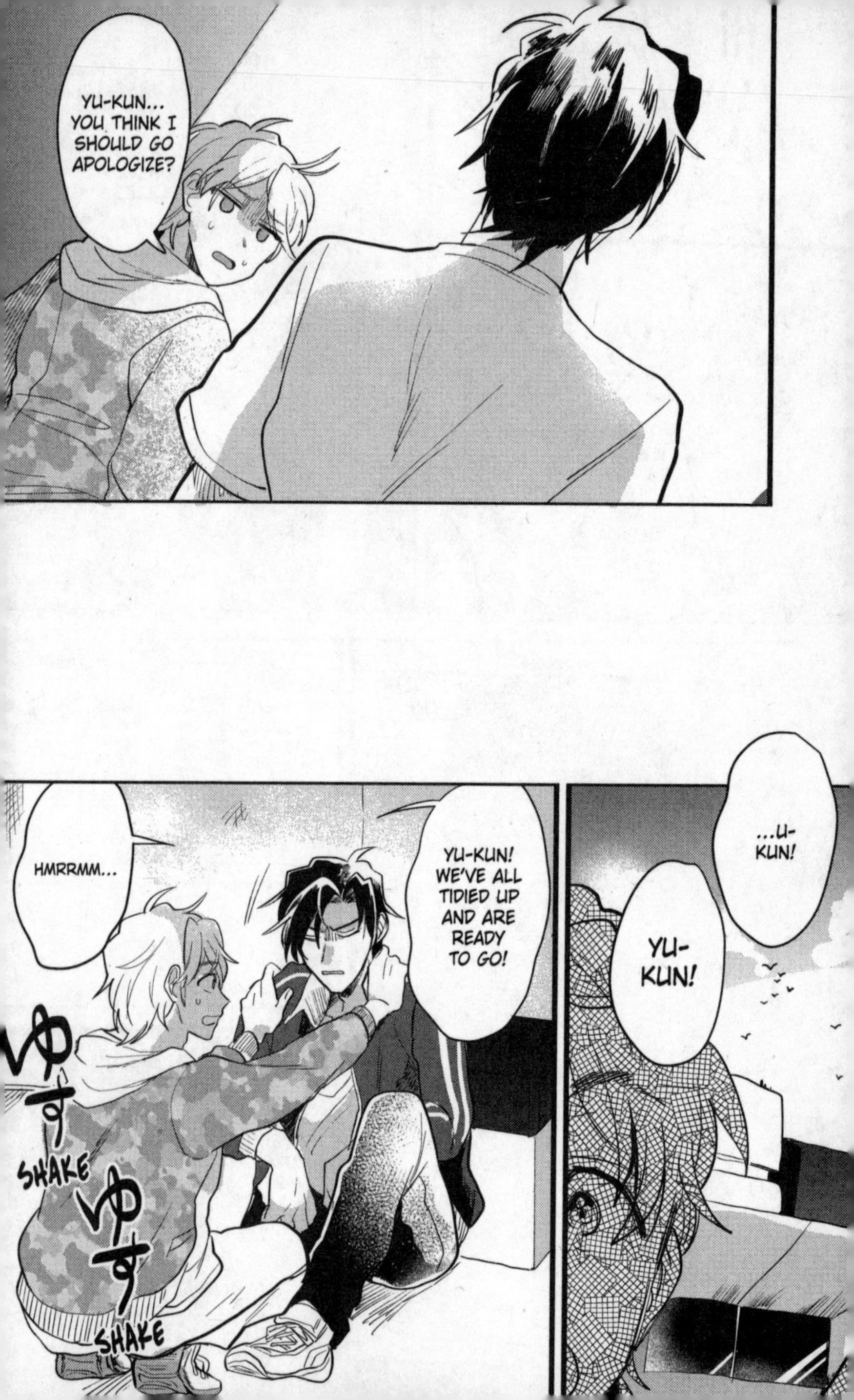
YU-KUN... YOU THINK I SHOULD GO APOLOGIZE?
...U-KUN!
YU-KUN!
YU-KUN! WE'VE ALL TIDIED UP AND ARE READY TO GO!
HMRRMM...
ゆす
SHAKE
ゆす
SHAKE

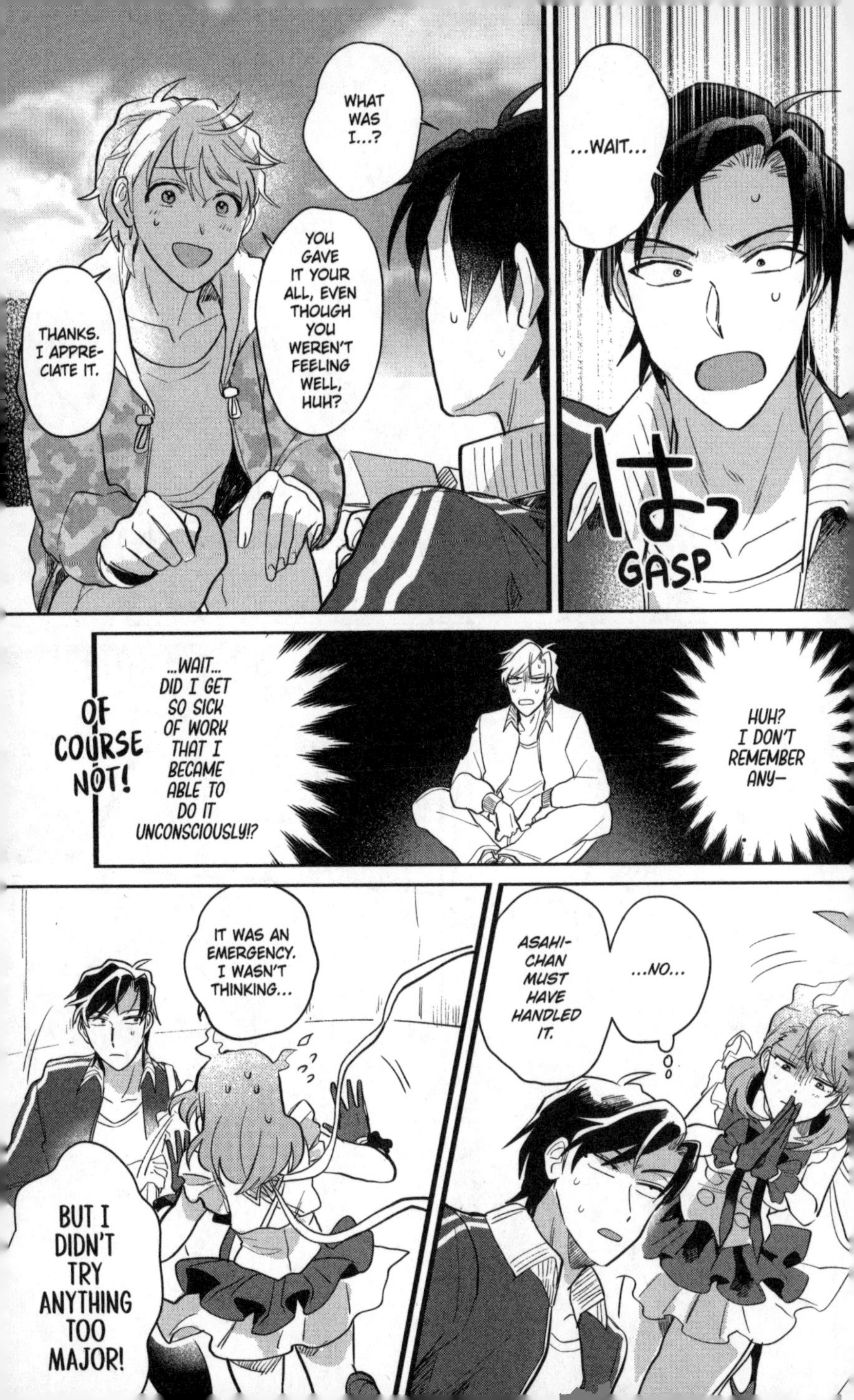
...WAIT...
はっ
GASP
WHAT WAS I...?
YOU GAVE IT YOUR ALL, EVEN THOUGH YOU WEREN'T FEELING WELL, HUH?
THANKS. I APPRECIATE IT.
HUH? I DON'T REMEMBER ANY—
...WAIT... DID I GET SO SICK OF WORK THAT I BECAME ABLE TO DO IT UNCONSCIOUSLY!?
OF COURSE NOT!
...NO...
ASAHI-CHAN MUST HAVE HANDLED IT.
IT WAS AN EMERGENCY. I WASN'T THINKING...
BUT I DIDN'T TRY ANYTHING TOO MAJOR!

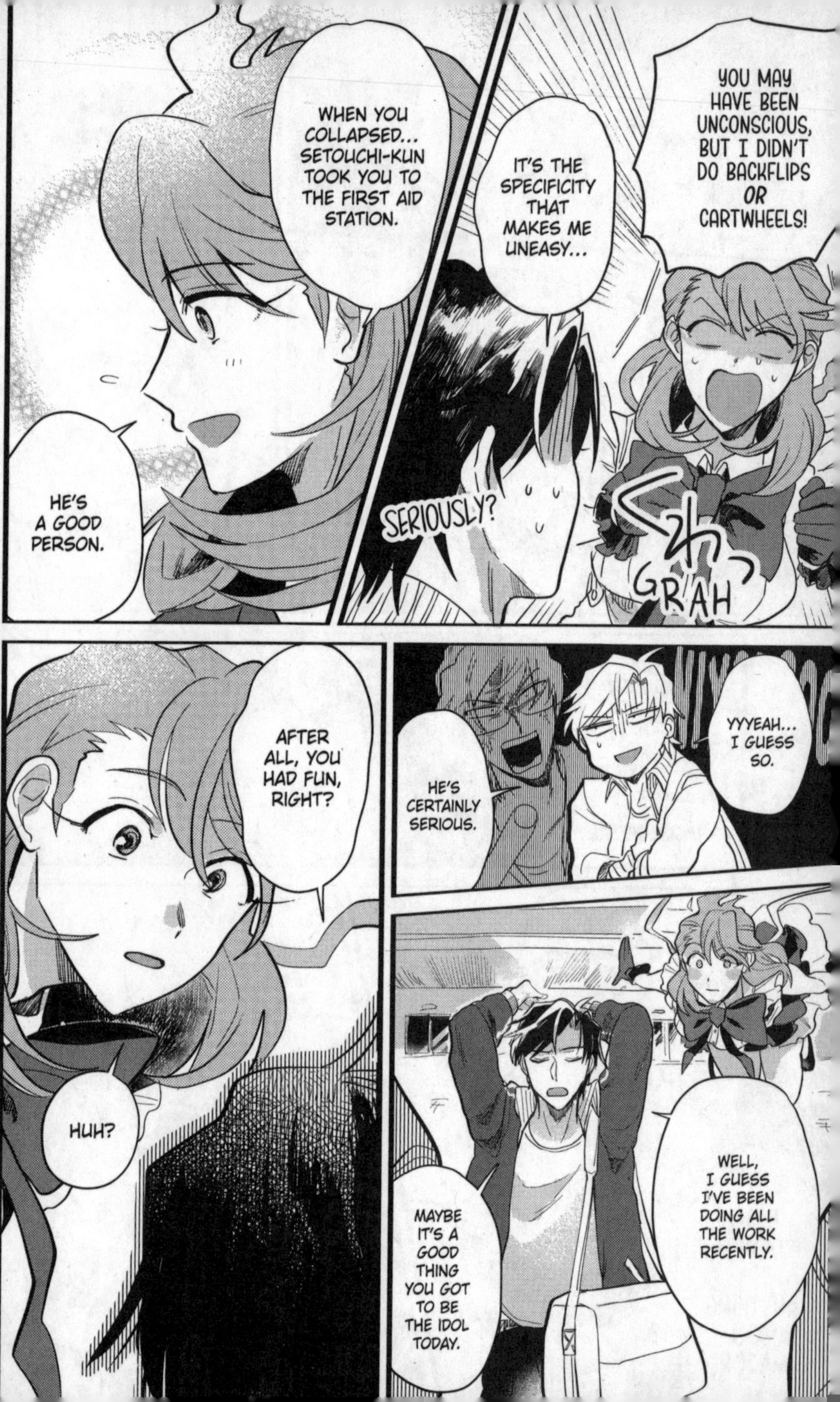
YOU MAY HAVE BEEN UNCONSCIOUS, BUT I DIDN'T DO BACKFLIPS OR CARTWHEELS!
くわっ GRAH
IT'S THE SPECIFICITY THAT MAKES ME UNEASY...
SERIOUSLY?
WHEN YOU COLLAPSED... SETOUCHI-KUN TOOK YOU TO THE FIRST AID STATION.
HE'S A GOOD PERSON.
YYYEAH... I GUESS SO.
HE'S CERTAINLY SERIOUS.
WELL, I GUESS I'VE BEEN DOING ALL THE WORK RECENTLY.
MAYBE IT'S A GOOD THING YOU GOT TO BE THE IDOL TODAY.
AFTER ALL, YOU HAD FUN, RIGHT?
HUH?

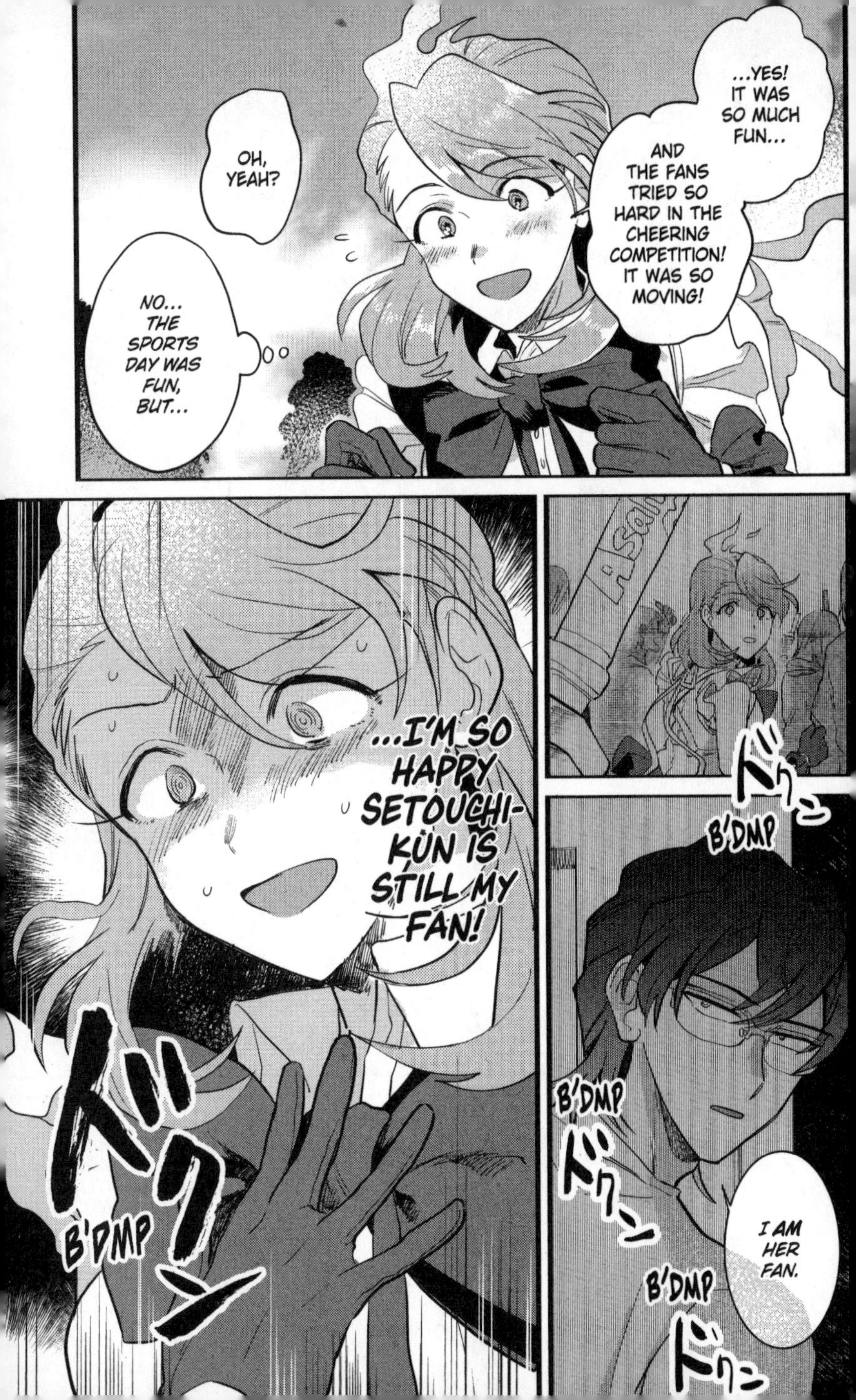
...YES! IT WAS SO MUCH FUN...
AND THE FANS TRIED SO HARD IN THE CHEERING COMPETITION! IT WAS SO MOVING!
OH, YEAH?
NO... THE SPORTS DAY WAS FUN, BUT...
ドクン
B'DMP
I AM HER FAN.
B'DMP
ドクン
B'DMP
ドクン
...I'M SO HAPPY SETOUCHI-KUN IS STILL MY FAN!
ドクン
B'DMP

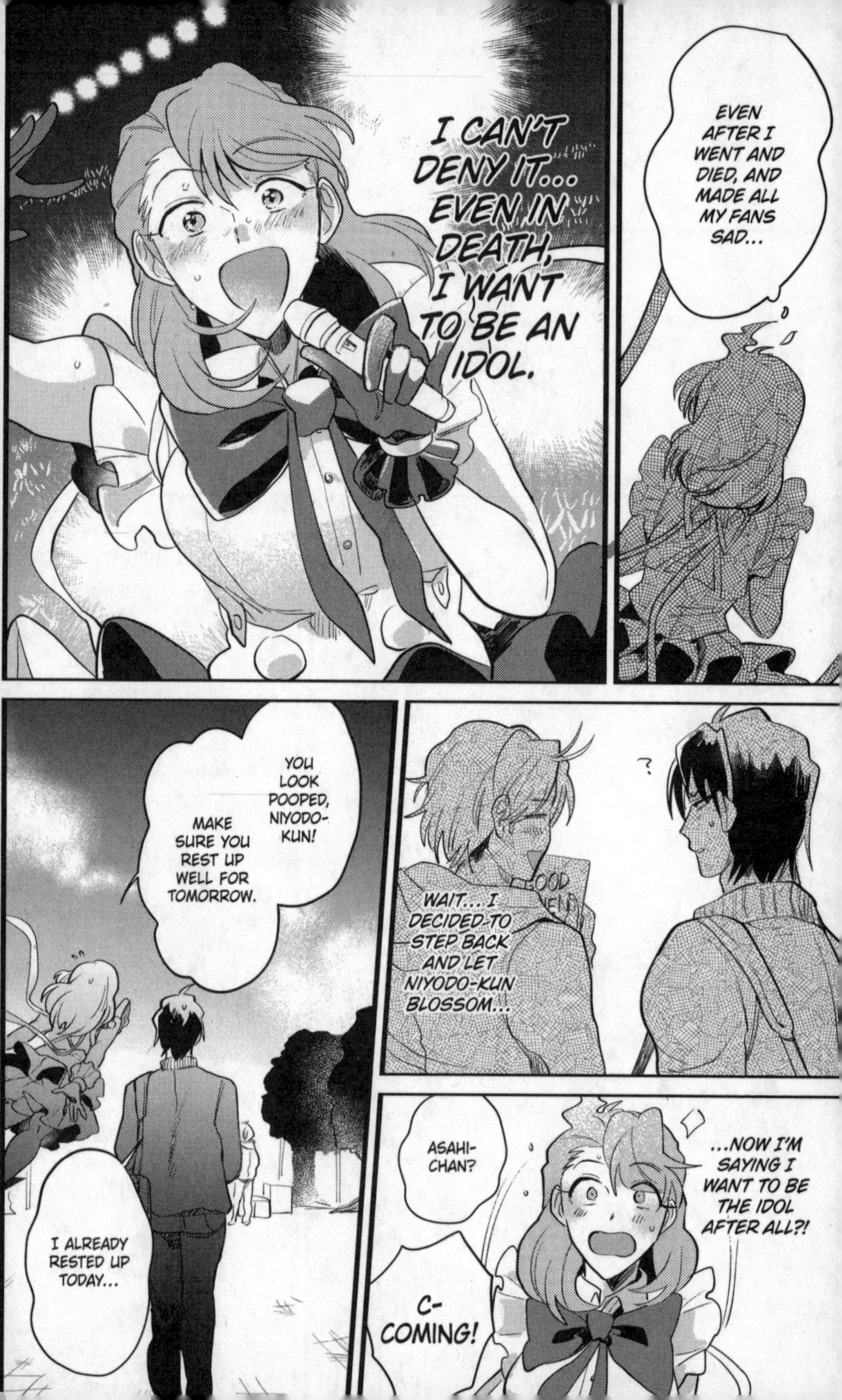
EVEN AFTER I WENT AND DIED, AND MADE ALL MY FANS SAD...
I CAN'T DENY IT... EVEN IN DEATH, I WANT TO BE AN IDOL.
WAIT... I DECIDED TO STEP BACK AND LET NIYODO-KUN BLOSSOM...
...NOW I'M SAYING I WANT TO BE THE IDOL AFTER ALL?!
ASAHI-CHAN?
C-COMING!
YOU LOOK POOPED, NIYODO-KUN!
MAKE SURE YOU REST UP WELL FOR TOMORROW.
I ALREADY RESTED UP TODAY...

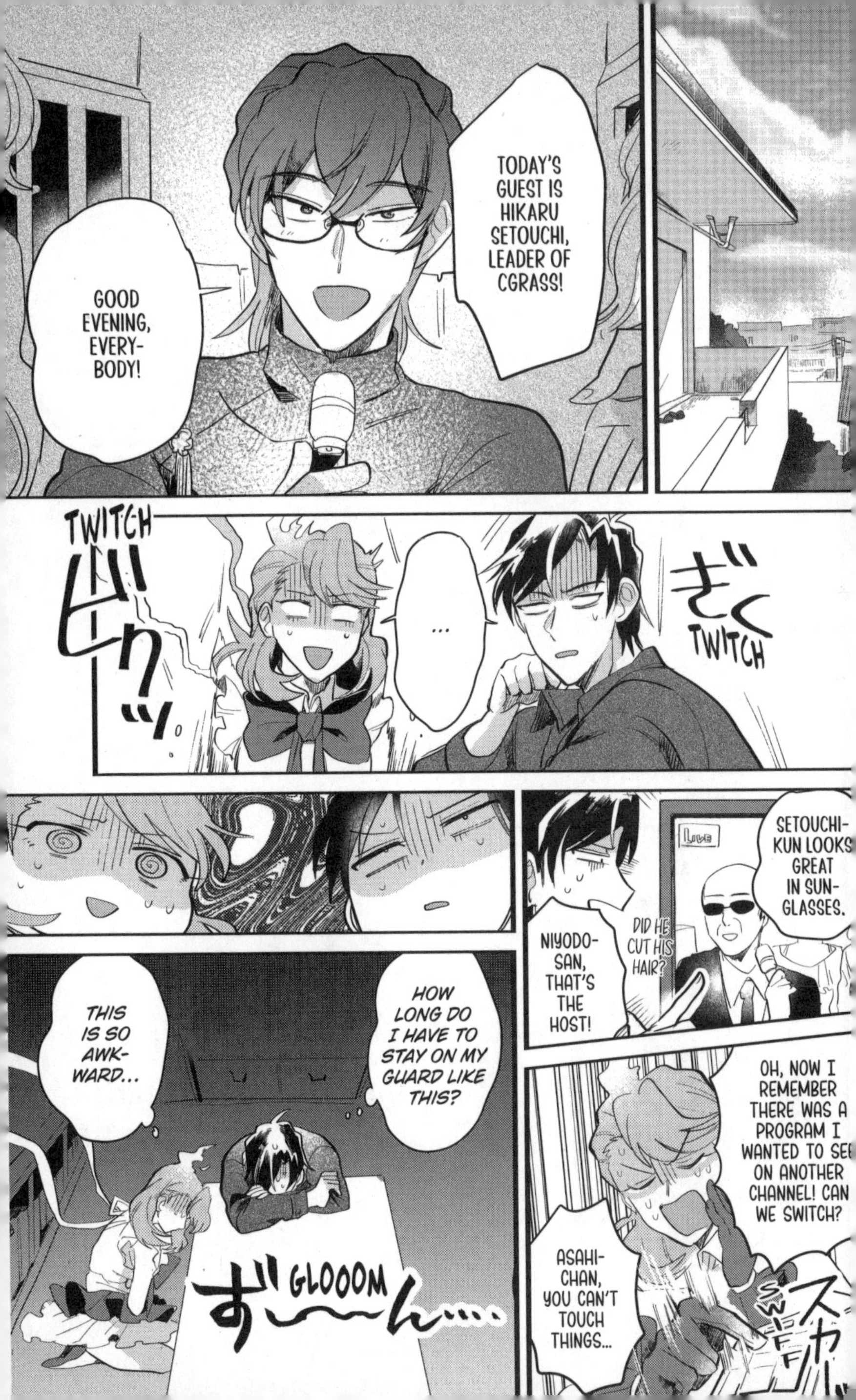
TODAY'S GUEST IS HIKARU SETOUCHI, LEADER OF CGRASS!
GOOD EVENING, EVERY-BODY!
ぎく
TWITCH
...
TWITCH
ビクッ
SETOUCHI-KUN LOOKS GREAT IN SUN-GLASSES.
DID HE CUT HIS HAIR?
NIYODO-SAN, THAT'S THE HOST!
HOW LONG DO I HAVE TO STAY ON MY GUARD LIKE THIS?
THIS IS SO AWK-WARD...
GLOOOM
ずーん...
OH, NOW I REMEMBER THERE WAS A PROGRAM I WANTED TO SEE ON ANOTHER CHANNEL! CAN WE SWITCH?
ASAHI-CHAN, YOU CAN'T TOUCH THINGS...
スカッ
SWIFF

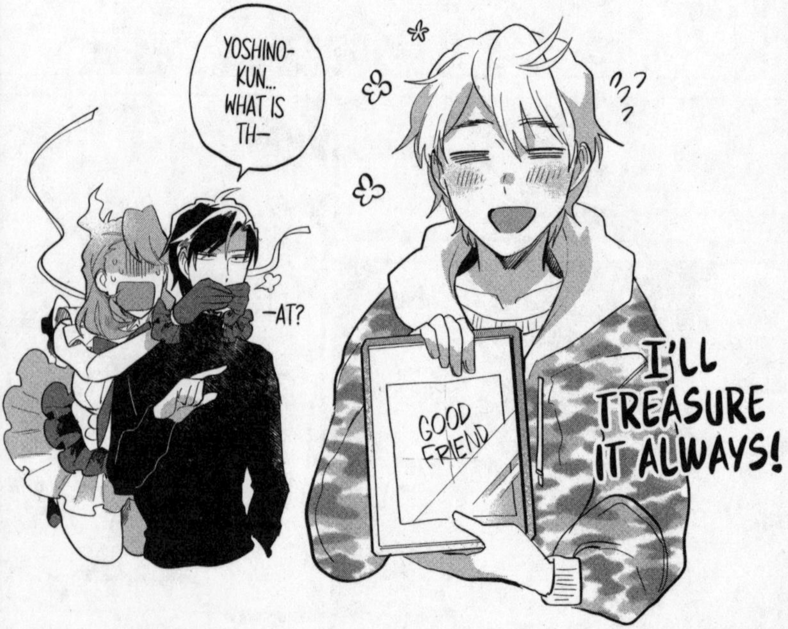
GOOD FRIEND
I'LL TREASURE IT ALWAYS!
YOSHINO-KUN... WHAT IS TH—
—AT?

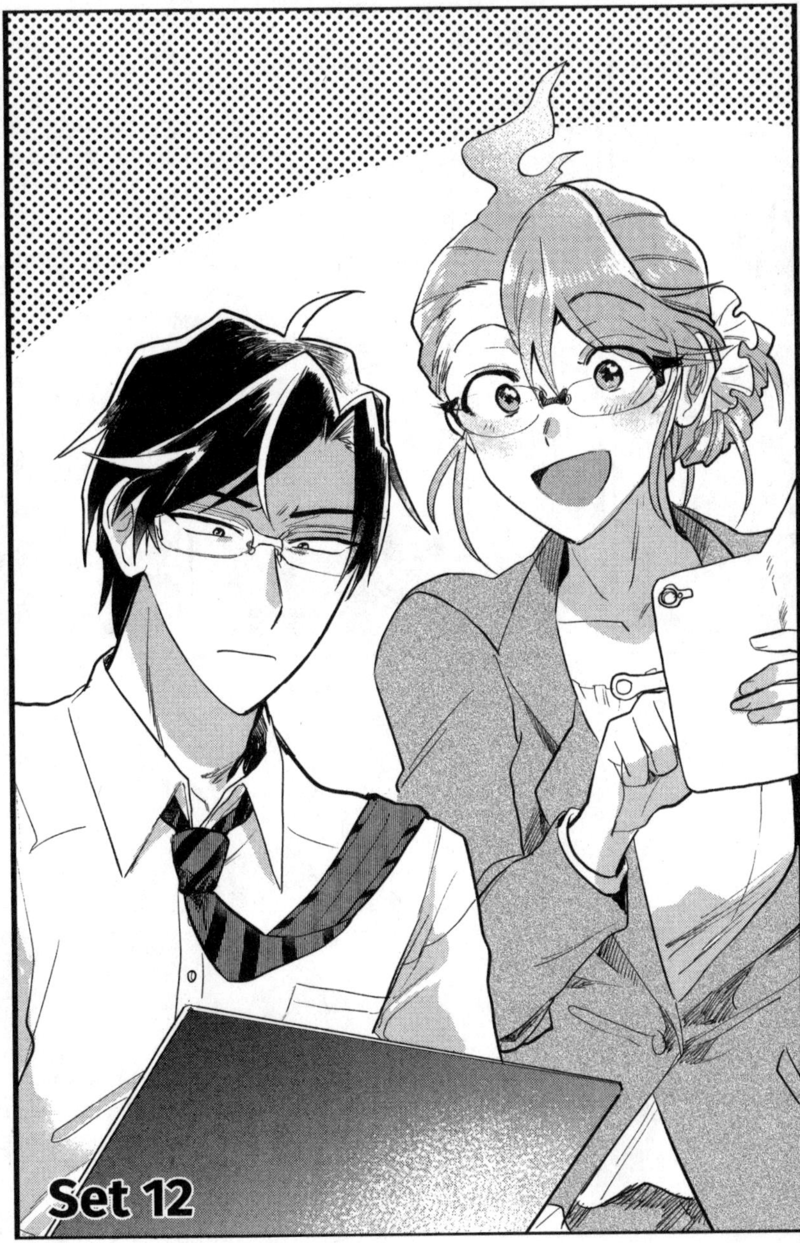
Set 12

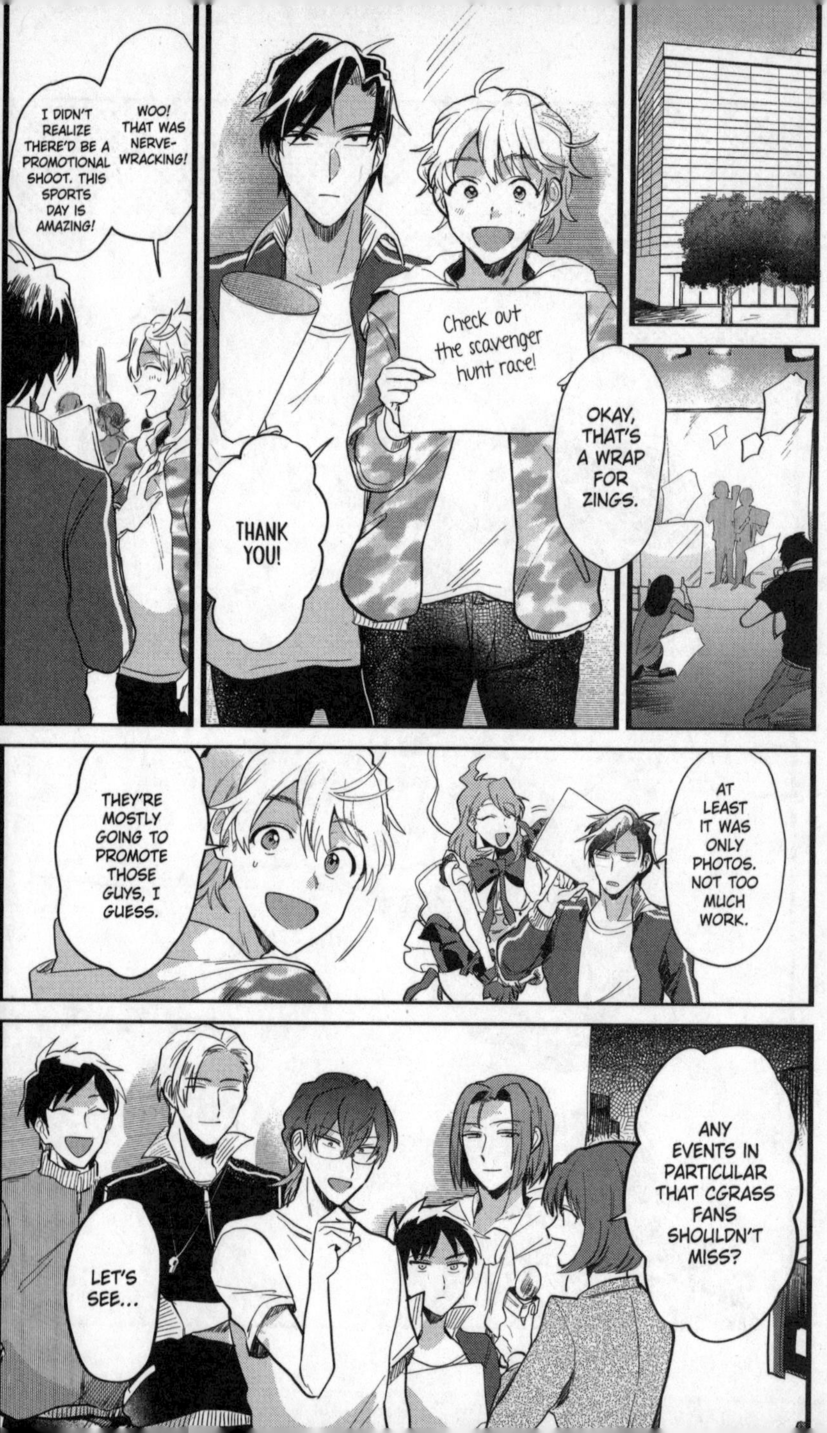
OKAY, THAT'S A WRAP FOR ZINGS.
Check out the scavenger hunt race!
THANK YOU!
WOO! THAT WAS NERVE-WRACKING!
I DIDN'T REALIZE THERE'D BE A PROMOTIONAL SHOOT. THIS SPORTS DAY IS AMAZING!
AT LEAST IT WAS ONLY PHOTOS. NOT TOO MUCH WORK.
THEY'RE MOSTLY GOING TO PROMOTE THOSE GUYS, I GUESS.
ANY EVENTS IN PARTICULAR THAT CGRASS FANS SHOULDN'T MISS?
LET'S SEE...

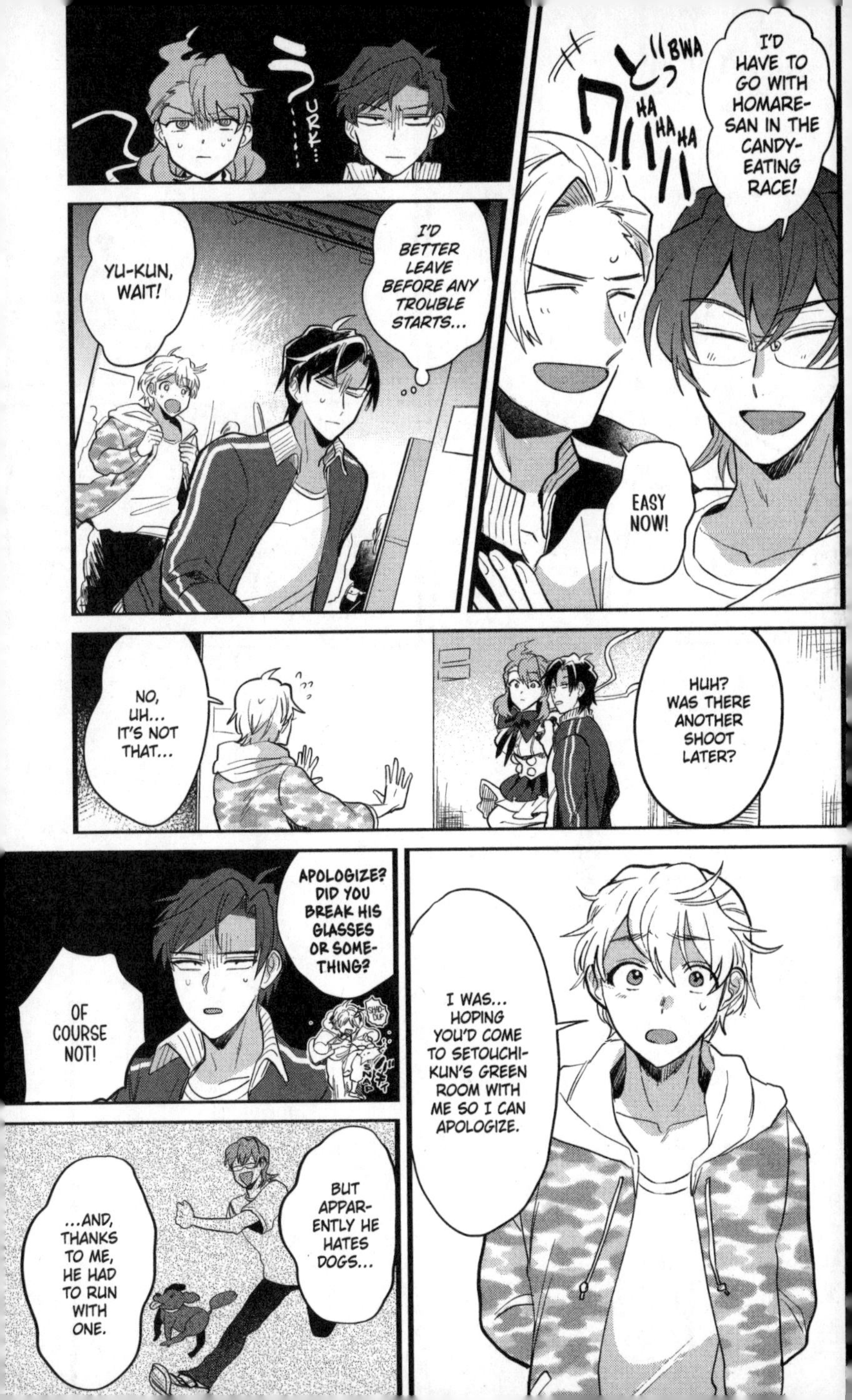
I'D HAVE TO GO WITH HOMARE-SAN IN THE CANDY-EATING RACE!
BWA HA HA HA
EASY NOW!
URK...
I'D BETTER LEAVE BEFORE ANY TROUBLE STARTS...
YU-KUN, WAIT!
HUH? WAS THERE ANOTHER SHOOT LATER?
NO, UH... IT'S NOT THAT...
I WAS... HOPING YOU'D COME TO SETOUCHI-KUN'S GREEN ROOM WITH ME SO I CAN APOLOGIZE.
APOLOGIZE? DID YOU BREAK HIS GLASSES OR SOME-THING?
OF COURSE NOT!
BUT APPAR-ENTLY HE HATES DOGS...
...AND, THANKS TO ME, HE HAD TO RUN WITH ONE.

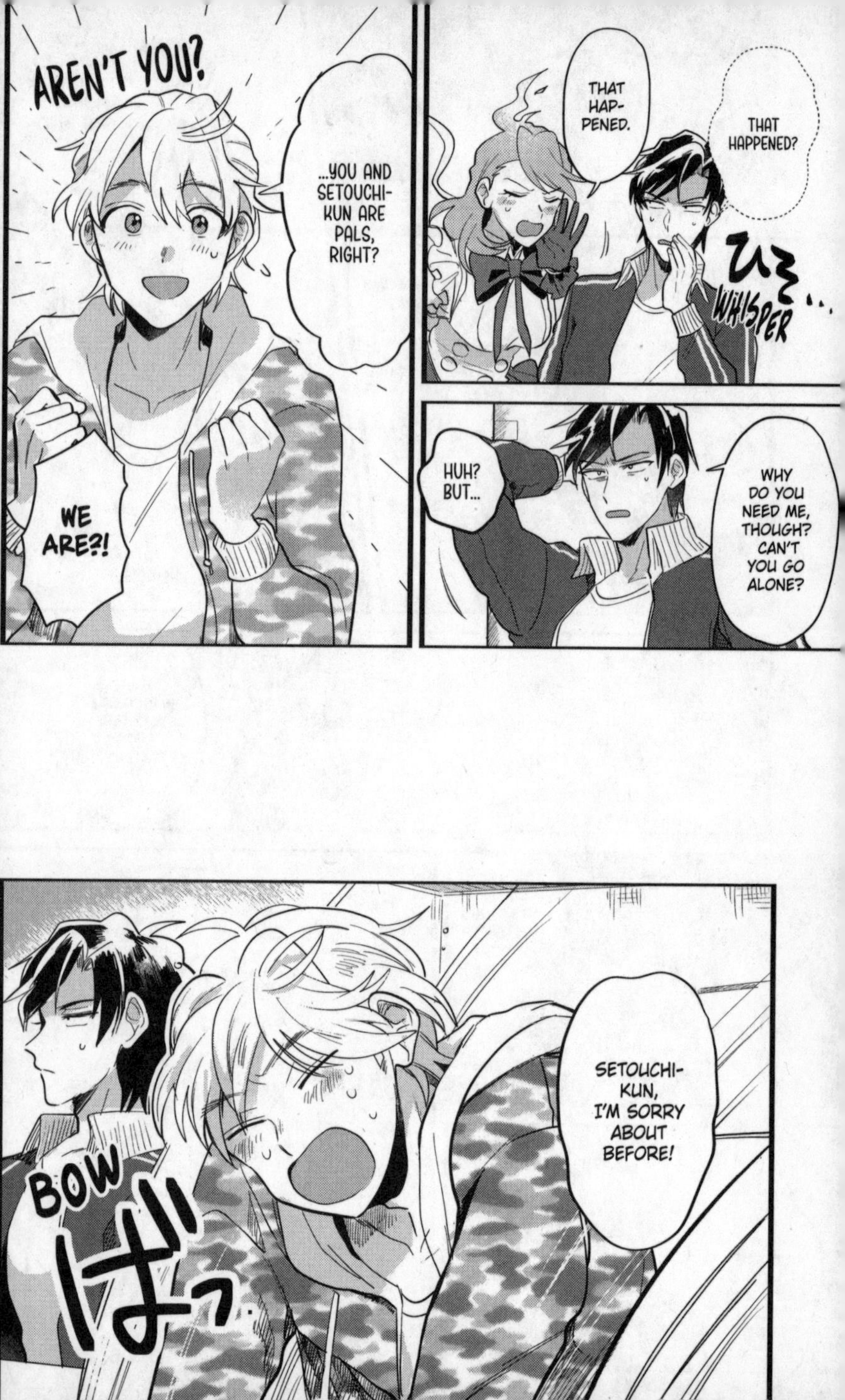
THAT HAP-PENED.
THAT HAPPENED?
ひそ…
WHISPER
WHY DO YOU NEED ME, THOUGH? CAN'T YOU GO ALONE?
HUH? BUT...
...YOU AND SETOUCHI-KUN ARE PALS, RIGHT?
AREN'T YOU?
WE ARE?!
SETOUCHI-KUN, I'M SORRY ABOUT BEFORE!
BOW
ばっ

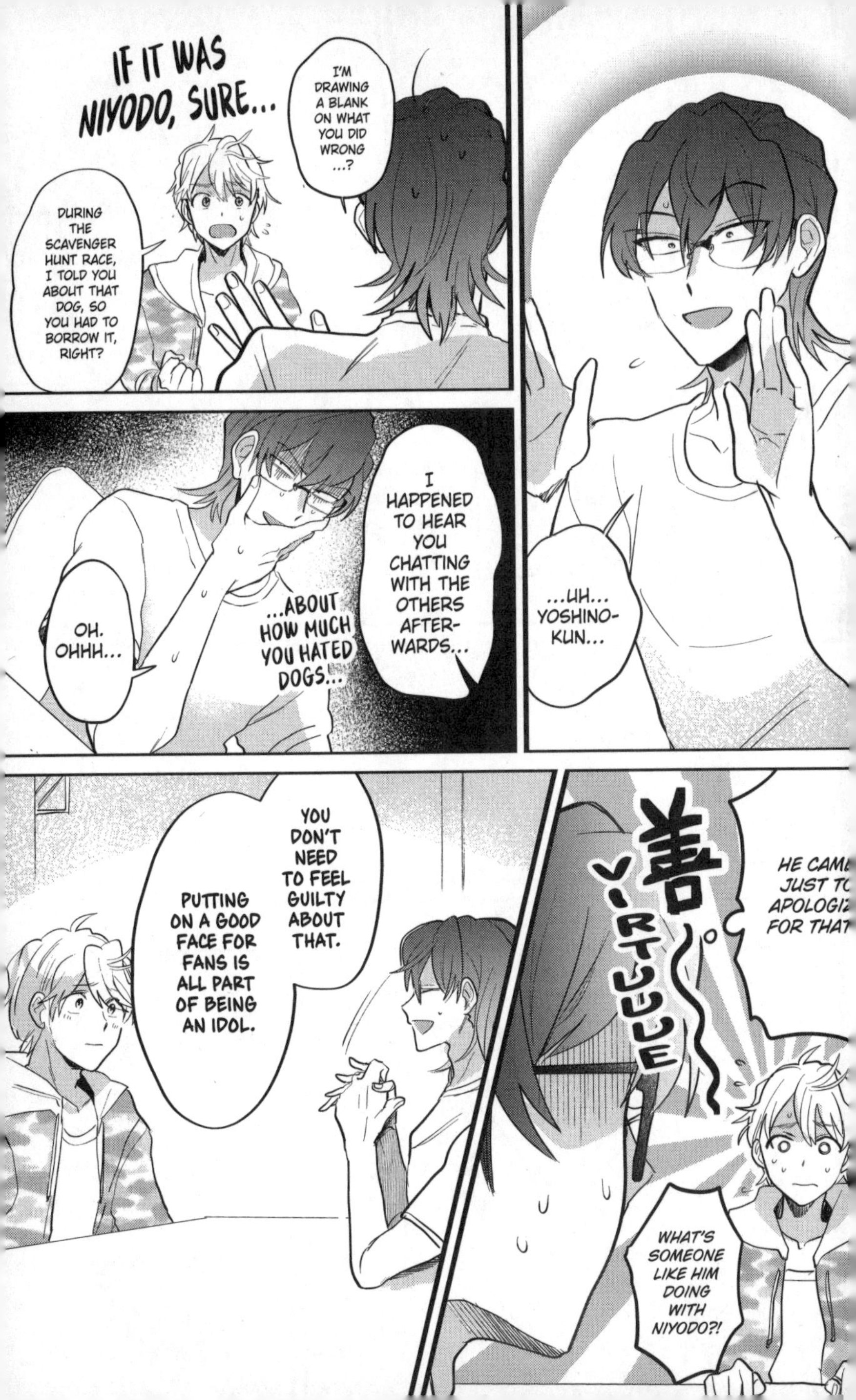
...UH... YOSHINO-KUN...
I'M DRAWING A BLANK ON WHAT YOU DID WRONG ...?
IF IT WAS NIYODO, SURE...
DURING THE SCAVENGER HUNT RACE, I TOLD YOU ABOUT THAT DOG, SO YOU HAD TO BORROW IT, RIGHT?
I HAPPENED TO HEAR YOU CHATTING WITH THE OTHERS AFTER-WARDS...
...ABOUT HOW MUCH YOU HATED DOGS...
OH. OHHH...
善 VIRTUE
HE CAME JUST TO APOLOGIZ FOR THAT
WHAT'S SOMEONE LIKE HIM DOING WITH NIYODO?!
YOU DON'T NEED TO FEEL GUILTY ABOUT THAT.
PUTTING ON A GOOD FACE FOR FANS IS ALL PART OF BEING AN IDOL.

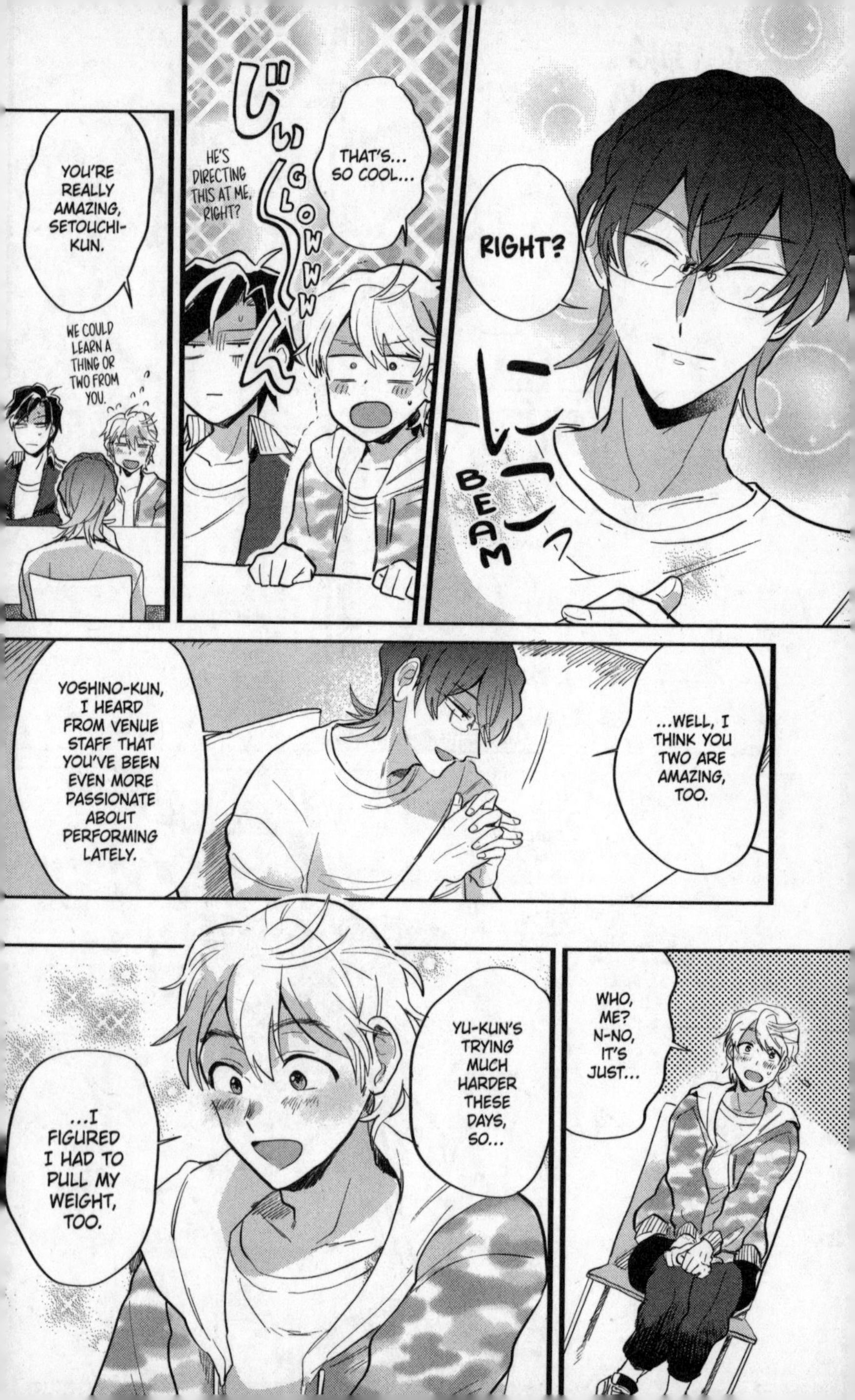
RIGHT?
BEAM
THAT'S... SO COOL...
HE'S DIRECTING THIS AT ME, RIGHT?
GLOWWW
YOU'RE REALLY AMAZING, SETOUCHI-KUN.
WE COULD LEARN A THING OR TWO FROM YOU.
...WELL, I THINK YOU TWO ARE AMAZING, TOO.
YOSHINO-KUN, I HEARD FROM VENUE STAFF THAT YOU'VE BEEN EVEN MORE PASSIONATE ABOUT PERFORMING LATELY.
WHO, ME? N-NO, IT'S JUST...
YU-KUN'S TRYING MUCH HARDER THESE DAYS, SO...
...I FIGURED I HAD TO PULL MY WEIGHT, TOO.

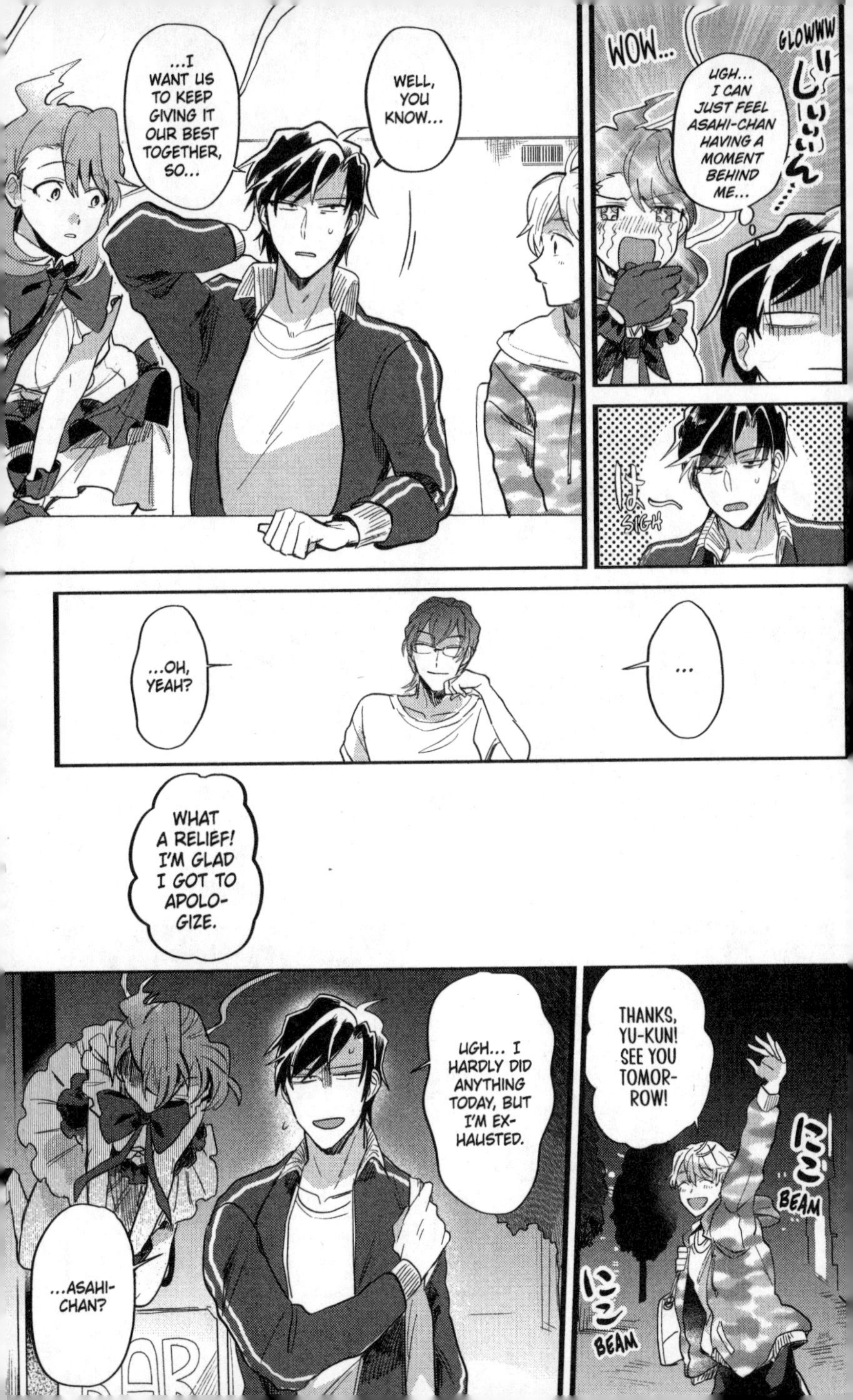
WOW...
GLOWWW
UGH... I CAN JUST FEEL ASAHI-CHAN HAVING A MOMENT BEHIND ME...
はー
SIGH
WELL, YOU KNOW...
...I WANT US TO KEEP GIVING IT OUR BEST TOGETHER, SO...
...
...OH, YEAH?
WHAT A RELIEF! I'M GLAD I GOT TO APOLO-GIZE.
THANKS, YU-KUN! SEE YOU TOMOR-ROW!
にこ
BEAM
にこ
BEAM
UGH... I HARDLY DID ANYTHING TODAY, BUT I'M EX-HAUSTED.
...ASAHI-CHAN?

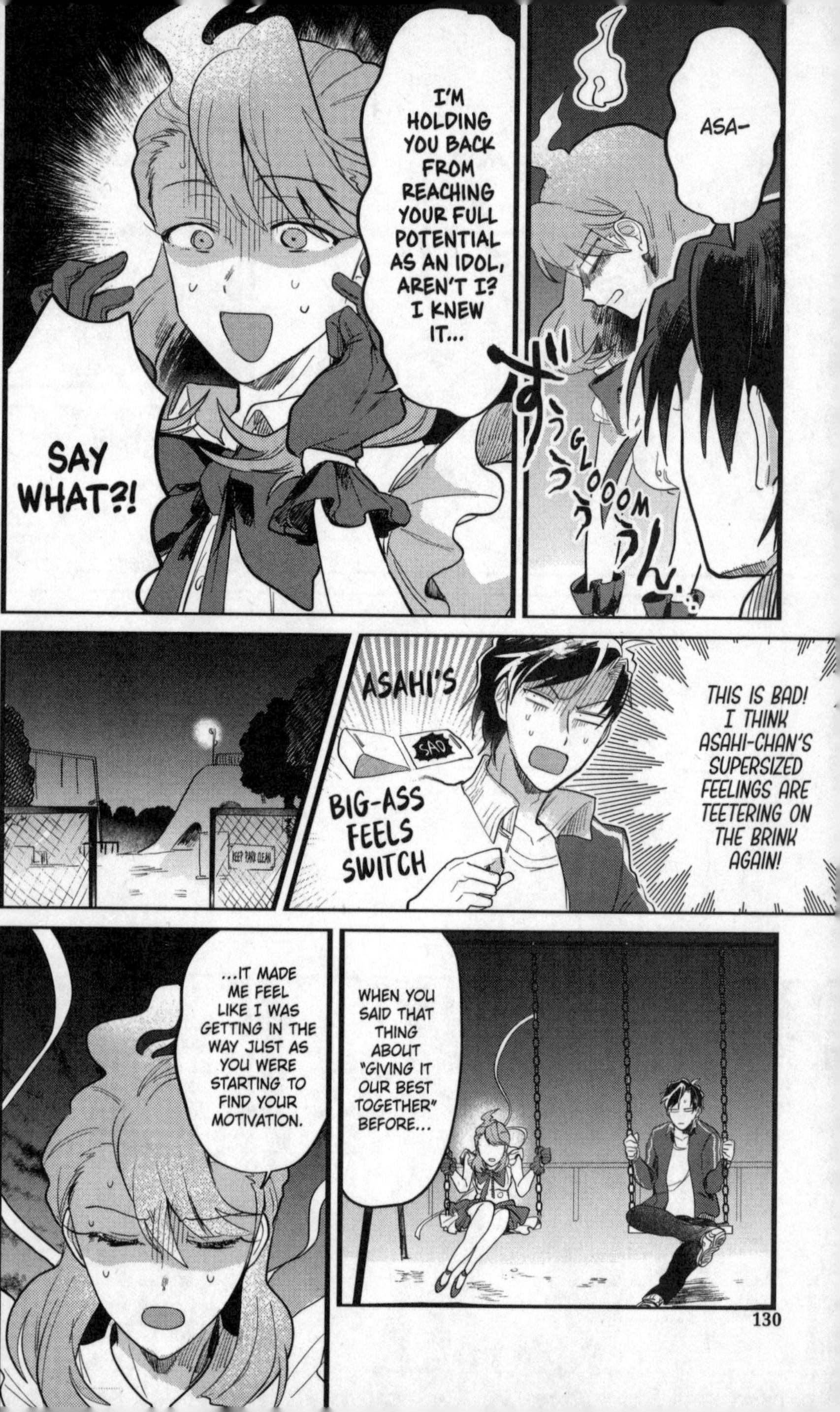

ASA-
GLOOOM
I'M HOLDING YOU BACK FROM REACHING YOUR FULL POTENTIAL AS AN IDOL, AREN'T I? I KNEW IT...
SAY WHAT?!
THIS IS BAD! I THINK ASAHI-CHAN'S SUPERSIZED FEELINGS ARE TEETERING ON THE BRINK AGAIN!
ASAHI'S BIG-ASS FEELS SWITCH
KEEP PARK CLEAN
WHEN YOU SAID THAT THING ABOUT "GIVING IT OUR BEST TOGETHER" BEFORE...
...IT MADE ME FEEL LIKE I WAS GETTING IN THE WAY JUST AS YOU WERE STARTING TO FIND YOUR MOTIVATION.

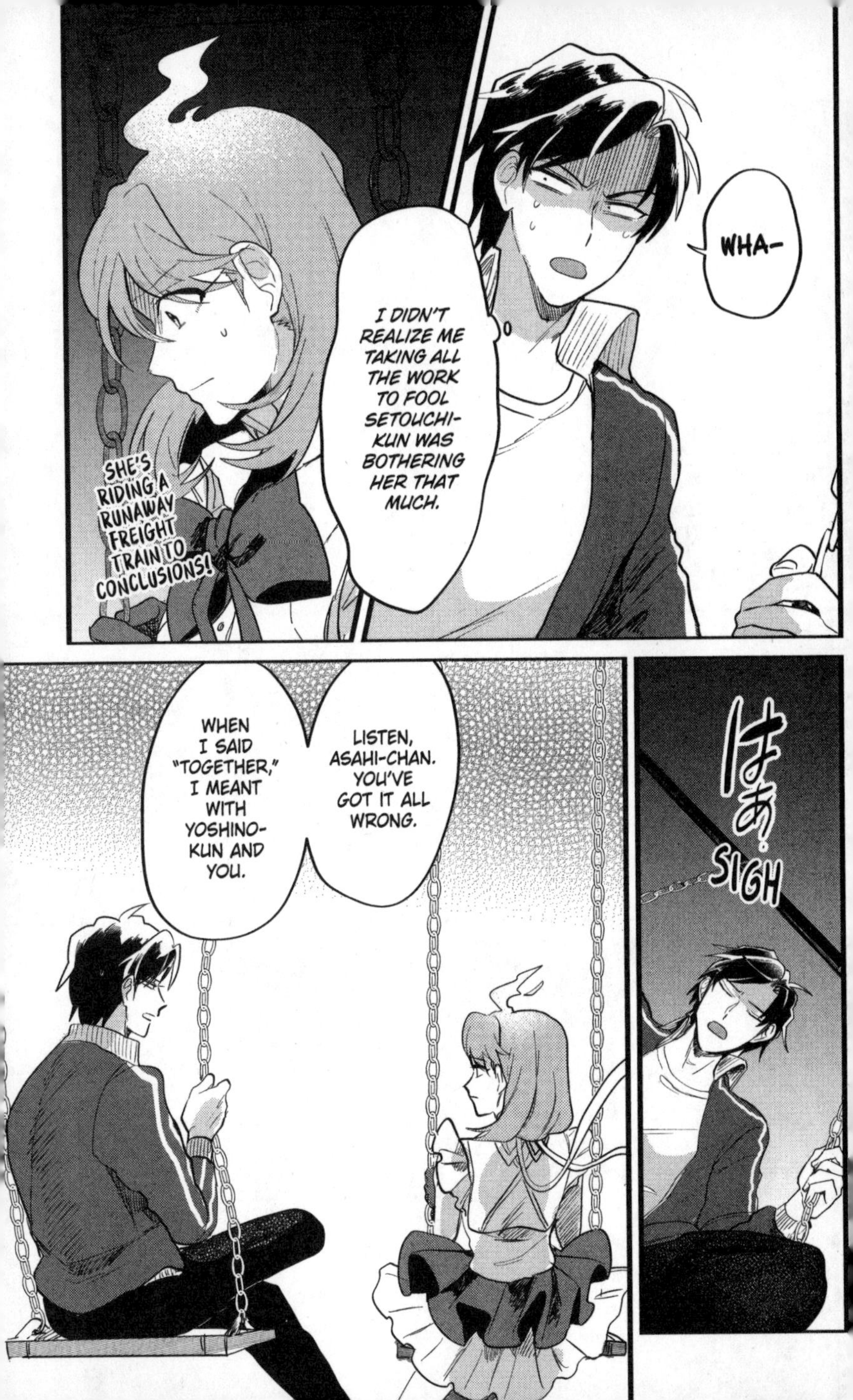
WHA-
I DIDN'T REALIZE ME TAKING ALL THE WORK TO FOOL SETOUCHI-KUN WAS BOTHERING HER THAT MUCH.
SHE'S RIDING A RUNAWAY FREIGHT TRAIN TO CONCLUSIONS!
はあ
SIGH
LISTEN, ASAHI-CHAN. YOU'VE GOT IT ALL WRONG.
WHEN I SAID "TOGETHER," I MEANT WITH YOSHINO-KUN AND YOU.

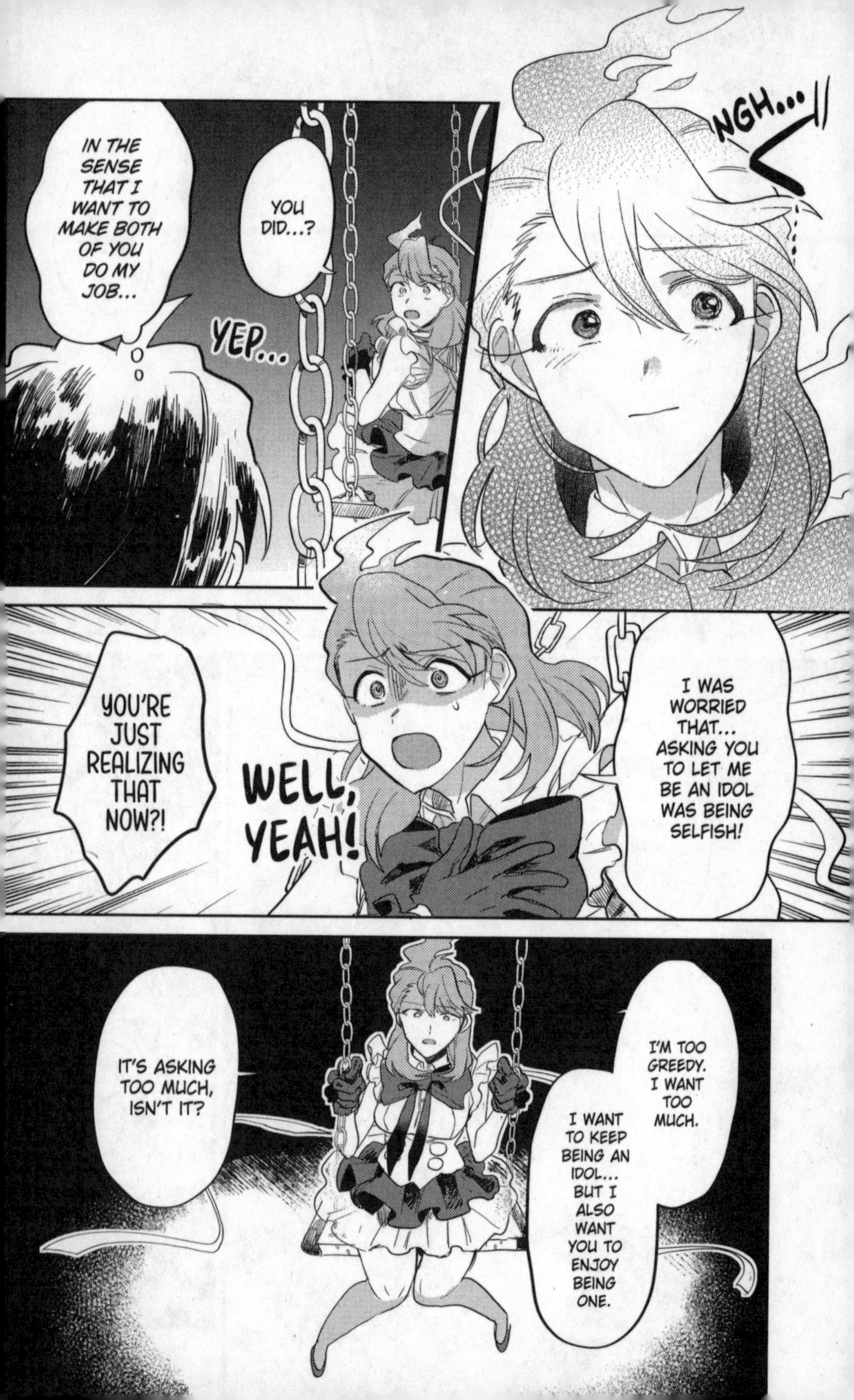
NGH...
YOU DID...?
IN THE SENSE THAT I WANT TO MAKE BOTH OF YOU DO MY JOB...
YEP...
I WAS WORRIED THAT... ASKING YOU TO LET ME BE AN IDOL WAS BEING SELFISH!
WELL, YEAH!
YOU'RE JUST REALIZING THAT NOW?!
I'M TOO GREEDY. I WANT TOO MUCH.
I WANT TO KEEP BEING AN IDOL... BUT I ALSO WANT YOU TO ENJOY BEING ONE.
IT'S ASKING TOO MUCH, ISN'T IT?

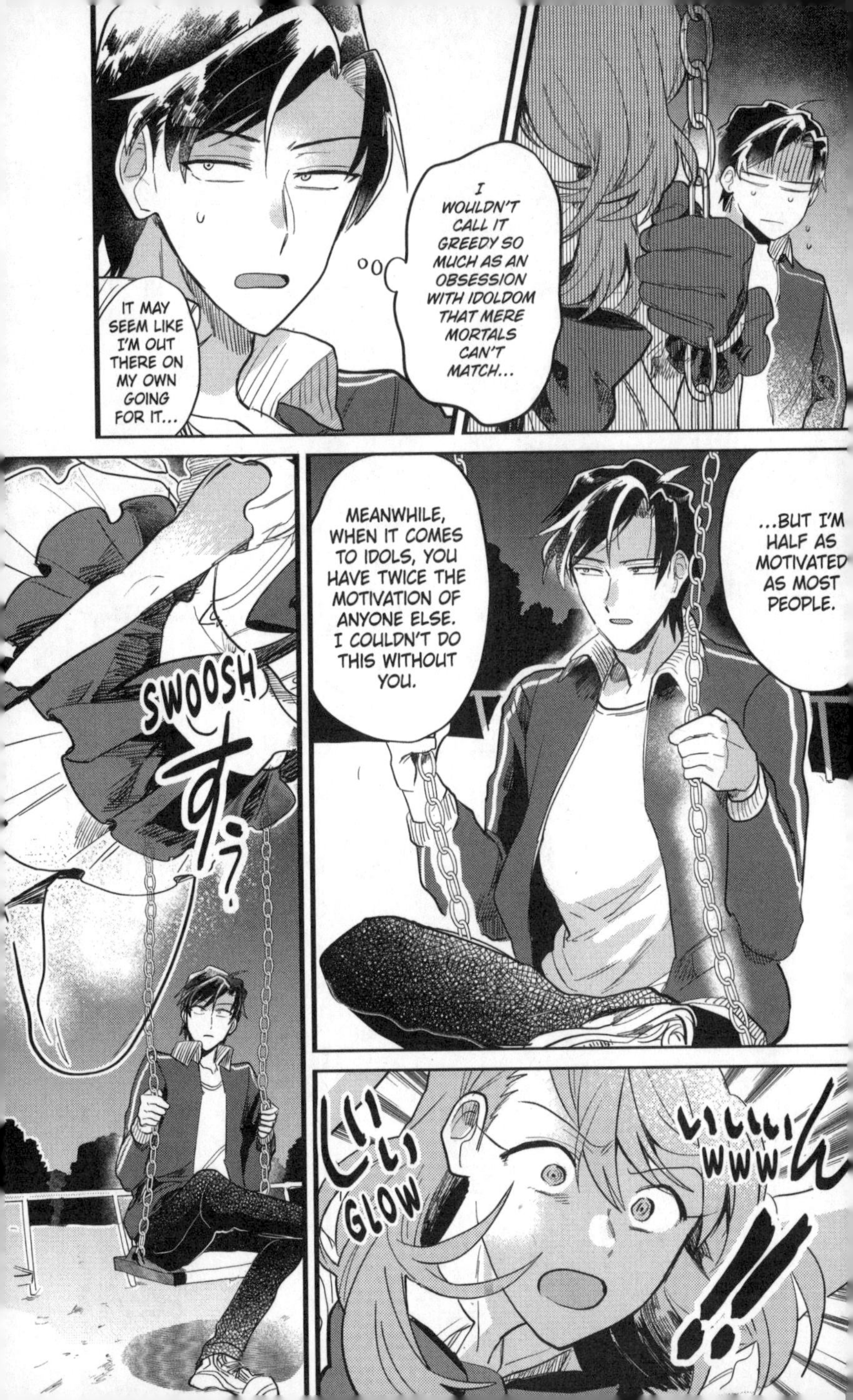
I WOULDN'T CALL IT GREEDY SO MUCH AS AN OBSESSION WITH IDOLDOM THAT MERE MORTALS CAN'T MATCH…
IT MAY SEEM LIKE I'M OUT THERE ON MY OWN GOING FOR IT…
…BUT I'M HALF AS MOTIVATED AS MOST PEOPLE.
MEANWHILE, WHEN IT COMES TO IDOLS, YOU HAVE TWICE THE MOTIVATION OF ANYONE ELSE. I COULDN'T DO THIS WITHOUT YOU.
GLOW
WWW
SWOOSH

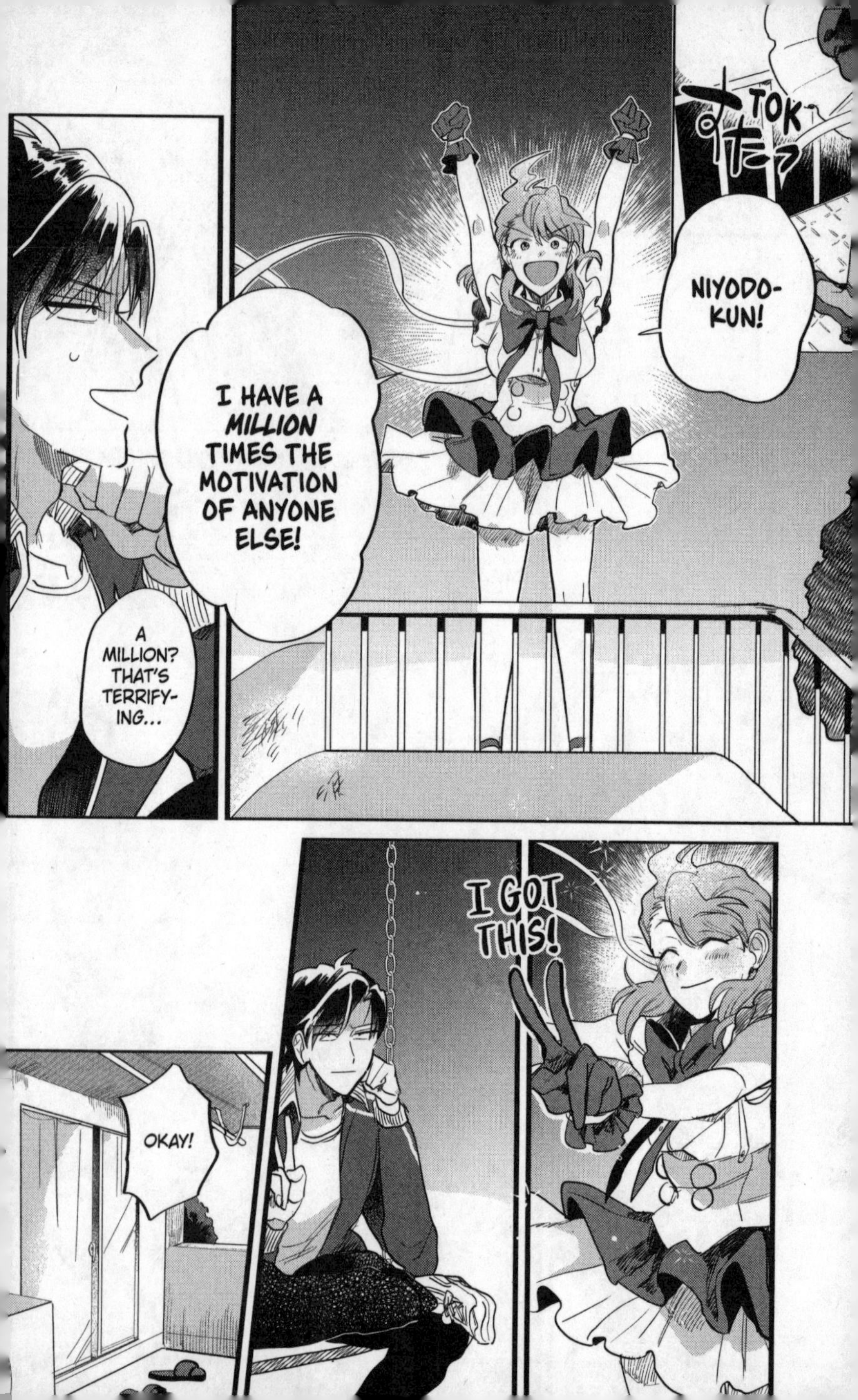
TOK
NIYODO-KUN!
I HAVE A *MILLION* TIMES THE MOTIVATION OF ANYONE ELSE!
A MILLION? THAT'S TERRIFYING...
I GOT THIS!
OKAY!

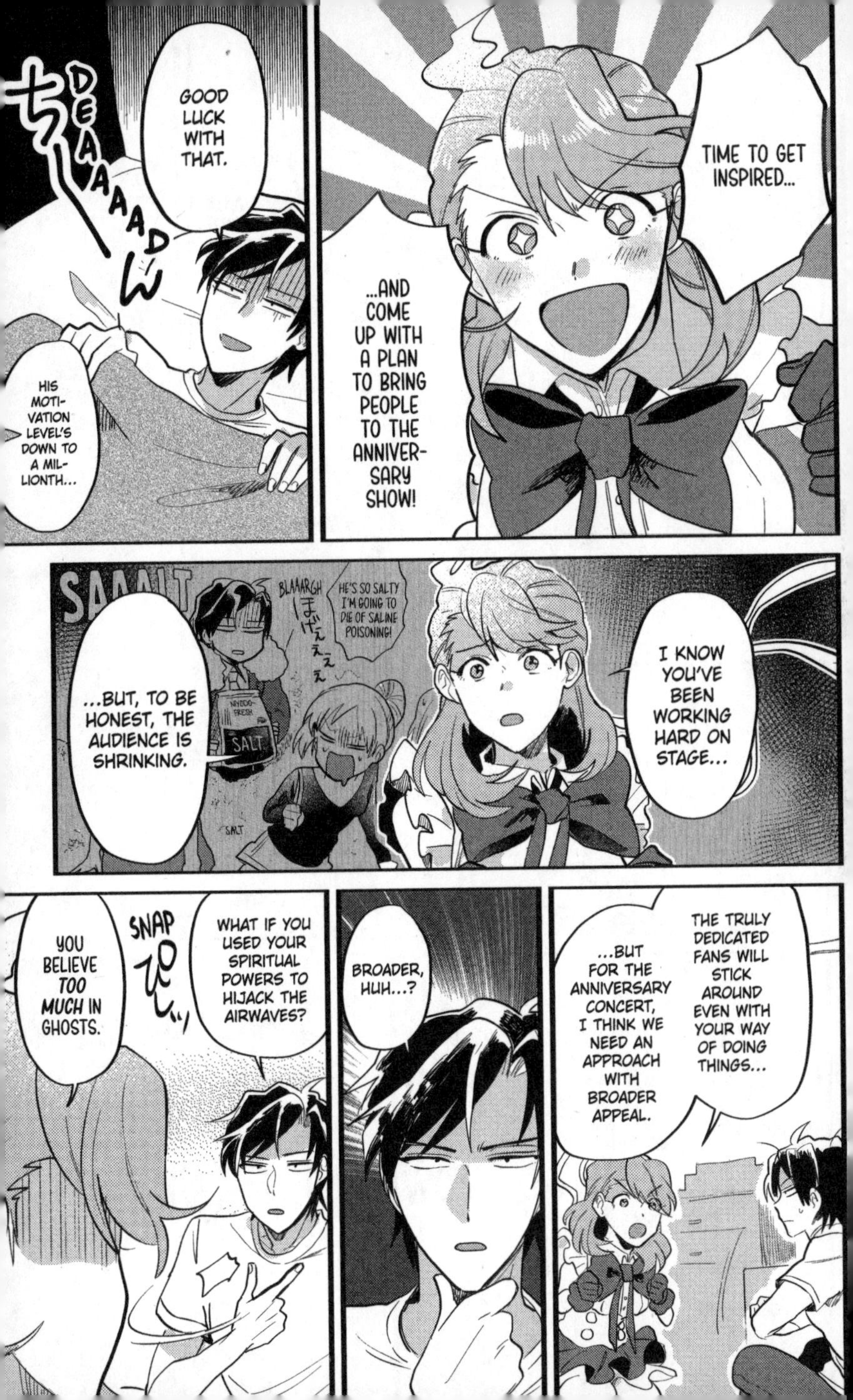
TIME TO GET INSPIRED...
...AND COME UP WITH A PLAN TO BRING PEOPLE TO THE ANNIVERSARY SHOW!
GOOD LUCK WITH THAT.
DEAAAAADW
ち
HIS MOTIVATION LEVEL'S DOWN TO A MILLIONTH...
I KNOW YOU'VE BEEN WORKING HARD ON STAGE...
...BUT, TO BE HONEST, THE AUDIENCE IS SHRINKING.
HE'S SO SALTY I'M GOING TO DIE OF SALINE POISONING!
BLAAARGH
SAAALT
NIYODO FRESH
SALT
SALT
THE TRULY DEDICATED FANS WILL STICK AROUND EVEN WITH YOUR WAY OF DOING THINGS...
...BUT FOR THE ANNIVERSARY CONCERT, I THINK WE NEED AN APPROACH WITH BROADER APPEAL.
BROADER, HUH...?
WHAT IF YOU USED YOUR SPIRITUAL POWERS TO HIJACK THE AIRWAVES?
SNAP
YOU BELIEVE *TOO MUCH* IN GHOSTS.

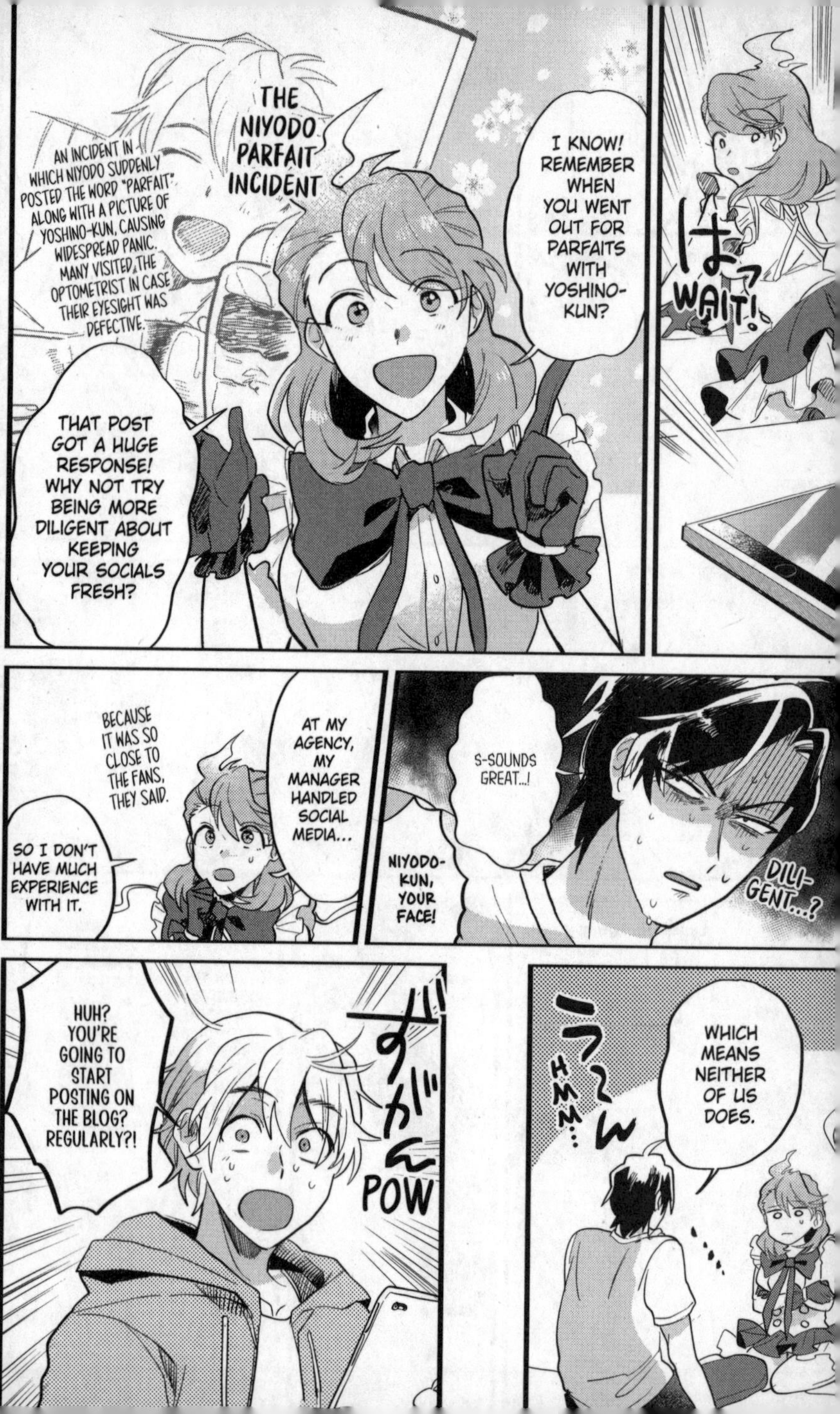
はっ
WAIT!
I KNOW! REMEMBER WHEN YOU WENT OUT FOR PARFAITS WITH YOSHINO-KUN?
THE NIYODO PARFAIT INCIDENT
AN INCIDENT IN WHICH NIYODO SUDDENLY POSTED THE WORD "PARFAIT" ALONG WITH A PICTURE OF YOSHINO-KUN, CAUSING WIDESPREAD PANIC. MANY VISITED THE OPTOMETRIST IN CASE THEIR EYESIGHT WAS DEFECTIVE.
THAT POST GOT A HUGE RESPONSE! WHY NOT TRY BEING MORE DILIGENT ABOUT KEEPING YOUR SOCIALS FRESH?
DILI-GENT...?
S-SOUNDS GREAT...!
NIYODO-KUN, YOUR FACE!
AT MY AGENCY, MY MANAGER HANDLED SOCIAL MEDIA...
BECAUSE IT WAS SO CLOSE TO THE FANS, THEY SAID.
SO I DON'T HAVE MUCH EXPERIENCE WITH IT.
うーん
HMM...
WHICH MEANS NEITHER OF US DOES.
...
ずがん
POW
HUH? YOU'RE GOING TO START POSTING ON THE BLOG? REGULARLY?!

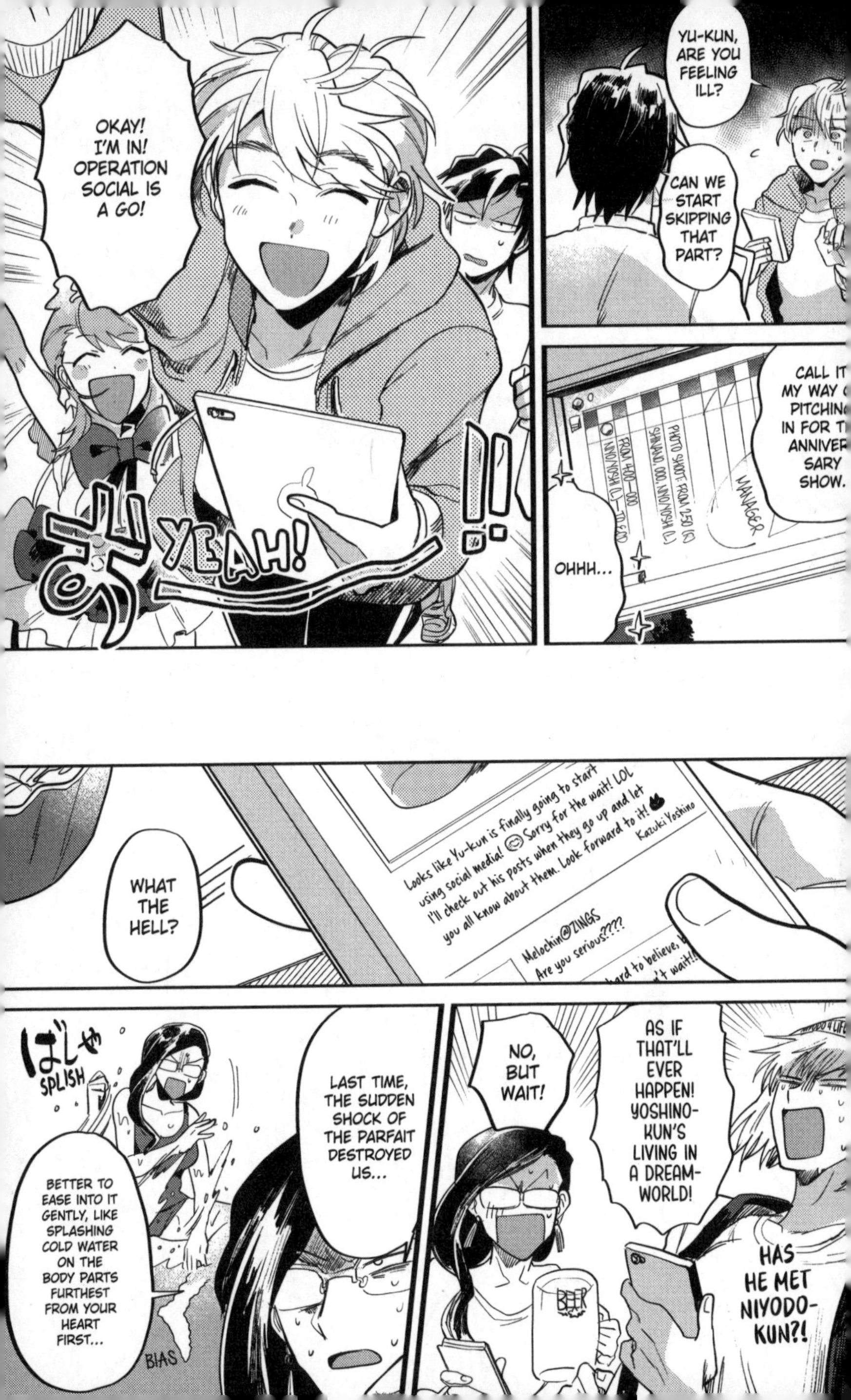
YU-KUN, ARE YOU FEELING ILL?
CAN WE START SKIPPING THAT PART?
MANAGER
OHHH...
OKAY! I'M IN! OPERATION SOCIAL IS A GO!
YEAH!!!
WHAT THE HELL?
Looks like Yu-kun is finally going to start using social media! Sorry for the wait! LOL I'll check out his posts when they go up and let you all know about them. Look forward to it!
Kazuki Yoshino
Melochin@ZINGS
Are you serious????
HAS HE MET NIYODO-KUN?!
AS IF THAT'LL EVER HAPPEN! YOSHINO-KUN'S LIVING IN A DREAM-WORLD!
NO, BUT WAIT!
BEER
LAST TIME, THE SUDDEN SHOCK OF THE PARFAIT DESTROYED US...
ばしゃ
SPLISH
BETTER TO EASE INTO IT GENTLY, LIKE SPLASHING COLD WATER ON THE BODY PARTS FURTHEST FROM YOUR HEART FIRST...
BIAS

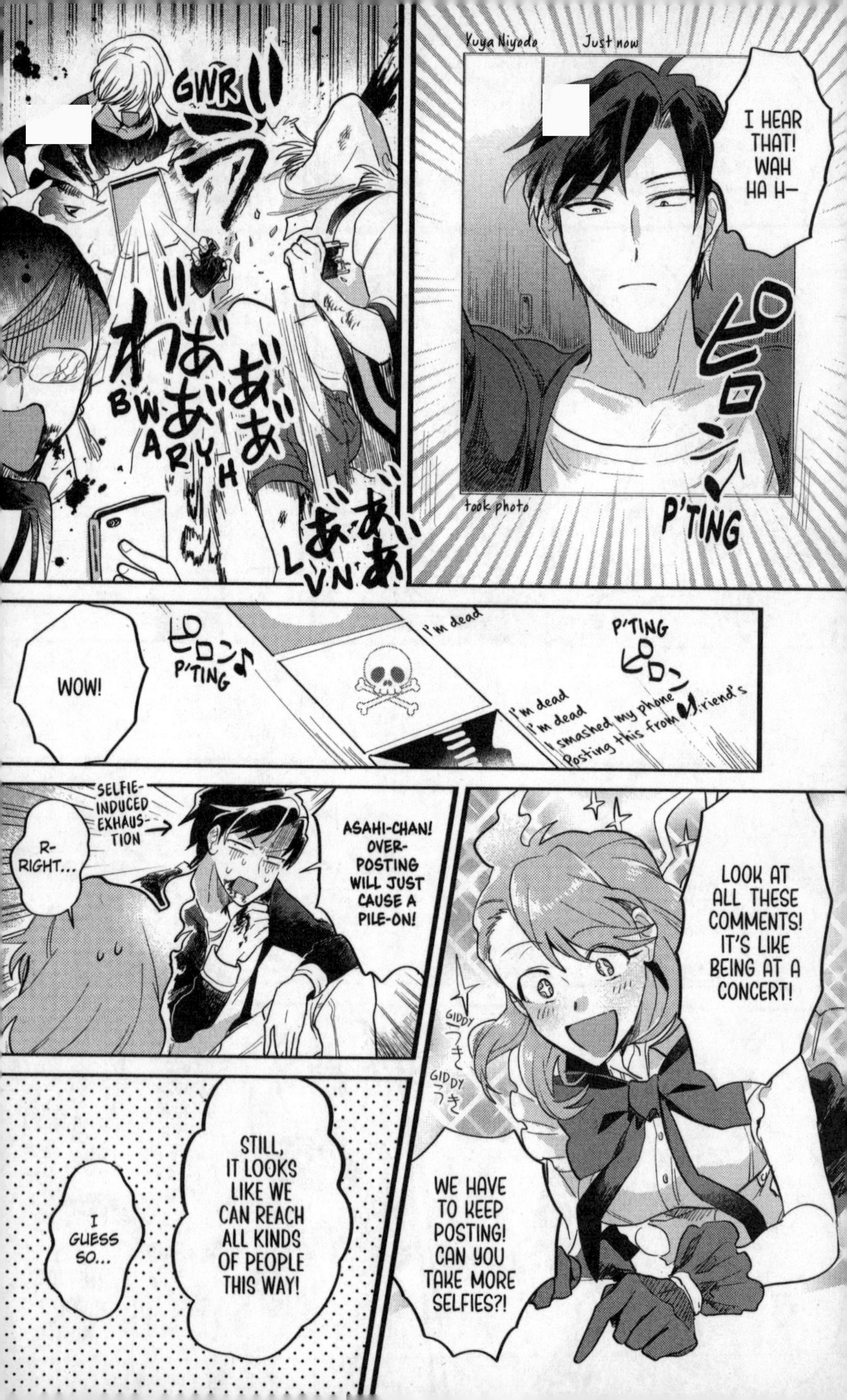

Yuya Niyodo
Just now
I HEAR THAT! WAH HA H—
ピロン♪
P'TING
took photo
GWR
わあああああ
BWARYH
あああ
LVN
P'TING
ピロン
I'm dead
I'm dead
I'm dead
smashed my phone
Posting this from riend's
ピロン♪
P'TING
WOW!
LOOK AT ALL THESE COMMENTS! IT'S LIKE BEING AT A CONCERT!
GIDDY うき
GIDDY うき
WE HAVE TO KEEP POSTING! CAN YOU TAKE MORE SELFIES?!
ASAHI-CHAN! OVER-POSTING WILL JUST CAUSE A PILE-ON!
SELFIE-INDUCED EXHAUSTION
R-RIGHT...
STILL, IT LOOKS LIKE WE CAN REACH ALL KINDS OF PEOPLE THIS WAY!
I GUESS SO...

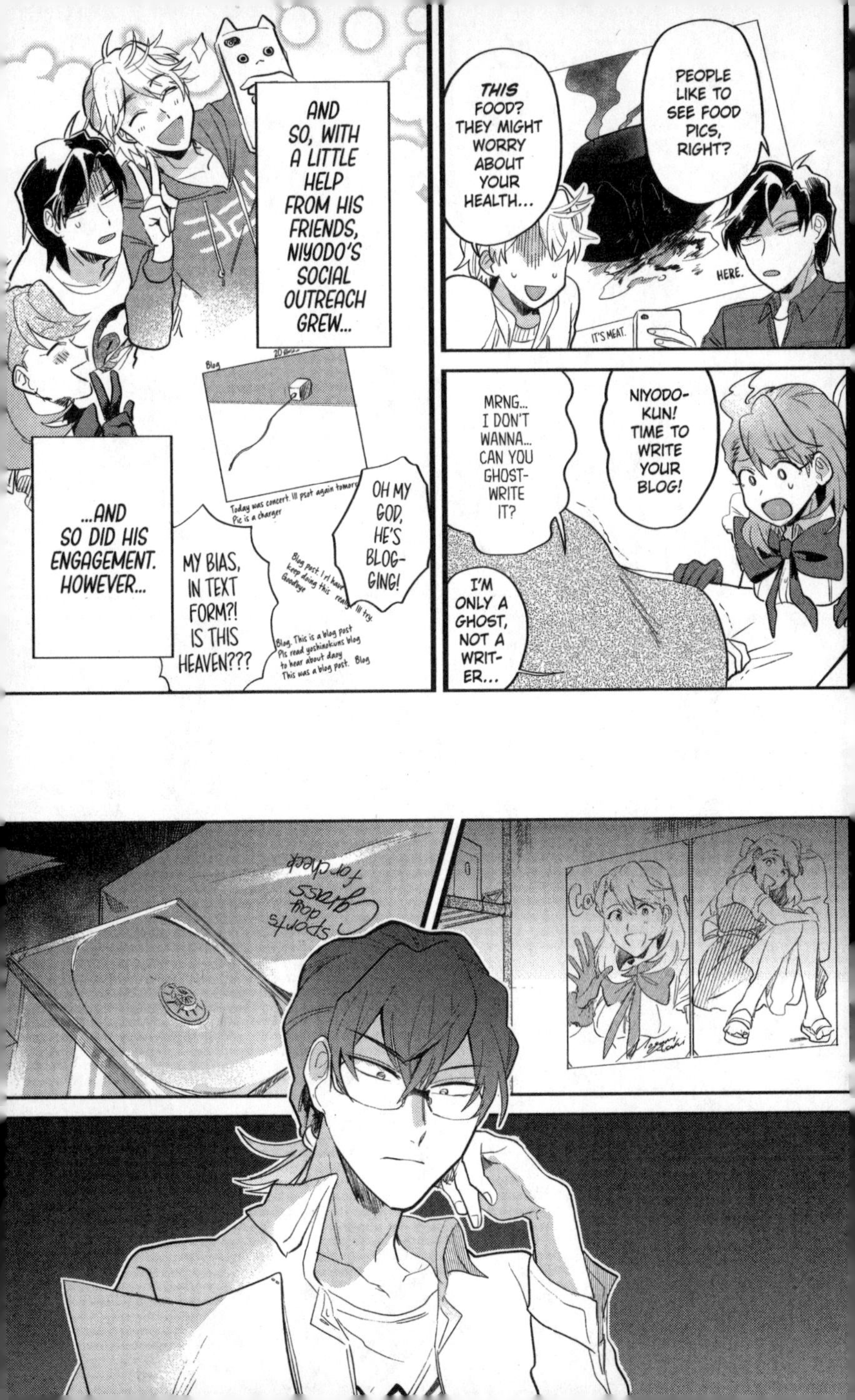
PEOPLE LIKE TO SEE FOOD PICS, RIGHT?
HERE.
IT'S MEAT.
THIS FOOD? THEY MIGHT WORRY ABOUT YOUR HEALTH...
NIYODO-KUN! TIME TO WRITE YOUR BLOG!
MRNG... I DON'T WANNA... CAN YOU GHOST-WRITE IT?
I'M ONLY A GHOST, NOT A WRITER...
AND SO, WITH A LITTLE HELP FROM HIS FRIENDS, NIYODO'S SOCIAL OUTREACH GREW...
Blog
Today was concert. Ill psot again tomor
Pic is a charger
OH MY GOD, HE'S BLOGGING!
Blog post. I rl have keep doing this really Ill try. Goodbye
MY BIAS, IN TEXT FORM?! IS THIS HEAVEN???
Blog. This is a blog post Pls read yoshinokuns blog to hear about daoy This was a blog post. Blog
...AND SO DID HIS ENGAGEMENT. HOWEVER...

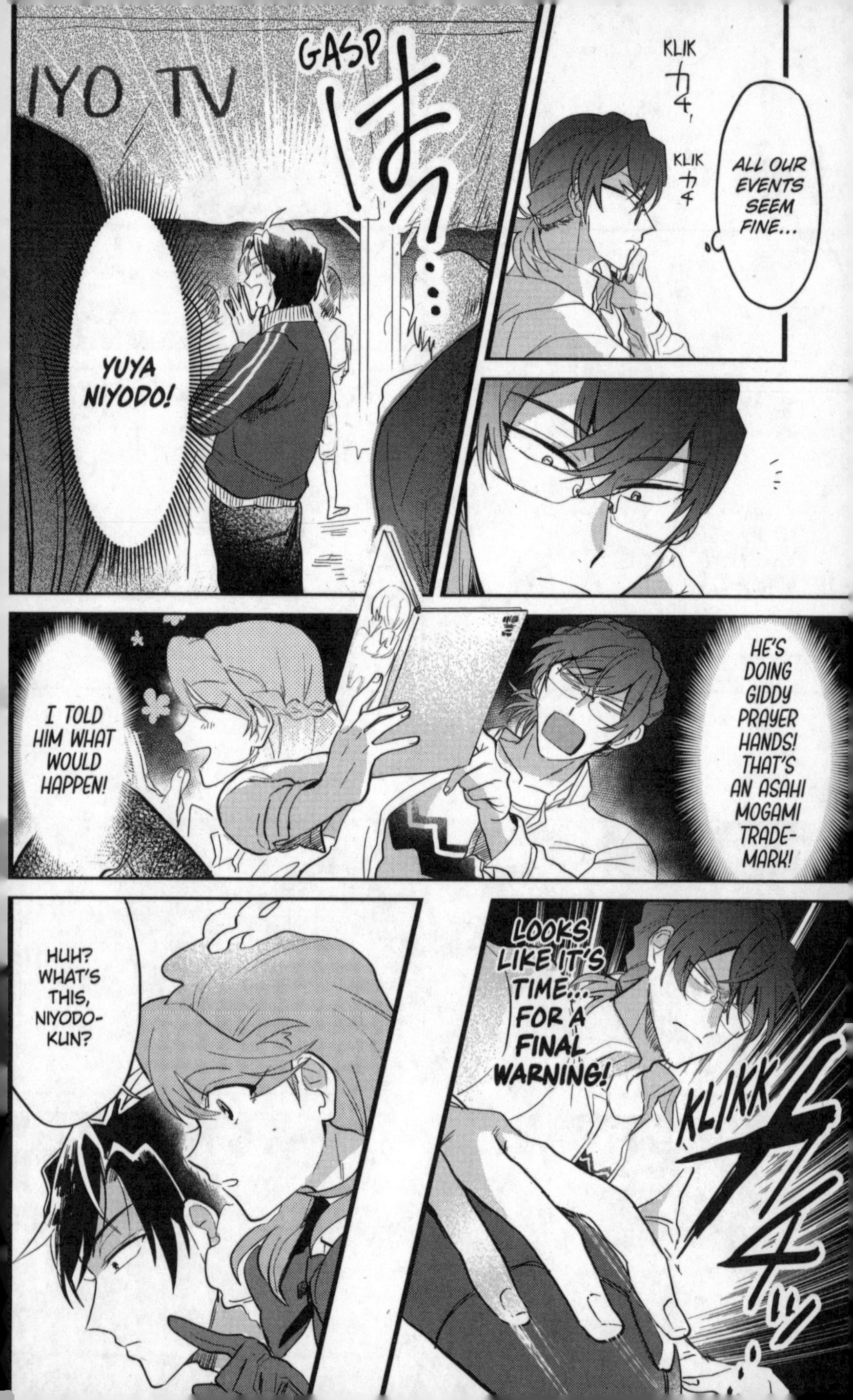
KLIK
KLIK
ALL OUR EVENTS SEEM FINE...
IYO TV
GASP
YUYA NIYODO!
HE'S DOING GIDDY PRAYER HANDS! THAT'S AN ASAHI MOGAMI TRADE-MARK!
I TOLD HIM WHAT WOULD HAPPEN!
LOOKS LIKE IT'S TIME... FOR A FINAL WARNING!
KLIKK
HUH? WHAT'S THIS, NIYODO-KUN?

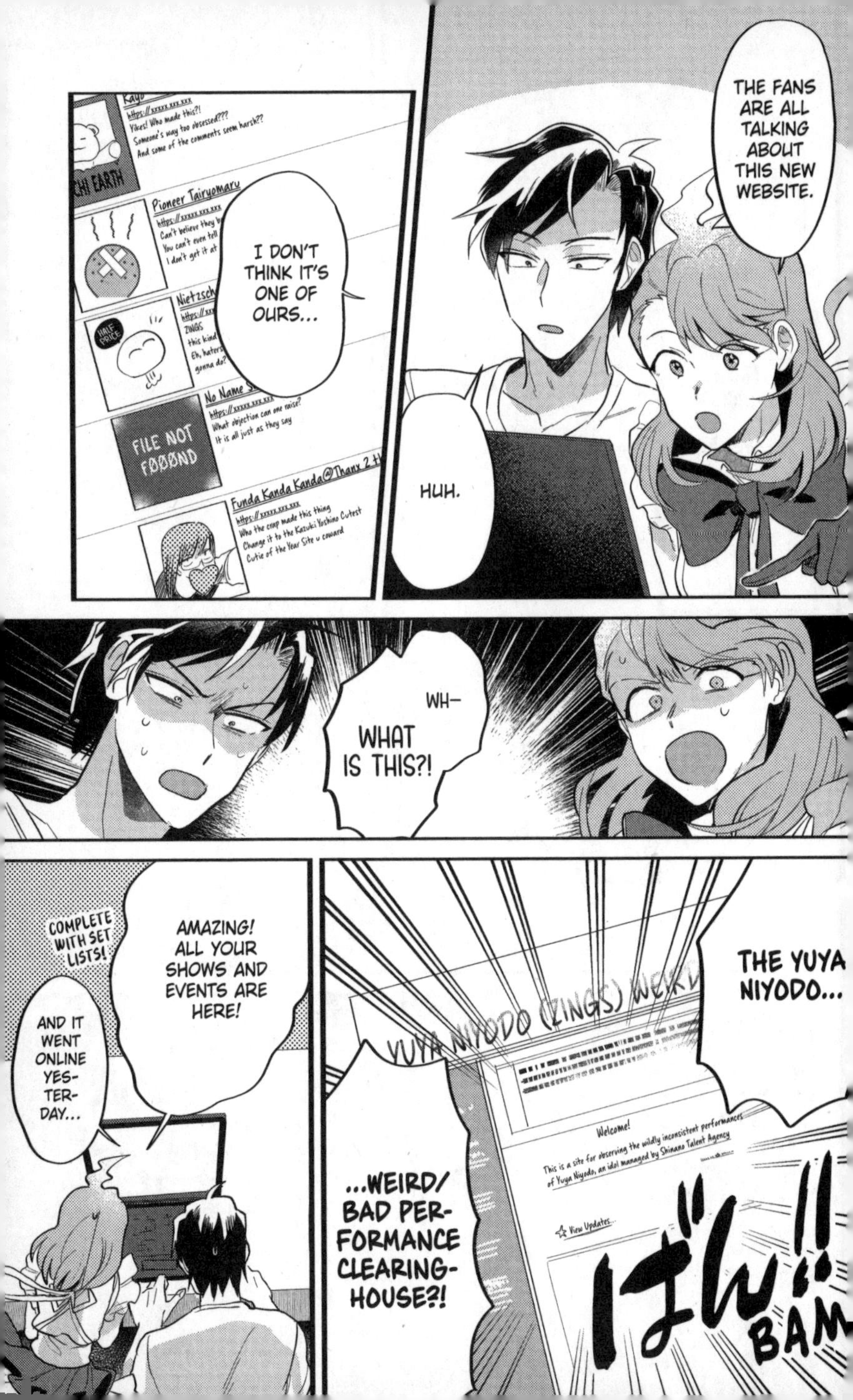
THE FANS ARE ALL TALKING ABOUT THIS NEW WEBSITE.
HUH.
Kayo
https://xxxxx.xxx.xxx
Yikes! Who made this?!
Someone's way too obsessed???
And some of the comments seem harsh??
Pioneer Tairyomaru
https://xxxxx.xxx.xxx
Can't believe they b
You can't even tell
I don't get it at
Nietzsch
ZINGS
this kind
Eh, haters
gonna do?
HALF PRICE
No Name S
https://xxxxx.xxx.xxx
What objection can one raise?
It is all just as they say
FILE NOT FØØØND
Funda Kanda Kanda@Thanx 2 H
https://xxxxx.xxx.xxx
Who the crap made this thing
Change it to the Kazuki Yoshino Cutest
Cutie of the Year Site u coward
I DON'T THINK IT'S ONE OF OURS...
WH—
WHAT IS THIS?!
THE YUYA NIYODO...
...WEIRD/BAD PERFORMANCE CLEARINGHOUSE?!
YUYA NIYODO (ZINGS) WEIRD
Welcome!
This is a site for observing the wildly inconsistent performances of Yuya Niyodo, an idol managed by Shinano Talent Agency
☆ View Updates...
ばん!!
BAM
AMAZING! ALL YOUR SHOWS AND EVENTS ARE HERE!
COMPLETE WITH SET LISTS!
AND IT WENT ONLINE YESTERDAY...

CAREFUL USE OF QUOTATIONS FROM ARTICLES AND VIDEO LINKS TO OFFICIAL SITES ONLY, SO AS NOT TO RUN AFOUL OF THE LAW...

Entertainment Web

All images and movies on this site are official materials made available by the Shinano Talent Agency and properly embedded. Quotations are all the property of the Shinano Talent Agency. Please contact us in case of any concerns.

(0.8~)
clearly phoning it in. Motions lack symmetry and

SITE STRUCTURE DIVIDED INTO CATEGORIES FOR EASE OF VIEWING, AND SORTABLE BY DATE...

★ Stage banter fail #

∥ ∥ ∥ XX/XX/XXXX Yoisha concert ∥ ∥ ∥
Yoshino: "This is our third show at Yoisha."
Miyado: "Yes."
Yoshino: "Miyado, you have to keep the conversation going!"
Miyado: "But I don't have anything to say!"
Yoshino: "Just forget it."

BANTER ENDS!...

→ Yoisha posts
→ Banter posts

| Song 1 | XMAS | Serious face, no change of expression |
| Song 2 | RUN | Glanced offstage several times, seemingly ben... |

THE ADMIN'S JUST CALLED "MR. SCARF"

...

WHO COULD HAVE MADE SUCH A POLISHED SITE...?

RELIABLE WEBSITE DESIGN! CALL NOW FOR A CONSULTATION!

WHAT IS HIS PROBLEM?!

SETOUCHI-KUN!!!

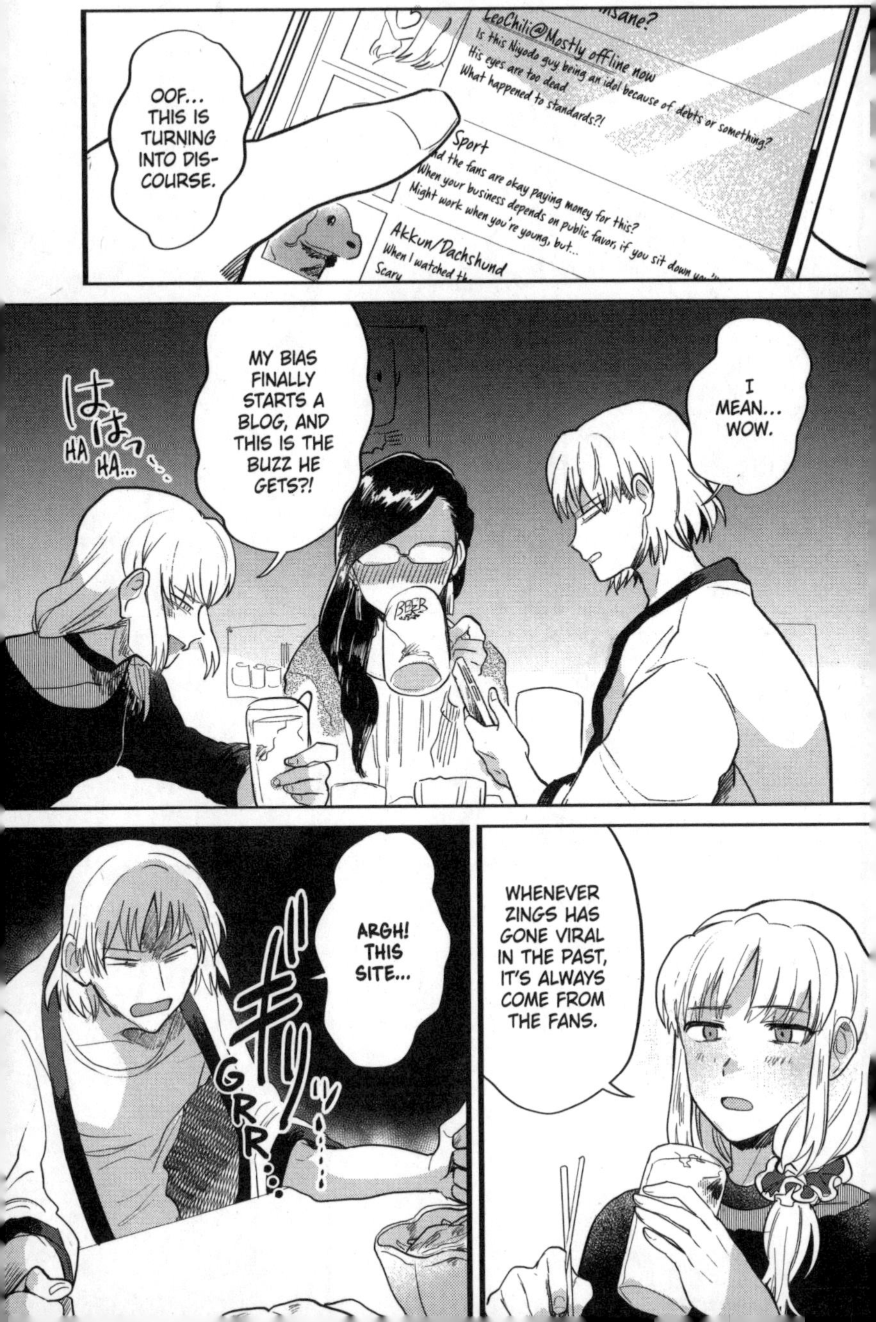
LeoChili@Mostly offline now
Is this Niyodo guy being an idol because of debts or something?
His eyes are too dead
What happened to standards?!
Sport
the fans are okay paying money for this?
When your business depends on public favor, if you sit down
Might work when you're young, but...
Akkun/Dachshund
Scary
OOF... THIS IS TURNING INTO DIS-COURSE.
I MEAN... WOW.
MY BIAS FINALLY STARTS A BLOG, AND THIS IS THE BUZZ HE GETS?!
ははっ…
HA HA...
WHENEVER ZINGS HAS GONE VIRAL IN THE PAST, IT'S ALWAYS COME FROM THE FANS.
ARGH! THIS SITE...
ギリッ
GRR...

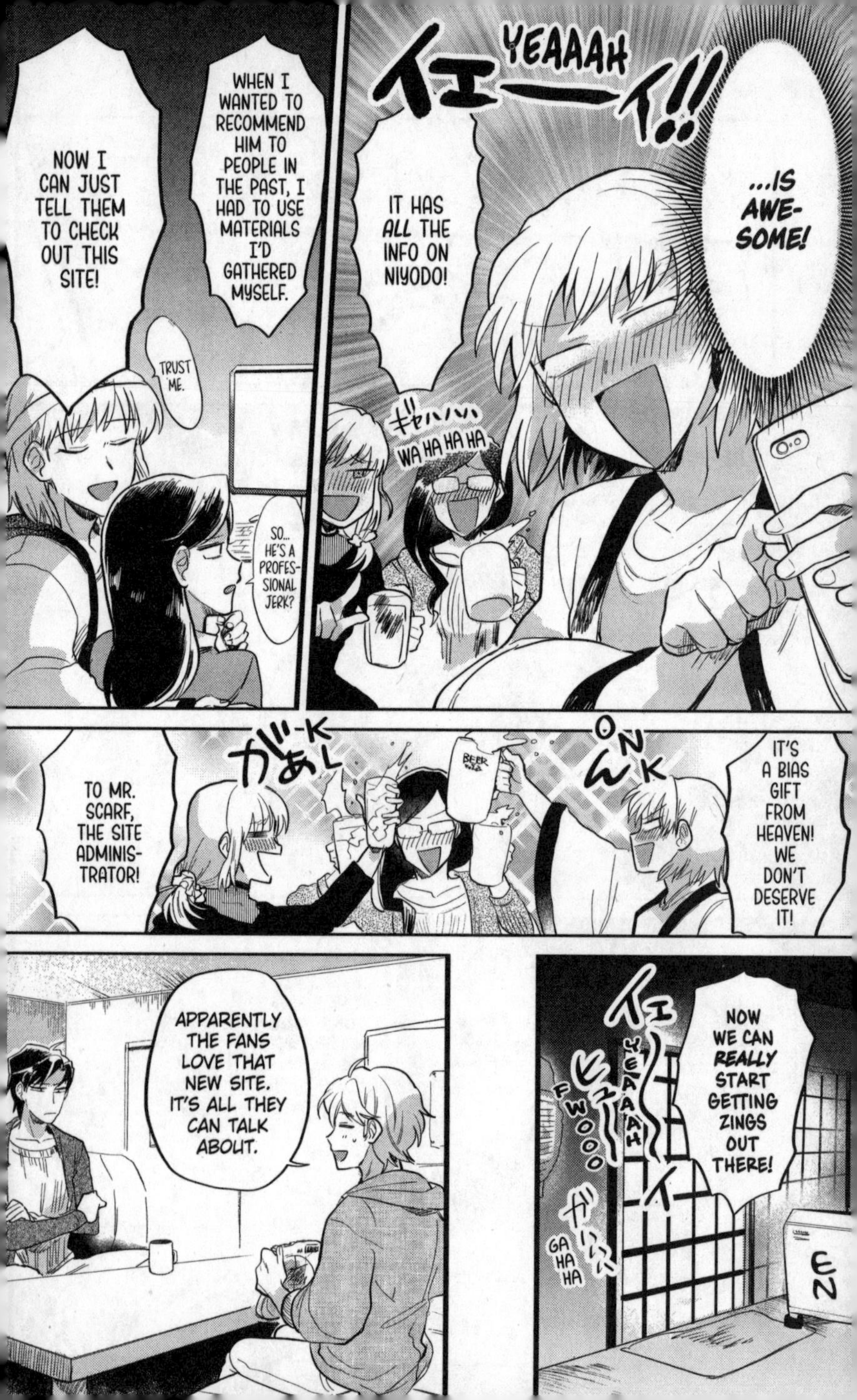
イエーーイ!!
YEAAAH
...IS AWESOME!
IT HAS ALL THE INFO ON NIYODO!
WA HA HA HA
WHEN I WANTED TO RECOMMEND HIM TO PEOPLE IN THE PAST, I HAD TO USE MATERIALS I'D GATHERED MYSELF.
NOW I CAN JUST TELL THEM TO CHECK OUT THIS SITE!
TRUST ME.
SO... HE'S A PROFESSIONAL JERK?
IT'S A BIAS GIFT FROM HEAVEN! WE DON'T DESERVE IT!
BEER
TO MR. SCARF, THE SITE ADMINISTRATOR!
NOW WE CAN REALLY START GETTING ZINGS OUT THERE!
YEAAAH
FWOOOO
GA HA HA
APPARENTLY THE FANS LOVE THAT NEW SITE. IT'S ALL THEY CAN TALK ABOUT.

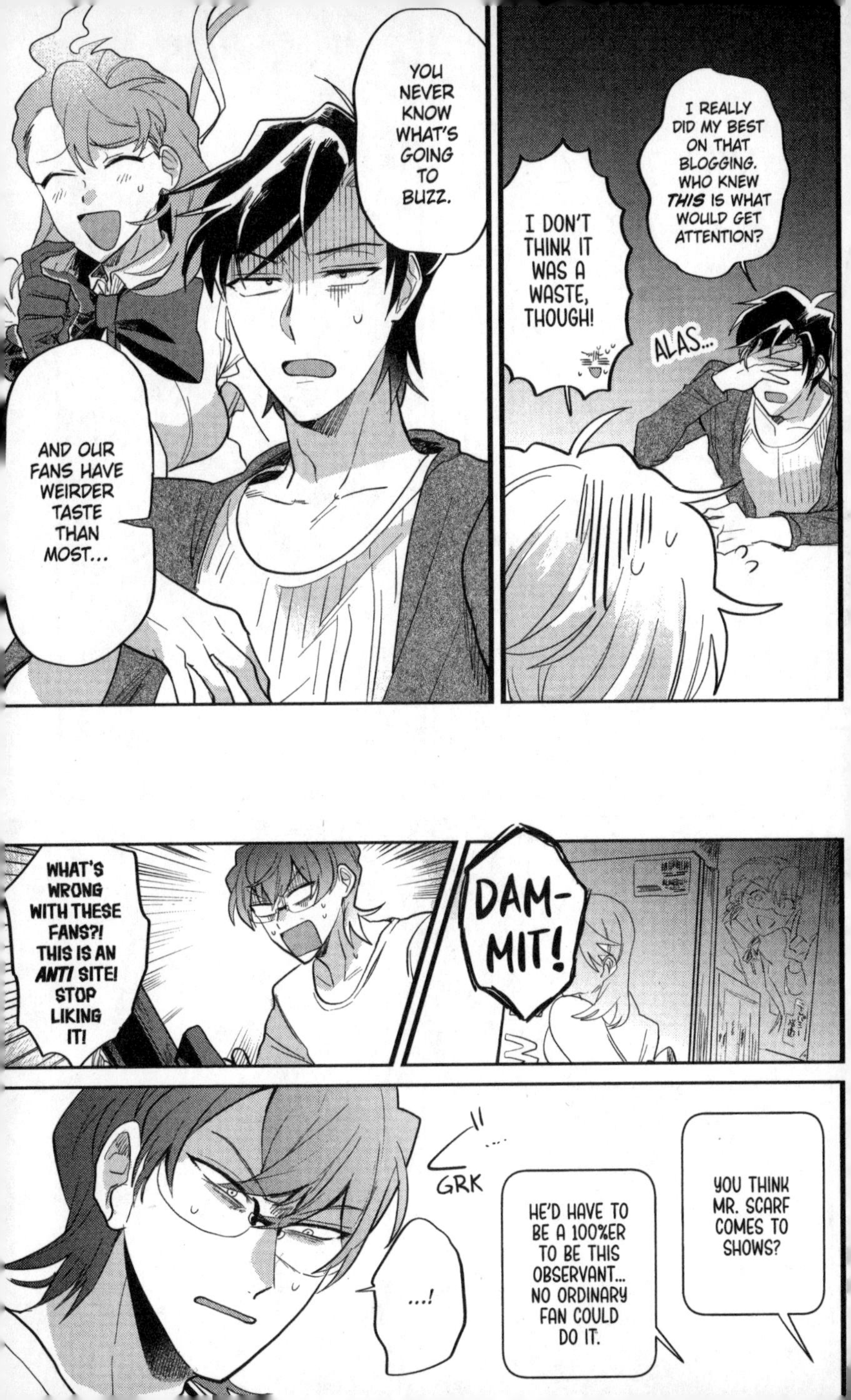
I REALLY DID MY BEST ON THAT BLOGGING. WHO KNEW *THIS* IS WHAT WOULD GET ATTENTION?
ALAS...
I DON'T THINK IT WAS A WASTE, THOUGH!
YOU NEVER KNOW WHAT'S GOING TO BUZZ.
AND OUR FANS HAVE WEIRDER TASTE THAN MOST...
DAM-MIT!
WHAT'S WRONG WITH THESE FANS?! THIS IS AN *ANTI* SITE! STOP LIKING IT!
YOU THINK MR. SCARF COMES TO SHOWS?
HE'D HAVE TO BE A 100%ER TO BE THIS OBSERVANT... NO ORDINARY FAN COULD DO IT.
GRK
...!

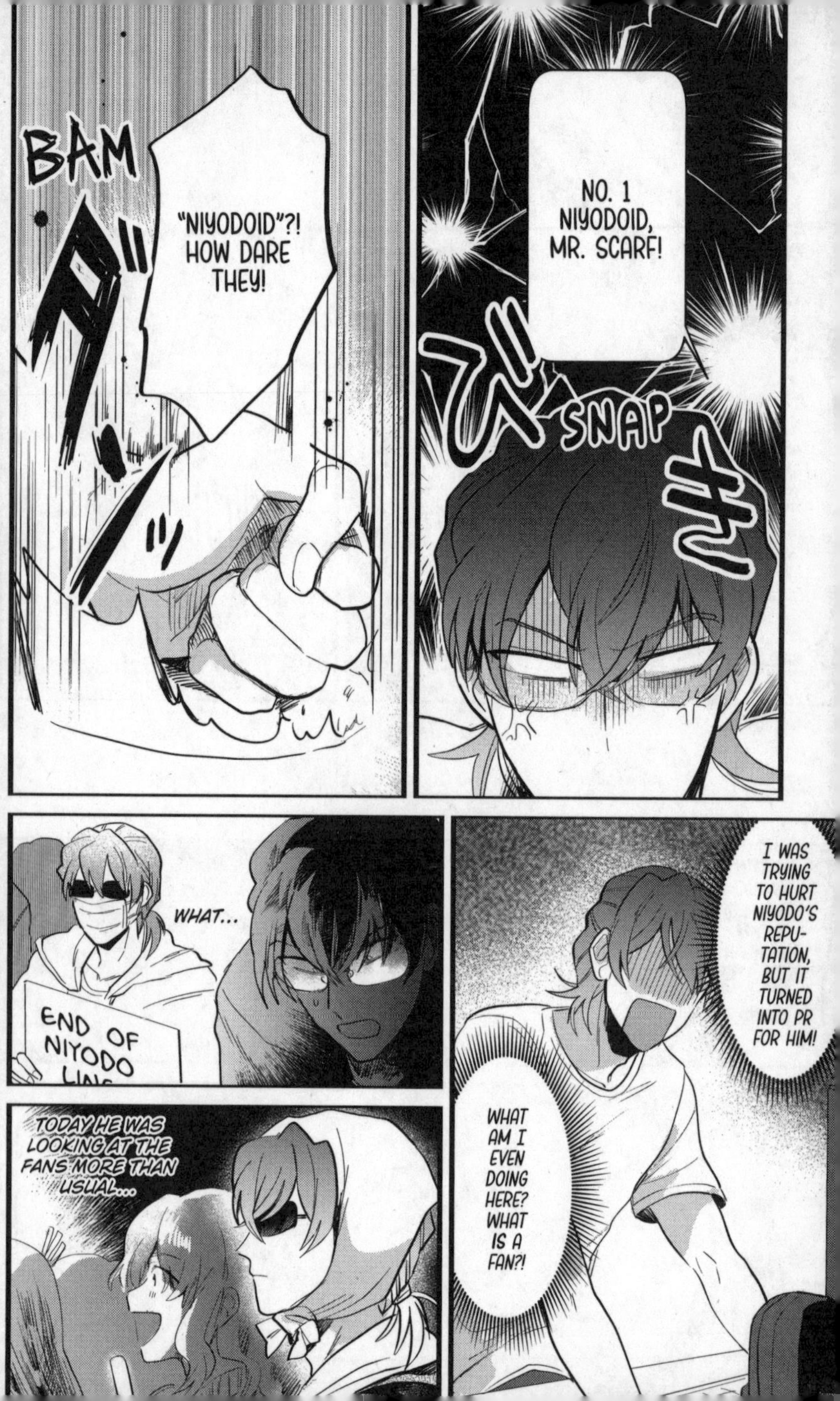
NO. 1 NIYODOID, MR. SCARF!
SNAP
BAM
"NIYODOID"?! HOW DARE THEY!
I WAS TRYING TO HURT NIYODO'S REPUTATION, BUT IT TURNED INTO PR FOR HIM!
WHAT AM I EVEN DOING HERE? WHAT IS A FAN?!
WHAT...
END OF NIYODO
TODAY HE WAS LOOKING AT THE FANS MORE THAN USUAL...

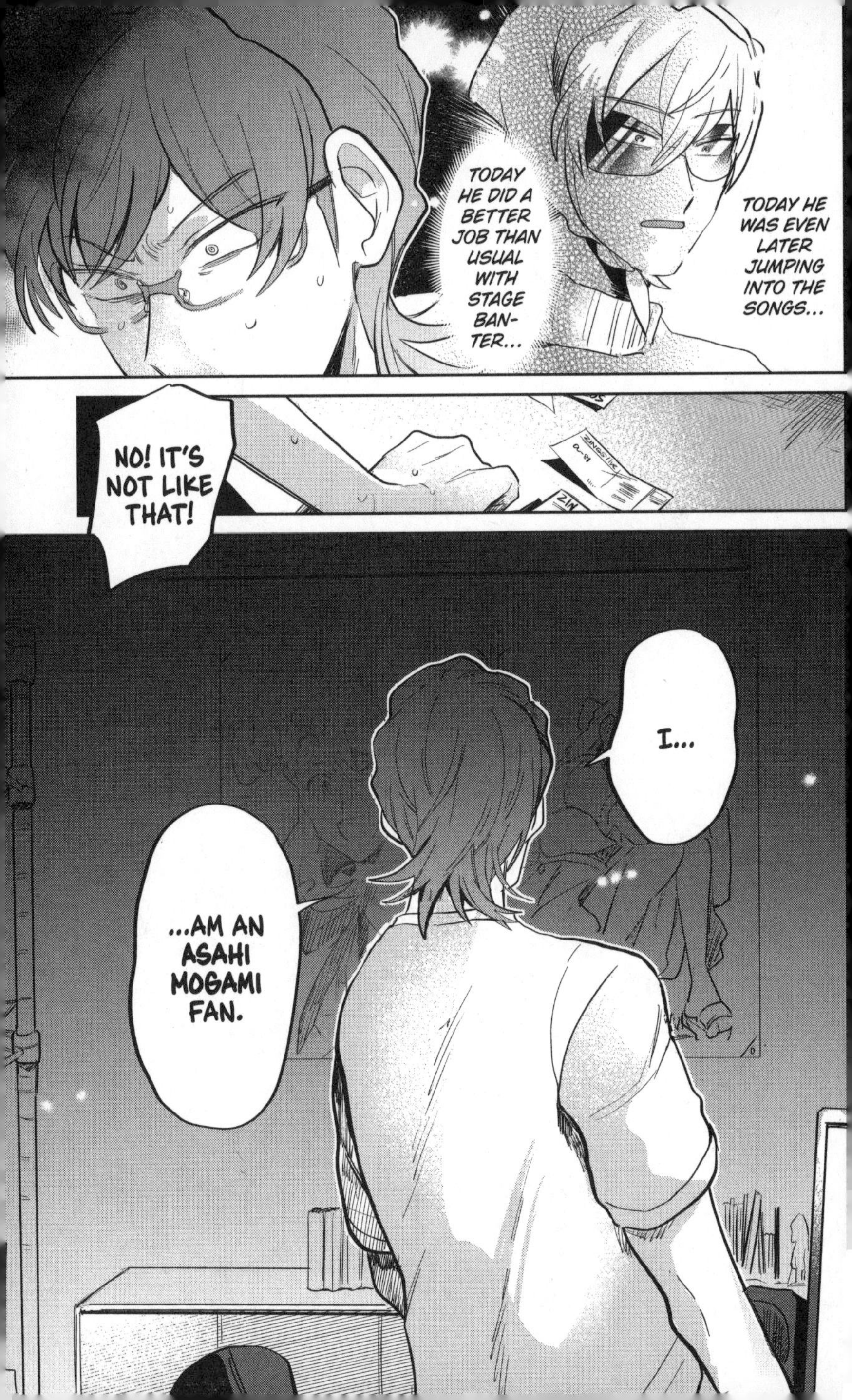
TODAY HE WAS EVEN LATER JUMPING INTO THE SONGS...
TODAY HE DID A BETTER JOB THAN USUAL WITH STAGE BAN-TER...
NO! IT'S NOT LIKE THAT!
I...
...AM AN ASAHI MOGAMI FAN.

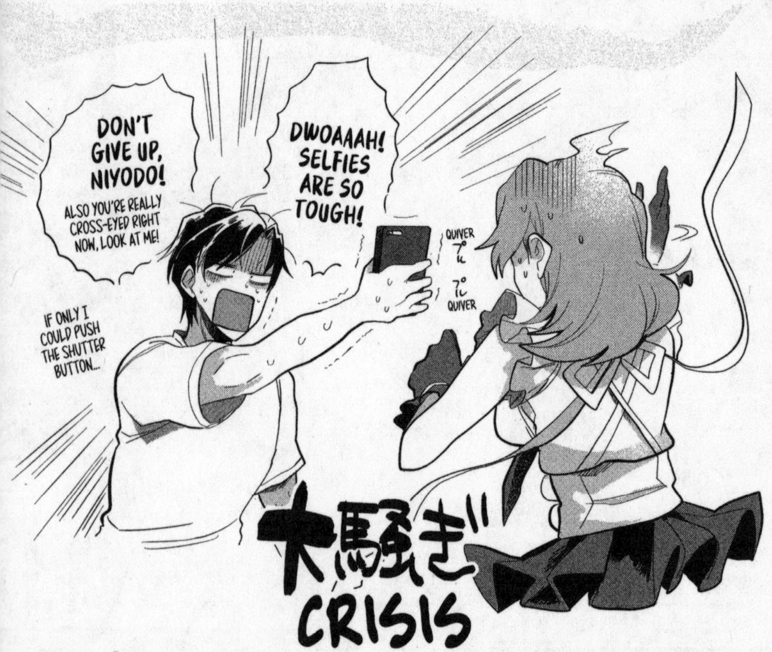
QUIVER プル
プル QUIVER
DWOAAAH! SELFIES ARE SO TOUGH!
DON'T GIVE UP, NIYODO!
ALSO YOU'RE REALLY CROSS-EYED RIGHT NOW, LOOK AT ME!
IF ONLY I COULD PUSH THE SHUTTER BUTTON...
大騒ぎ CRISIS

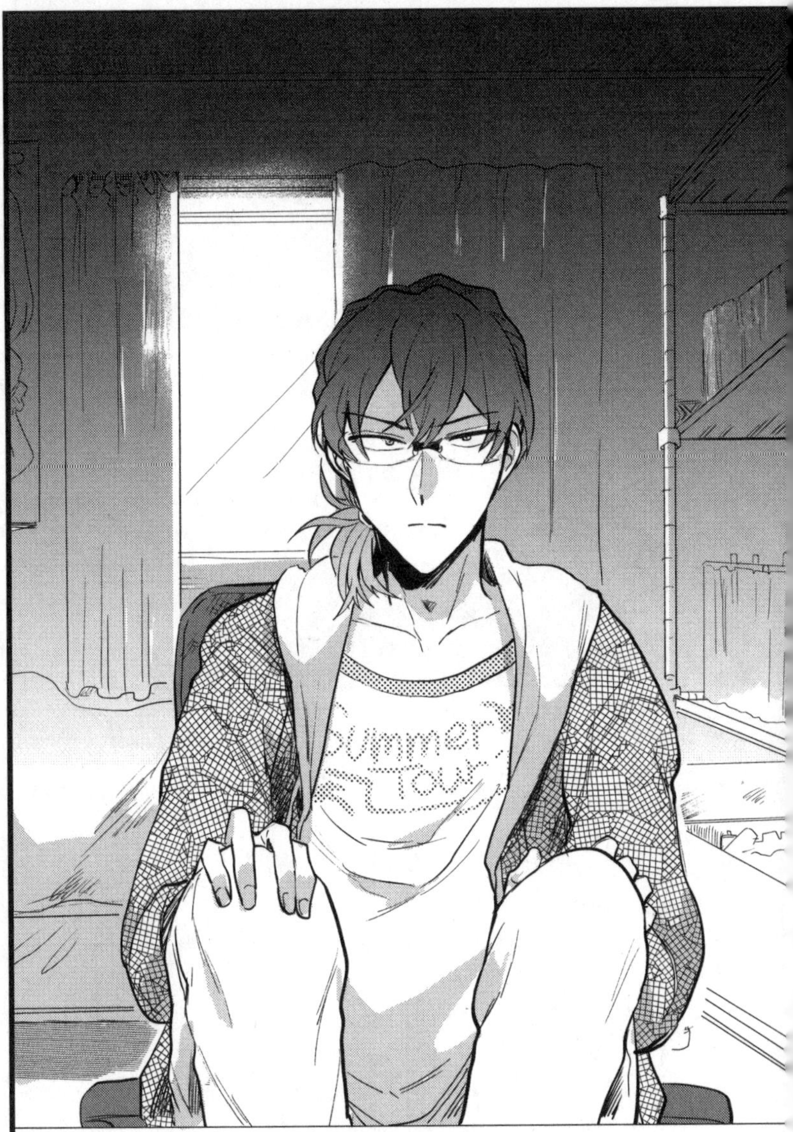
Summer Tour

Set 13

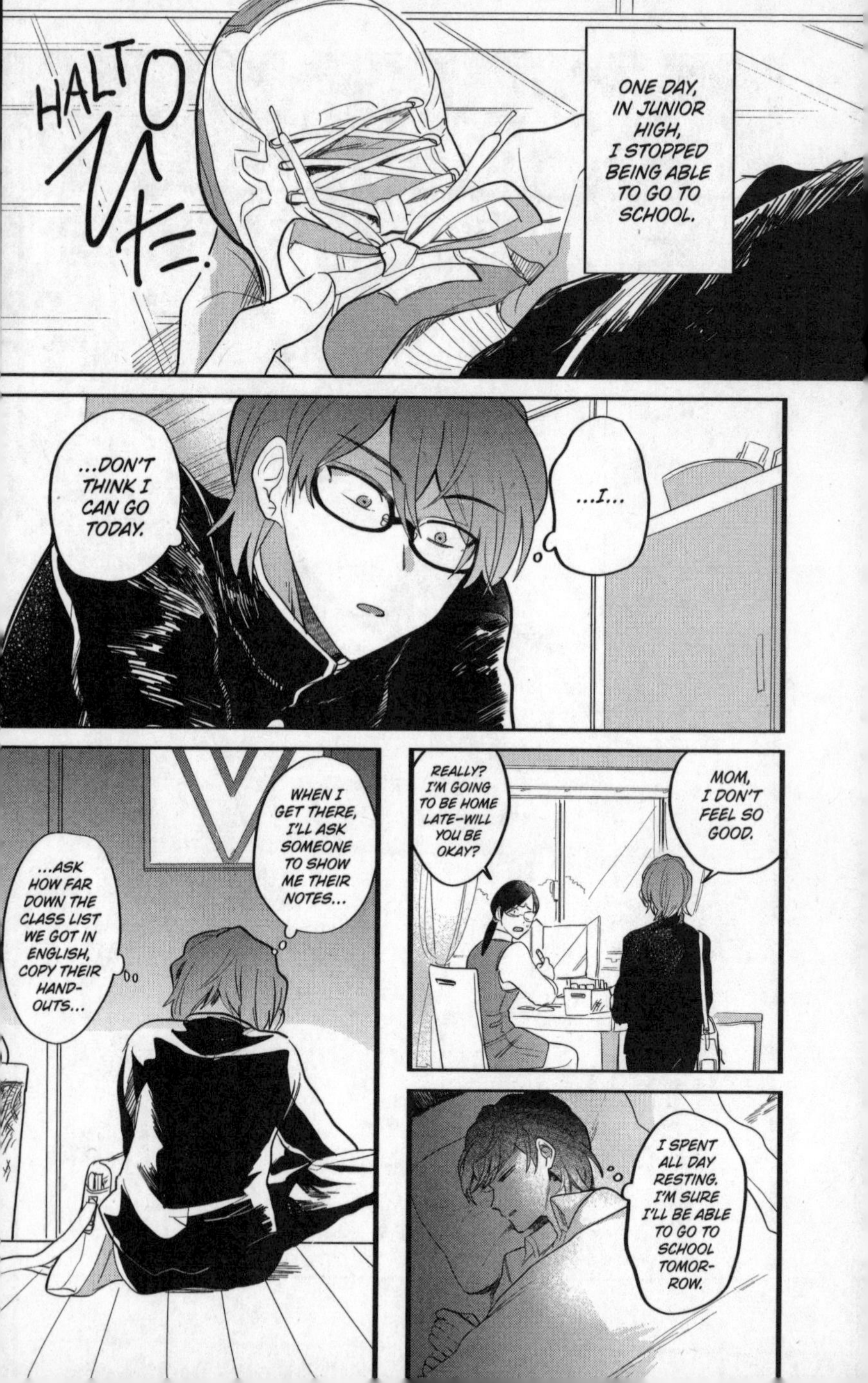
ONE DAY, IN JUNIOR HIGH, I STOPPED BEING ABLE TO GO TO SCHOOL.
HALT
...I...
...DON'T THINK I CAN GO TODAY.
MOM, I DON'T FEEL SO GOOD.
REALLY? I'M GOING TO BE HOME LATE—WILL YOU BE OKAY?
I SPENT ALL DAY RESTING. I'M SURE I'LL BE ABLE TO GO TO SCHOOL TOMOR-ROW.
WHEN I GET THERE, I'LL ASK SOMEONE TO SHOW ME THEIR NOTES...
...ASK HOW FAR DOWN THE CLASS LIST WE GOT IN ENGLISH, COPY THEIR HAND-OUTS...

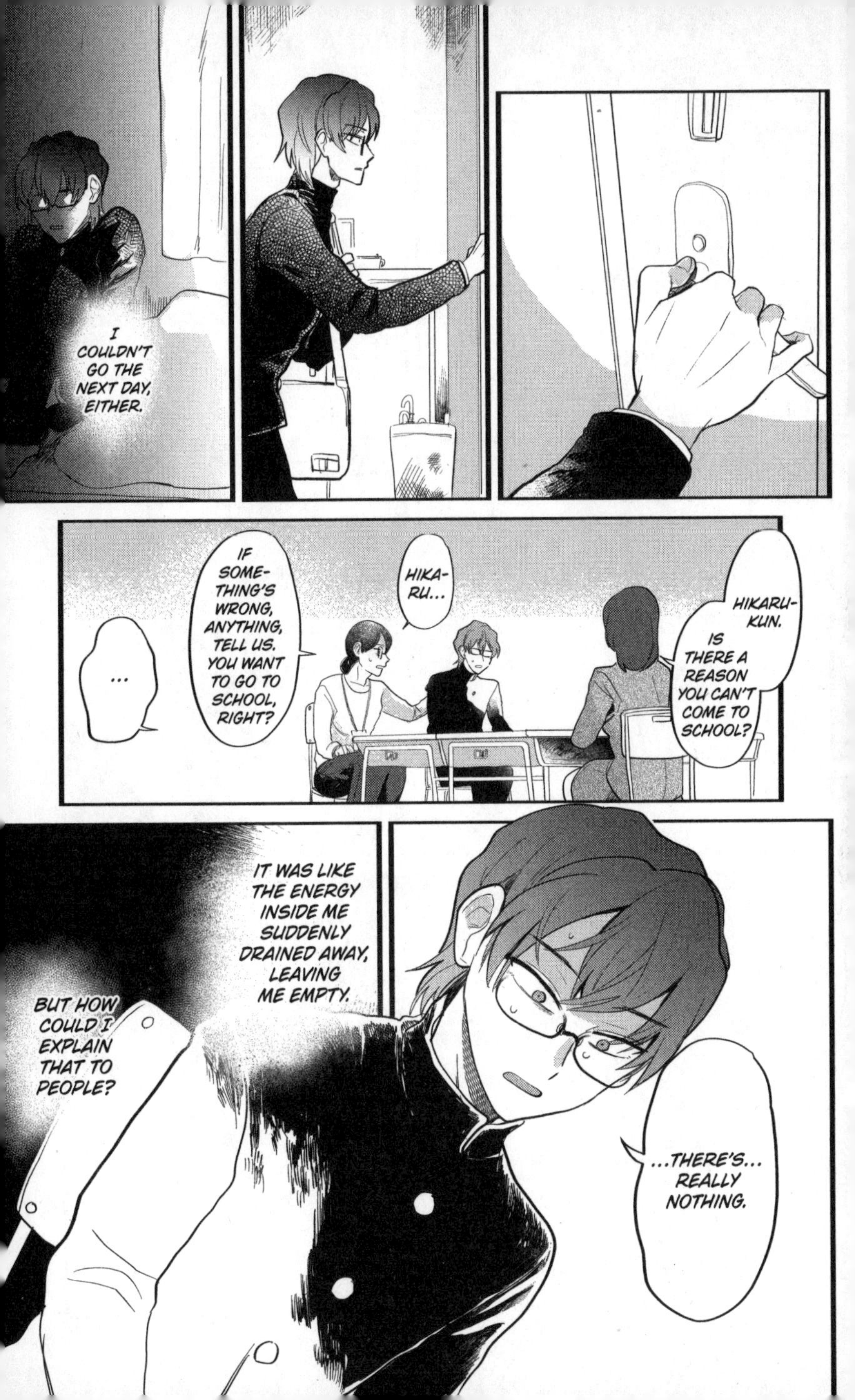
I COULDN'T GO THE NEXT DAY, EITHER.
HIKARU-KUN. IS THERE A REASON YOU CAN'T COME TO SCHOOL?
HIKARU...
IF SOMETHING'S WRONG, ANYTHING, TELL US. YOU WANT TO GO TO SCHOOL, RIGHT?
...
...THERE'S... REALLY NOTHING.
IT WAS LIKE THE ENERGY INSIDE ME SUDDENLY DRAINED AWAY, LEAVING ME EMPTY.
BUT HOW COULD I EXPLAIN THAT TO PEOPLE?

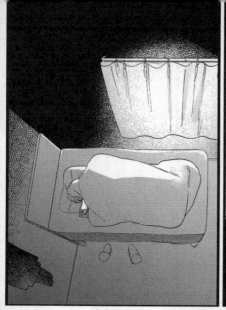

EVERYONE WAS GOING TO SCHOOL LIKE NORMAL, STUDYING LIKE NORMAL... THEY DIDN'T NEED A REASON.

SO, WHAT WAS I DOING?

I WONDER WHERE THE MUSIC IN THIS VIDEO IS FROM...

HELLO, EVERYBODY!

AN IDOL GROUP...?

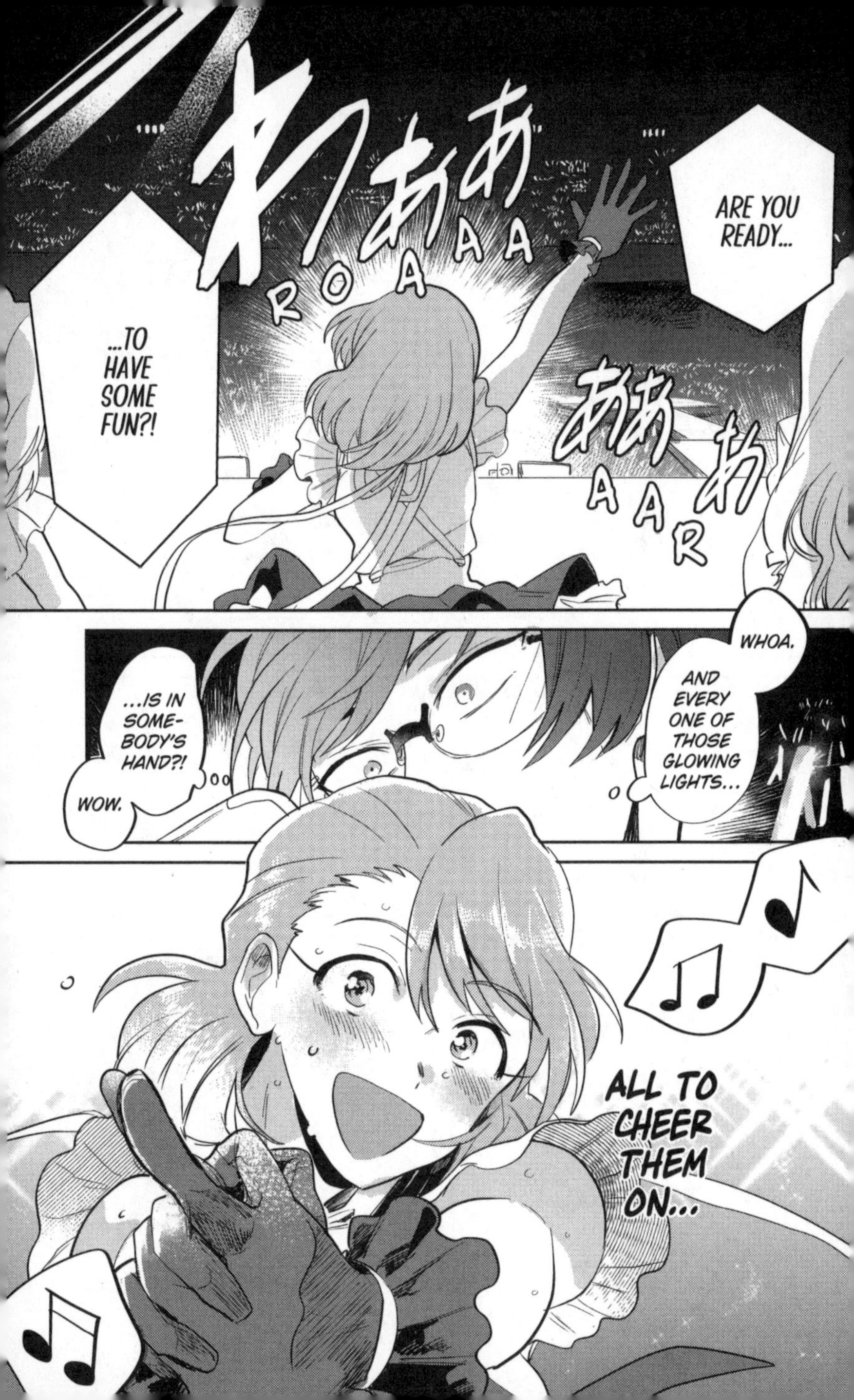
ARE YOU READY...
わああ
ROAAA
...TO HAVE SOME FUN?!
あああ
AAR
WHOA.
AND EVERY ONE OF THOSE GLOWING LIGHTS...
...IS IN SOMEBODY'S HAND?!
WOW.
ALL TO CHEER THEM ON...

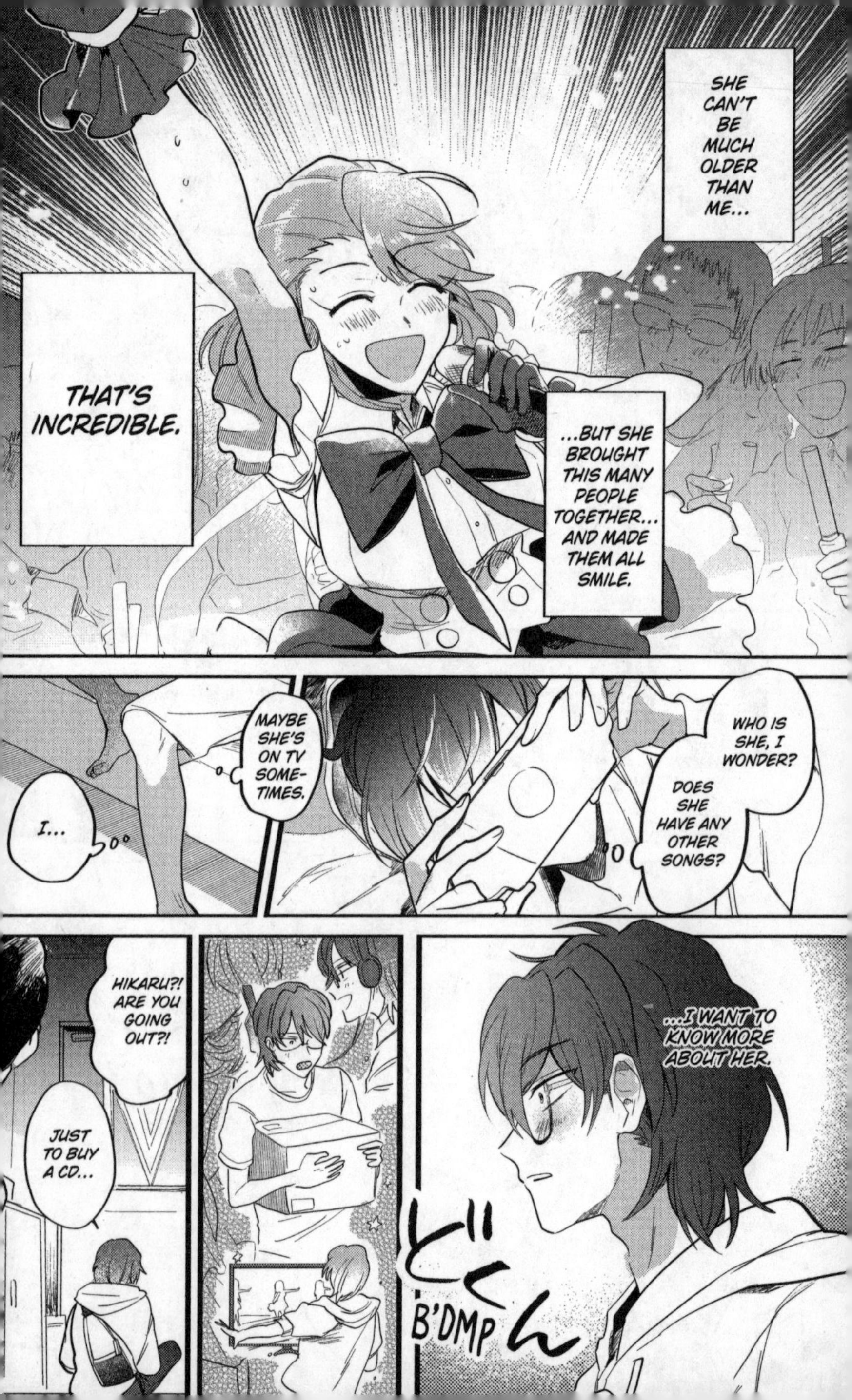
SHE CAN'T BE MUCH OLDER THAN ME...
...BUT SHE BROUGHT THIS MANY PEOPLE TOGETHER... AND MADE THEM ALL SMILE.
THAT'S INCREDIBLE.
WHO IS SHE, I WONDER?
DOES SHE HAVE ANY OTHER SONGS?
MAYBE SHE'S ON TV SOMETIMES.
I...
...I WANT TO KNOW MORE ABOUT HER.
どくん
B'DMP
HIKARU?! ARE YOU GOING OUT?!
JUST TO BUY A CD...

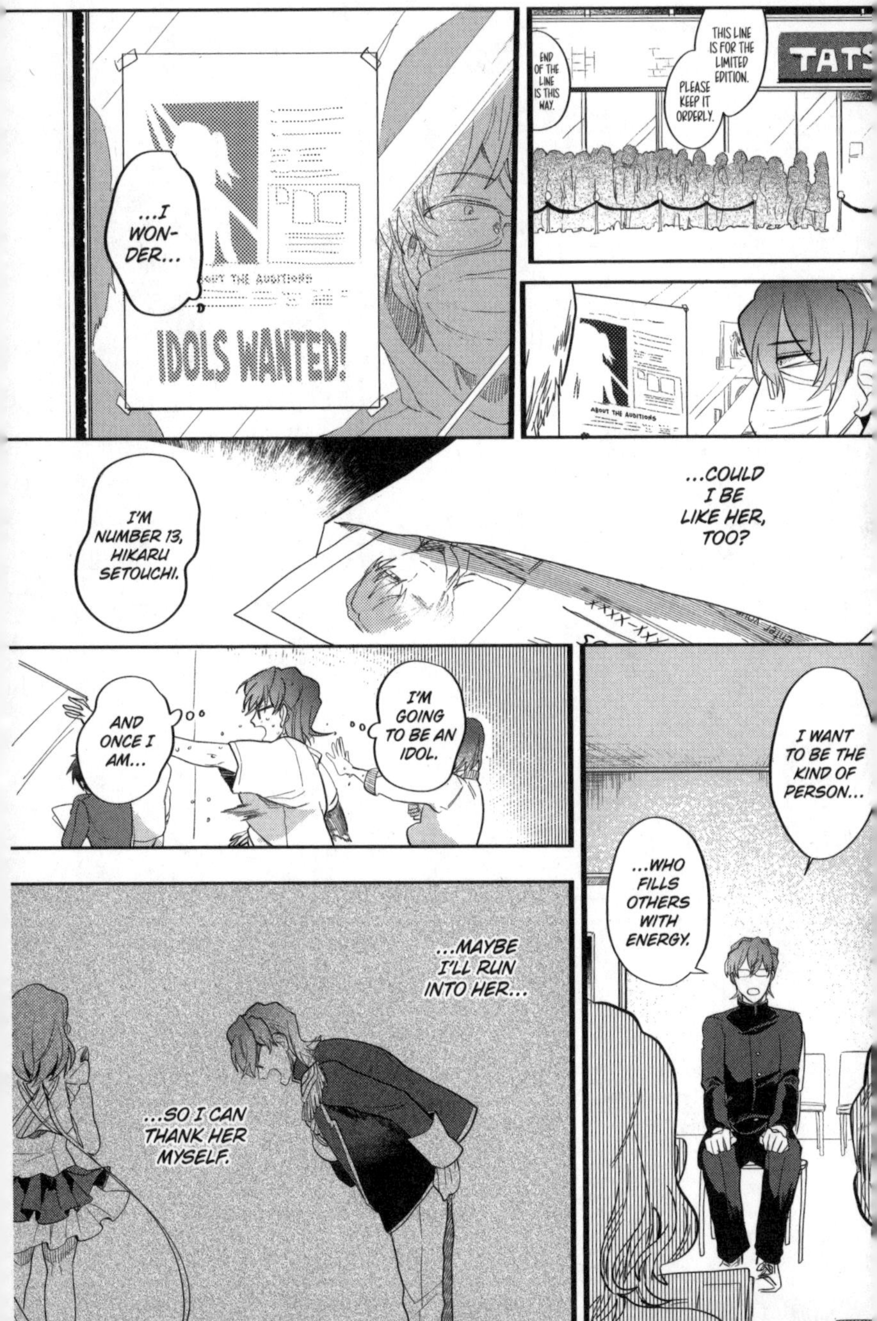
TATS
THIS LINE IS FOR THE LIMITED EDITION.
PLEASE KEEP IT ORDERLY.
END OF THE LINE IS THIS WAY.
ABOUT THE AUDITIONS
...I WONDER...
IDOLS WANTED!
...COULD I BE LIKE HER, TOO?
I'M NUMBER 13, HIKARU SETOUCHI.
I WANT TO BE THE KIND OF PERSON...
...WHO FILLS OTHERS WITH ENERGY.
I'M GOING TO BE AN IDOL.
AND ONCE I AM...
...MAYBE I'LL RUN INTO HER...
...SO I CAN THANK HER MYSELF.

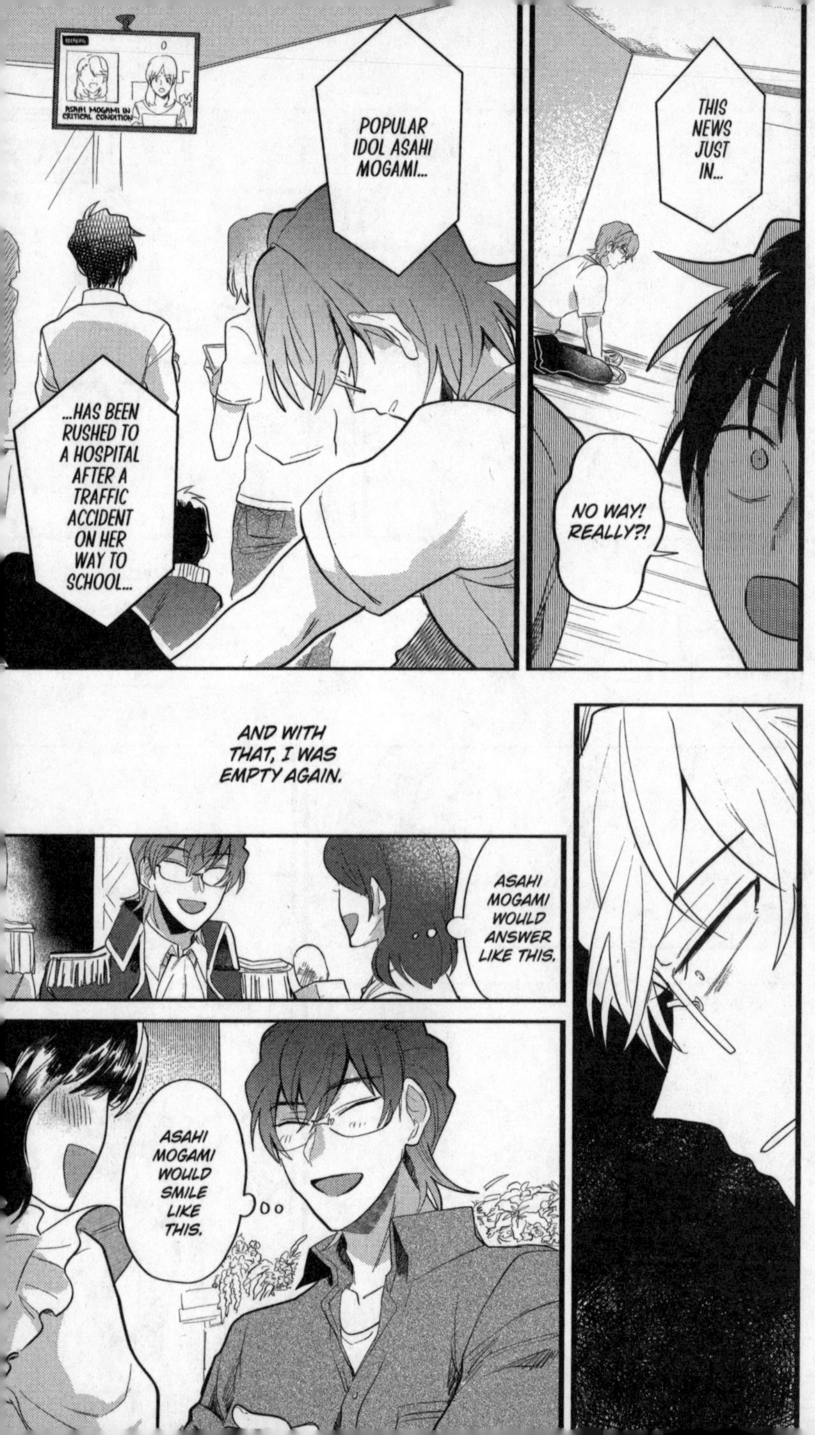
THIS NEWS JUST IN...
NO WAY! REALLY?!
ASAHI MOGAMI IN CRITICAL CONDITION
POPULAR IDOL ASAHI MOGAMI...
...HAS BEEN RUSHED TO A HOSPITAL AFTER A TRAFFIC ACCIDENT ON HER WAY TO SCHOOL...
AND WITH THAT, I WAS EMPTY AGAIN.
ASAHI MOGAMI WOULD ANSWER LIKE THIS.
ASAHI MOGAMI WOULD SMILE LIKE THIS.

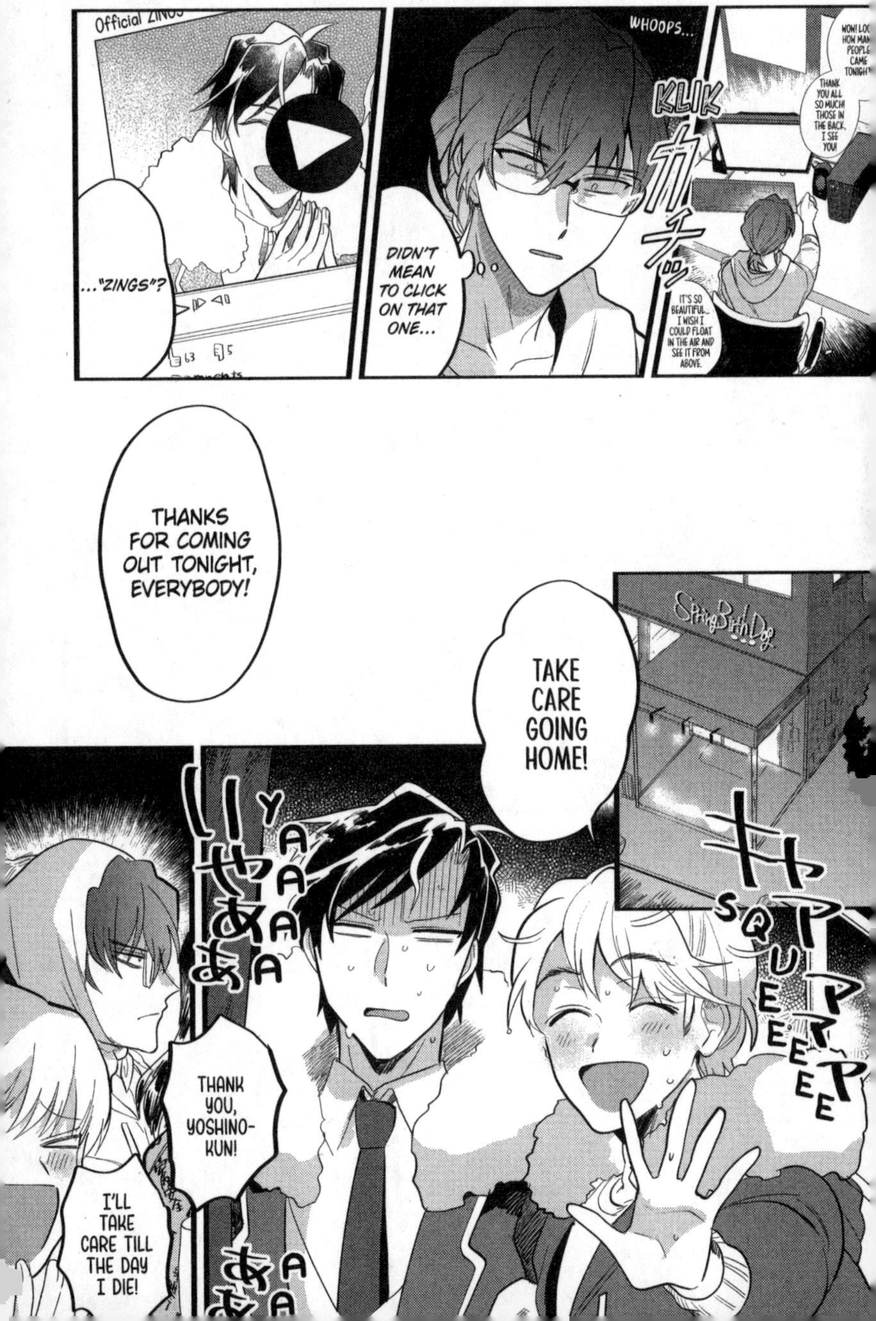
WOW! LOO HOW MAN PEOPLE CAME TONIGHT
THANK YOU ALL SO MUCH! THOSE IN THE BACK, I SEE YOU!
KLIK
カチッ
IT'S SO BEAUTIFUL... I WISH I COULD FLOAT IN THE AIR AND SEE IT FROM ABOVE.
WHOOPS...
DIDN'T MEAN TO CLICK ON THAT ONE...
Official ZINGS
...“ZINGS”?
THANKS FOR COMING OUT TONIGHT, EVERYBODY!
TAKE CARE GOING HOME!
SpringBirthDog
キャ
SQUEEEE
いやああ
YAAAA
THANK YOU, YOSHINO-KUN!
I'LL TAKE CARE TILL THE DAY I DIE!
ああ
AA

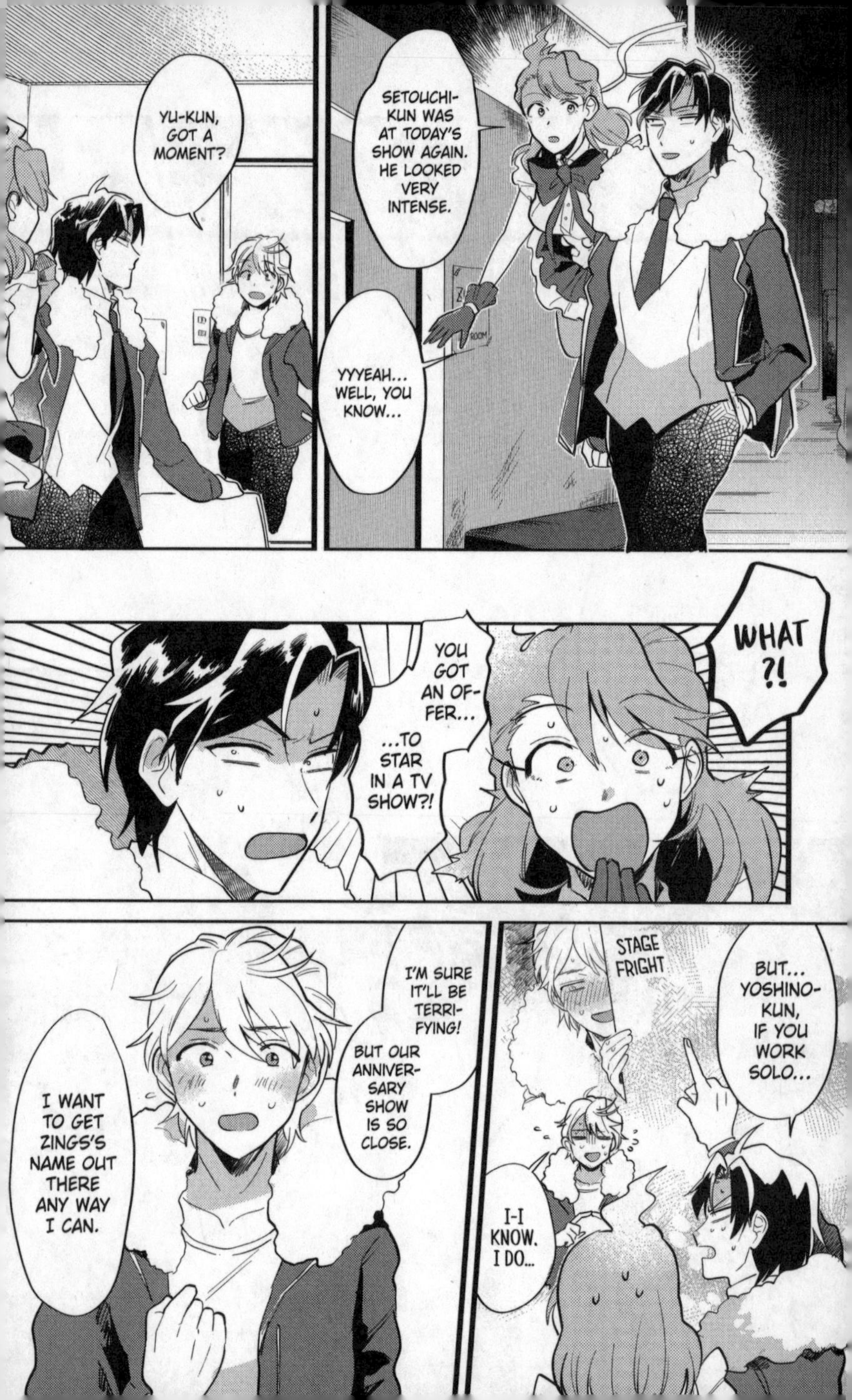
SETOUCHI-KUN WAS AT TODAY'S SHOW AGAIN. HE LOOKED VERY INTENSE.
YYYEAH... WELL, YOU KNOW...
YU-KUN, GOT A MOMENT?
WHAT?!
YOU GOT AN OFFER...
...TO STAR IN A TV SHOW?!
BUT... YOSHINO-KUN, IF YOU WORK SOLO...
STAGE FRIGHT
I-I KNOW. I DO...
I'M SURE IT'LL BE TERRIFYING!
BUT OUR ANNIVERSARY SHOW IS SO CLOSE.
I WANT TO GET ZINGS'S NAME OUT THERE ANY WAY I CAN.

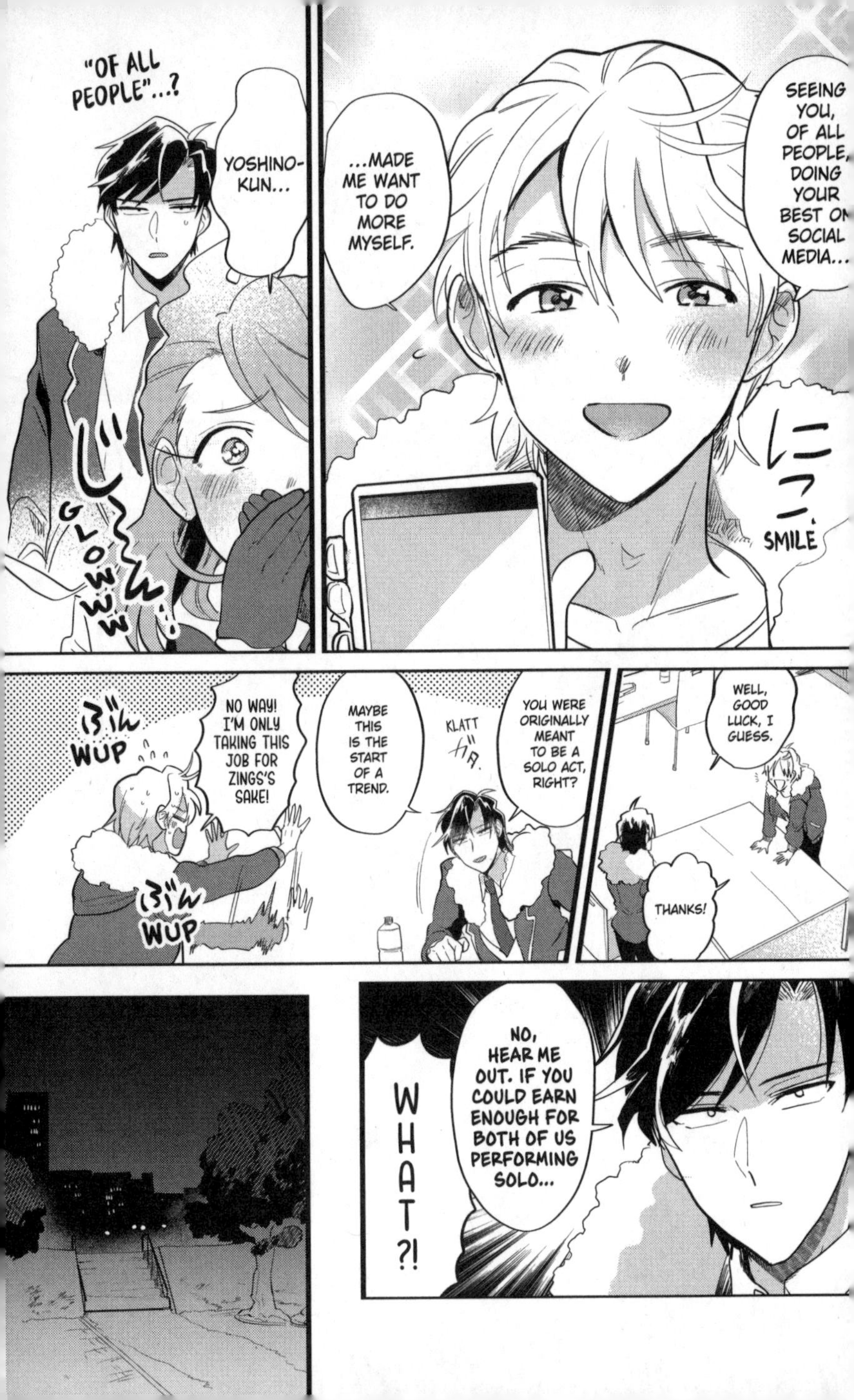
SEEING YOU, OF ALL PEOPLE, DOING YOUR BEST ON SOCIAL MEDIA...
...MADE ME WANT TO DO MORE MYSELF.
にっこ
SMILE
YOSHINO-KUN...
"OF ALL PEOPLE"...?
じーん
GLOWWW
WELL, GOOD LUCK, I GUESS.
THANKS!
YOU WERE ORIGINALLY MEANT TO BE A SOLO ACT, RIGHT?
ガタ
KLATT
MAYBE THIS IS THE START OF A TREND.
NO WAY! I'M ONLY TAKING THIS JOB FOR ZINGS'S SAKE!
ぶん
WUP
ぶん
WUP
NO, HEAR ME OUT. IF YOU COULD EARN ENOUGH FOR BOTH OF US PERFORMING SOLO...
WHAT?!

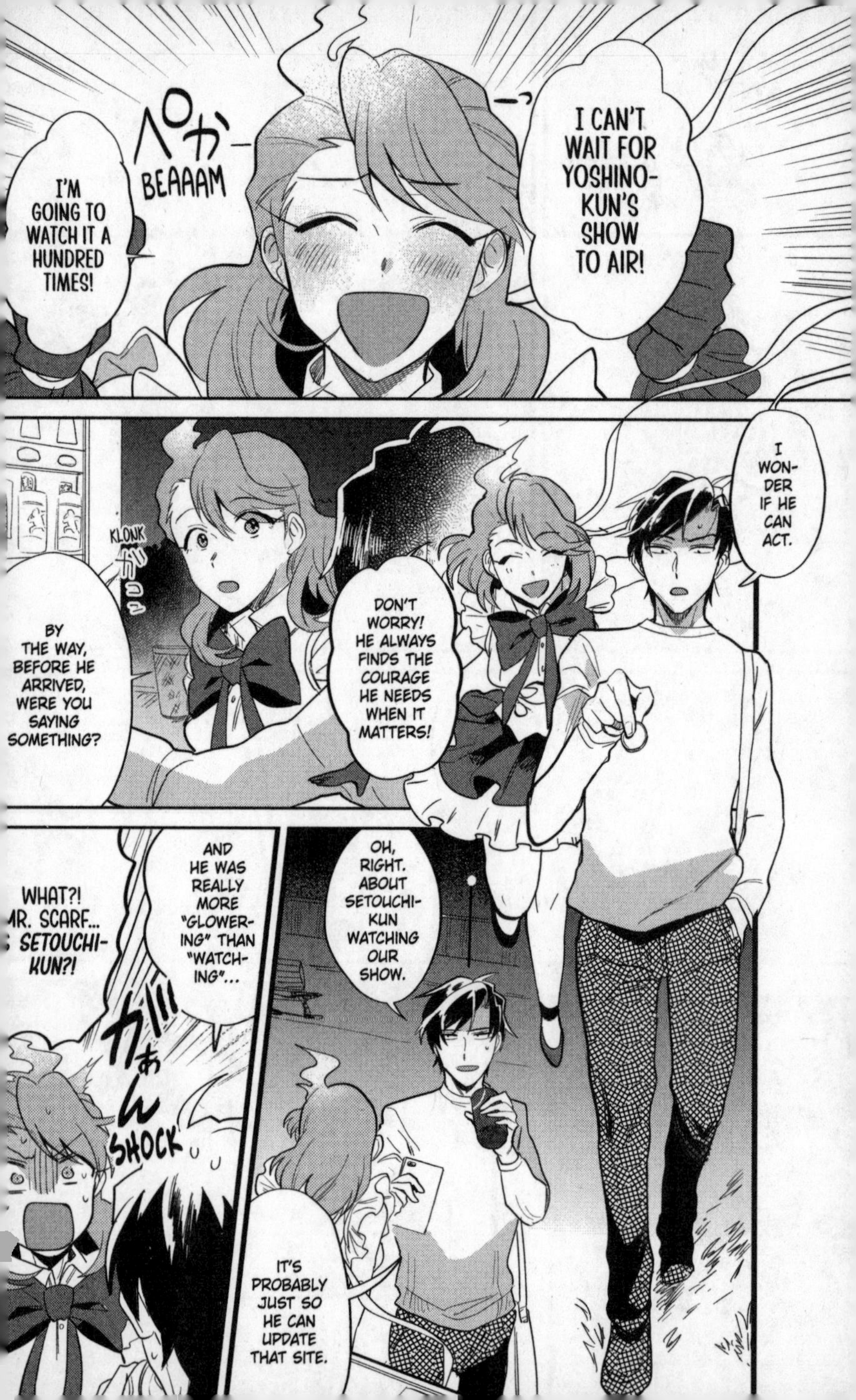
I CAN'T WAIT FOR YOSHINO-KUN'S SHOW TO AIR!
ぺかー
BEAAAM
I'M GOING TO WATCH IT A HUNDRED TIMES!
I WONDER IF HE CAN ACT.
DON'T WORRY! HE ALWAYS FINDS THE COURAGE HE NEEDS WHEN IT MATTERS!
KLONK
BY THE WAY, BEFORE HE ARRIVED, WERE YOU SAYING SOMETHING?
OH, RIGHT. ABOUT SETOUCHI-KUN WATCHING OUR SHOW.
AND HE WAS REALLY MORE "GLOWERING" THAN "WATCHING"...
IT'S PROBABLY JUST SO HE CAN UPDATE THAT SITE.
WHAT?! MR. SCARF... SETOUCHI-KUN?!
SHOCK

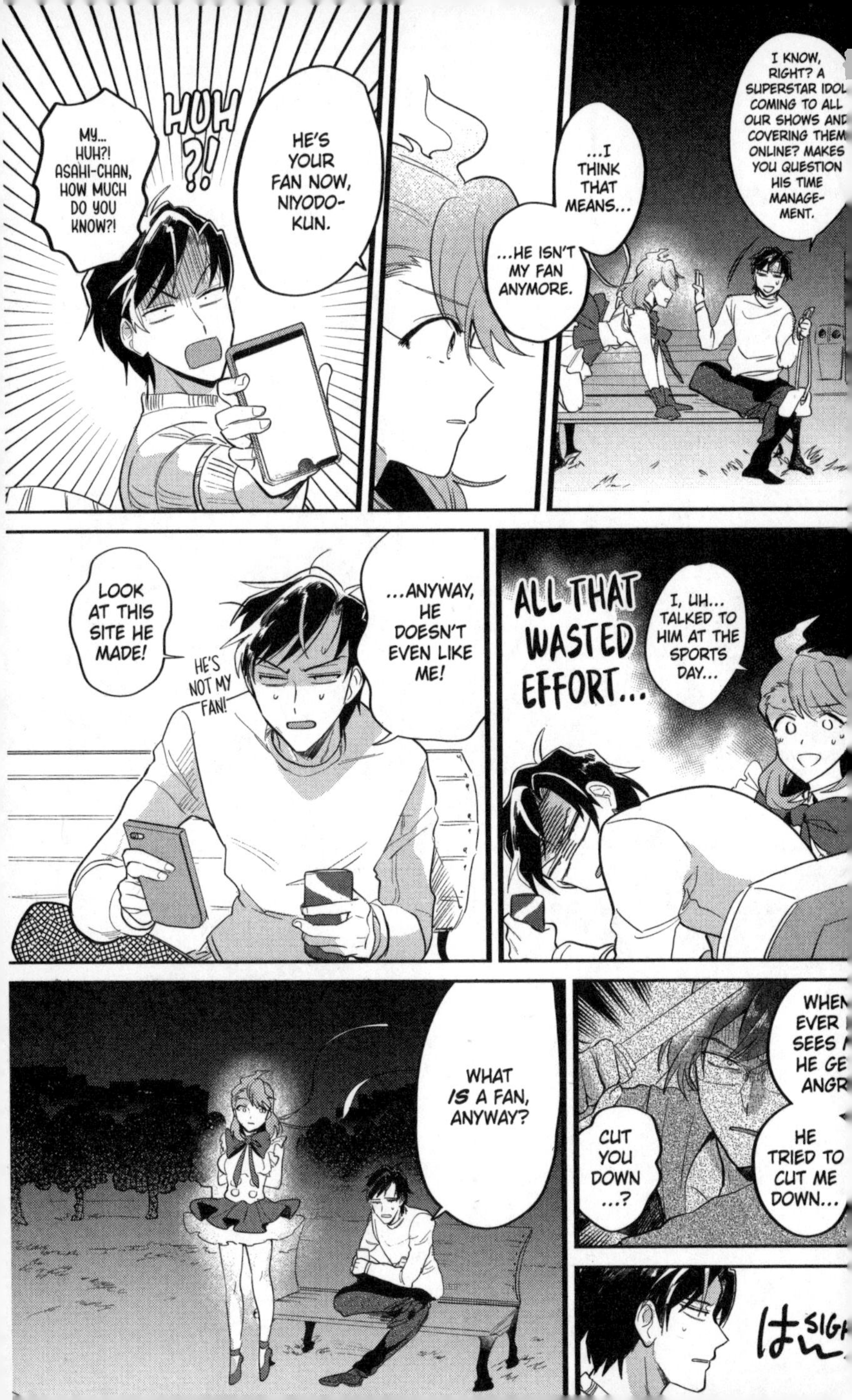
I KNOW, RIGHT? A SUPERSTAR IDOL COMING TO ALL OUR SHOWS AND COVERING THEM ONLINE? MAKES YOU QUESTION HIS TIME MANAGEMENT.
...I THINK THAT MEANS...
...HE ISN'T MY FAN ANYMORE.
HE'S YOUR FAN NOW, NIYODO-KUN.
HUH ?!
MY... HUH?! ASAHI-CHAN, HOW MUCH DO YOU KNOW?!
I, UH... TALKED TO HIM AT THE SPORTS DAY...
ALL THAT WASTED EFFORT...
...ANYWAY, HE DOESN'T EVEN LIKE ME!
HE'S NOT MY FAN!
LOOK AT THIS SITE HE MADE!
WHEN EVER SEES HE GE ANGR
HE TRIED TO CUT ME DOWN...
CUT YOU DOWN ...?
はぁ SIGH
WHAT IS A FAN, ANYWAY?

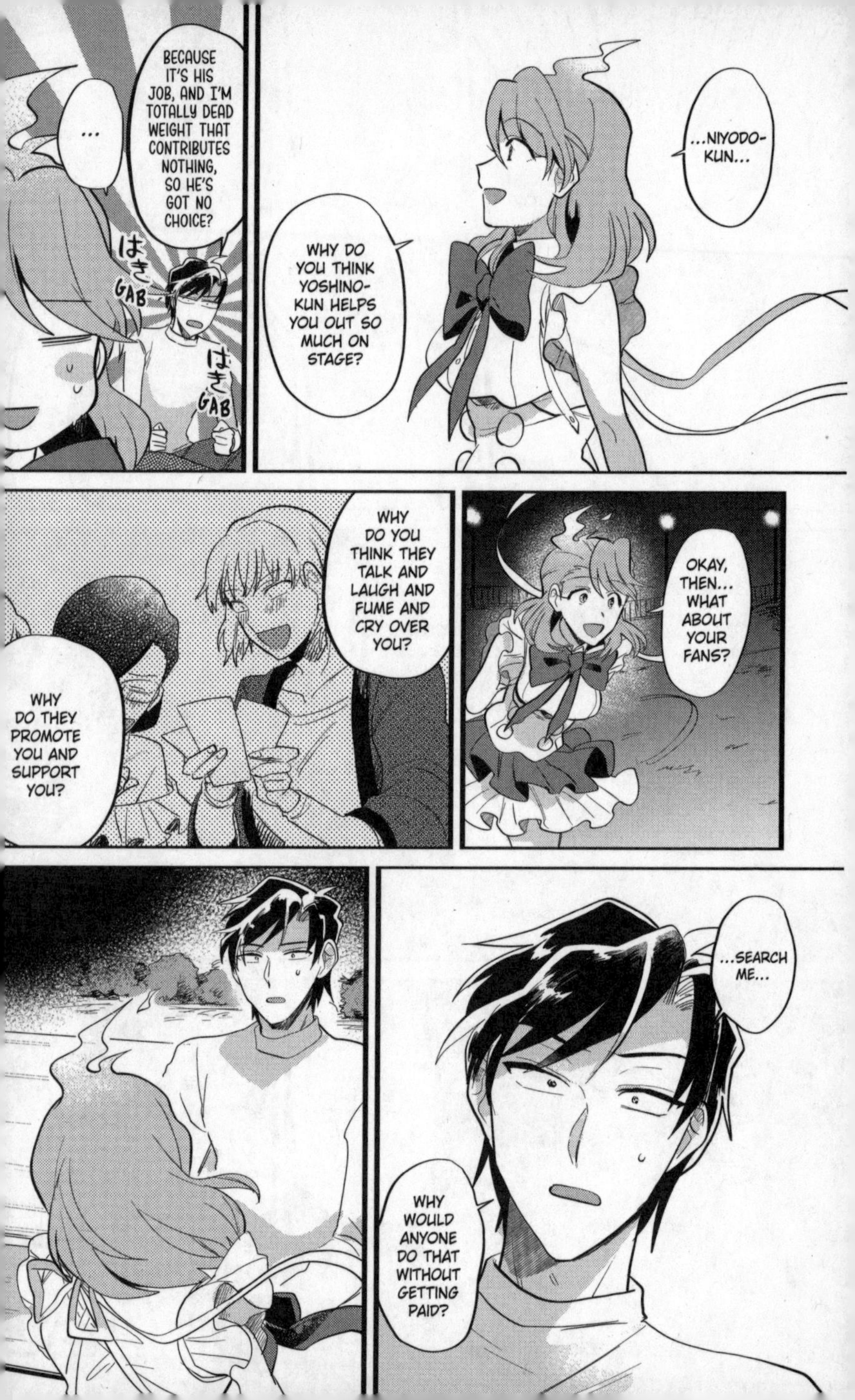
...NIYODO-KUN...
WHY DO YOU THINK YOSHINO-KUN HELPS YOU OUT SO MUCH ON STAGE?
BECAUSE IT'S HIS JOB, AND I'M TOTALLY DEAD WEIGHT THAT CONTRIBUTES NOTHING, SO HE'S GOT NO CHOICE?
はき GAB
はき GAB
...
OKAY, THEN... WHAT ABOUT YOUR FANS?
WHY DO YOU THINK THEY TALK AND LAUGH AND FUME AND CRY OVER YOU?
WHY DO THEY PROMOTE YOU AND SUPPORT YOU?
...SEARCH ME...
WHY WOULD ANYONE DO THAT WITHOUT GETTING PAID?

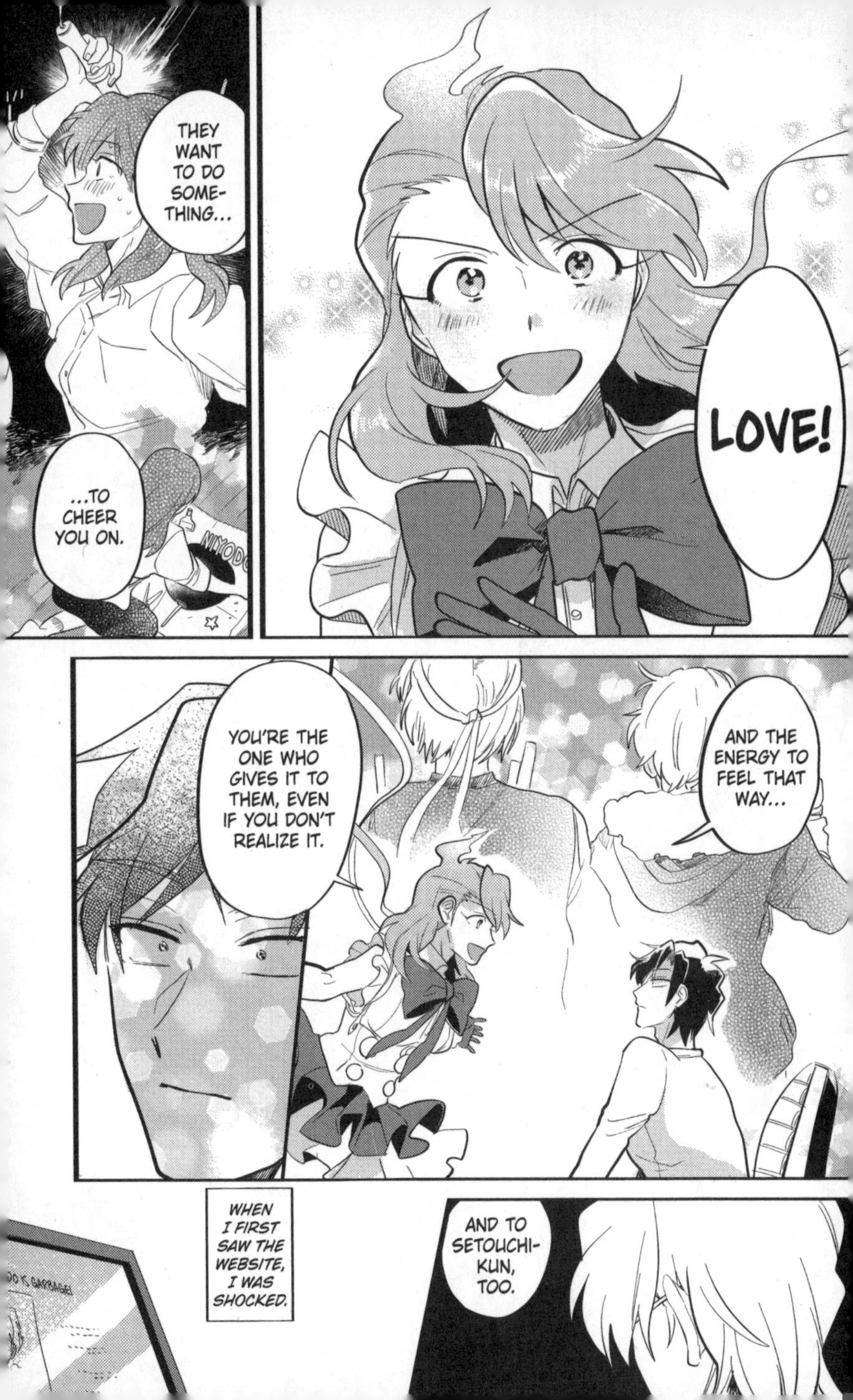
LOVE!
THEY WANT TO DO SOME-THING...
...TO CHEER YOU ON.
AND THE ENERGY TO FEEL THAT WAY...
YOU'RE THE ONE WHO GIVES IT TO THEM, EVEN IF YOU DON'T REALIZE IT.
AND TO SETOUCHI-KUN, TOO.
WHEN I FIRST SAW THE WEBSITE, I WAS SHOCKED.

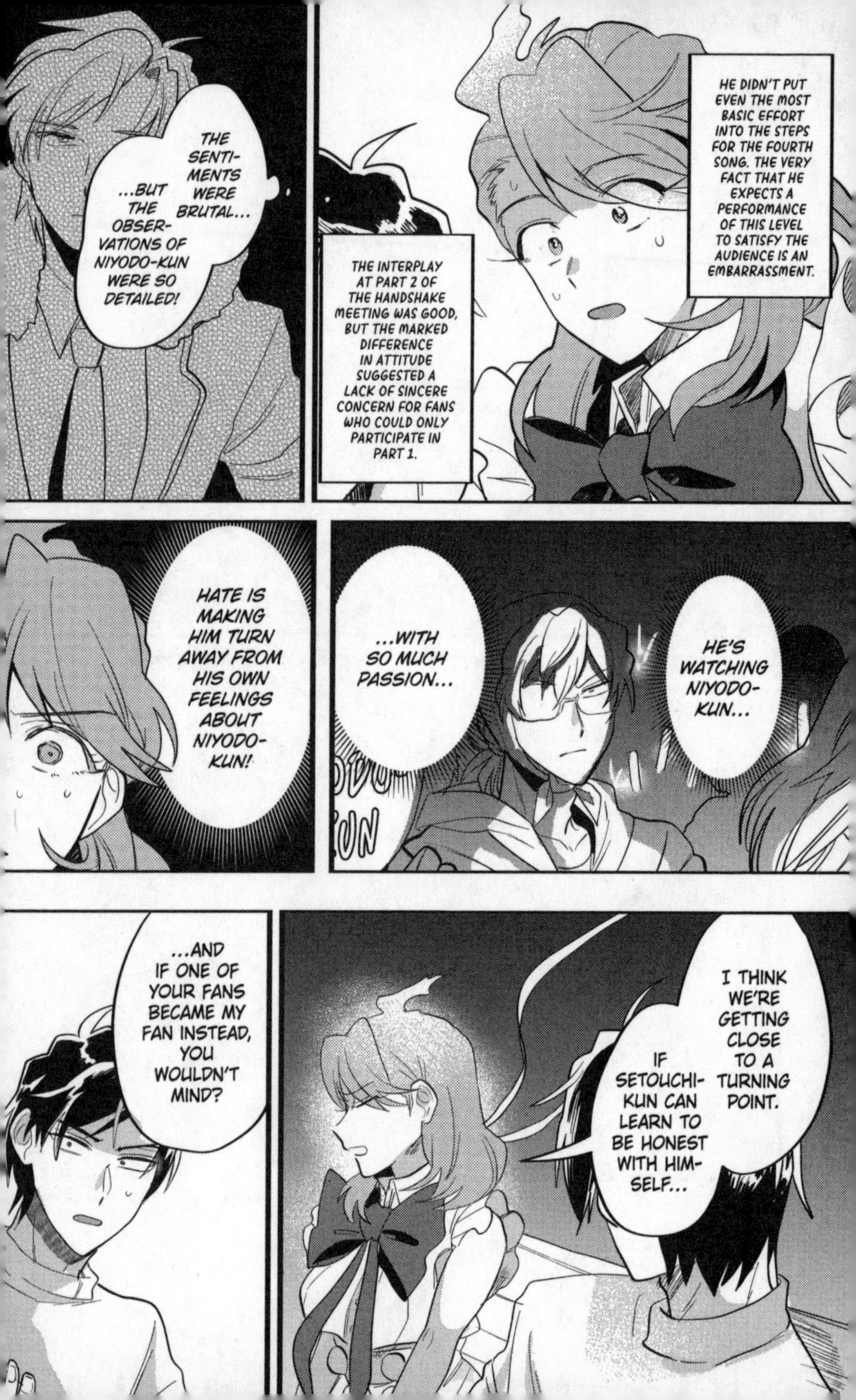
HE DIDN'T PUT EVEN THE MOST BASIC EFFORT INTO THE STEPS FOR THE FOURTH SONG. THE VERY FACT THAT HE EXPECTS A PERFORMANCE OF THIS LEVEL TO SATISFY THE AUDIENCE IS AN EMBARRASSMENT.
THE INTERPLAY AT PART 2 OF THE HANDSHAKE MEETING WAS GOOD, BUT THE MARKED DIFFERENCE IN ATTITUDE SUGGESTED A LACK OF SINCERE CONCERN FOR FANS WHO COULD ONLY PARTICIPATE IN PART 1.
THE SENTIMENTS WERE BRUTAL... ...BUT THE OBSERVATIONS OF NIYODO-KUN WERE SO DETAILED!
HE'S WATCHING NIYODO-KUN...
...WITH SO MUCH PASSION...
HATE IS MAKING HIM TURN AWAY FROM HIS OWN FEELINGS ABOUT NIYODO-KUN!
I THINK WE'RE GETTING CLOSE TO A TURNING POINT.
IF SETOUCHI-KUN CAN LEARN TO BE HONEST WITH HIMSELF...
...AND IF ONE OF YOUR FANS BECAME MY FAN INSTEAD, YOU WOULDN'T MIND?

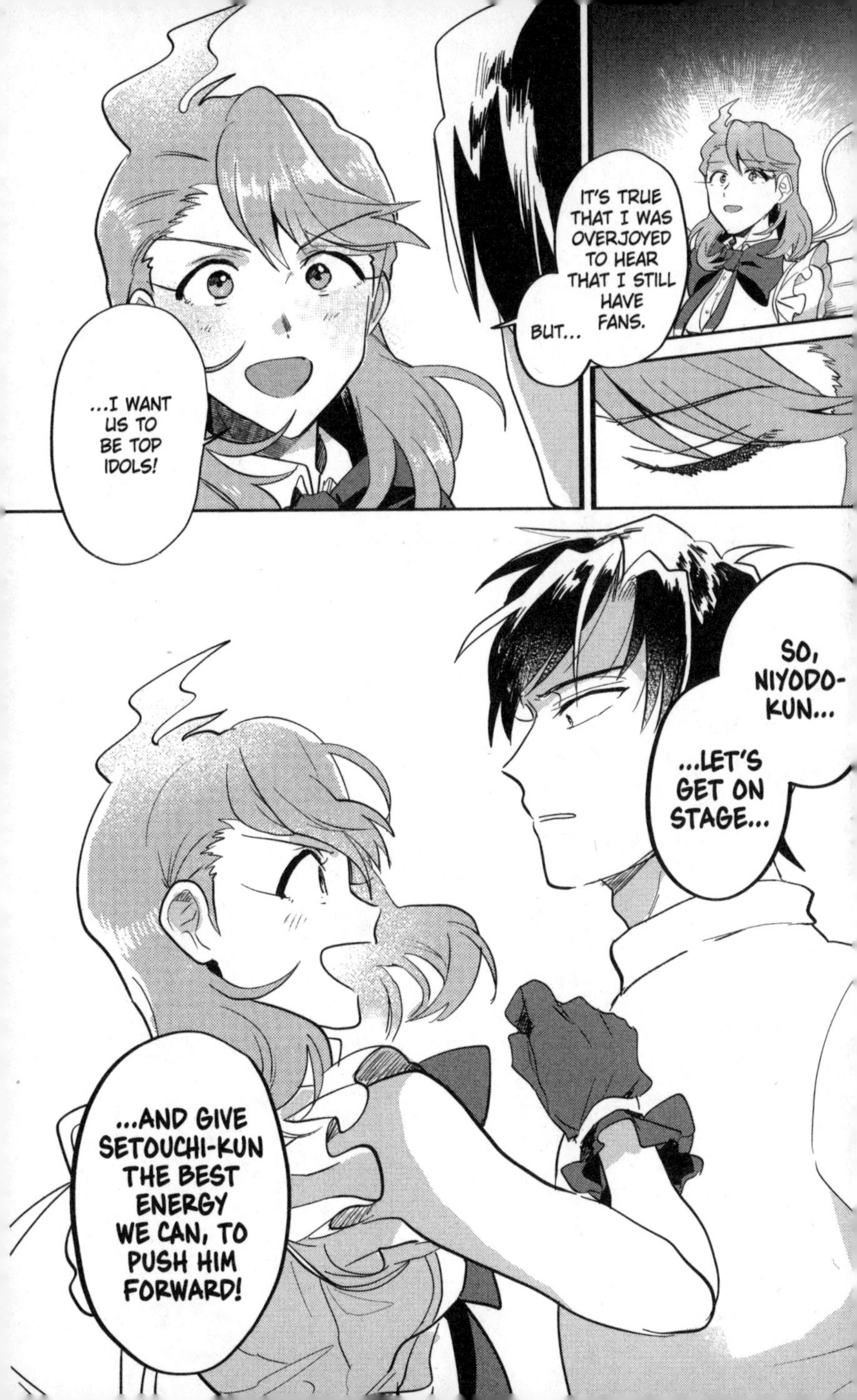
IT'S TRUE THAT I WAS OVERJOYED TO HEAR THAT I STILL HAVE FANS.
BUT...
...I WANT US TO BE TOP IDOLS!
SO, NIYODO-KUN...
...LET'S GET ON STAGE...
...AND GIVE SETOUCHI-KUN THE BEST ENERGY WE CAN, TO PUSH HIM FORWARD!

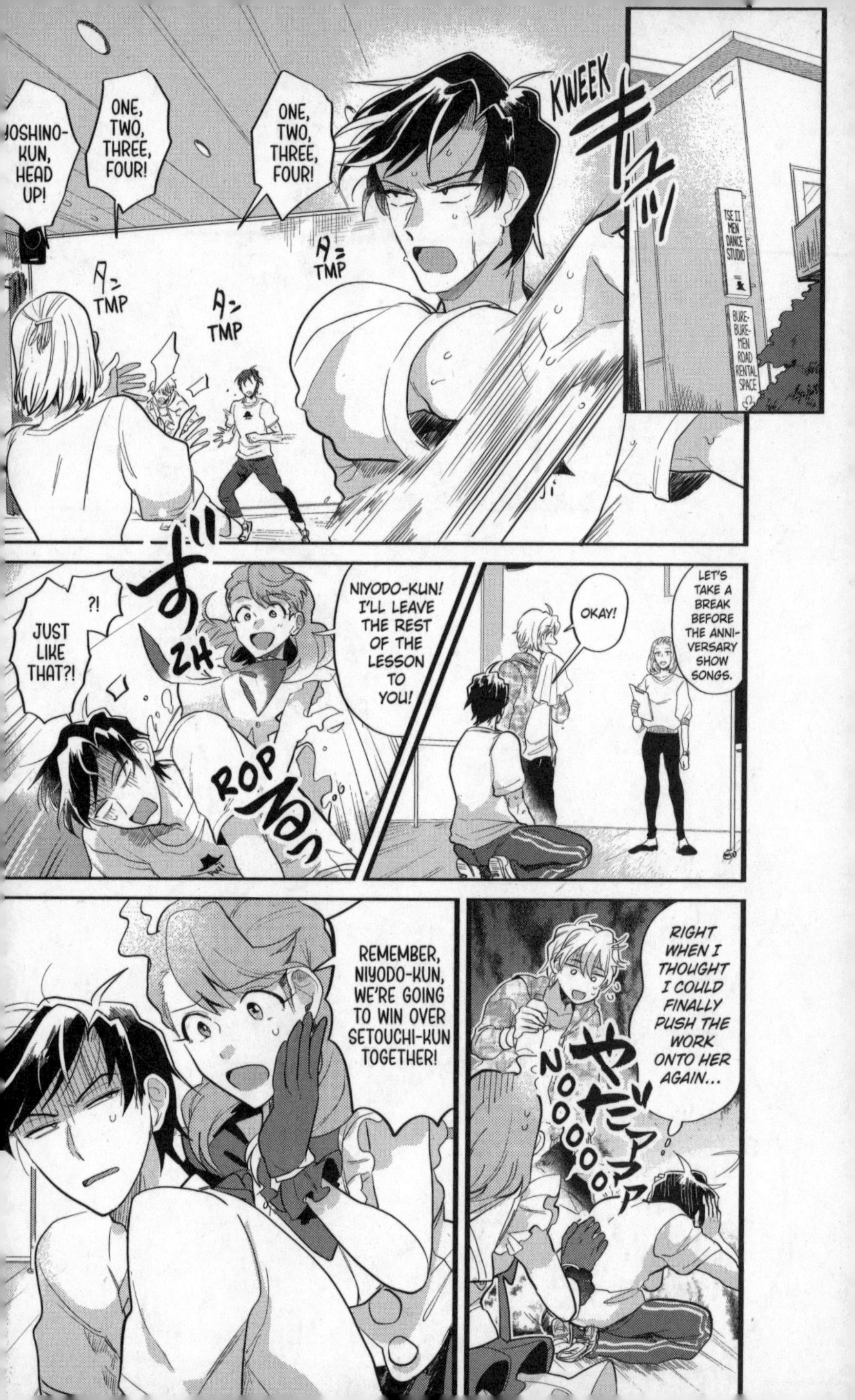
KWEEK
TSE II MEN DANCE STUDIO
BURE-BUKE-MEN ROAD RENTAL SPACE
ONE, TWO, THREE, FOUR!
TMP
ONE, TWO, THREE, FOUR!
YOSHINO-KUN, HEAD UP!
TMP
TMP
LET'S TAKE A BREAK BEFORE THE ANNIVERSARY SHOW SONGS.
OKAY!
NIYODO-KUN! I'LL LEAVE THE REST OF THE LESSON TO YOU!
ZH
?!
JUST LIKE THAT?!
ROP
RIGHT WHEN I THOUGHT I COULD FINALLY PUSH THE WORK ONTO HER AGAIN...
NOOOOOOO
REMEMBER, NIYODO-KUN, WE'RE GOING TO WIN OVER SETOUCHI-KUN TOGETHER!

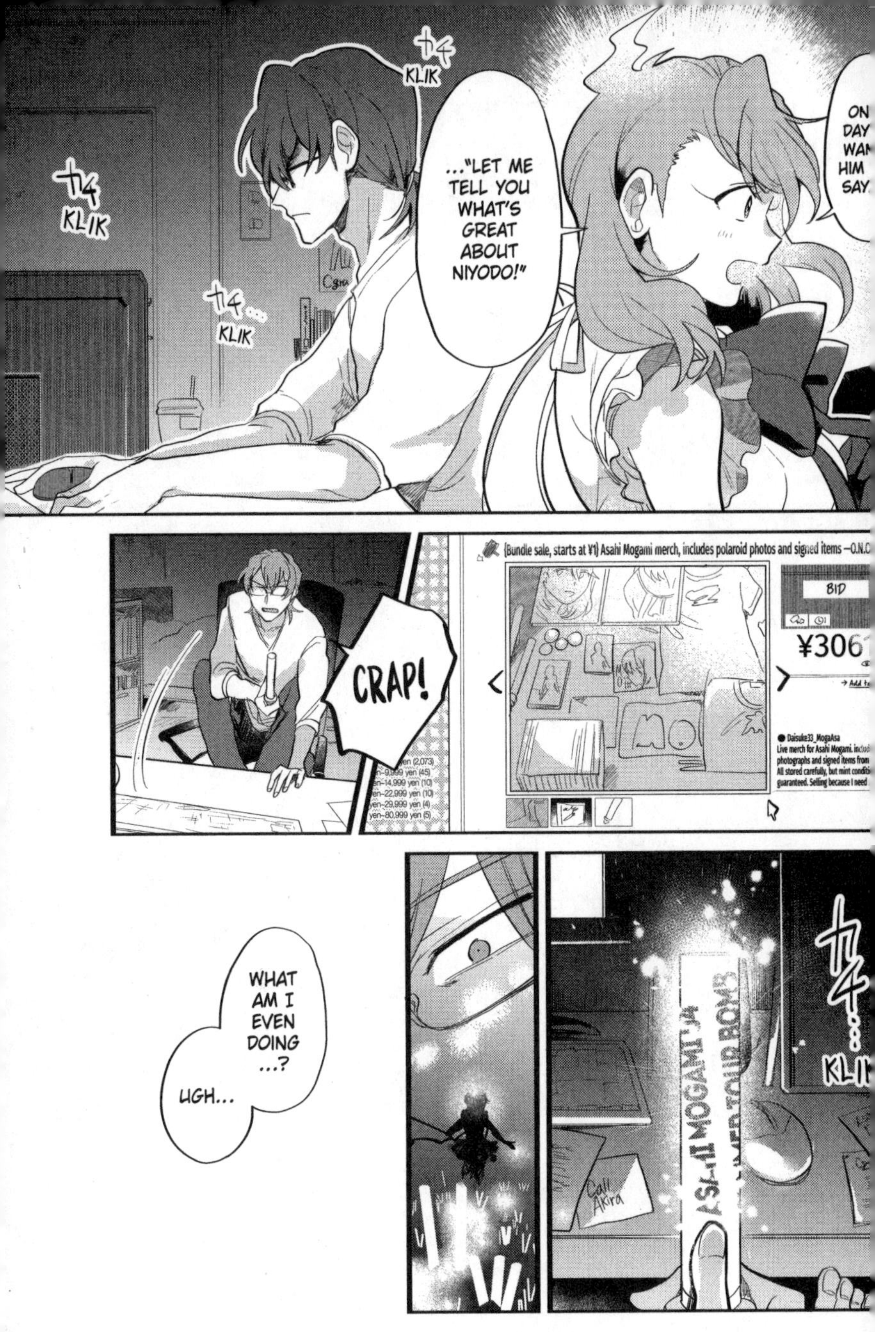
ON DAY WAN HIM SAY
..."LET ME TELL YOU WHAT'S GREAT ABOUT NIYODO!"
KLIK
KLIK
KLIK
(Bundle sale, starts at ¥1) Asahi Mogami merch, includes polaroid photos and signed items —O.N.C
BID
¥3061
→ Add t
Daisuke33_MogaAsa
Live merch for Asahi Mogami. includ
photographs and signed items from
All stored carefully, but mint conditi
guaranteed. Selling because I need
yen (2,073)
-9,999 yen (45)
yen-14,999 yen (10)
yen-22,999 yen (10)
yen-29,999 yen (4)
yen-80,999 yen (5)
CRAP!
KLIK
Call Akira
WHAT AM I EVEN DOING ...?
UGH...

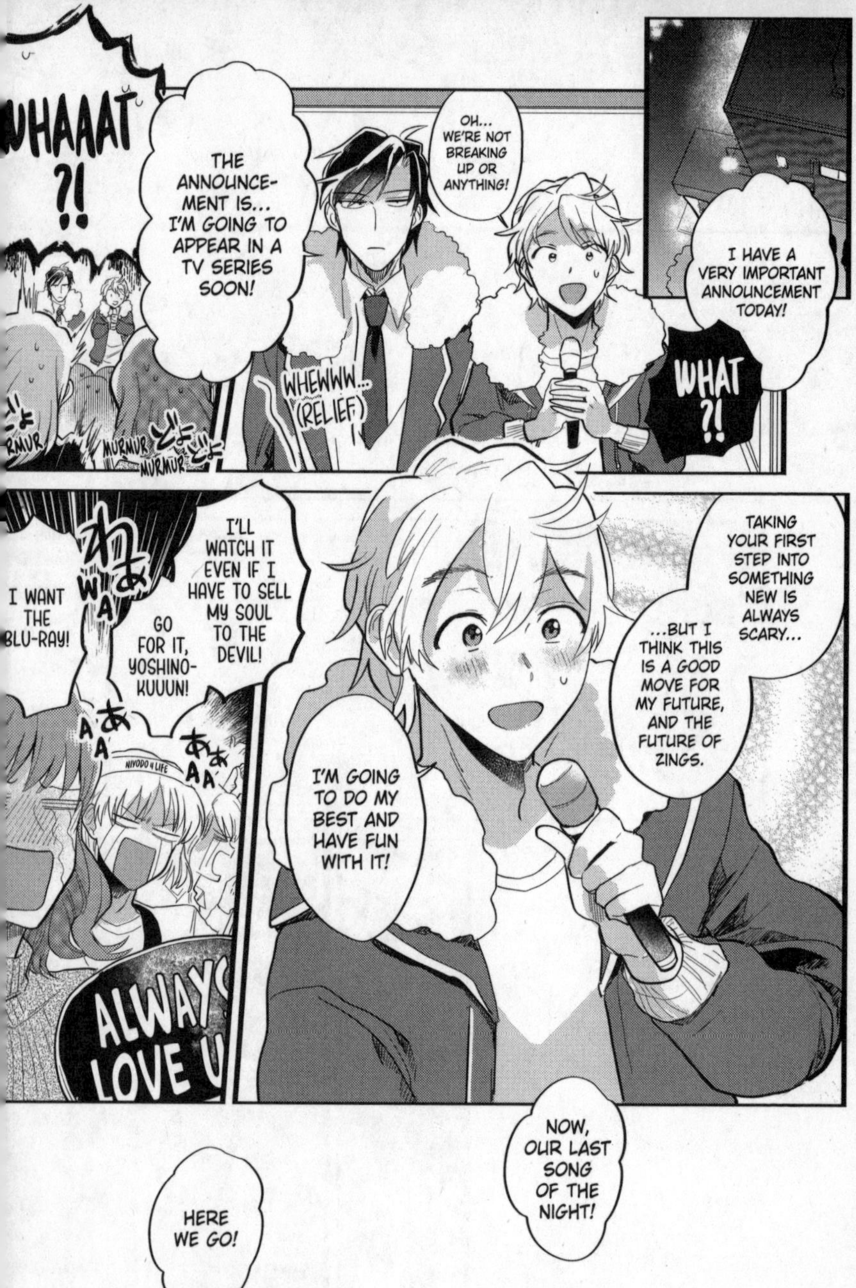
I HAVE A VERY IMPORTANT ANNOUNCEMENT TODAY!
WHAT ?!
OH... WE'RE NOT BREAKING UP OR ANYTHING!
THE ANNOUNCEMENT IS... I'M GOING TO APPEAR IN A TV SERIES SOON!
WHEWWW... (RELIEF)
WHAAAT ?!
MURMUR MURMUR
TAKING YOUR FIRST STEP INTO SOMETHING NEW IS ALWAYS SCARY...
...BUT I THINK THIS IS A GOOD MOVE FOR MY FUTURE, AND THE FUTURE OF ZINGS.
I'M GOING TO DO MY BEST AND HAVE FUN WITH IT!
I'LL WATCH IT EVEN IF I HAVE TO SELL MY SOUL TO THE DEVIL!
GO FOR IT, YOSHINO-KUUUN!
I WANT THE BLU-RAY!
WAA
AA
NIYODO 4 LIFE
ALWAYS LOVE U
NOW, OUR LAST SONG OF THE NIGHT!
HERE WE GO!

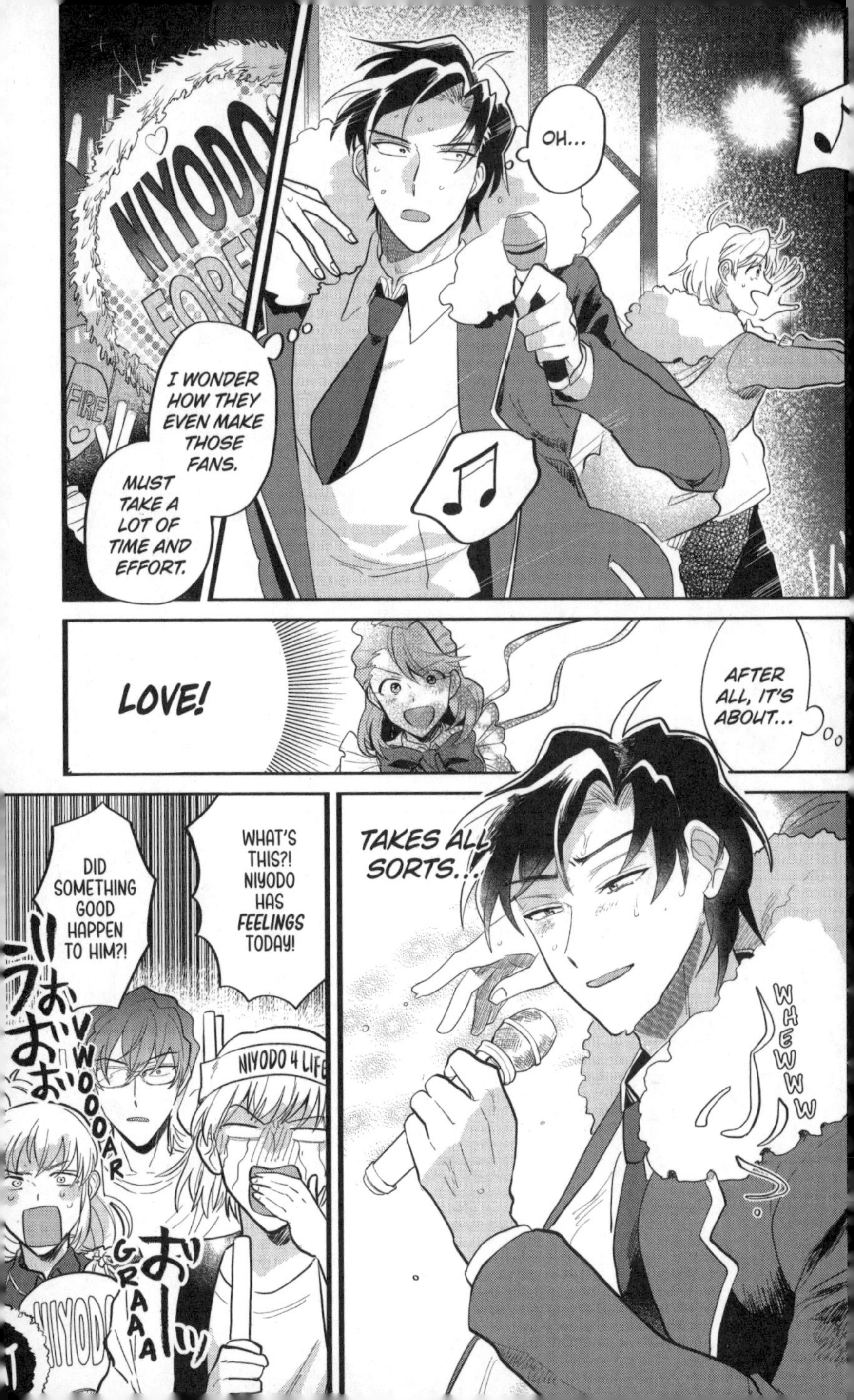
OH...
NIYODO
FORE
FIRE
I WONDER HOW THEY EVEN MAKE THOSE FANS.
MUST TAKE A LOT OF TIME AND EFFORT.
AFTER ALL, IT'S ABOUT...
LOVE!
TAKES ALL SORTS...
WHEWWWW
WHAT'S THIS?! NIYODO HAS FEELINGS TODAY!
DID SOMETHING GOOD HAPPEN TO HIM?!
NIYODO 4 LIFE
うおおお
VWOOOOAR
おおー
GRAAAA
NIYODO

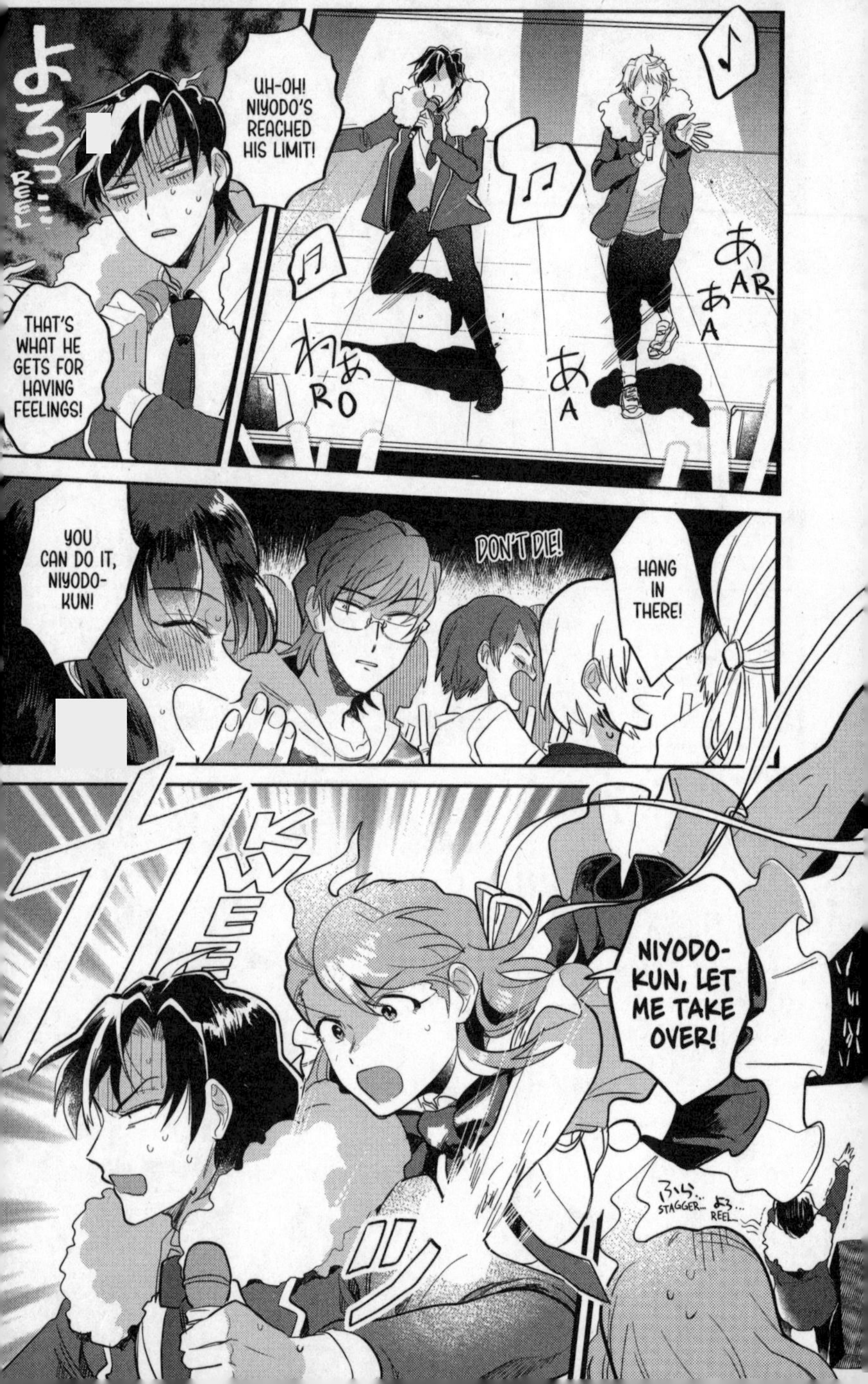
♪
AR
A
RO
A
UH-OH! NIYODO'S REACHED HIS LIMIT!
REEL
THAT'S WHAT HE GETS FOR HAVING FEELINGS!
HANG IN THERE!
DON'T DIE!
YOU CAN DO IT, NIYODO-KUN!
NIYODO-KUN, LET ME TAKE OVER!
KWEEE
STAGGER... REEL...

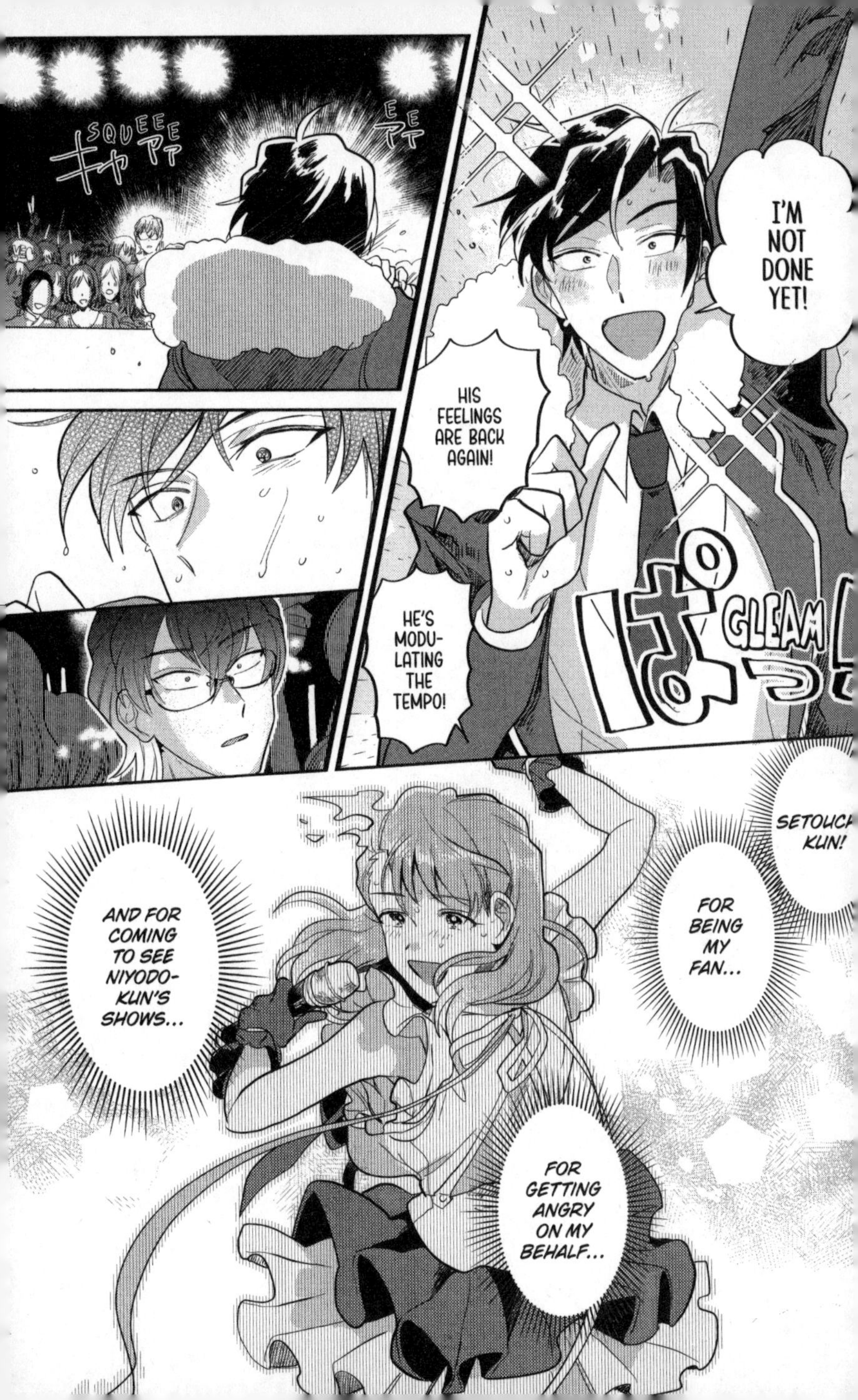
I'M NOT DONE YET!
HIS FEELINGS ARE BACK AGAIN!
GLEAM
HE'S MODU-LATING THE TEMPO!
SQUEEEE
EE
SETOUCH KUN!
FOR BEING MY FAN...
AND FOR COMING TO SEE NIYODO-KUN'S SHOWS...
FOR GETTING ANGRY ON MY BEHALF...

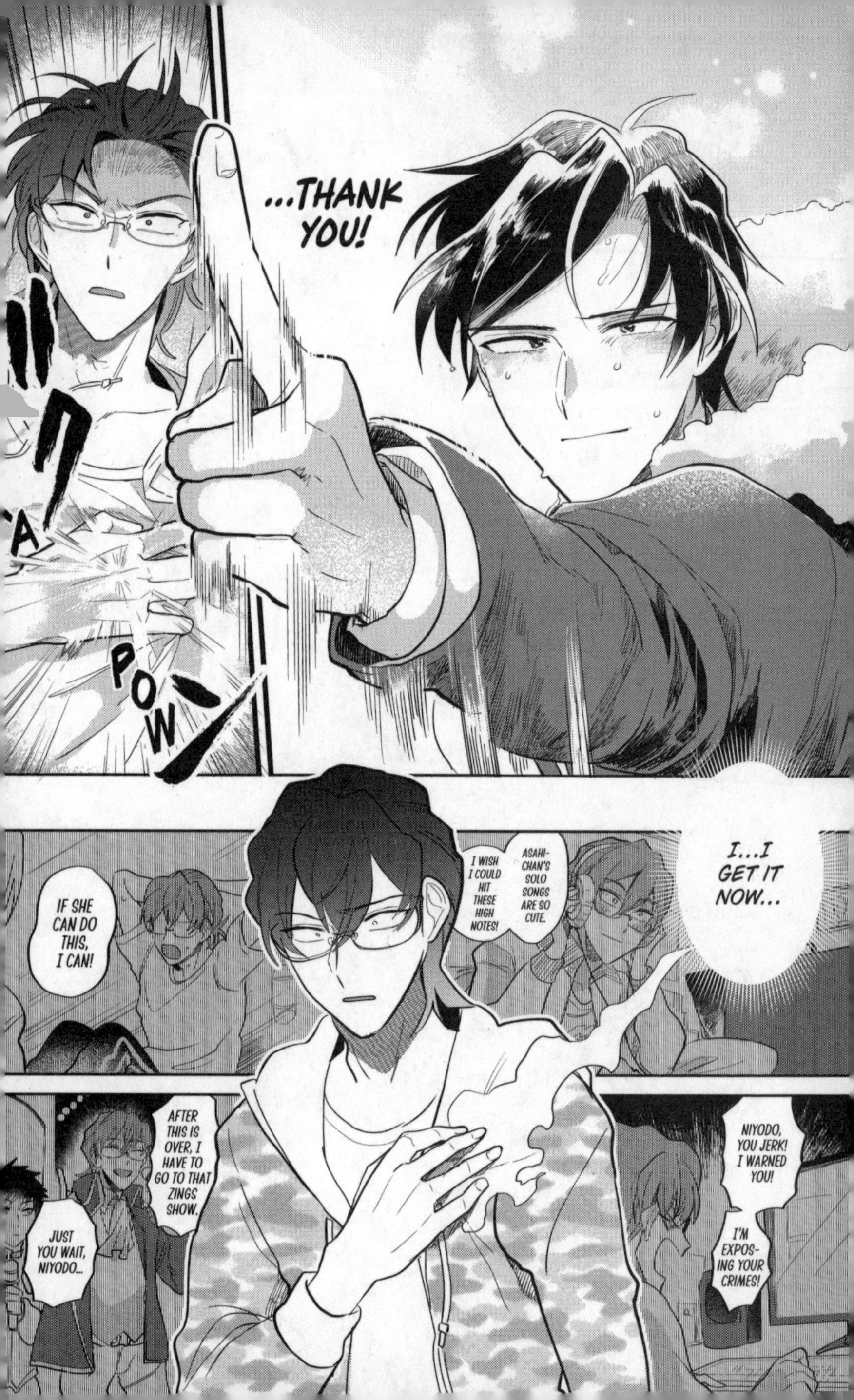
...THANK YOU!
POW
I...I GET IT NOW...
ASAHI-CHAN'S SOLO SONGS ARE SO CUTE.
I WISH I COULD HIT THESE HIGH NOTES!
IF SHE CAN DO THIS, I CAN!
NIYODO, YOU JERK! I WARNED YOU!
I'M EXPOS-ING YOUR CRIMES!
AFTER THIS IS OVER, I HAVE TO GO TO THAT ZINGS SHOW.
JUST YOU WAIT, NIYODO...

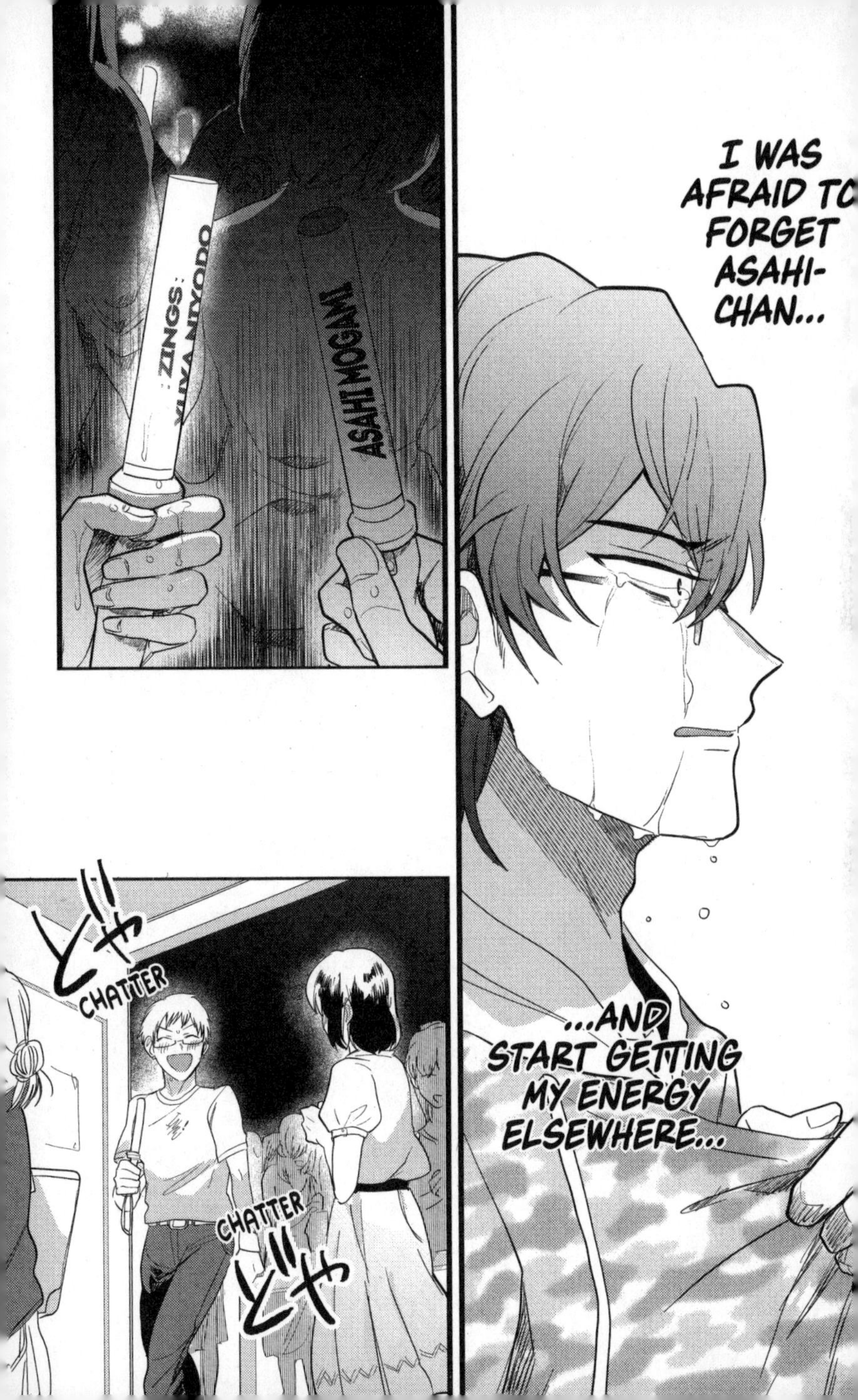
I WAS AFRAID TO FORGET ASAHI-CHAN...
...AND START GETTING MY ENERGY ELSEWHERE...
ZINGS: YUYA NIYODO
ASAHI MOGAMI
どや
CHATTER
CHATTER
どや

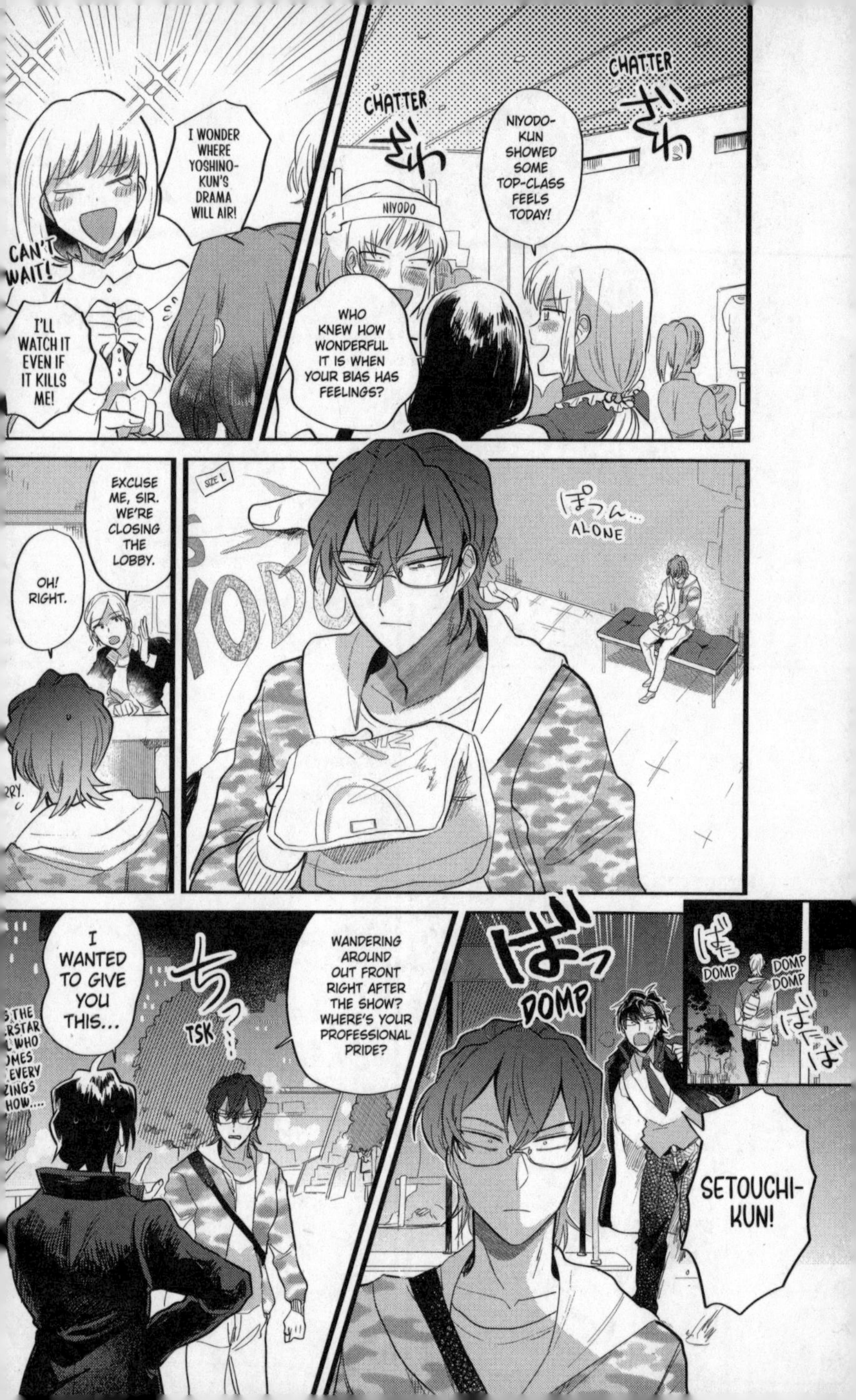
CHATTER
ざわ
NIYODO
NIYODO-KUN SHOWED SOME TOP-CLASS FEELS TODAY!
WHO KNEW HOW WONDERFUL IT IS WHEN YOUR BIAS HAS FEELINGS?
CHATTER
ざわ
I WONDER WHERE YOSHINO-KUN'S DRAMA WILL AIR!
CAN'T WAIT!
I'LL WATCH IT EVEN IF IT KILLS ME!
ぽつん…
ALONE
SIZE L
EXCUSE ME, SIR. WE'RE CLOSING THE LOBBY.
OH! RIGHT.
ばた
DOMP
DOMP DOMP
ばたばた
ばっ
DOMP
SETOUCHI-KUN!
WANDERING AROUND OUT FRONT RIGHT AFTER THE SHOW? WHERE'S YOUR PROFESSIONAL PRIDE?
ちっ
TSK...
I WANTED TO GIVE YOU THIS...

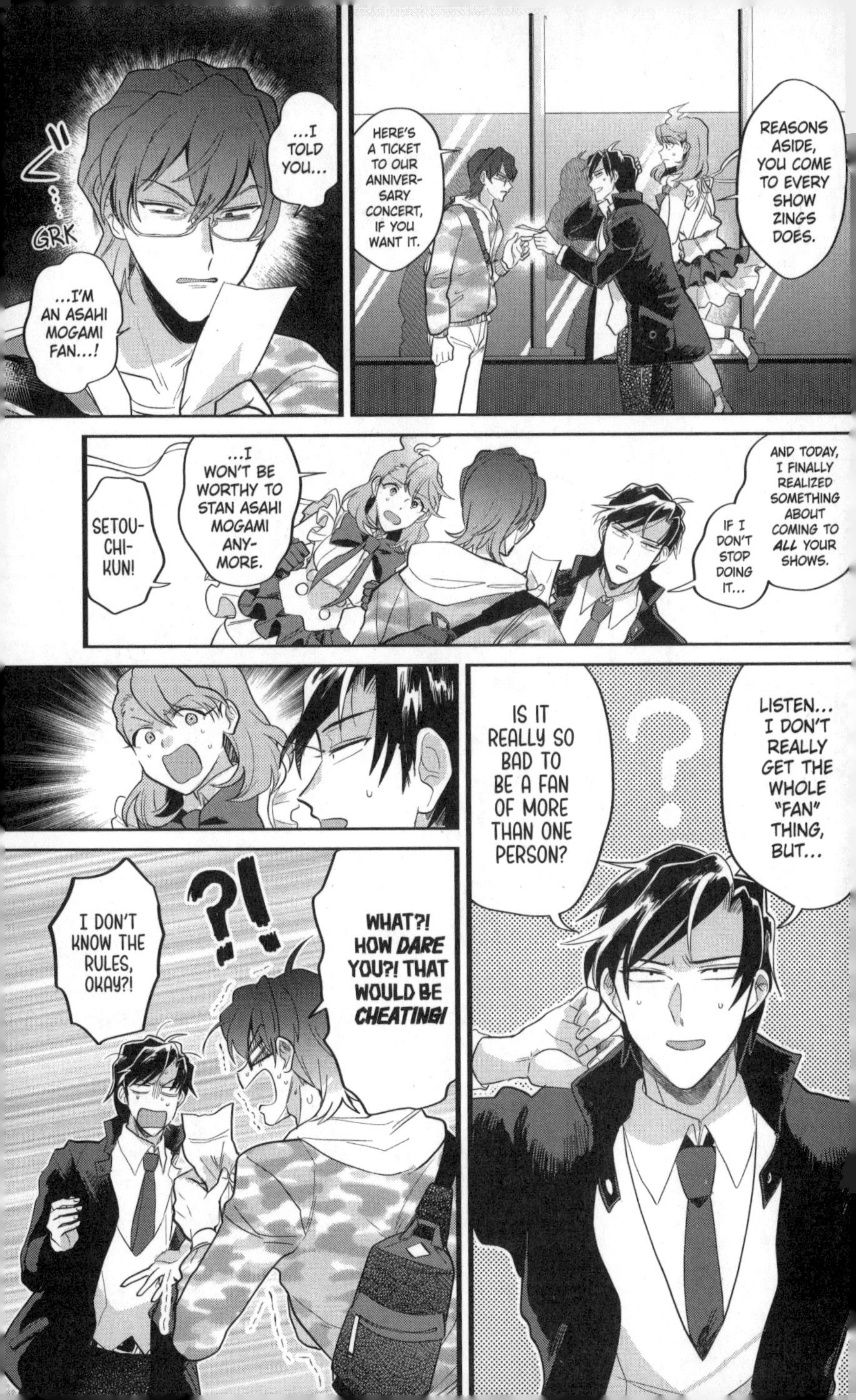
REASONS ASIDE, YOU COME TO EVERY SHOW ZINGS DOES.
HERE'S A TICKET TO OUR ANNIVERSARY CONCERT, IF YOU WANT IT.
...I TOLD YOU...
GRK
...I'M AN ASAHI MOGAMI FAN...!
AND TODAY, I FINALLY REALIZED SOMETHING ABOUT COMING TO *ALL* YOUR SHOWS.
IF I DON'T STOP DOING IT...
...I WON'T BE WORTHY TO STAN ASAHI MOGAMI ANYMORE.
SETOUCHI-KUN!
LISTEN... I DON'T REALLY GET THE WHOLE "FAN" THING, BUT...
IS IT REALLY SO BAD TO BE A FAN OF MORE THAN ONE PERSON?
WHAT?! HOW *DARE* YOU?! THAT WOULD BE *CHEATING!*
I DON'T KNOW THE RULES, OKAY?!

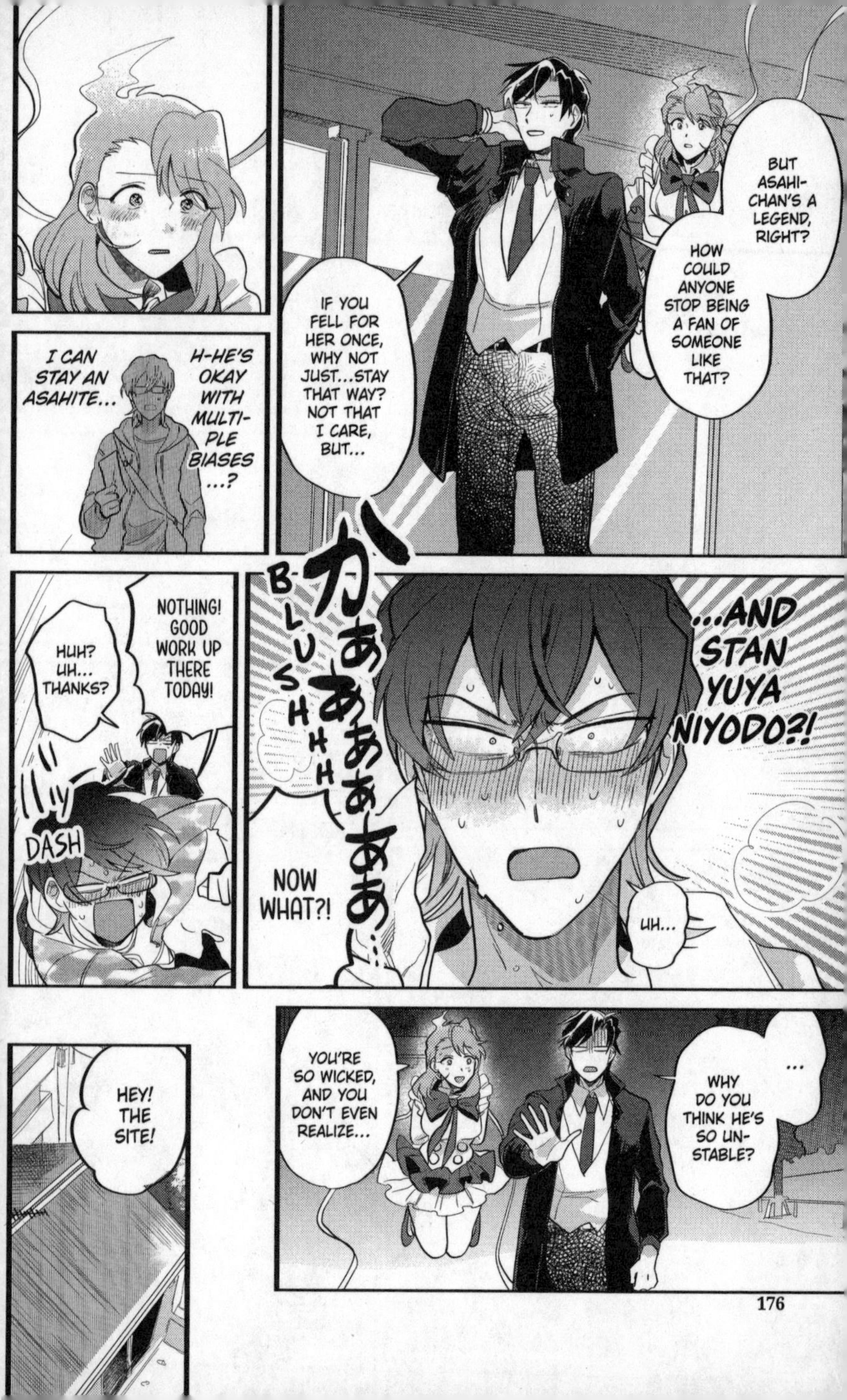
BUT ASAHI-CHAN'S A LEGEND, RIGHT?
HOW COULD ANYONE STOP BEING A FAN OF SOMEONE LIKE THAT?
IF YOU FELL FOR HER ONCE, WHY NOT JUST...STAY THAT WAY? NOT THAT I CARE, BUT...
H-HE'S OKAY WITH MULTI-PLE BIASES ...?
I CAN STAY AN ASAHITE...
...AND STAN YUYA NIYODO?!
UH...
かあああああああ
BLUSHHHH
NOW WHAT?!
NOTHING! GOOD WORK UP THERE TODAY!
HUH? UH... THANKS?
DASH
...
WHY DO YOU THINK HE'S SO UN-STABLE?
YOU'RE SO WICKED, AND YOU DON'T EVEN REALIZE...
HEY! THE SITE!

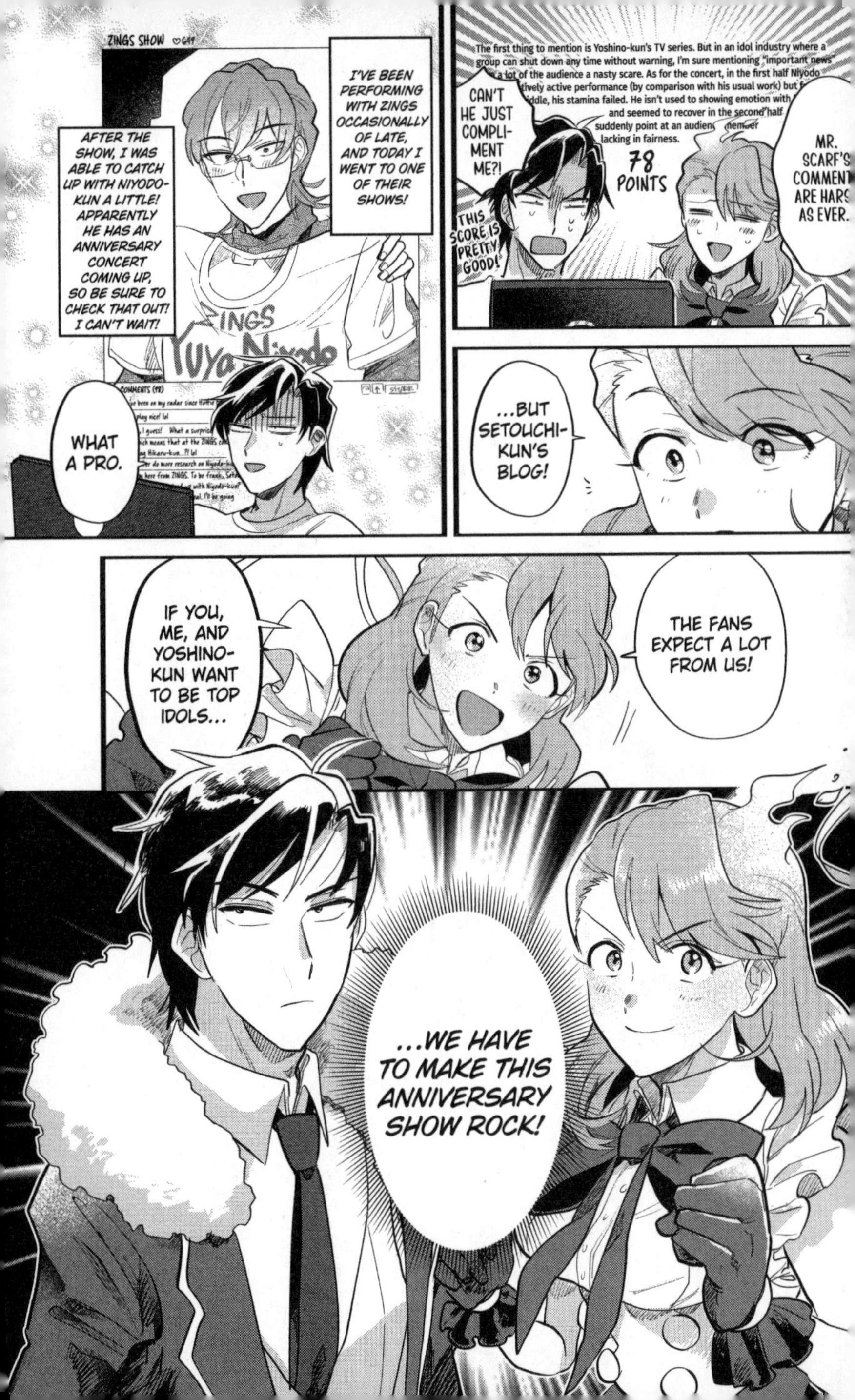
The first thing to mention is Yoshino-kun's TV series. But in an idol industry where a group can shut down any time without warning, I'm sure mentioning "important news" a lot of the audience a nasty scare. As for the concert, in the first half Niyodo tively active performance (by comparison with his usual work) but iddle, his stamina failed. He isn't used to showing emotion with and seemed to recover in the second half suddenly point at an audien member lacking in fairness.
MR. SCARF'S COMMENT ARE HARS AS EVER.
78 POINTS
CAN'T HE JUST COMPLI-MENT ME?!
THIS SCORE IS PRETTY GOOD!
...BUT SETOUCHI-KUN'S BLOG!
ZINGS SHOW
I'VE BEEN PERFORMING WITH ZINGS OCCASIONALLY OF LATE, AND TODAY I WENT TO ONE OF THEIR SHOWS!
AFTER THE SHOW, I WAS ABLE TO CATCH UP WITH NIYODO-KUN A LITTLE! APPARENTLY HE HAS AN ANNIVERSARY CONCERT COMING UP, SO BE SURE TO CHECK THAT OUT! I CAN'T WAIT!
COMMENTS (98)
WHAT A PRO.
THE FANS EXPECT A LOT FROM US!
IF YOU, ME, AND YOSHINO-KUN WANT TO BE TOP IDOLS...
...WE HAVE TO MAKE THIS ANNIVERSARY SHOW ROCK!

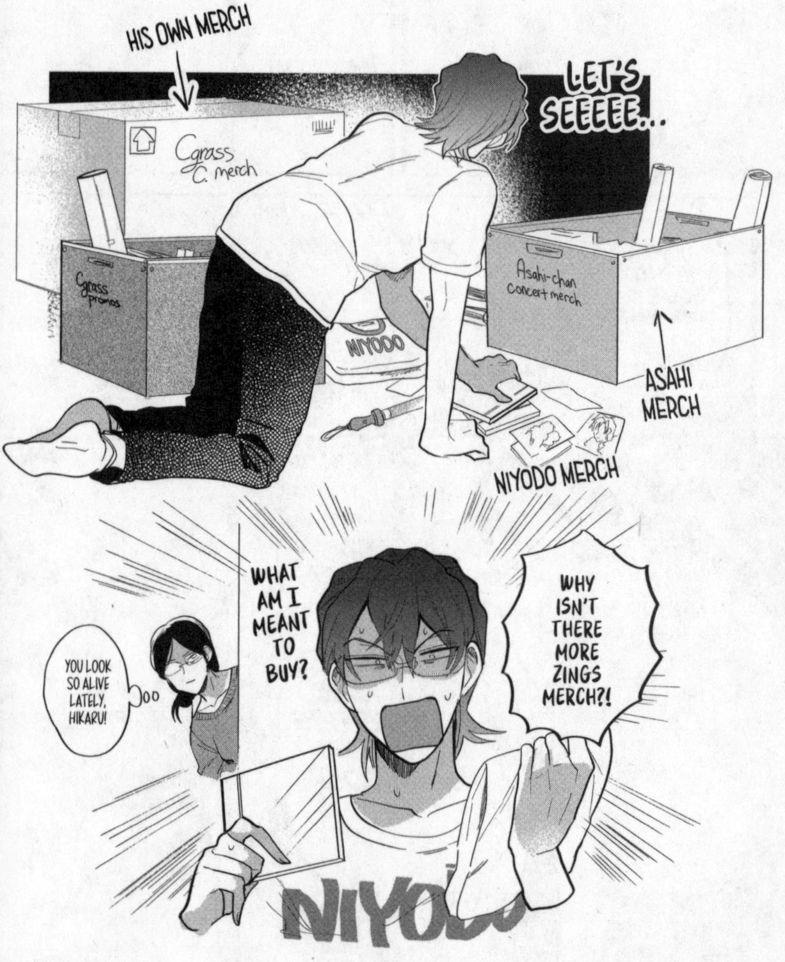
LET'S SEEEEEE...
ASAHI MERCH
Asahi-chan concert merch
NIYODO MERCH
NIYODO
HIS OWN MERCH
Cgrass C. merch
Cgrass promos
WHY ISN'T THERE MORE ZINGS MERCH?!
WHAT AM I MEANT TO BUY?
YOU LOOK SO ALIVE LATELY, HIKARU!
NIYODO

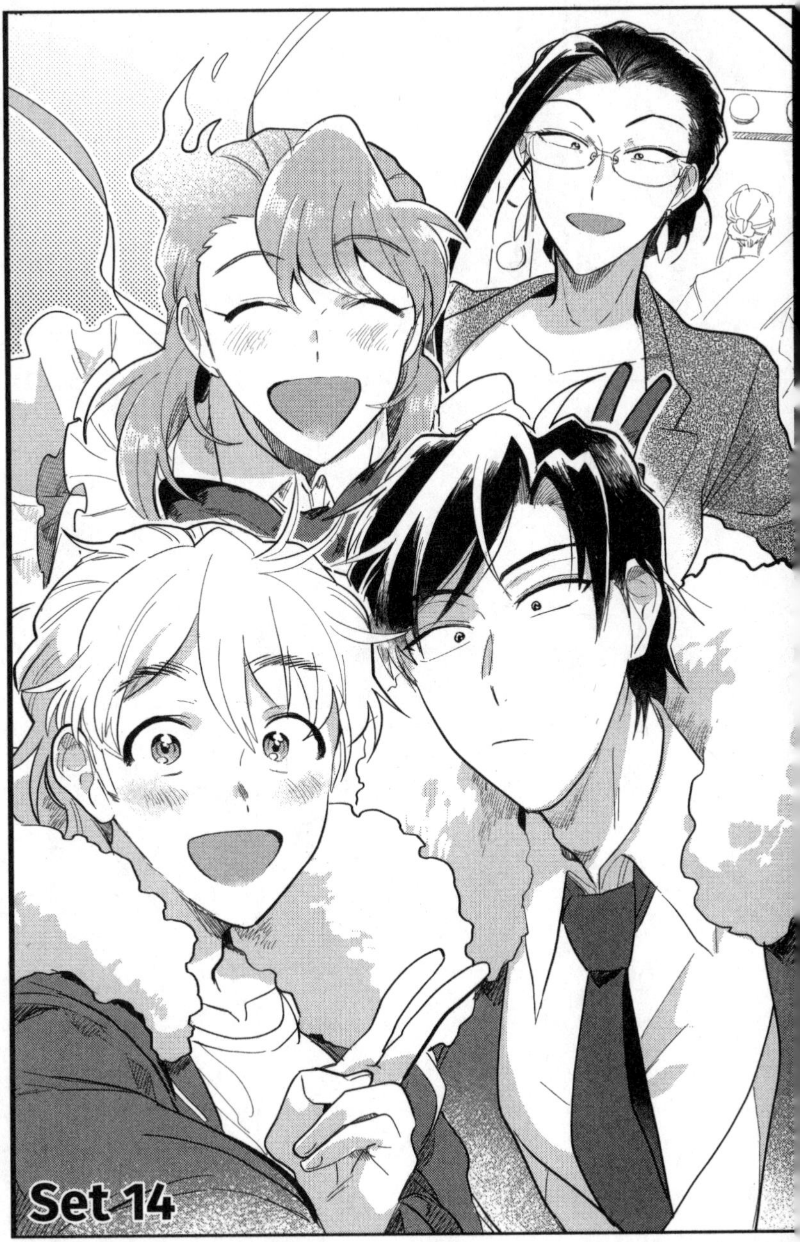
Set 14

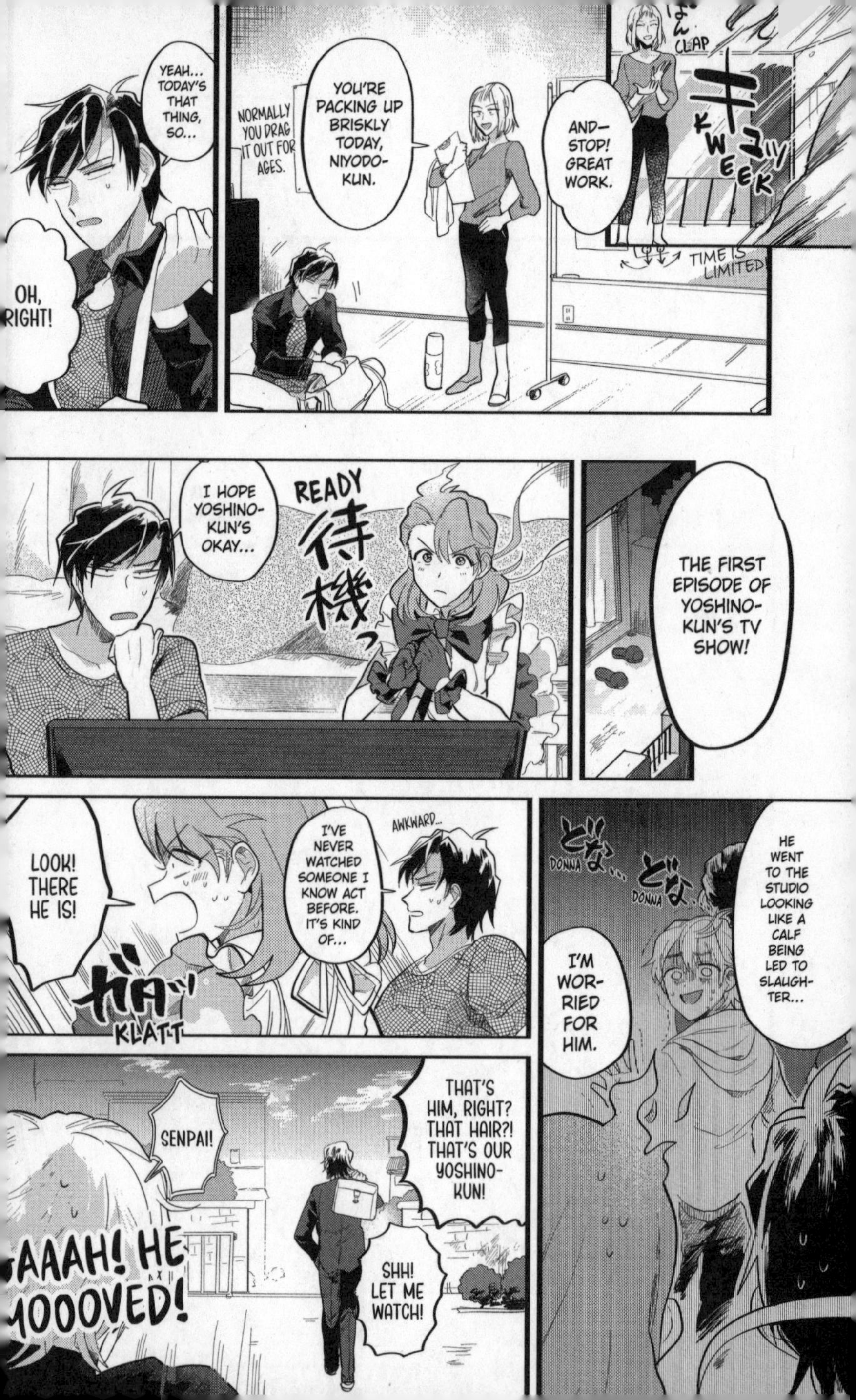

ぱん CLAP
AND— STOP! GREAT WORK.
キュッ KWEEEK
TIME IS LIMITED
YOU'RE PACKING UP BRISKLY TODAY, NIYODO-KUN.
NORMALLY YOU DRAG IT OUT FOR AGES.
YEAH... TODAY'S THAT THING, SO...
OH, RIGHT!
THE FIRST EPISODE OF YOSHINO-KUN'S TV SHOW!
READY 待機っ
I HOPE YOSHINO-KUN'S OKAY...
どな... DONNA
どな.. DONNA
HE WENT TO THE STUDIO LOOKING LIKE A CALF BEING LED TO SLAUGHTER...
I'M WORRIED FOR HIM.
AWKWARD...
I'VE NEVER WATCHED SOMEONE I KNOW ACT BEFORE. IT'S KIND OF...
LOOK! THERE HE IS!
ガタッ KLATT
THAT'S HIM, RIGHT? THAT HAIR?! THAT'S OUR YOSHINO-KUN!
SHH! LET ME WATCH!
SENPAI!
AAAH! HE OOOVED!

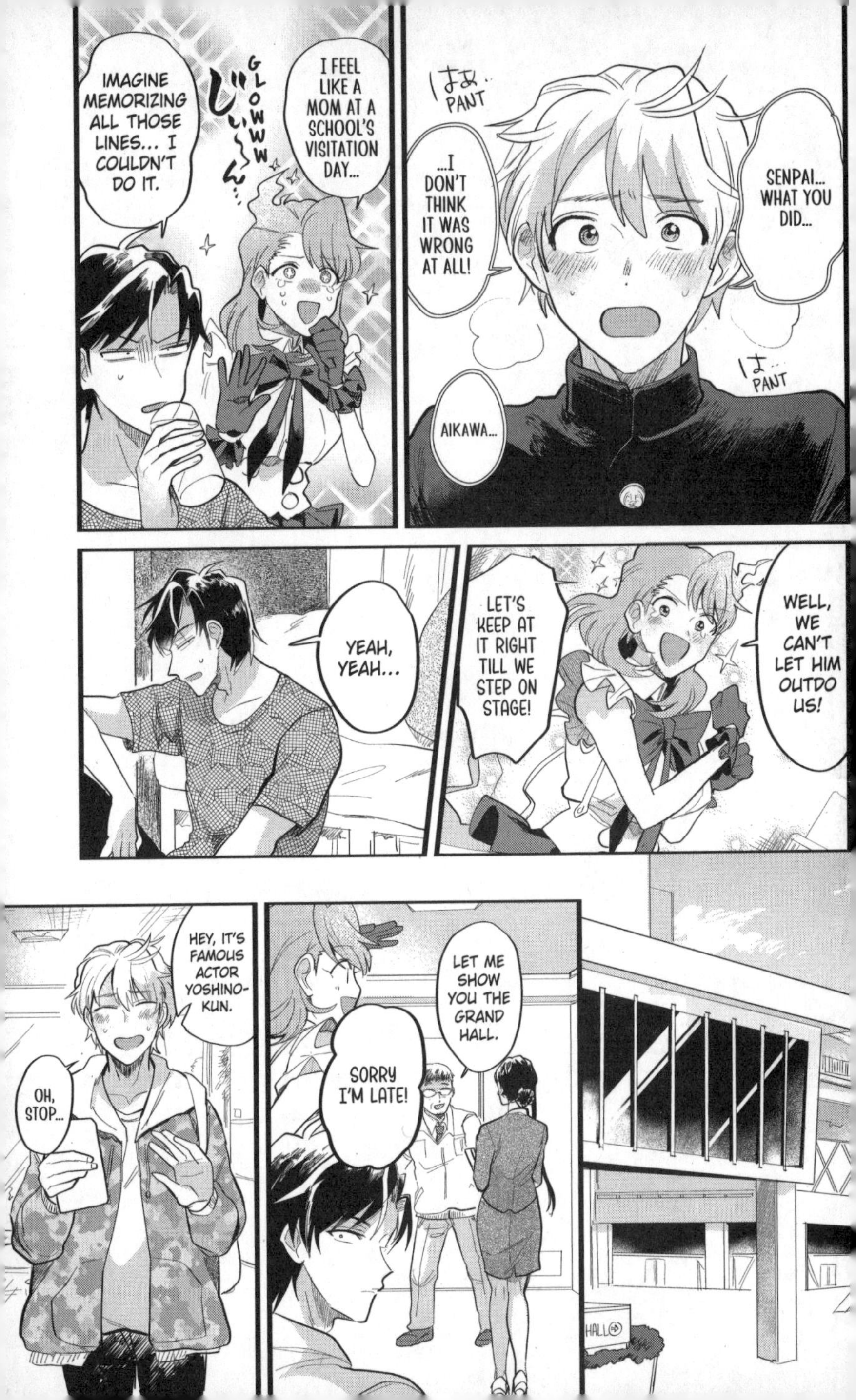
はあ… PANT
SENPAI... WHAT YOU DID...
...I DON'T THINK IT WAS WRONG AT ALL!
は… PANT
AIKAWA...
I FEEL LIKE A MOM AT A SCHOOL'S VISITATION DAY...
GLOWWW じぃ〜ん…
IMAGINE MEMORIZING ALL THOSE LINES... I COULDN'T DO IT.
WELL, WE CAN'T LET HIM OUTDO US!
LET'S KEEP AT IT RIGHT TILL WE STEP ON STAGE!
YEAH, YEAH...
HALL
LET ME SHOW YOU THE GRAND HALL.
SORRY I'M LATE!
HEY, IT'S FAMOUS ACTOR YOSHINO-KUN.
OH, STOP...

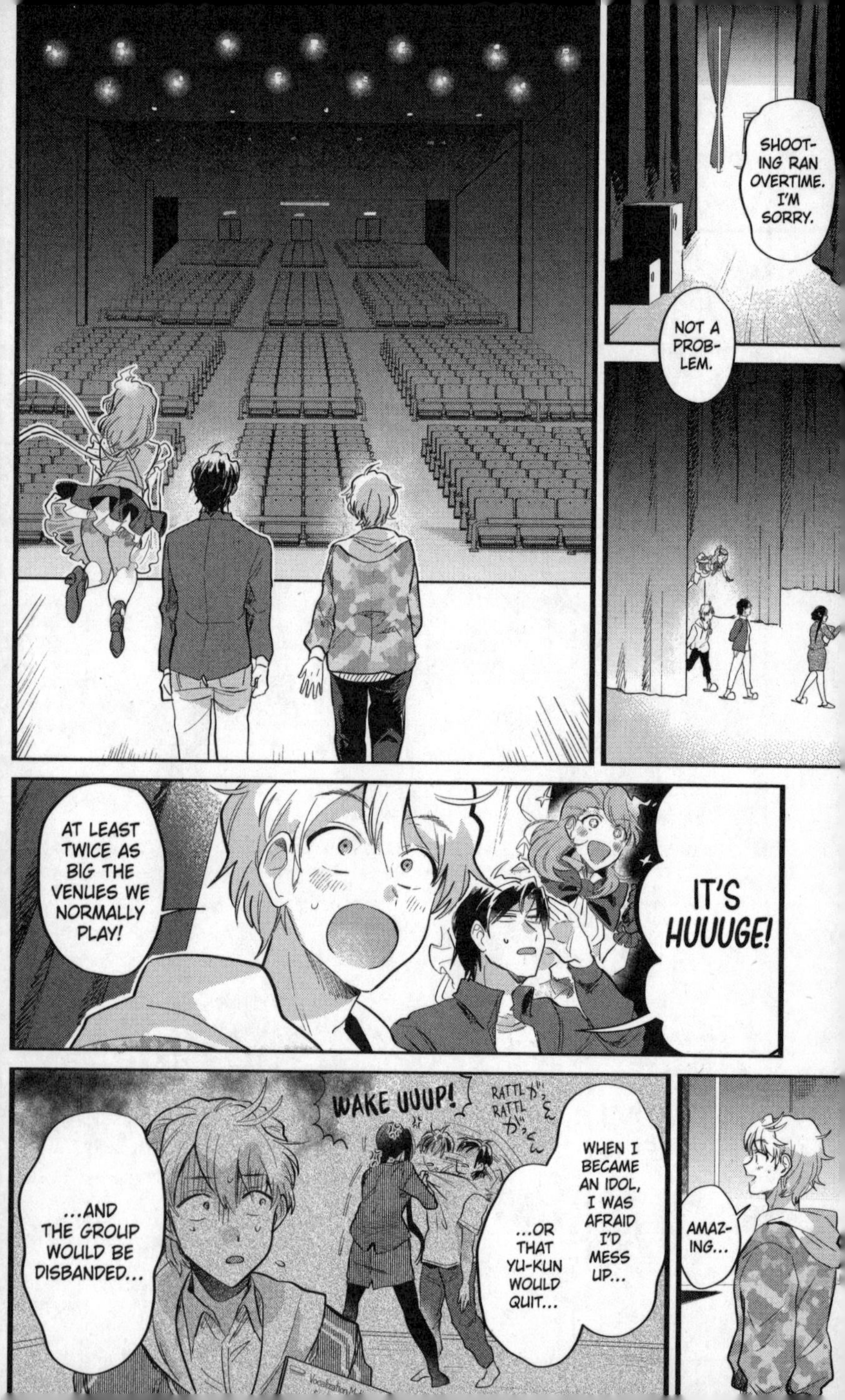
SHOOTING RAN OVERTIME. I'M SORRY.
NOT A PROBLEM.
IT'S HUUUGE!
AT LEAST TWICE AS BIG THE VENUES WE NORMALLY PLAY!
AMAZING...
RATTL RATTL
WHEN I BECAME AN IDOL, I WAS AFRAID I'D MESS UP...
WAKE UUUP!
...OR THAT YU-KUN WOULD QUIT...
...AND THE GROUP WOULD BE DISBANDED...

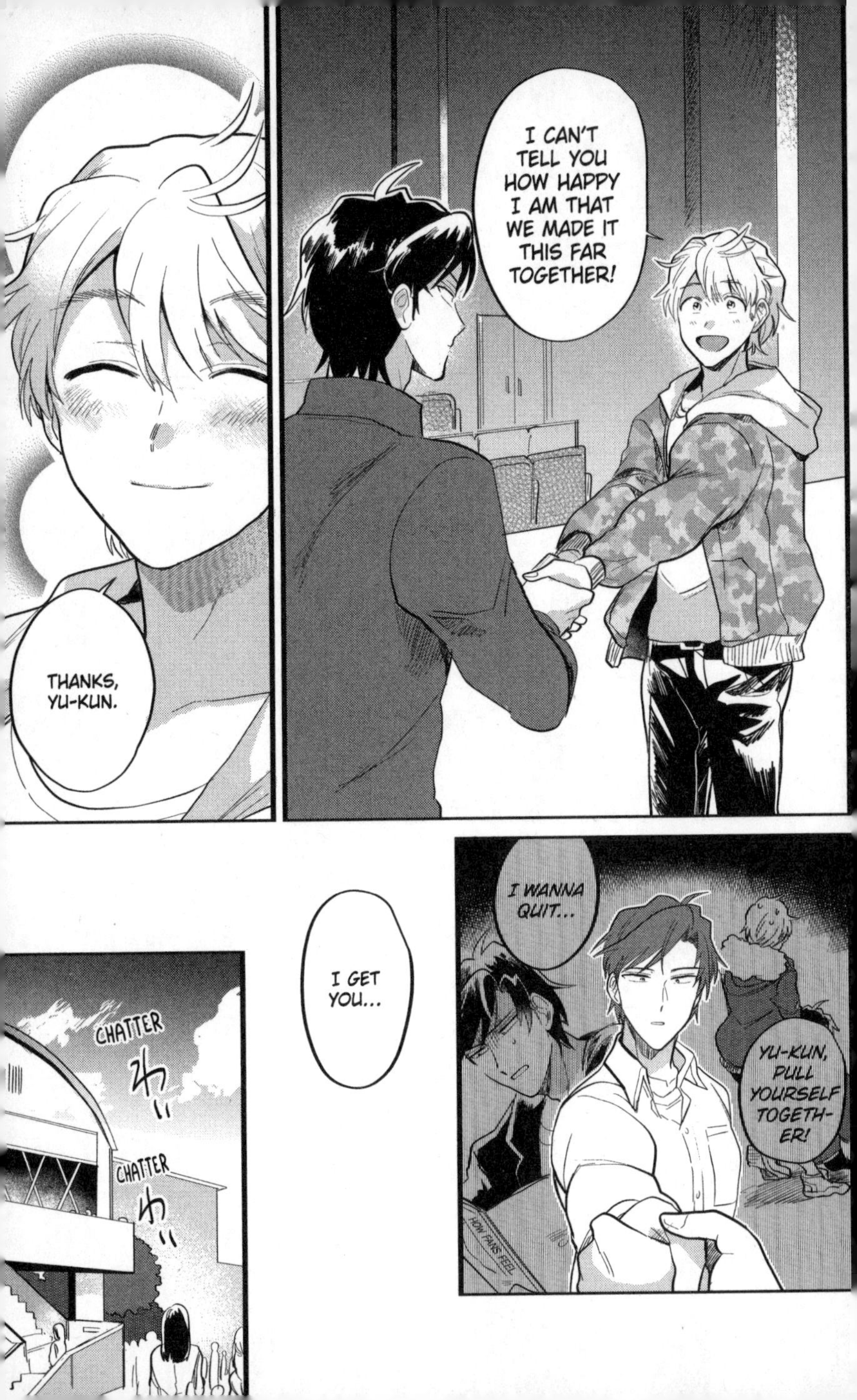
I CAN'T TELL YOU HOW HAPPY I AM THAT WE MADE IT THIS FAR TOGETHER!
THANKS, YU-KUN.
I WANNA QUIT...
YU-KUN, PULL YOURSELF TOGETH-ER!
HOW FANS FEEL
I GET YOU...
CHATTER
CHATTER

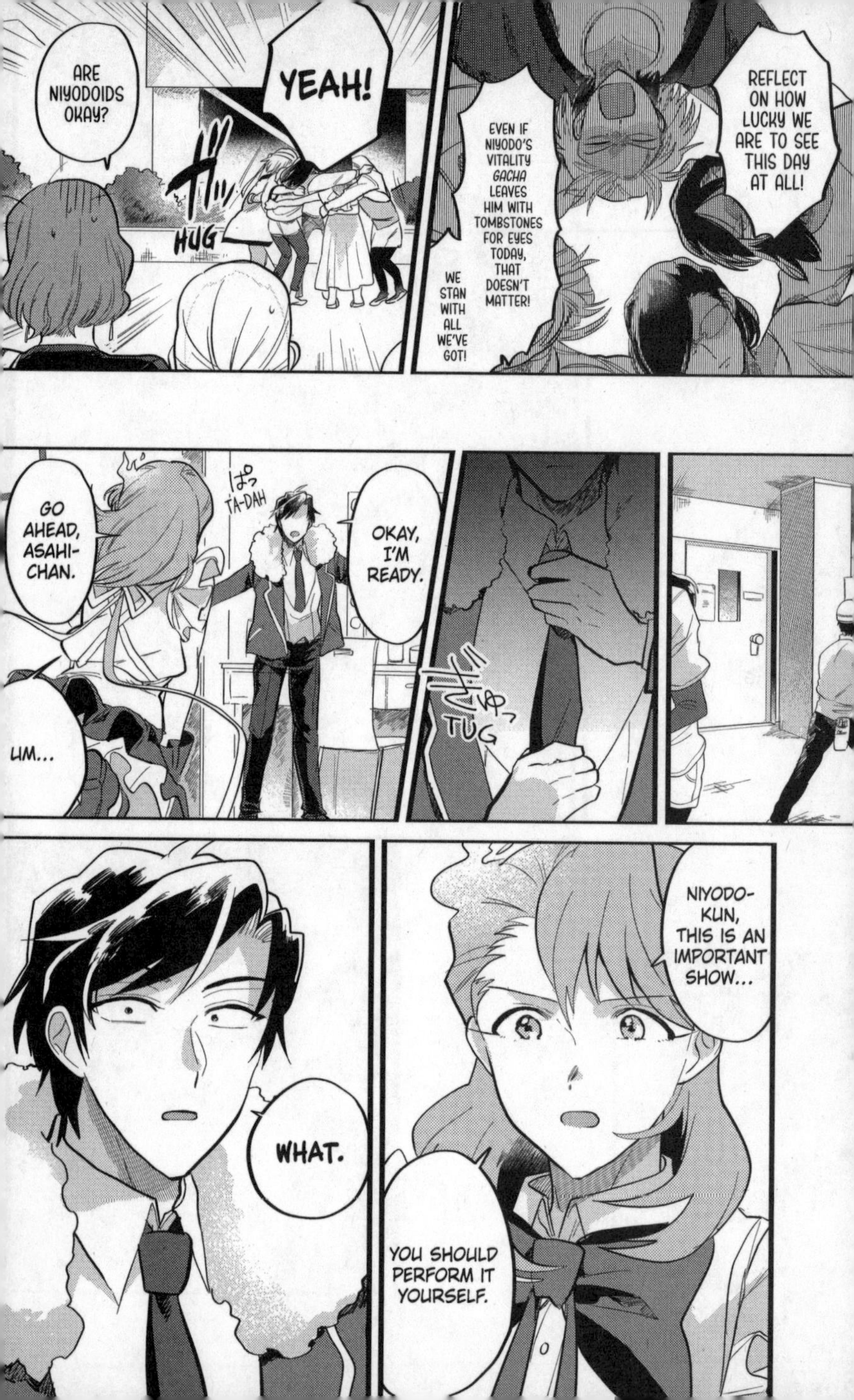
REFLECT ON HOW LUCKY WE ARE TO SEE THIS DAY AT ALL!
EVEN IF NIYODO'S VITALITY *GACHA* LEAVES HIM WITH TOMBSTONES FOR EYES TODAY, THAT DOESN'T MATTER!
WE STAN WITH ALL WE'VE GOT!
YEAH!
ARE NIYODOIDS OKAY?
HUG
TUG
OKAY, I'M READY.
TA-DAH
GO AHEAD, ASAHI-CHAN.
UM...
NIYODO-KUN, THIS IS AN IMPORTANT SHOW...
YOU SHOULD PERFORM IT YOURSELF.
WHAT.

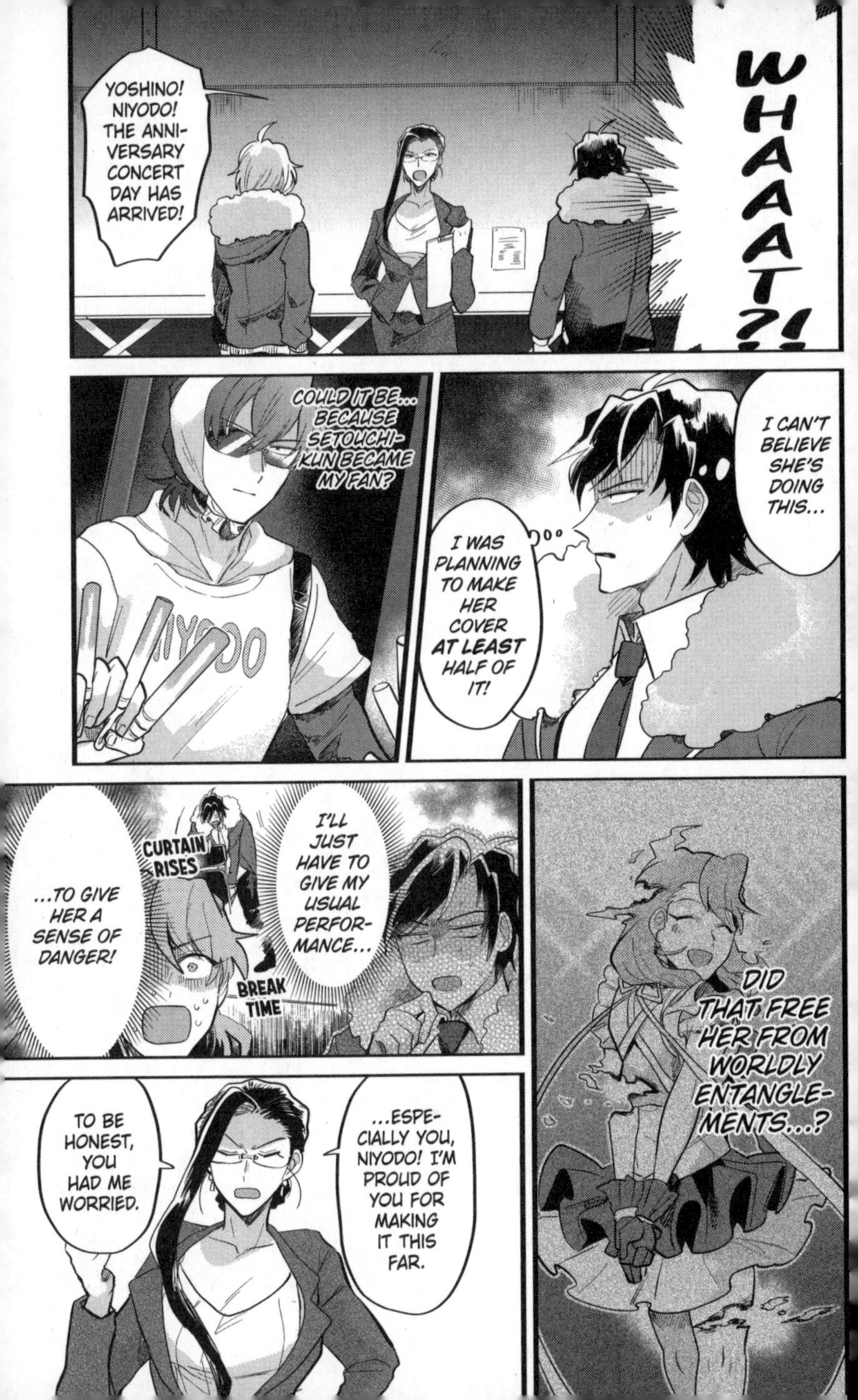
WHAAAT?!
YOSHINO! NIYODO! THE ANNIVERSARY CONCERT DAY HAS ARRIVED!
I CAN'T BELIEVE SHE'S DOING THIS...
I WAS PLANNING TO MAKE HER COVER AT LEAST HALF OF IT!
COULD IT BE... BECAUSE SETOUCHI-KUN BECAME MY FAN?
DID THAT FREE HER FROM WORLDLY ENTANGLEMENTS...?
I'LL JUST HAVE TO GIVE MY USUAL PERFORMANCE...
CURTAIN RISES
...TO GIVE HER A SENSE OF DANGER!
BREAK TIME
...ESPECIALLY YOU, NIYODO! I'M PROUD OF YOU FOR MAKING IT THIS FAR.
TO BE HONEST, YOU HAD ME WORRIED.

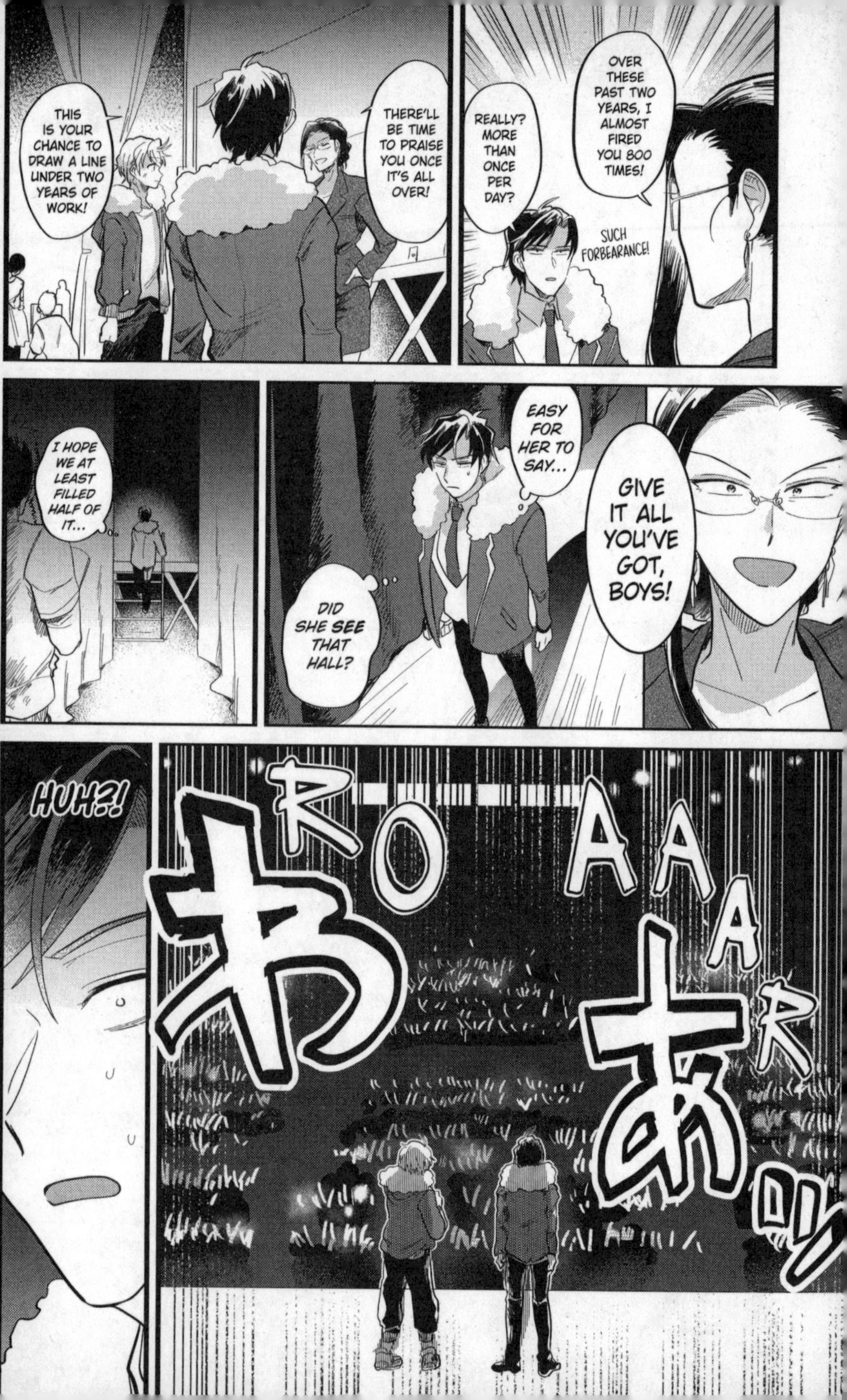
OVER THESE PAST TWO YEARS, I ALMOST FIRED YOU 800 TIMES!
REALLY? MORE THAN ONCE PER DAY?
SUCH FORBEARANCE!
THERE'LL BE TIME TO PRAISE YOU ONCE IT'S ALL OVER!
THIS IS YOUR CHANCE TO DRAW A LINE UNDER TWO YEARS OF WORK!
GIVE IT ALL YOU'VE GOT, BOYS!
EASY FOR HER TO SAY...
DID SHE SEE THAT HALL?
I HOPE WE AT LEAST FILLED HALF OF IT...
ROAAAR
おあ
HUH?!

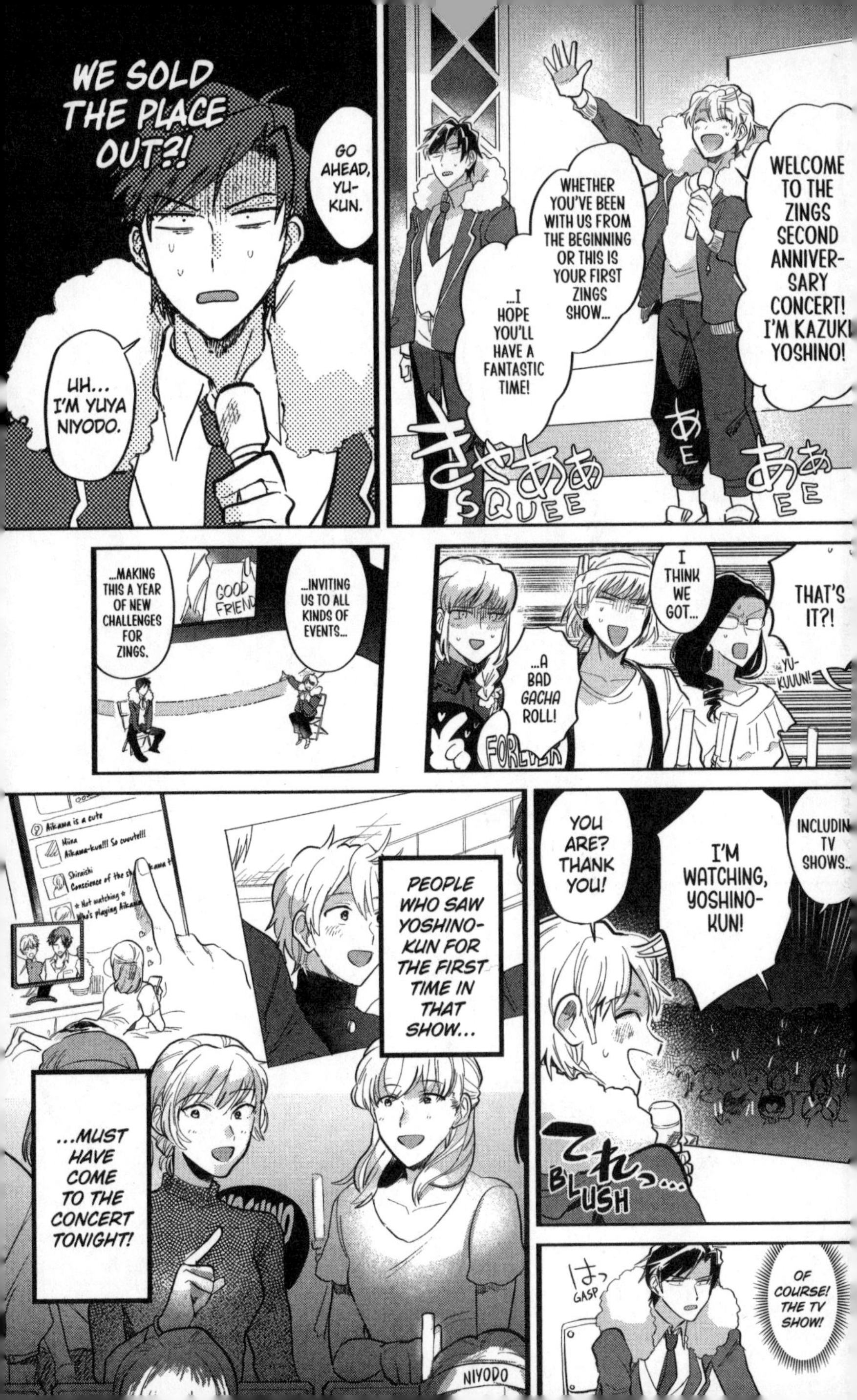
WELCOME TO THE ZINGS SECOND ANNIVERSARY CONCERT! I'M KAZUKI YOSHINO!
WHETHER YOU'VE BEEN WITH US FROM THE BEGINNING OR THIS IS YOUR FIRST ZINGS SHOW...
...I HOPE YOU'LL HAVE A FANTASTIC TIME!
きゃあああ
SQUEE
あ
E
ああ
EE
GO AHEAD, YU-KUN.
WE SOLD THE PLACE OUT?!
UH... I'M YUYA NIYODO.
THAT'S IT?!
I THINK WE GOT...
...A BAD GACHA ROLL!
YU-KUUUN!
...INVITING US TO ALL KINDS OF EVENTS...
...MAKING THIS A YEAR OF NEW CHALLENGES FOR ZINGS.
GOOD FRIEND
INCLUDIN TV SHOWS...
I'M WATCHING, YOSHINO-KUN!
YOU ARE? THANK YOU!
てれっ
BLUSH
はっ
GASP
OF COURSE! THE TV SHOW!
Aikawa is a cute
Miina
Aikawa-kun!!! So cuuute!!!
Shiraishi
☆ Not watching ☆
PEOPLE WHO SAW YOSHINO-KUN FOR THE FIRST TIME IN THAT SHOW...
...MUST HAVE COME TO THE CONCERT TONIGHT!
NIYODO

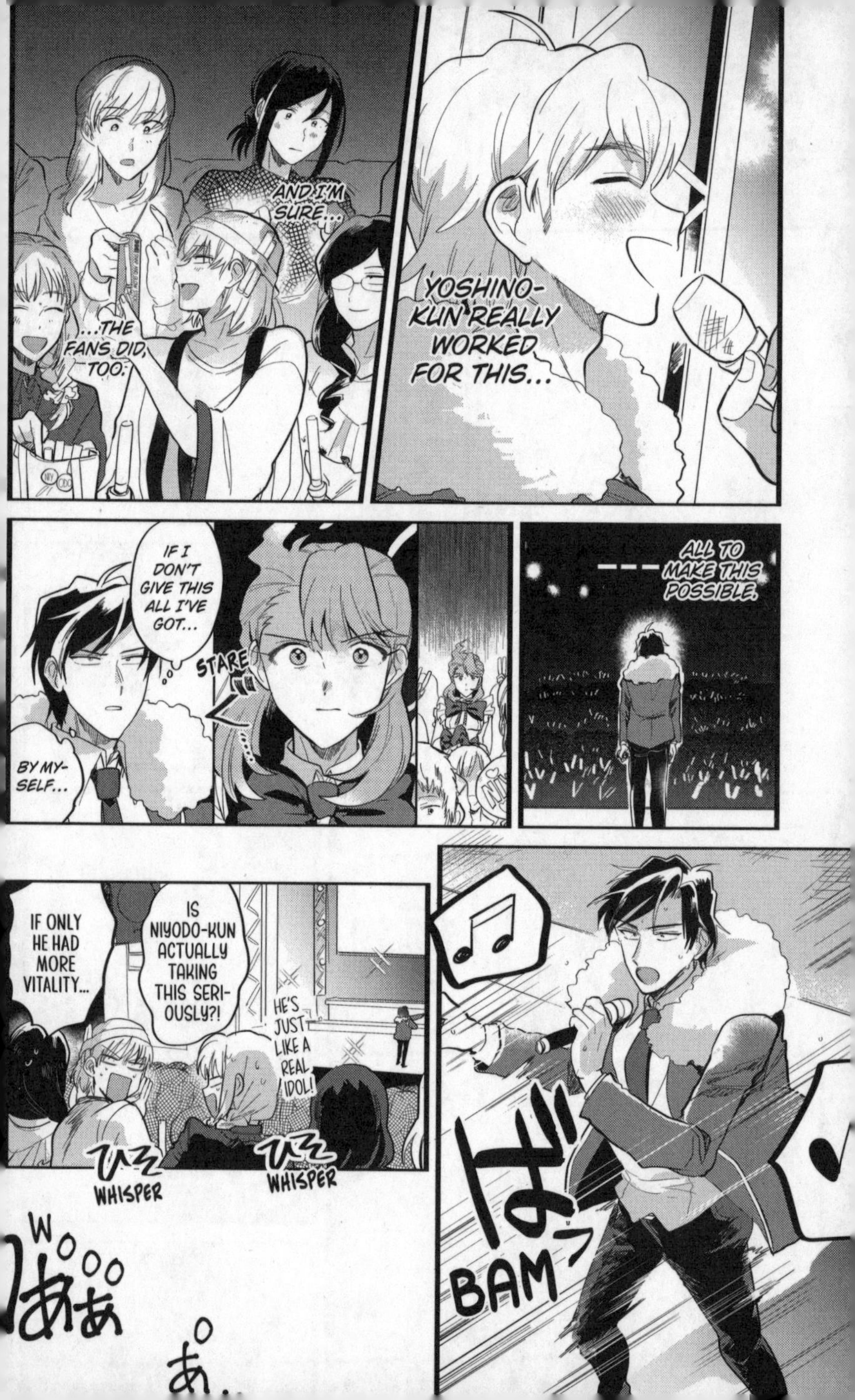
YOSHINO-KUN REALLY WORKED FOR THIS...
AND I'M SURE...
...THE FANS DID, TOO.
——ALL TO MAKE THIS POSSIBLE.
IF I DON'T GIVE THIS ALL I'VE GOT...
STARE
BY MY-SELF...
ぱっ BAM
IS NIYODO-KUN ACTUALLY TAKING THIS SERI-OUSLY?!
IF ONLY HE HAD MORE VITALITY...
HE'S JUST LIKE A REAL IDOL!
ひそ WHISPER
ひそ WHISPER
WOOO
ああ
あ.

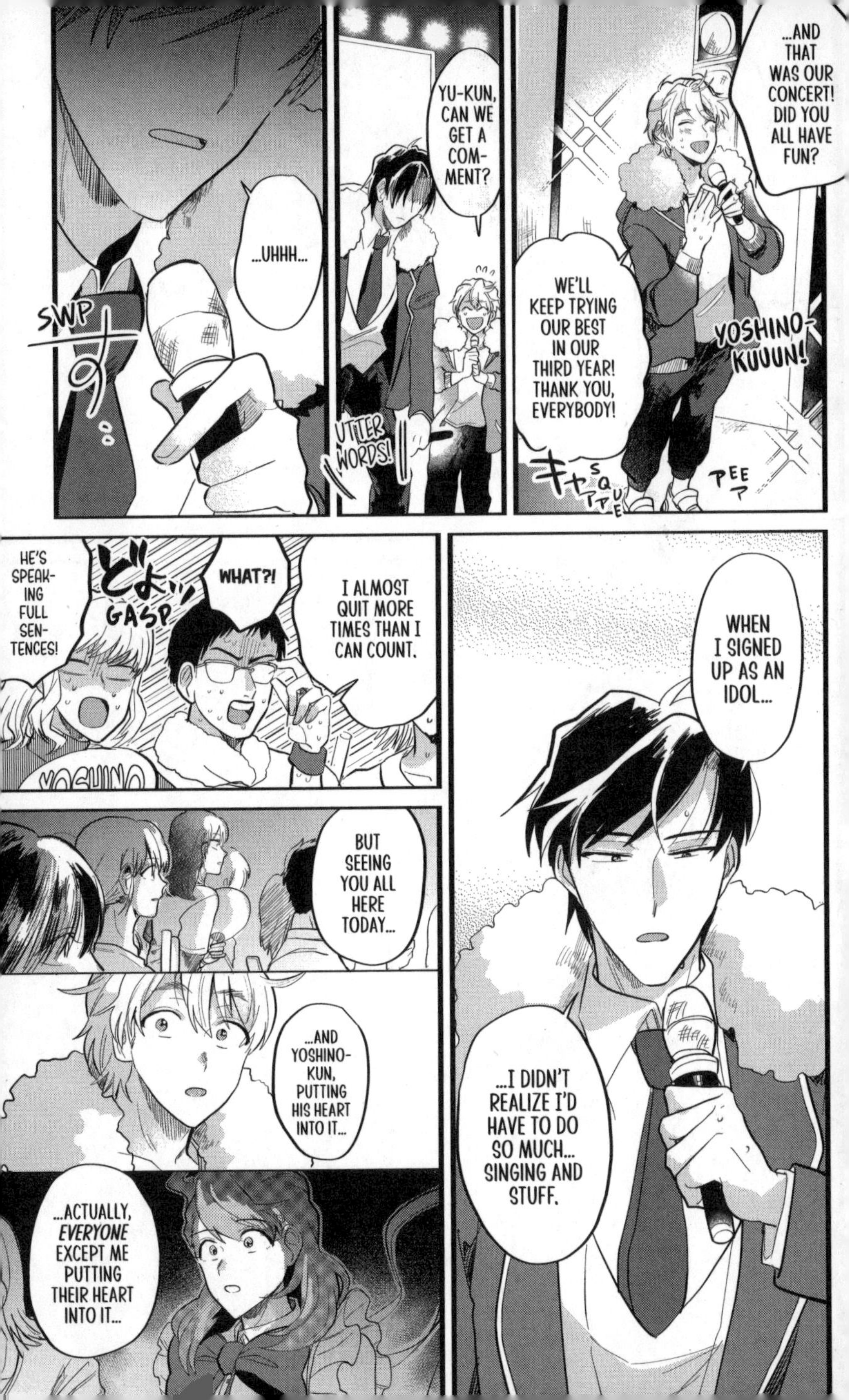
...AND THAT WAS OUR CONCERT! DID YOU ALL HAVE FUN?
WE'LL KEEP TRYING OUR BEST IN OUR THIRD YEAR! THANK YOU, EVERYBODY!
YOSHINO-KUUUN!
SQUEE
PEE
YU-KUN, CAN WE GET A COM-MENT?
UTTER WORDS!
...UHHH...
SWP
WHEN I SIGNED UP AS AN IDOL...
...I DIDN'T REALIZE I'D HAVE TO DO SO MUCH... SINGING AND STUFF.
I ALMOST QUIT MORE TIMES THAN I CAN COUNT.
WHAT?!
GASP
HE'S SPEAK-ING FULL SEN-TENCES!
YOSHINO
BUT SEEING YOU ALL HERE TODAY...
...AND YOSHINO-KUN, PUTTING HIS HEART INTO IT...
...ACTUALLY, *EVERYONE* EXCEPT ME PUTTING THEIR HEART INTO IT...

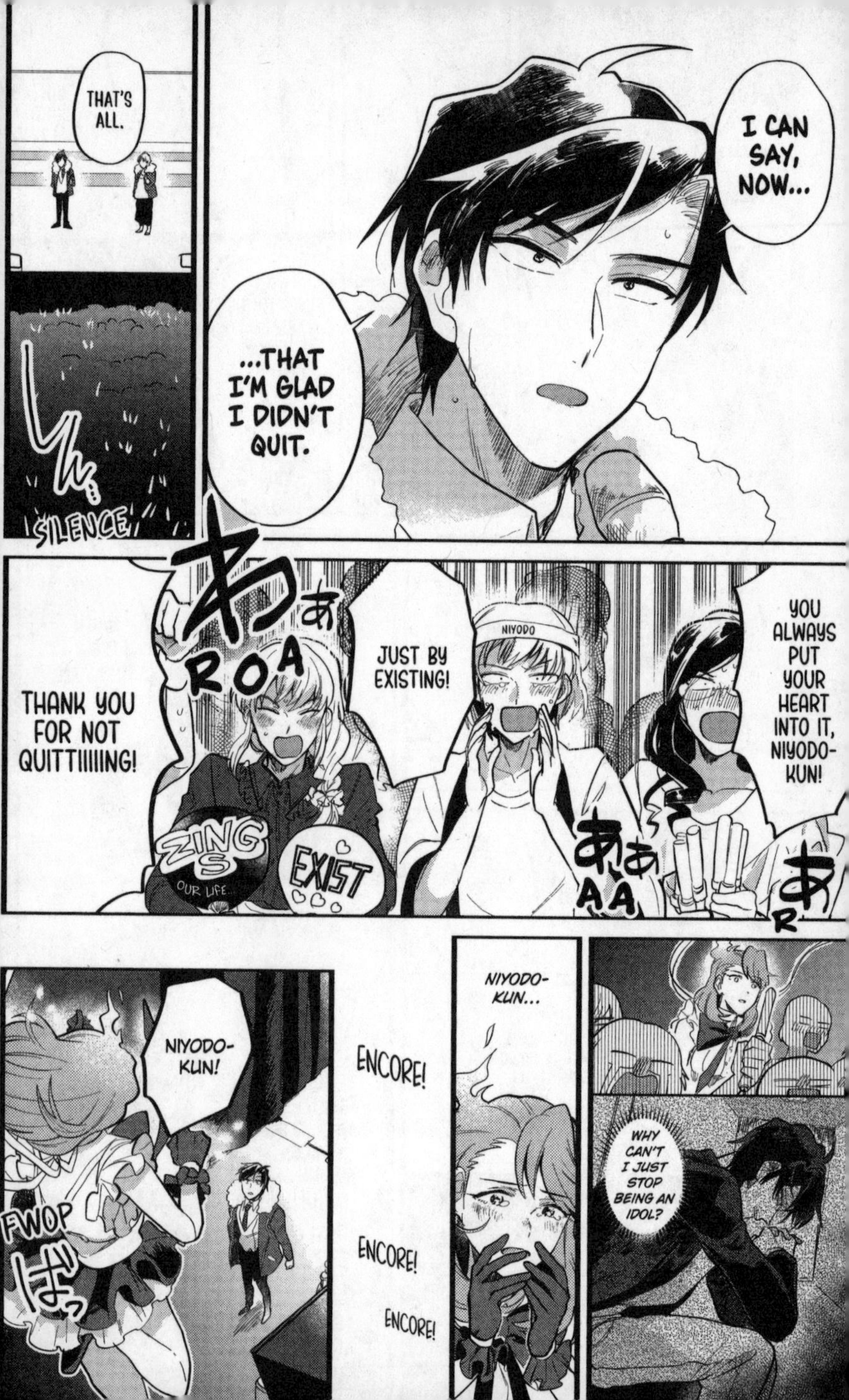

I CAN SAY, NOW...
...THAT I'M GLAD I DIDN'T QUIT.
THAT'S ALL.
しん
SILENCE
YOU ALWAYS PUT YOUR HEART INTO IT, NIYODO-KUN!
あ
R
ああ
AA
NIYODO
JUST BY EXISTING!
わ あ
ROA
THANK YOU FOR NOT QUITTIIIIING!
ZING S
OUR LIFE
EXIST
WHY CAN'T I JUST STOP BEING AN IDOL?
NIYODO-KUN...
ENCORE!
ENCORE!
ENCORE!
NIYODO-KUN!
FWOP
ぱっ

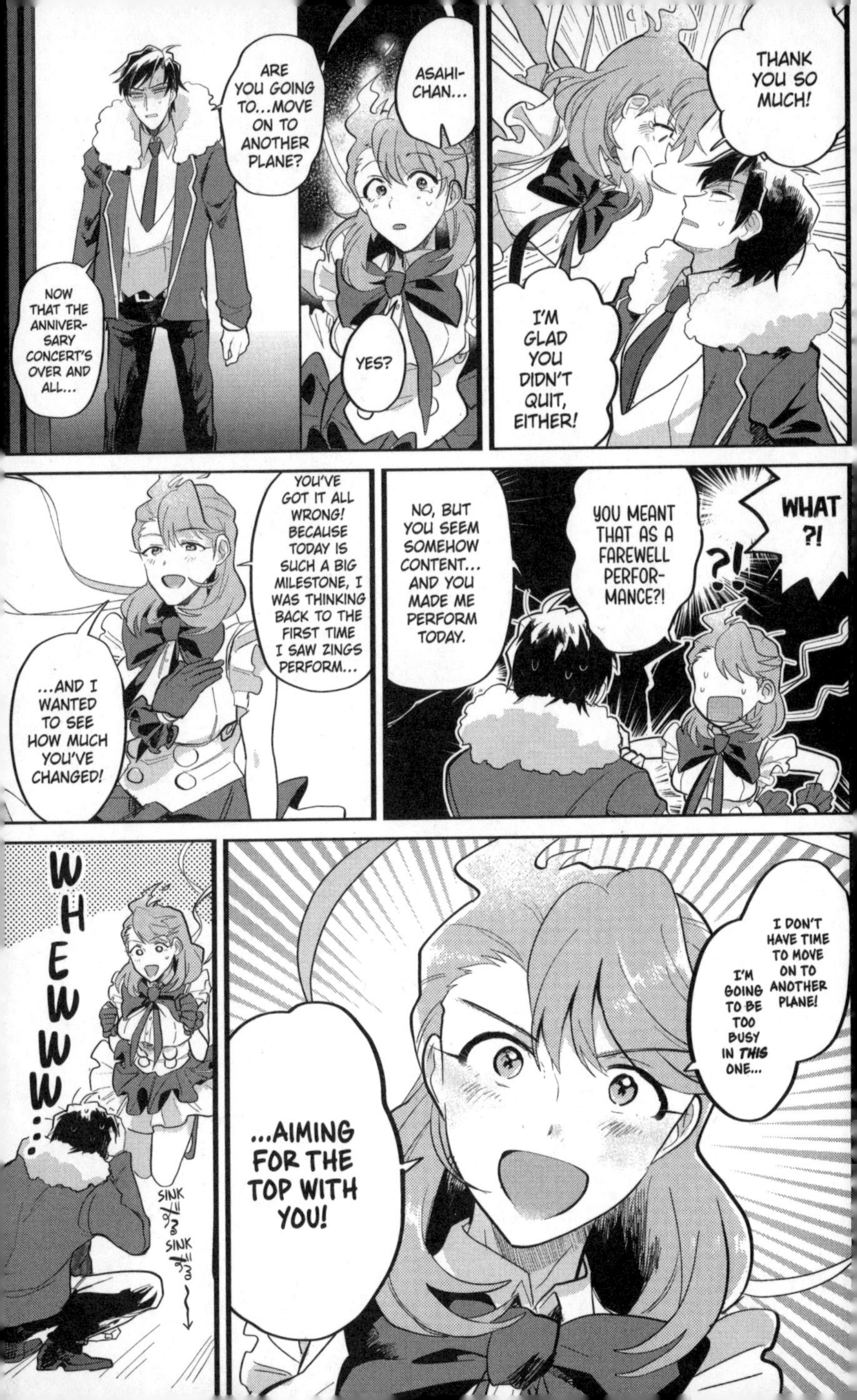

THANK YOU SO MUCH!
I'M GLAD YOU DIDN'T QUIT, EITHER!
ASAHI-CHAN...
YES?
ARE YOU GOING TO...MOVE ON TO ANOTHER PLANE?
NOW THAT THE ANNIVERSARY CONCERT'S OVER AND ALL...
WHAT?!
?!
YOU MEANT THAT AS A FAREWELL PERFORMANCE?!
NO, BUT YOU SEEM SOMEHOW CONTENT... AND YOU MADE ME PERFORM TODAY.
YOU'VE GOT IT ALL WRONG! BECAUSE TODAY IS SUCH A BIG MILESTONE, I WAS THINKING BACK TO THE FIRST TIME I SAW ZINGS PERFORM...
...AND I WANTED TO SEE HOW MUCH YOU'VE CHANGED!
I DON'T HAVE TIME TO MOVE ON TO ANOTHER PLANE!
I'M GOING TO BE TOO BUSY IN *THIS* ONE...
...AIMING FOR THE TOP WITH YOU!
WHEWWWW...
SINK
SINK

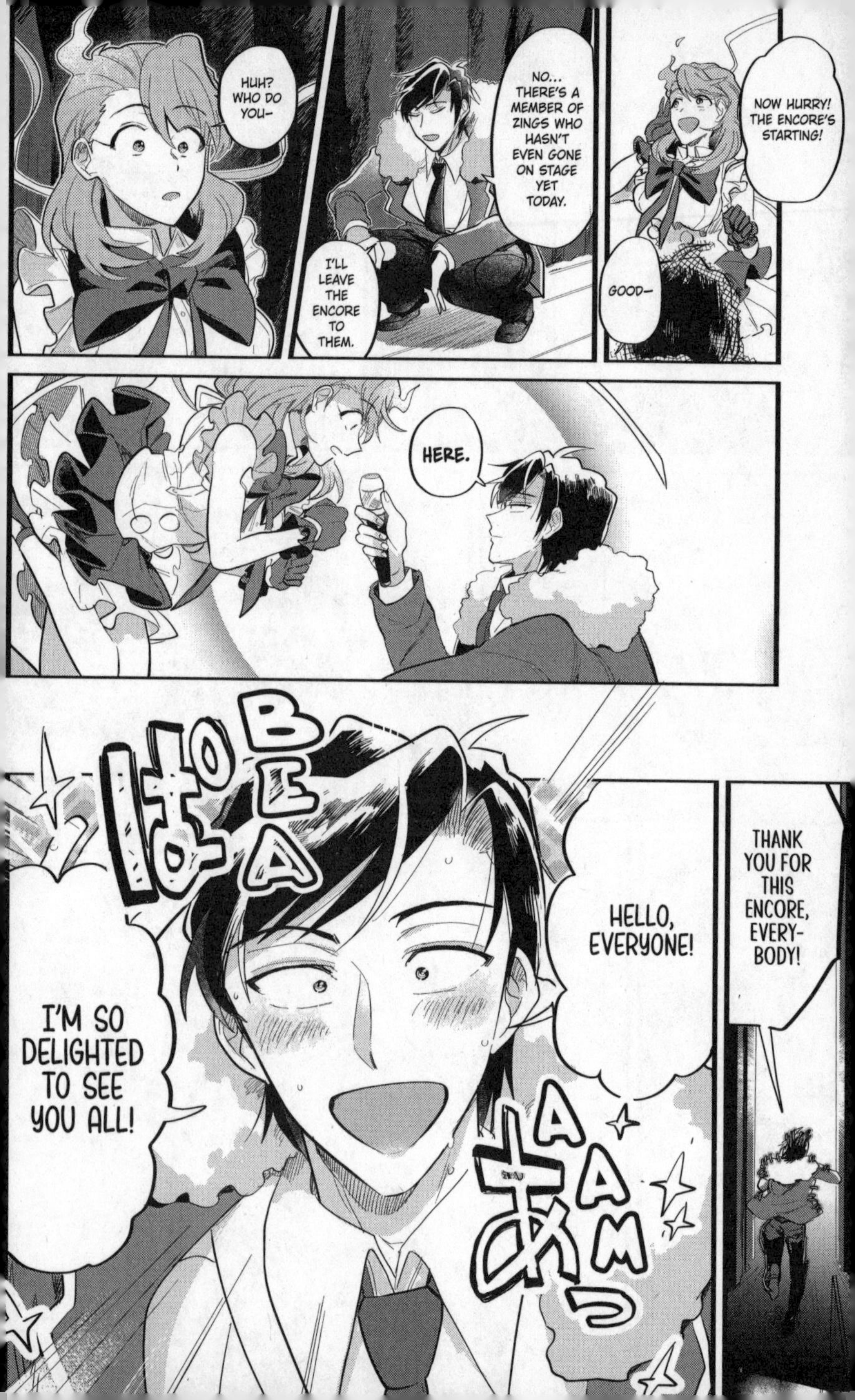
NOW HURRY! THE ENCORE'S STARTING!
GOOD—
NO... THERE'S A MEMBER OF ZINGS WHO HASN'T EVEN GONE ON STAGE YET TODAY.
I'LL LEAVE THE ENCORE TO THEM.
HUH? WHO DO YOU—
HERE.
THANK YOU FOR THIS ENCORE, EVERY-BODY!
HELLO, EVERYONE!
I'M SO DELIGHTED TO SEE YOU ALL!
BEA
AAM

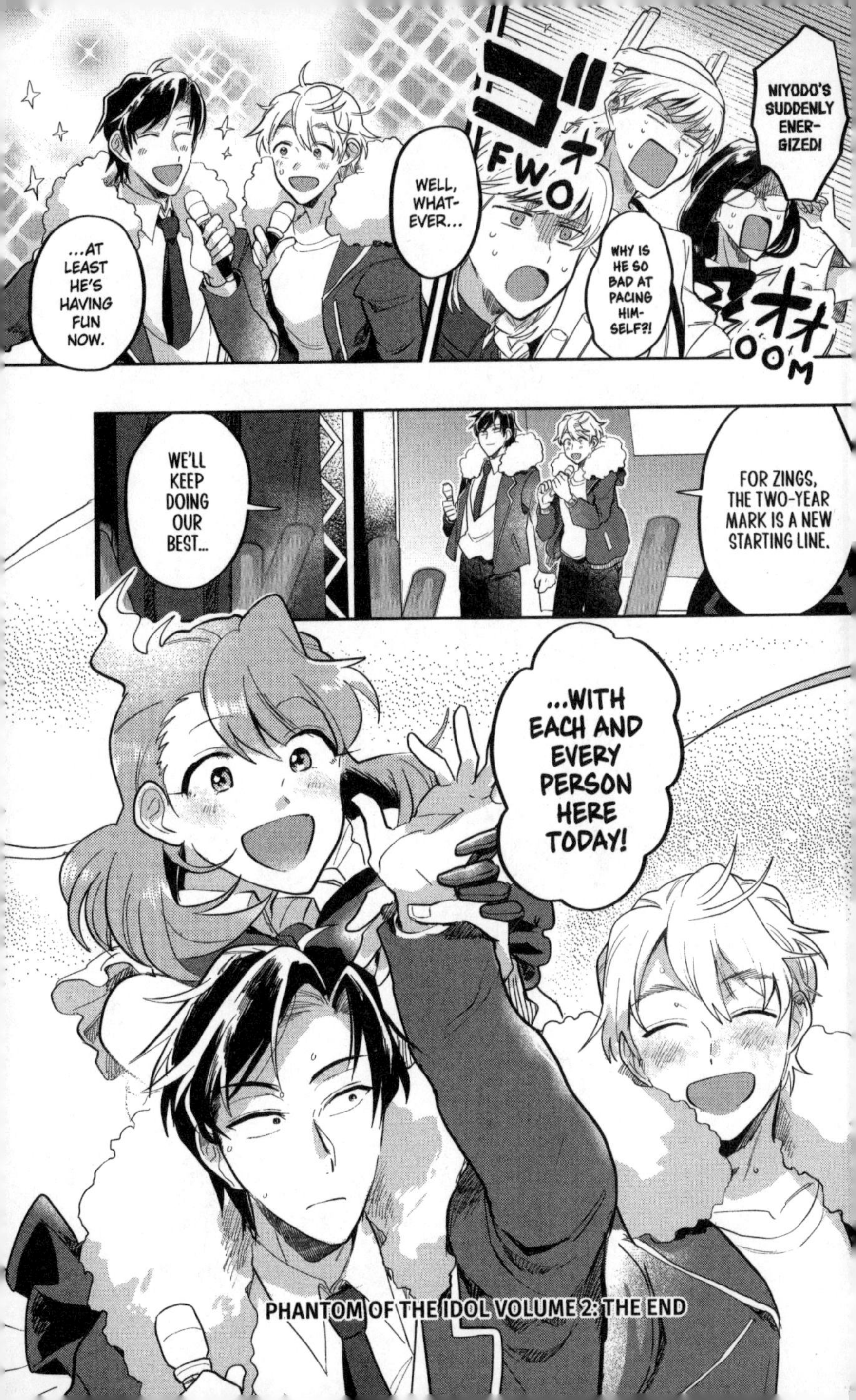
NIYODO'S SUDDENLY ENER-GIZED!
FWO
OOM
WHY IS HE SO BAD AT PACING HIM-SELF?!
WELL, WHAT-EVER...
...AT LEAST HE'S HAVING FUN NOW.
FOR ZINGS, THE TWO-YEAR MARK IS A NEW STARTING LINE.
WE'LL KEEP DOING OUR BEST...
...WITH EACH AND EVERY PERSON HERE TODAY!
PHANTOM OF THE IDOL VOLUME 2: THE END

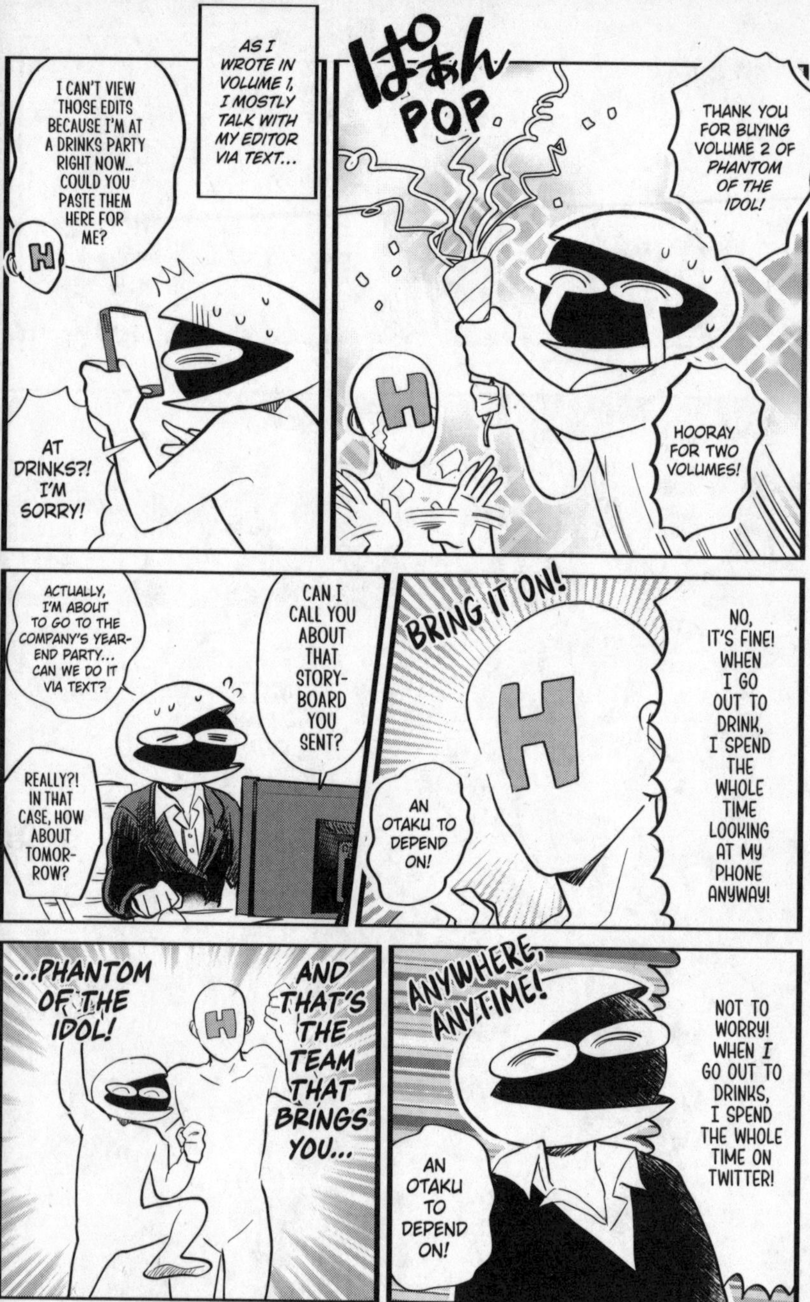
ぱあん
POP
THANK YOU FOR BUYING VOLUME 2 OF *PHANTOM OF THE IDOL!*
HOORAY FOR TWO VOLUMES!
AS I WROTE IN VOLUME 1, I MOSTLY TALK WITH MY EDITOR VIA TEXT...
I CAN'T VIEW THOSE EDITS BECAUSE I'M AT A DRINKS PARTY RIGHT NOW... COULD YOU PASTE THEM HERE FOR ME?
AT DRINKS?! I'M SORRY!
BRING IT ON!
NO, IT'S FINE! WHEN I GO OUT TO DRINK, I SPEND THE WHOLE TIME LOOKING AT MY PHONE ANYWAY!
AN OTAKU TO DEPEND ON!
CAN I CALL YOU ABOUT THAT STORY-BOARD YOU SENT?
ACTUALLY, I'M ABOUT TO GO TO THE COMPANY'S YEAR-END PARTY... CAN WE DO IT VIA TEXT?
REALLY?! IN THAT CASE, HOW ABOUT TOMOR-ROW?
ANYWHERE, ANYTIME!
NOT TO WORRY! WHEN *I* GO OUT TO DRINKS, I SPEND THE WHOLE TIME ON TWITTER!
AN OTAKU TO DEPEND ON!
AND THAT'S THE TEAM THAT BRINGS YOU...
...PHANTOM OF THE IDOL!

MAKE SURE TO JOIN IN AT DRINKS, EVERYONE.

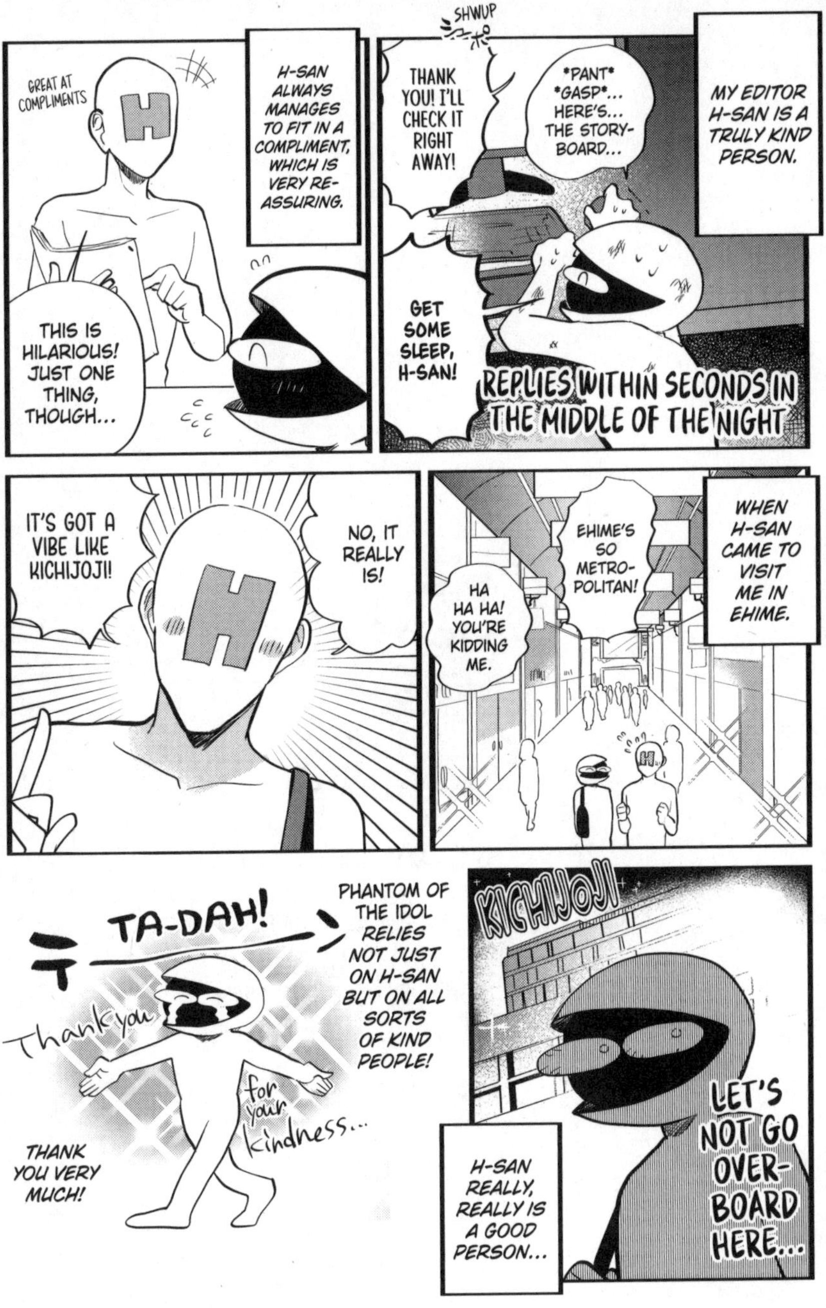
MY EDITOR H-SAN IS A TRULY KIND PERSON.
PANT *GASP*... HERE'S... THE STORY-BOARD...
SHWUP
THANK YOU! I'LL CHECK IT RIGHT AWAY!
GET SOME SLEEP, H-SAN!
REPLIES WITHIN SECONDS IN THE MIDDLE OF THE NIGHT
H-SAN ALWAYS MANAGES TO FIT IN A COMPLIMENT, WHICH IS VERY RE-ASSURING.
GREAT AT COMPLIMENTS
THIS IS HILARIOUS! JUST ONE THING, THOUGH...
WHEN H-SAN CAME TO VISIT ME IN EHIME.
EHIME'S SO METRO-POLITAN!
HA HA HA! YOU'RE KIDDING ME.
NO, IT REALLY IS!
IT'S GOT A VIBE LIKE KICHIJOJI!
KICHIJOJI
H-SAN REALLY, REALLY IS A GOOD PERSON...
LET'S NOT GO OVER-BOARD HERE...
PHANTOM OF THE IDOL RELIES NOT JUST ON H-SAN BUT ON ALL SORTS OF KIND PEOPLE!
TA-DAH!
Thank you
for your kindness...
THANK YOU VERY MUCH!

ISOFLAVONE HIJIKI

PEOPLE DOING THEIR BEST AT STUFF,
OTHER PEOPLE SUPPORTING THEM PASSIONATELY,
PEOPLE WITH NO MOTIVATION AND WITH TOO MUCH,
I LOVE THEM ALL!—IS THE FEELING I PUT INTO THIS!

I HOPE YOU ENJOY IT!

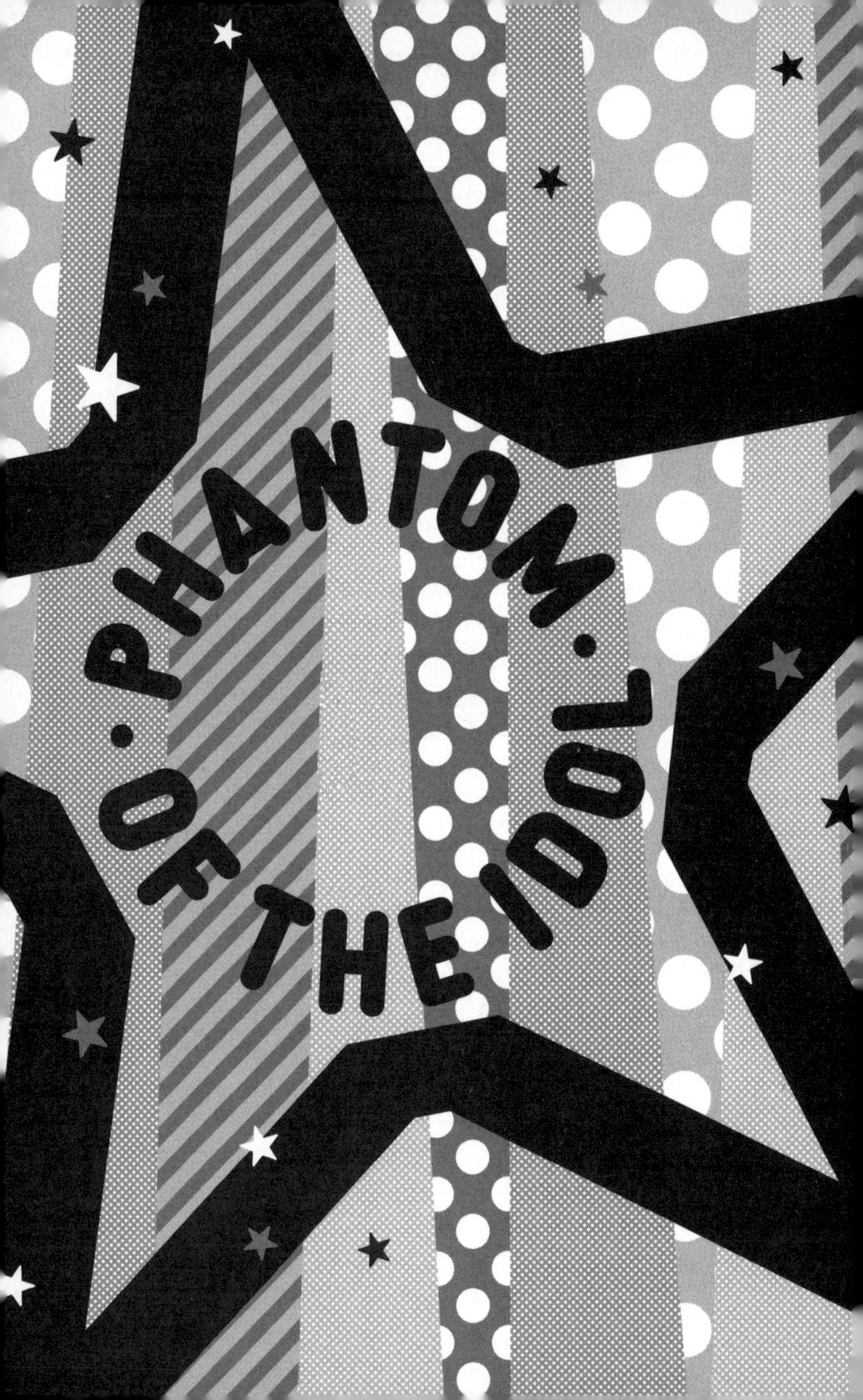
PHANTOM OF THE IDOL

Translation Notes

Flower stand, page 16
These are placed in the lobby at important concerts to congratulate the performers for their success. (They're also given to celebrate other professional successes, like new store openings.)

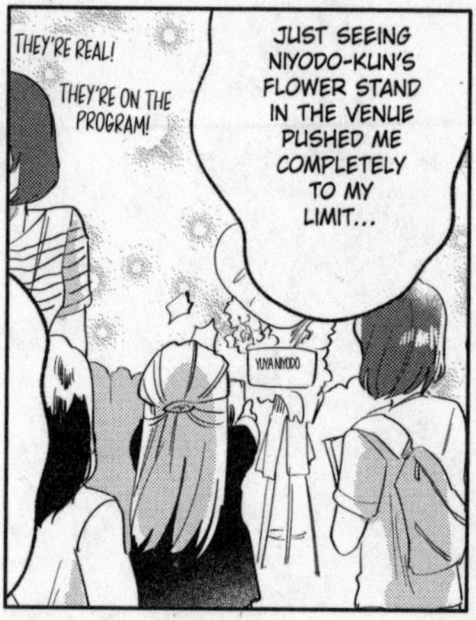
JUST SEEING NIYODO-KUN'S FLOWER STAND IN THE VENUE PUSHED ME COMPLETELY TO MY LIMIT...
THEY'RE REAL!
THEY'RE ON THE PROGRAM!
YUYA NIYODO

Ita-bag, page 28
A bag so thoroughly decorated with badges and other merch relating to one's bias that it is "painful" (*itai*) for others to witness. The mark of a truly obsessed fan. A portable relative to the "ita-sha" (a car lovingly decorated as a shrine to one's bias or favorite anime character).

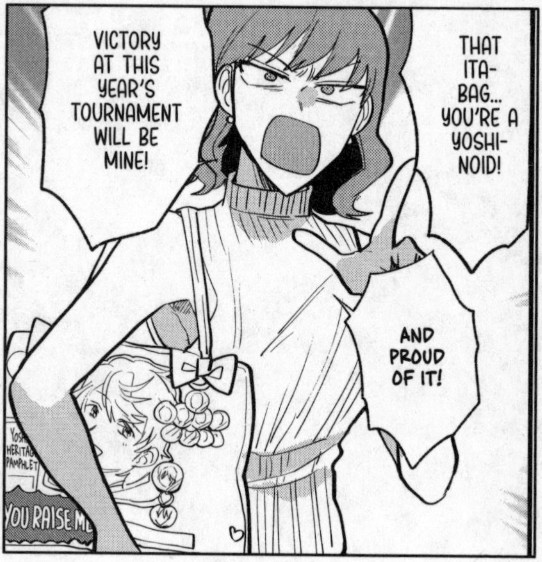
THAT ITA-BAG... YOU'RE A YOSHI-NOID!
VICTORY AT THIS YEAR'S TOURNAMENT WILL BE MINE!
AND PROUD OF IT!
YOU RAISE ME

Bizarre Scenes, page 31
May be a reference to *Nani kore chin hyakkei* (What Is This?! 100 Bizarre Scenes), a television show where guests—often including idols—react to strange images and videos.

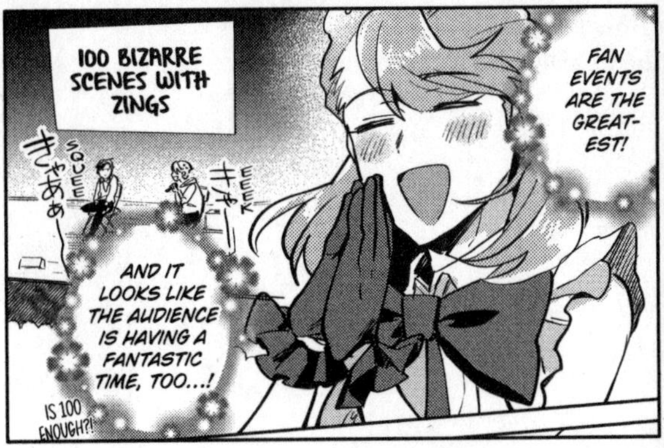
FAN EVENTS ARE THE GREAT-EST!
100 BIZARRE SCENES WITH ZINGS
EEEK
SQUEE
AND IT LOOKS LIKE THE AUDIENCE IS HAVING A FANTASTIC TIME, TOO...!
IS 100 ENOUGH?!

Mr. Scarf, page 83
Setouchi's unique scarf-wearing style is called a *hokkamuri* in Japanese, and is the stereotypical headgear for burglars and others looking to hide their identities.

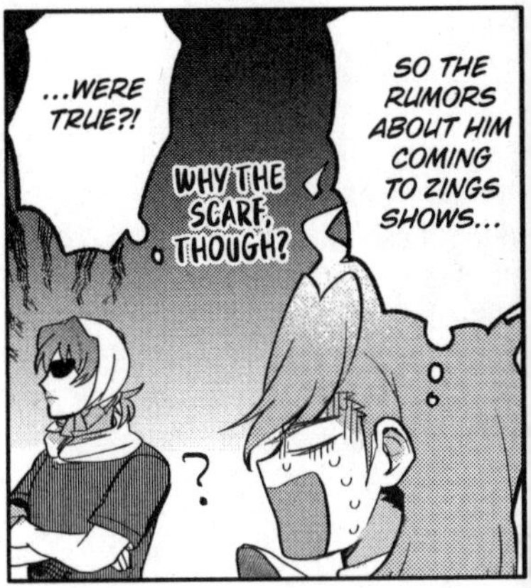
SO THE RUMORS ABOUT HIM COMING TO ZINGS SHOWS...
...WERE TRUE?!
WHY THE SCARF, THOUGH?
?

Cavalry battle, page 106
A game often played at school sports days in Japan. Students divide into teams of four. Three member are the "horse," and carry the fourth member around as "rider" trying to steal bandanas from other teams.

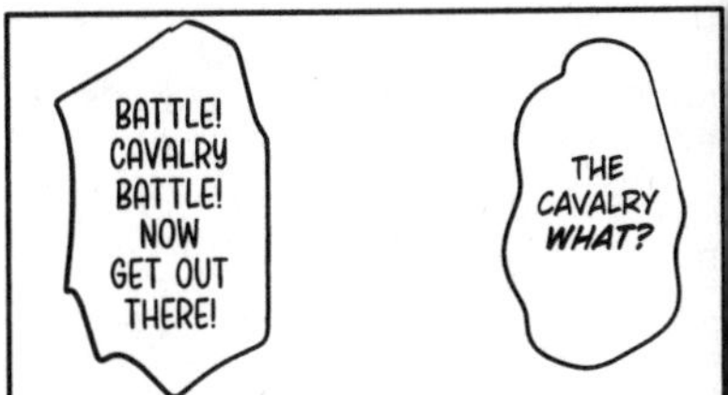
THE CAVALRY WHAT?
BATTLE! CAVALRY BATTLE! NOW GET OUT THERE!

"How precious to behold—the kindness of a companion!", page 112
An altered version of the song "*Aogeba totoshi*" ("How precious to behold"), the opening lyrics of which roughly translate to "How precious to behold—the kindness of my teacher."

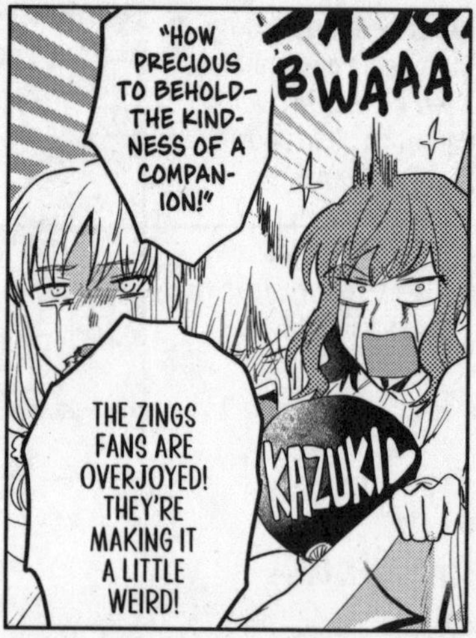
BWAAA
"HOW PRECIOUS TO BEHOLD-THE KINDNESS OF A COMPANION!"
KAZUKI♥
THE ZINGS FANS ARE OVERJOYED! THEY'RE MAKING IT A LITTLE WEIRD!

He's so salty, page 135
In Japanese idol culture, an idol who makes no effort to engage with fans or make them feel welcome is offering "salty treatment" (*shio taio*). The opposite of "salty treatment" is "godly treatment" (*kami taio*).

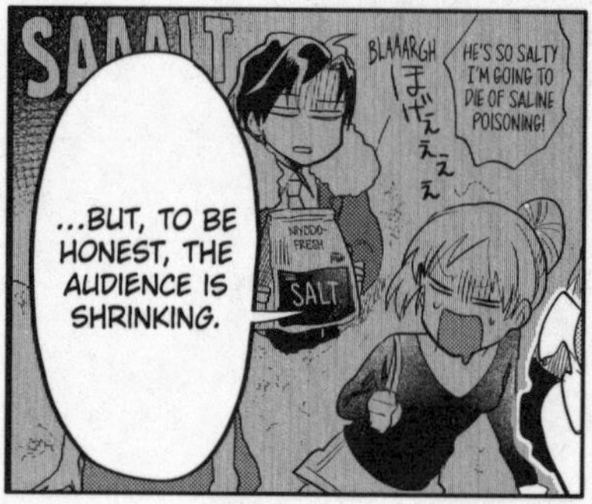
HE'S SO SALTY I'M GOING TO DIE OF SALINE POISONING!
BLAAARGH
ほげええええ
SAAALT
NYODO-FRESH
SALT
...BUT, TO BE HONEST, THE AUDIENCE IS SHRINKING.

Splashing cold water on the body parts furthest from your heart first, page 137
Japanese people are taught to do this when getting into cold water.

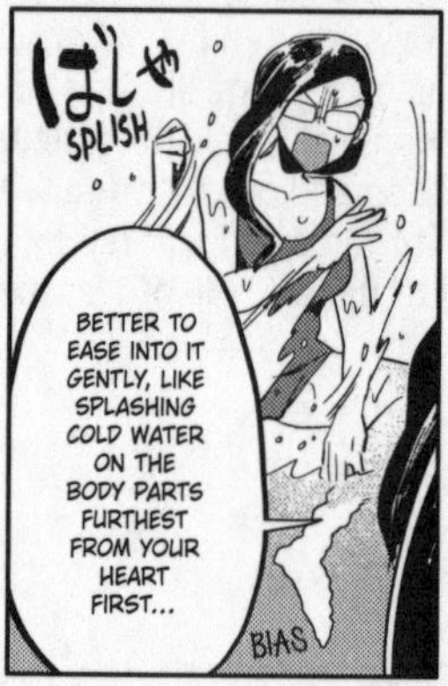
ぱしゃ
SPLISH
BETTER TO EASE INTO IT GENTLY, LIKE SPLASHING COLD WATER ON THE BODY PARTS FURTHEST FROM YOUR HEART FIRST...
BIAS

Young characters and steampunk setting, like *Howl's Moving Castle* and *Battle Angel Alita*

Beyond the Clouds © 2018 Nicke / Ki-oon

A boy with a talent for machines and a mysterious girl whose wings he's fixed will take you beyond the clouds! In the tradition of the high-flying, resonant adventure stories of Studio Ghibli comes a gorgeous tale about the longing of young hearts for adventure and friendship!

Knight of the Ice ©Yayoi Ogawa
Yayoi Ogawa

SKATING THRILLS AND ICY CHILLS WITH THIS NEW TINGLY ROMANCE SERIES!

A rom-com on ice, perfect for fans of *Princess Jellyfish* and *Wotakoi*. Kokoro is the talk of the figure-skating world, winning trophies and hearts. But little do they know... he's actually a huge nerd! From the beloved creator of *You're My Pet* (*Tramps Like Us*).

Chitose is a serious young woman, working for the health magazine *SASSO*. Or at least, she would be, if she wasn't constantly getting distracted by her childhood friend, international figure skating star Kokoro Kijinami! In the public eye and on the ice, Kokoro is a gallant, flawless knight, but behind his glittery costumes and breathtaking spins lies a secret: He's actually a hopelessly romantic otaku, who can only land his quad jumps when Chitose is on hand to recite a spell from his favorite magical girl anime!

A SMART, NEW ROMANTIC COMEDY FOR FANS OF *SHORTCAKE CAKE* AND *TERRACE HOUSE*!

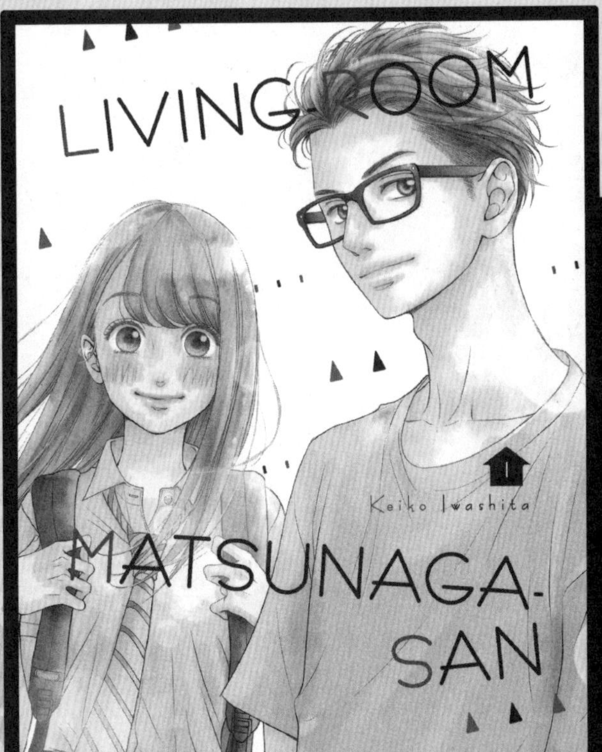
LIVING-ROOM
1
Keiko Iwashita
MATSUNAGA-SAN

KC KODANSHA COMICS

A romance manga starring high school girl Meeko, who learns to live on her own in a boarding house whose living room is home to the odd (but handsome) Matsunaga-san. She begins to adjust to her new life away from her parents, but Meeko soon learns that no matter how far away from home she is, she's still a young girl at heart — especially when she finds herself falling for Matsunaga-san.

The boys are back, in 400-page hardcovers that are as pretty and badass as they are!

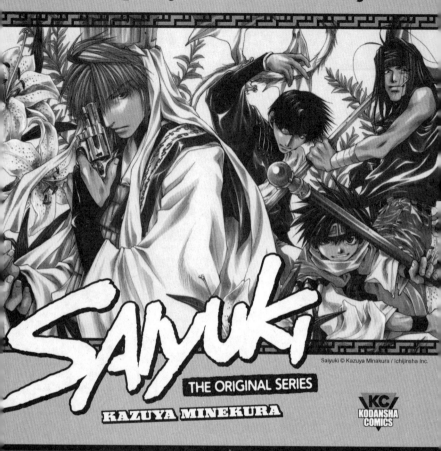

Saiyuki © Kazuya Minakura / Ichijinsha Inc.

SAIYUKI

THE ORIGINAL SERIES

KAZUYA MINEKURA

"AN EDGY COMIC LOOK AT AN ANCIENT CHINESE TALE." —YALSA

Genjo Sanzo is a Buddhist priest in the city of Togenkyo, which is being ravaged by yokai spirits that have fallen out of balance with the natural order. His superiors send him on a journey far to the west to discover why this is happening and how to stop it. His companions are three yokai with human souls. But this is no day trip — the four will encounter many discoveries and horrors on the way.

FEATURES NEW TRANSLATION, COLOR PAGES, AND BEAUTIFUL WRAPAROUND COVER ART!

PERFECT WORLD

Rie Aruga

A TOUCHING NEW SERIES ABOUT LOVE AND COPING WITH DISABILITY

An office party reunites Tsugumi with her high school crush Itsuki. He's realized his dream of becoming an architect, but along the way, he experienced a spinal injury that put him in a wheelchair. Now Tsugumi's rekindled feelings will butt up against prejudices she never considered — and Itsuki will have to decide if he's ready to let someone into his heart...

"Depicts with great delicacy and courage the difficulties some with disabilities experience getting involved in romantic relationships... Rie Aruga refuses to romanticize, pushing her heroine to face the reality of disability. She invites her readers to the same tasks of empathy, knowledge and recognition."
—Slate.fr

"An important entry [in manga romance]... The emotional core of both plot and characters indicates thoughtfulness... [Aruga's] research is readily apparent in the text and artwork, making this feel like a real story."
—Anime News Network

SAINT ☆ YOUNG MEN

A LONG AWAITED ARRIVAL IN PREMIUM 2-IN-1 HARDCOVER

After centuries of hard work, Jesus and Buddha take a break from their heavenly duties to relax among the people of Japan, and their adventures in this lighthearted buddy comedy are sure to bring mirth and merriment to all!

"Brilliant…the physical comedy and facial expressions will make you literally LOL."
—Sam Humphries (host of *DC Daily*; writer, *Green Lanterns, Legendary Star-Lord*)

Saint Young Men © Hikaru Nakamura/Kodansha Ltd.

The adorable new odd-couple cat comedy manga from the creator of the beloved *Chi's Sweet Home*, in full color!

Sue & Tai-chan

Konami Kanata

Sue is an aging housecat who's looking forward to living out her life in peace... but her plans change when the mischievous black tomcat Tai-chan enters the picture! Hey! Sue never signed up to be a catsitter! *Sue & Tai-chan* is the latest from the reigning meow-narch of cute kitty comics, Konami Kanata.

KC
KODANSHA
COMICS

A Kodansha Trade Paperback Original

Phantom of the Idol 2 copyright © 2019 Hijiki Isoflavone
English translation copyright © 2022 Hijiki Isoflavone

Published in the United States by
Kodansha USA Publishing, LLC, New York.

Publication rights for this English edition arranged through
Kodansha Ltd., Tokyo.

First published in Japan in 2019 by Ichijinsha Inc., Tokyo
as *Kami Kuzu Aidoru*, volume 2.

ISBN 978-1-64651-585-1

Printed in the United States of America.

9 8 7 6 5 4 3 2 1

Translation: Max Greenway
Lettering: Michael Martin
Editing: Maggie Le
Kodansha USA Publishing edition cover design by Matthew Akuginow

Publisher: Kiichiro Sugawara

Director of Publishing Services: Ben Applegate
Director of Publishing Operations: Dave Barrett
Associate Director of Publishing Operations: Stephen Pakula
Publishing Services Managing Editors: Alanna Ruse, Madison Salters
Production Manager: Angela Zurlo

KODANSHA.US

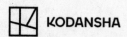 KODANSHA